Acclaim for **M I C H A** ...

S E C R E T L I F E

Chosen by the editors of The New York Times
Book Review *as a Notable Book for 1995*

"*Secret Life* is a profoundly perceptive, agonizing, and even witty exploration of the concatenation of circumstances and character that make up a life." —Katherine Powers, *Boston Globe*

"Michael Ryan tells his story with style and jocular charm, and even the disquieted reader won't be able to put it down." —*San Francisco Focus*

"The author renders his years in Catholic schools in Pennsylvania with near-perfect pitch. Without this spirit of humor, *Secret Life* might well have been unreadable, and it's quite the opposite."
—Mark Childress, *Times Literary Supplement*

"Ryan is so fascinating a memoirist, so vivid and interesting a writer, that his book is a wonderful social history of the years from 1946 to the present. It is also a painful and sometimes hilarious story about a boy's growing up." —David Guy, *Durham News & Observer*

"What this unusually honest book does, and does very well, is to demonstrate one possible outcome of early sexual molestation."
—Anthony Storr, *London Times*

"This autobiography is so well-written, so rich in psychological detail and intrigue, that it should stand long after its raison d'etre has faded."
—*Reader's Review*

"This searing memoir, superbly crafted, will generate a great amount of discussion: its frankness, frankness for the sake of art and expiation, will compel many, many readers."

— Thomas Keneally, author of *Schindler's List*

"This memoir of psychosexual addiction and abuse is a miracle of tact, intelligence, and understanding. Few books have told as harrowing a story of a family's struggle to rise and stay in the middle class, and of the sexual and emotional costs to one of its children. *Secret Life* is brilliantly and beautifully written, with clarity and unusual grace. It is a report of a Hell ruled by Eros from someone who managed, against all odds, to escape." — Charles Baxter, author of *A Relative Stranger*

"*Secret Life* tells the story of a childhood, and is as deftly and vividly rendered as any memoir of the sort that I have read. This is also the story of how a loathsome act can help to beget counterparts, of how a child grew into a sexual predator so compulsively self-destructive that he hardly noticed how many other lives he injured. I found this book extraordinarily compelling."

— Tracy Kidder, author of *The Soul of a New Machine*

"An extraordinary portrait of a man, an era, a family, an addiction, and release. Beautifully written, mesmerizing, sometimes funny, and always incredibly honest, it grabbed me from the first page and would not let me go until I was finished. What a great read. The inner landscape of this one man's soul and psyche is at once stark and chilling and tender and familiar. I cannot recommend this book highly enough." — Anne Lamott, author of *Bird by Bird*

"Ryan writes with extreme clarity, memorable wit, maturity, and compassion. At every turn, he chooses to be accountable for his life and to identify humanness where another might see iniquity. This wonderful book made me laugh out loud, kept me up nights, broke my heart, and gave me hope." — Dennis McFarland, author of *The Music Room*

MICHAEL RYAN

SECRET LIFE

Michael Ryan's first book of poems won the Yale Series of Younger Poets Award and was nominated for a National Book Award in 1974. *God Hunger*, his most recent book, won the Lenore Marshall/*Nation* Award for the most outstanding book of poems published in 1989. He has received many other awards for his poems and essays, including a Whiting Writers Award and a Guggenheim Fellowship.

SECRET LIFE

SECRET LIFE

An Autobiography

MICHAEL RYAN

Vintage Books

A Division of Random House, Inc.

New York

Grateful acknowledgment is made to the following for permission to reprint previously
published material: *House of Bryant*: Excerpt from "All I Have to Do Is Dream," words
and music by Boudleaux Bryant, copyright © 1958 (renewed 1968) by House of Bryant
Publications. Reprinted by permission of House of Bryant. *The Lowery Group*: Excerpt
from "Young Love," words and music by Carole Joyner and Ric Cartey. EU 456777
October 30, 1956; RE 204458 May 29, 1984. Reprinted
by permission of The Lowery Group.

The names, distinguishing traits, and places of most
of the people represented here have been changed.

The Library of Congress has cataloged the Pantheon edition as follows:
Ryan, Michael, 1946–
Secret life : an autobiography / Michael Ryan.
p. cm.
ISBN 0-679-40775-8
1. Ryan, Michael, 1946– —Biography. 2. Poets, American—20th Century—Biography.
3. Adult child sexual abuse victims—United States—Biography. I. Title.
PS3568.Y39Z47 1995
811'.54—dc20
[B] 94-43814
CIP
Vintage ISBN: 0-679-76776-2

Random House Web address: http://www.randomhouse.com/

Author photograph © Joan Alden

molest: ME *molesten*: OFR *molester*: L *molestare*: *molestus*, troublesome: *moles*, a burden: IE base *molo-*, to strive

CONTENTS

SECRET LIFE

SOUL SICKNESS

Every sex addict has his own thing, the thing he likes the most, although "like" is hardly the word for the inexorable pull I felt and sought and sometimes still feel but with God's help one day at a time do not act on. It's as if an electronic magnet in my solar plexus were switched on. At its most intense, I'd go into a kind of trance, dissociated, beamed in from Mars, my mouth dry and my heart pounding, my usual waking consciousness hovering somewhere outside my body while I was taken by the pull. One of my partners once said to me, "You are like another person when we go into sex." That's how I put it, too: *go into* sex. Any way I could get there was fine. But the best way was anonymous sex, with a teenage girl, initiated by a secret touch. I spent most of my adult life in public watching for her, checking every prospect for what I called The Look—pouting, furious, damaged, sullen—short skirts, tight jeans, halter tops, spiked-heel pumps. When I saw her, it was like getting hit in the face by a door. I'd double back if circumstances permitted and stare and stare. I'd tie my shoelace or pretend to window-shop trying to catch her eye. On the few occasions I managed to talk to her I blew it. I became tongue-tied. Everything I could think of to say sounded preposterously banal. I felt like a pervert, his evil intent blaring like a bullhorn. Yet I wanted her more than anything, so she stood as a constant reproach because I was obviously not sexy enough or good-looking enough or fearless enough to get her. She was what everything I could get was not. I was able to write (from midnight to 6 A.M.), I could teach, I could laugh, I could enjoy reading or exercising or cooking, but there was often this thing between me and enjoyment: my thing, the thing I liked the most but never got.

What I got were approximations and compromises—students, strangers, almost anyone who was attracted to me. When I was in the same room with someone I wanted but hadn't had—whatever my relationship to her, her husband, or to anyone else—the social world was a thin, irritating haze covering the real world of sex where we should be together. I wanted to touch her, I wanted to have some part of my body in contact with hers. Sitting at a table, my attention was under the table no matter how engaging the dinner conversation. I always knew where her legs and feet were. There could be looks or words, but looks and words weren't enough for me. The signal had to be palpable. Then I'd store it in my fantasy bank, and sneak in there later like a miser to toy with it and shape it into a porno video I'd play over and over again in my mind.

This is who I was to myself. It was who I had always been. I had always hidden myself from my family. It was not that I wasn't the person my friends knew, but I was also someone else, and not just someone else, *really* someone else, this secret person being the real one. My primary loyalty was to sex. No human relationship took precedence over it. Not marriage, not friendship, and certainly not ethics. Achievements were meaningless unless converted into sexual rewards. The more inappropriate someone was for me (the more inappropriate *I* was for me), the more it excited me. The more someone repelled me (morally), the more I wanted her. When I pressed my knee against an anonymous knee in a movie or on a plane, or tried to hustle someone in a disco, or seduced a student half my age I knew I'd soon get bored with, it didn't matter as much if the person repelled me because I repelled myself. The other person could be absolutely anyone. Just the desire to use people like this repelled me, much less doing it, but when I did it, I reveled in my power. I thought any man would do what I did if he were powerful enough. Yet since my appetite was infinite, I wasn't nearly powerful enough either. I never got what I *really* wanted, and I hated myself for that, and hated life, and hated myself again for caring about sex more than anything or anybody, including the people I loved. Then I hated myself for loving so badly. It was like living inside a spin dryer. Finally, what I cared about was me, and not even me but the addict-me, this no-I driving me to be with no one, to be no one.

—

IN JANUARY 1991, on a plane to California to begin my first permanent teaching job in a decade, I took out a yellow pad and wrote down what they call in twelve-step programs for sexual addiction "bottom-line behavior"—behavior driven by shame and producing shame, which, in my case, could get me arrested, killed, or fired, and did in fact get me fired by Princeton University in 1981. This is what I wrote on my yellow pad:

- no sex with students
- no teenagers
- no anonymous sex
- no secret touching

My motives were not noble. If I were fired from this teaching job, I'd never get another one. I was a month away from my forty-fifth birthday. How do you change the person you have always been? How do you change your sexuality, how do you change what turns you on? I had no idea. All I knew was that I was in deep trouble. I couldn't trust my instincts, much less my fantasies. I couldn't trust myself. And I was so tired of being myself, disgruntled and predatory and hungry, creeping around with a secret agenda, trivialized by it, racked by the self-loathing I was beginning to understand I had both blocked and enacted with my sexual behavior. Well, it wasn't being blocked any-more. I felt like a piece of shit with eyes. I felt wrong in the innermost fabric of my being.

Exactly one year before, my (second) marriage had exploded. As much as I could love anyone, I loved my wife. We had been together nine years, since just after I had been fired by Princeton and had un-dergone the public humiliation that followed it. Her love probably kept me alive. In the first six months since our breakup, I had sometimes unprotected sex with a Radcliffe sophomore I met in a health-food store who turned out to be under treatment for depression and as ther-apy danced to steel drums and smoked ganja with Rastafarians in the park, a flight attendant who had moved to Boston to be near a man she found out was married, a woman from Prague I met after my poetry reading at the West Side Y who wore homburgs like the character in the Kundera novel, a grad student I met at the Sarah Lawrence-NYU Creative Writing Programs volleyball game who was the girlfriend of a rock star who slept with prostitutes, my acupuncturist, the wife of a struggling poet who admired me, an anesthesiologist I met at my health club, the owner of a pet shop I also met at my health club, an ex-student from Princeton who had written a fine first novel, and an in-dustrial waste executive who lived next door to the apartment building where I had lived with my wife. What these people had in common was that they were willing to sleep with me. I didn't know any of them when I went to bed with them. I liked them or I didn't, I admired them or I didn't, they were beautiful or they weren't—it just didn't matter. It was what I knew how to do to assuage my loneliness. Only it didn't assuage my loneliness. The charge became fainter each time. After six months they started to seem like bodies strewn by the roadside, a feeling not ameliorated by the rationalization that I might also be a body strewn by their roadsides. The last time I had had sex with a man was in 1981, a couple of months before I was fired by Princeton and coincidentally the first cases of AIDS were discovered. Although I figured I'd probably have shown symptoms after nine years if I had it, the newspapers kept publishing new estimates for the incubation period, some as high as fourteen years, and there were nights I'd wake soaked with sweat—one of the early symptoms—from dreams about dying. I was afraid to get tested, and it was possible I was spreading it or getting it. I'd think of this in bed with these women, afterward and during. My behavior was dangerous and degrading and deceitful. I wanted to stop it.

But I couldn't. Just as every addict has his own thing, so every addict has his own "bottom," which may well be below death, as it was for my father, who died a practicing alcoholic. How far down that bottom is may have to do with power and pride and how deeply the addiction is rooted in the addict's personality and beliefs—or bottoming out may simply be the grace of God, or luck (the secular term for grace). There's certainly no rational reason why I wasn't killed any number of times—by an outraged husband or father or sexual partner, male or female, or by HIV. "I'm alive and I'm not in jail" is sometimes the most one can say after one stops the addictive behavior and experiences full force the suicidal self-hatred behind such compulsive risk-taking. A sex addict does indeed "exchange life in its entirety for sex," as does a drug addict for drugs or an alcoholic for alcohol. As an addiction, they are all what Sherwin Nuland calls in *How We Die* "chronic habitual suicide." They are all ways to keep from killing yourself which at the point of some shadowy crossover start to kill you. You marshal all your intelligence and charm and power to keep the addiction alive—if necessary, at the expense of your own life. Everything and everyone in your life, who you are and what you believe, falls in line around it. The amazing thing is how any addict ever stops using before he dies. The substance I used was human beings. For me nothing could be more absorbing, transporting, and shameful—which of course is why I used human beings instead of something else. Getting fired by Princeton did not make me stop. Losing my wife did not make me stop. Risking my life and the lives of my sexual partners did not make me stop.

What made me stop or, more accurately, made me see I had no

choice but to find a way to stop, occurred in late summer of 1990. I found myself driving a car to upstate New York for the purpose of seducing a friend's fifteen-year-old daughter. "Found myself" is the right way to describe it, although I had prepared it over the course of weeks as methodically as an assassin. All the charge I didn't get from the parade of adult seductions I got from the idea of seducing this young girl: finally, after all these years, my thing. This time it was going to happen. She was perfect: sophisticated and difficult and furious at her parents, like a bomb about to explode. She was, as Doris Lessing described a character, "in that state so many young girls go through— a state of sexual obsession that can be like a sort of trance." Just the kind of trance I liked. Her skin radiated it, her body language screamed it. My preternatural alertness to signals howled on overload, the pull magnified exponentially to the hundredth power. "She thinks you're really cute," her mother reported to me on the phone, thinking I'd find it amusing. I found it amusing all right. I was going to give it to her seventeen ways from Sunday. My mental porno video was already shot and edited. I'd arrive in the early afternoon, when her father was still at work. The house had a swimming pool in the backyard. We'd take a little dip. She'd look unbelievable in her bikini, smiling at me shyly when she first came out of the house. We'd play underwater games. This is when I would first touch her. I'd put my hands on her from behind. It would be like lightning hitting my fingers. She'd love it and let me know she loved it. She'd touch me, too. The connection would be made, the message clear. Afterward, all evening, our desire would be excruciating for both of us. Maybe we'd play footsie under the dinner table or I'd brush the back of her thigh while she was clearing the dishes. In the kitchen or hallway we'd steal a deep kiss. That night while her parents were asleep, she would sneak down to my room in her nightie, and that's when we'd do it seventeen ways from Sunday, and continue doing it every chance we got. Her ecstasy would be unbounded. She'd have so many titanic orgasms she'd think she was an earthquake. She would be tied to me. She would remember me for the rest of her life.

The fantasy was so real that while I was making preparations for the visit it seemed like it had already happened. The day I left, I packed a bag, made some sandwiches, checked the maps, and filled the car with gas, just as I would for any road trip. I had misgivings, but they were all about getting caught. The conflict in myself I simply would not entertain. I buried it under years of fantasy and frustration. By God I was going to do this, that was all there was to it. I knew I could be arrested, her mother would hate me, and her father might kill me, but I did not think for a moment of the emotional damage to the girl, and at no time did I realize that I was about to go molest a child. Had I realized that, I couldn't have wanted to do it.

So what happened I still can't explain. I turned back. I drove all the way from Boston to Albany, five hours, and as I got closer to their house, the reality of what I was about to try to do gradually replaced the fantasy, and I panicked. It would be false to say I saw how insane it was, how insane I was. I pulled over into a rest area and sat there with my hands on the steering wheel and my forehead on my knuckles. It was Labor Day weekend. Families were pulling in to use the rest rooms—minivans and campers, parents holding their children's hands as they walked them to the john. When I used the john myself, I saw a father in a stall helping his son to pee. The boy had spiky blond hair that looked as soft as down. His shorts were crumpled around his ankles and his tiny butt was like a white peach. His father was coaxing him to take his time, to relax. It was an unbearably tender thing. Outside, kids pestered their parents for Cokes and snacks. Everybody looked fat, ugly, and stupid, but nobody else was alone. I didn't want their lives and I didn't want mine either. There was no life I wanted. I had no one in Boston to go back to, no reason to be anywhere. My friends were out of town or picnicking with relatives. I never felt more lonely than this, but I was still not as lonely as I imagine a child molester is—the deepest loneliness inside the deepest shame, an unsurvivable loneliness. I sat in the car for I don't know how long before I took myself to the pay phone to call and cancel. I hadn't been trying to decide whether or not to cancel. My mind was blank, white, as if it had been erased. The goings and comings in the rest area were behind a glaze. I certainly didn't connect what I had planned to do with what was done to me when I was sexually molested, but now I think had I done this to her the split in me would have opened like a gorge, and I would have lost the possibility of compassion for myself, much less for anyone else, and then it would have been only a matter of time.

SECRET LIFE

I was sexually molested when I was five years old, probably for about a year (I can remember the change of seasons), probably from one spring through the next winter, 1951–1952, during the last part of the Korean War. I was sitting in our backyard playing in the dirt when a man appeared in front of me with a camera and took my picture. He was young and handsome—but I believe that was what I thought later, after I was under his spell. He was an adult—they all seemed the same age except for the grandmothers and grandfathers who were old (*old* was a different species of adult). This one was interested in me. When I looked up and saw him snap my picture, I was startled but not frightened. He came over and squatted in front of me. I hadn't moved. His hair was dark brown and slicked straight back like my father's. I was sitting in the dirt with my knees akimbo pushing miniature metal trucks around inside the circle my legs made. He asked me if I liked him taking my picture. I liked it okay. He asked if my mother was home, and when I told him she was, he knocked on the screen door.

His name was Bob Stoller, he explained to my mother. He was our neighbor's son just back from Korea, our neighbor who lived up the block (I wasn't allowed to go off the block or cross the street by myself). He was just back from Korea and was trying to get started as a professional photographer, and would my mother mind if he took my picture? He could do this one right here in the yard (did he tell her he'd already taken one without her permission?) and we'd see how it turned out.

It turned out great. The Professional-Quality eight-by-ten glossy of me in my favorite gray-and-black Hopalong Cassidy sweater is still among the family albums in the bottom drawer of the secretary in my mother's living room. He brought our copy to us the next day—everyone liked it—and asked if I could come up to his studio so he could take a few in Kodacolor. In 1951, color was a very exotic medium. Only a Professional could take color photographs, and then mostly in a studio where the lighting was strictly controlled. My mother supposed it would be all right, did I want to do it? I did want to do it. I liked the picture, I liked Bob Stoller, and he had mentioned that he had brought back some guns from Korea that he would show me (no, they wouldn't shoot, the Army won't let you take them home that way). And he also owned an accordion. I loved the buttons on accordions. I was ready to go that minute.

Did we first have to get my father's approval? Was there a family discussion that evening, the black-and-white glossy passed around the dining-room table? I don't remember. I do remember that we all knew beforehand what Bob Stoller had in mind for the color photos: a diptych (he didn't call it that) in a hinged frame: on the left I would be dressed as an angel; on the right, a devil. We all thought this was a cute idea.

The appointment was made, and the day came. This first time Bob Stoller called for me, at the back door. I remember my mother saying goodbye to us and us walking up the alley to his back door and me asking more about the accordion and if I could see it right away. I remember his mother was at home when we got there. She greeted me when I walked into her kitchen, then disappeared.

His studio was set up in the attic, where he also kept his guns. The accordion he stored in a closet in the den on the ground floor. He opened the closet door and hauled it out, a bejeweled treasure chest, dazzling, the sun streaming through a window and glittering off the black and white enamel and chrome plating, a fantastic kind of turtle whose shell could be pried open to reveal the folded black cardboard innards. I tried to pick it up but couldn't—sitting on the floor it was bigger than I was—so Bob Stoller put it on my lap as I sat on the daybed, and I pressed all the little buttons on the left and the keyboard on the right (and would have been happy to do that all afternoon) but couldn't get it to make a sound. I begged him to play it for me, which he did. Effortlessly, he lifted it off my lap, and strapped it on, and pumped the great bellows in and out, tickling the buttons and keys, filling the room with polka music as I sat on the bed wide-eyed at this amazing display of power. The sound was deafening and I loved it. I wanted more and more, and this was the first time I saw something wrong. Maybe he felt ridiculous—seeing himself serenading a five-year-old with an accordion polka. Maybe he felt degraded. Maybe his mother simply left the house but would be back soon. In any case, he began to get irritated at my fixation on the accordion, or that's what I thought. He was impatient to get upstairs. Didn't I want to see the guns and have my picture taken?

The stairway to the attic was narrow and steep and unfinished and smelled like a cedar chest. It was like the rabbit hole in *Alice in Wonderland*, only climbing not falling through the passage to another world. Before long it would be exactly that. Knowing what would happen there, I would feel a new emotion as he followed me up the stairs, a blend of wonder and dread. Even this first time the passage seemed mysterious and secret. At the top was a daybed, a rug, a chair, a bathroom, a kind of living space set off from the rest of the attic where he had established his box camera and a little pedestal surrounded by quartz lights. It was cold. Bob Stoller switched on an electric heater, and it whirred, the exposed coils turning from black to orange to red. I sat on the bed and he brought over the guns, their muzzles stuffed with dirty hard cotton, M-1's and dummy grenades and strange pistols with three-bullet barrels, even a German Luger that was not likely ever to have been in Korea. I guess he bought them somewhere. Maybe he had never been in Korea himself, but that didn't occur to me or to anyone else, as far as I know.

This is when he first touched me—not between the legs. He put his arm around me while we looked at the guns. He had piled them by the bed and on the bed, and he pulled them across our laps as we sat with our backs against the wall. I stroked the polished wood stocks and blue steel barrels of the rifles. He helped me aim across the attic at the box camera and bathroom doorknob. He helped me cock the hammers and pull the triggers. We did it for a long time. He didn't get impatient. It was a physical closeness I liked very much. The attention was all on me now, on whatever I wanted. I had never had a better time. His body was big and warm, the guns were fascinating. I was five years old.

Then it came time to take my picture. I had to put on a costume, which he showed to me: a red cape, a pair of stubby wooden horns glued to a circle of black elastic that went under my chin, and a tiny diaphanous red jockstrap. It was time for me to pretend I was a little devil. I had to take off all my clothes and put the costume on, but if I felt embarrassed, I could go over to the dressing stall (like the ones with curtains in cheap department stores). I knew how to undress myself and even to untie my shoes, though I couldn't always tie them up again. He asked if I was sure I could manage, and when I said I could (I wanted to be grown-up), he left me in the stall and pulled the curtain across.

When I had all my clothes off—it was freezing—Bob Stoller suddenly pulled the curtain back. I felt terror—I'll never forget it—I was naked and he loomed over me. Standing straight up, I didn't reach his waist. He seemed twice as big now as before, and the light behind him made him into a dark hulk. It was so sudden. I was going to put the costume on myself—what was he doing?

"I want to make sure you get it on right," he said. He pulled the jockstrap up, and kept adjusting it around me, touching me. I felt like a bar of iron was being shoved up into my stomach. I felt nauseated and dizzy, my legs wouldn't work. I pushed his hands away and said I could do it myself. I was about to cry.

Then he changed again. I think if he would have gotten mad, I might have run away. No one had ever talked to me about being touched, but he was still a stranger and I was upset. But then he was nice, wonderfully nice, just as he had been while we looked at the guns, the way he had been in the yard and playing the polka on the accordion. He helped me with the cape, which was like Superman's; he adjusted the horns, kidding me about their not being straight (this insane costume he must have spent hours making—how many little boys had worn it?). He rubbed my head with his palm the way my uncles did.

He calmed me down. Maybe he apologized. I got up on the pedestal, surrounded by the quartz lights, and he took my picture, talking to me the whole time in a soothing voice, saying nice things, telling me I was handsome. The jockstrap did feel kind of funny in a way I liked, but I was cold. My skin was all goose bumps. He brought over the heater. There was much touching and adjusting, but he didn't touch me there anymore and the heat felt good. I liked posing. I liked turning the way he told me, this way and that, him gesturing from behind the camera with his hands.

When he was finished shooting the devil pictures, he brought out the angel costume: a gold-lamé-bordered sheet with a hole in the middle, and a gold cloth-covered wire bent into two attached circles, one that sat on my head, one for the halo. He said I could put the costume on by myself in the dressing stall and could put my underpants back on if I wanted to, which I did. He didn't pull the curtain open. I pulled it open and stepped back up onto the pedestal into the cold air. He touched me again, arranging me for the picture, and he shot it.

How much time passed it's impossible now to say. It may have been a couple of hours, with this man's attention focused exclusively on me, courting me, making me feel special. I was handsome, I had good muscles, I was big for my age, I was smart, my hair was soft, I would probably become a good baseball player. We would be friends. I thought this would be wonderful. Since I was cold, why didn't I take a warm bath now and we would take more pictures next time, in a couple of days.

I didn't like baths, but I wanted to please him. He really wanted me to take a bath. I didn't connect it to his pulling open the curtain and touching me, and I just wanted to forget about that so we could be friends. Anyway, there was something nice about wearing these costumes. I was starting to feel beautiful, not like other children, better than them, different. A man liked me.

He drew the bath and left the bathroom again before I took off my underpants and got in. A minute later he knocked lightly on the door and poked his head in (the door was behind me) and asked how I was doing and if he could come in, making a little joke about not wanting to surprise me again. He sat down on the toilet with the lid down and talked to me a little about who knows what (how many hours of childish *talk* in a year? how could he not be bored senseless with it?), talked to me about taking baths by myself, which I said I did, figuring the more grown-up I was the more likely it was he'd want to be my friend. He asked me if, when I took a bath by myself and nobody else was around, did I ever play with it? Did I ever make it stiff so it stood out straight? I said I did, looking down shyly. It was true, I did, not often but sometimes, and I was astonished anyone else could know about this or guess it. I was also a little embarrassed, and also pleased to be sharing this secret, which Bob Stoller said he'd never tell anyone ever, it would be just between us two. It was our secret. He was still sitting on the toilet. Then he asked if I would touch myself and show him how I did it. He asked me to play with it so he could see.

The water was warm, the steam rising gently and making the air warm, too. Bob said to use both hands, to just put my fingers underneath it and tickle it and make it feel good. I started to do what he said and the familiar feeling came back as it stiffened, a dream feeling that before I had had only by myself; it never occurred to me that anyone else ever had it, it seemed naughty, but here was my friend sharing it with me and he didn't think it was bad and we were in this nice secret place together. I don't know how long I did it for him, not long probably. When it was still stiff, he brought over a towel and said to stand up in the tub and he would dry me off. I did stand up and he took the plug out and began rubbing me with the towel all over and now it felt good and dreamy and warm not like when he touched me before in the dressing stall and he told me to put my arms around his neck to steady myself while he did it and I did, in a swoon, the classic gesture of surrender and embrace.

If at that moment I had been able to scream and run away, or evaporate into the steamy air, I believe my whole life would have been different. But I was already gone. He had me and he knew it He carried me in his arms into the other room. The heater was already reset by the bed, aimed at the spot where he knew he would lay me down, talking to me the whole time the way a lover does. Was he kissing me? I think he was, but not on the mouth. Somehow he explained an even better secret we could share, that he could play with it in his mouth the way I had with my fingers, and still inside the dream feeling he was kneeling in front of me and tickling it with his tongue and lips.

Of course, I couldn't climax, and straddling his big head and steadying myself on it with his mouth on me was like the disappointing slow last moments of the ride on the mechanical bucking horse in front of the grocery store. I started to come out of the dream feeling. It felt so strange, and too frightening to be pleasant. I may have said something, I don't know, but the spell was broken by the time he stopped and asked me to do the same thing to him. He showed it to me. It was a lot bigger than mine, red and angry. He showed me how to do what he had done: pull my lips in over my teeth. He looked like my grandmother when she took out her dentures. He talked softly, cajoling, caressing and touching, rubbing me there. I was on his lap with no clothes on and his pants were around his ankles. He lowered me between his legs. His thing was right in front of my face. "Go ahead, Mike," he said. "Take it in your mouth."

Sometimes I still remember how it felt and tasted: hot—hotter than the temperature in my mouth—and it pushed my mouth open as wide as it could, too wide, it was too much in my mouth. But it was the taste that was unique, the flesh taste, cock taste, *this* cock taste. The sensation was odd, but it was the dream feeling I liked, that sometimes would be there while I was doing this to him. But there was always something I didn't like about it, something physically unpleasant, especially the first time, though it was not in my mouth long the first time, probably less than half a minute before he pulled it out and squeezed it purple in his fist, violently tight, and the cream gushed out. The semen didn't shoot up into the air—he must have been trying to keep it from doing that by squeezing it, I have no idea why, maybe he thought this would scare me too much. I watched amazed. I was still on my knees and it was right in front of my face. He didn't moan or do anything else unusual. He cleaned himself with a Kleenex (which he also had waiting right there) and said that this is what happened when you grew up. I didn't understand. He said everything was fine, there was nothing wrong, he would explain it to me in time. He took me on his lap again. We had a big secret now. We would be best friends, and he would teach me about things. But there was something very important. *Very* important. He held me under the arms, facing him. His face was big. If I ever told anyone, ever, for any reason, he would get into a lot of trouble. They would send him to jail. Why? Because no one else could understand our secret, just like my playing with myself in the bathtub, only now we shared it together. It was just ours, no one else's, not even our parents'. I must tell no one under any circumstances as long as I lived. Did I promise? I promised.

I kept that promise for most of my life. I didn't tell anyone. At home, of course nothing tangible had changed, which was at once reassuring and terrifying—reassuring because the furniture, my family, the noises, smells, and movement were familiar, negotiable, I could make my way through them and still be part of them but now only partially, only superficially; there was now a deeper reality than this one with boiled potatoes steaming on the table in a blue china bowl and the family gathering for dinner from their separate enterprises, this façade I'd never fully believe in again. There were some questions about my afternoon and I remember deflecting them successfully, though it's also possible that I may have dropped a hint or two about what really happened that could have been picked up. I was ashamed, I thought I'd be blamed and, moreover, I knew they didn't want me to tell them — just the way everyone laughed with pleasure when I, the baby of the family, pretended not to get the dirty jokes. But the biggest reason I didn't tell was because Bob Stoller made me believe his fate was in my hands. We had done something he said he would be blamed for more than me, something unimaginable that no one had ever done before, something that would horrify my parents and make me strange to them. And now I was strange, stranger than they'd ever know, than anyone would ever know (except Bob Stoller). And I could save Bob Stoller — the only person on earth who knew who I really was — by not telling. I was his savior. He was tied to me.

Was this when I began to be unable to sleep in the dark, when I began to have the fantasies that these parents were not my real parents? My real parents were kept prisoner in the basement, or, in another version, were in collusion with these people who pretended to be my parents, and came upstairs after I went to sleep, the four of them sitting in the living room and laughing about deceiving me. I was shocked many years later to read that this is a common fantasy of disturbed children. It embodies the child's feeling of being unloved, and I believed my parents couldn't love a little boy who had done the awful thing I had done. To tell them would leave me absolutely alone, whereas now I had Bob Stoller.

Did I think our friendship would never end? To a child the present feels endless, at least it did to me, and, trying to remember that year when I was five years old, the great majority of time when I was not being sexually molested (the rest of my life) hardly seems to have existed, although all the other people who were important to me were there—my parents, my grandpa (my mother's father), my older brother and sister—and I continued to play step ball with big, clumsy, sweet-tempered Kenny next door and war with the kids in the neighborhood in the vacant lots and construction sites, climbing on the thick wire struts reinforcing the concrete, relishing the perfume of fresh concrete and dirt. The other people in my life then are stuck in separate compartments in my memory, and I can't recapture the manifold texture of a particular day. Maybe this reflects my experience becoming split apart, immediately categorized, while underneath it all and truer than the rest was Bob Stoller.

How he managed to see me and how often during that year, I'm not sure. I became his model. Besides the angel-devil diptych (an image for my split self I accepted completely—did he design it that way?), I also was to be a sort of child-Bacchus standing atop a birdbath holding a beachball. I remember posing nude on the same pedestal in his attic studio, in the same cold air, holding the beachball behind my head. This was a conventional photographer's pose for bathing beauties in the early fifties. Travel ads, especially, often featured a bathing beauty in the pleasure spot standing ankle-deep in surf, holding a beachball behind her head. It gave me a stiff neck. Bob Stoller would sit in front of me molding chicken wire to my approximate shape around which he intended to pour concrete. Not exactly the most sophisticated idea of sculpting technique but an efficient way to get my clothes off. This project was also known to my parents, though I believe we told them I was clothed in shorts and a T-shirt which I'd bring along and never put on. And I'd also sneak up to his house at preappointed times and he'd be waiting at the back door. Once we were walking down the alley and my mother saw us, and once he bought me a Popsicle—it must have been summer—and I was still eating it when I got home and my mother asked where I got it. I told her Bob had bought it for me and it seems she might have wondered about a grown man's continuing friendship with a five-year-old boy. But it was a different era then, at least superficially innocent, and she had many distractions. I also can't estimate the effectiveness of the mask of innocence I used to hide the truth. I'm not sure how many times Bob Stoller had sex with me. I remember my reluctance every time, and the ways he'd overcome it by appeals to my sympathy and vanity, except—and this may be a trick of memory—the very last time, when his mother caught us, I was eager.

Maybe this is why I believe the most insidious part of sexual abuse is in the creation of desire in the molested child, the way it forms a shape for desire that can never again be fulfilled, only compulsively substituted for and repeated, unless—if he's lucky and can find help—he ceases to identify with the molester. From my reading I understand sexual abuse affects every victim differently, according to age, gender, the child's relationship to the molester, and whether or not the child kept the secret. Some victims, especially women, never identify with the molester, who is usually a man. But this identification, this no-I, was for me the hardest part to uproot. It is as if I were imprinted. The identification formed my identity. In memory the atmosphere of that last time is palpably different from any other. The place was different—his basement, not the attic studio; I knew we were going to do it beforehand, whereas, every other time I can recall, part of me didn't want to and had to be cajoled. Bob had told me his plan: I would sneak up to his house when his mother was out and we would go to his basement. We'd pretend to be looking at slides if she came home. Did he tell me he couldn't use me as his model anymore because his parents were becoming suspicious? Something like that. Something was closing in on us. He told me to ask my mother to sew elastic into the waistband of my jeans so that I could pull them up faster and not have to buckle my belt. Which I did. I remember standing in front of her in my underpants while she sewed. Bob had told me to come to his back door at a particular time, and my mother hadn't yet fixed my pants as I had asked her. I was jumping up and down, telling her to hurry up, she of course asking what the hurry was, and me saying I just wanted to go out. So I was late getting to his house, running full speed the circuitous route he had devised to make my being observed less likely, arriving breathless but wearing the pants he wanted.

"We'll have to hurry now," he said, and he took me downstairs, which was dark except for the light of a slide projector without a slide in front of it. I was still huffing and puffing, and he set me on his lap as he had many times, both of us facing the glaring screen. He put on a slide to soften the light, maybe some landscape shot from somebody's vacation, his mother waving at us from in front of the Grand Canyon. "Just catch your breath," he whispered, his hands on my chest and stomach. As my breath returned, so the dream feeling entered, gradually, as if it were part of my body. His talk became husky. I knew his hands would start moving soon, and soon after that nothing else would exist.

He was kneeling in front of me, my pants around my ankles, when we both heard the back door open at the top of the basement stairs. "Oh God," Bob Stoller said. "My mother. Pull up your pants. Pull up your pants." How glad I was I had my elastic waistband! My pants were up in a second, and everything was sure to be fine.

Bob went upstairs and I heard his mother screaming, "What are you doing down there? What are you doing?"

He told her we were looking at slides, but she didn't believe him. I knew we were in trouble. He came downstairs to tell me I had to go home now but everything would be all right, my parents wouldn't find out, he'd take care of his mother, he'd talk to me soon. It was that abrupt. I could hardly stand walking up Bob Stoller's basement stairs, feeling shame in every muscle as I passed through the kitchen, his mother, it seems, turning her shoulder and walking into another room at the moment I passed through the kitchen and out the back door, Bob Stoller touching my head as he gently closed the door behind me, me blinking my eyes trying to adjust to the sudden sunlight.

How long was it before I saw him again? It seems it may have been the next day. What was the night like for me between the afternoon we were caught and the next day? I don't remember at all; it is the blackest of blanks. The next time I saw him, when he told me he would be going away soon, I was surprised. It was daytime again, we were at his house, it seems his mother was in the room.

When the day came for him to leave, my mother saw him in front of his house packing his pickup truck and suggested my sister and I go say goodbye. My sister is four-and-a-half years older than me—she was nine—and I believe Bob Stoller molested her, too. She can remember him taking her picture, too, but nothing else. Sometimes, like me, she'd go to his house alone, and once he took us both for a whole day in the country in his pickup. We went to a site on which he planned to build a cabin of his own. When it was all built, he said, we could come stay with him there overnight. There was the foundation of a house that had burned down and the whole place was overgrown. It seemed rough and a little frightening and I was bored, but what I remember best was his calling me over to a tree to look at a funny branch. He was standing underneath the tree. He touched the end of one of its branches with a long stick, and the branch turned from gray to green and moved—it was a big insect that protected itself by perfect camouflage, grotesquely ugly, the ugliest thing I had ever seen. That evening—or was it another?—the three of us, my sister in the middle, went to a drive-in in his pickup, and afterwards he bought us foot-long hot dogs. There was no sex or talk of sex with the three of us together.

And yet at some point in that year, I knew that he did have sex with his cousin, a little girl my sister's age, who came for a long visit. He asked me before she arrived if I'd like to see her cunt (that's the word he used), but I said I wouldn't. It was to be part of an anatomy lesson, part of "the facts of life" he said I was old enough to learn. I remember meeting her and being with both her and Bob Stoller in his attic studio and her saying something knowing to me, something that indicated that Bob Stoller had told her about me. She had clipped dark hair and wore a plaid wool shirt. She smiled when she said it. I shied away, it made me feel a little sick. My sister became her friend.

And my sister began to have terrible attacks of hives that would send her to bed. She couldn't swallow pills. My parents would try to force her to swallow them, and she would scream at the top of her lungs and throw herself against the wall and floor. I thought she was being stupid. Once, we were in the car, my parents in the front and she and I in the back, and she had such a violent attack I had to move up front. Kneeling backward between my parents with my chin on the top of the front seat I was interested to see her flail from one side of the backseat to the other, flying from side to side and floor to ceiling as if jerked by a wire, as if she were possessed. This was the word my parents used: possessed. So I did, too. I proudly announced to the neighbors that my sister was possessed, until my parents told me I shouldn't. When she and I were walking by ourselves, and a man walked toward us on the same side of the street, my sister would say, "Michael, there's a *man*," and we'd have to cross to the other side. On a busy street we'd have to crisscross back and forth, and it always took us twice as long to get where we were going.

The goodbye to Bob Stoller was short and kind of sad, but I didn't allow myself to feel much. He shook hands with each of us; he was very vague about where he was going or if he'd ever be coming back. *He* was the one who seemed sad, and the odd thing about this and about my whole relationship with him is that he would express the emotions I actually felt, and in general reverse our roles: I was the one with the power, I was the one who could hurt him. He stood with his head bowed, scuffing his toe on the curb in front of the pickup packed with the attic studio furniture and his photography equipment tied down with ropes. It was an old black pickup with a square cab. We watched him drive away, and my sister and I walked back to our house not speaking.

He was gone, but nothing else changed. If I felt abandoned or betrayed, which I must have, I didn't register it consciously. There was simply a hole at the middle of the world. Appearances were just as flimsy as before but now there was nothing at all behind them. It never occurred to me to find another adult to replace Bob Stoller. What had happened to me was absolutely specific to him, and he was gone. I began not to be able to urinate. I would really have to go and would stand over the toilet while a few drops dribbled out. I'd be watching "Crusader Rabbit," my favorite television cartoon program (he was a hero rabbit), and I'd keep having to run to the bathroom and interrupt the story. I'd hold it as long as I could, then run to the bathroom again and try to push my pee out, then run back as quickly as I could, five six seven times during a half-hour program. My mother made an appointment with a doctor whose office was downtown, near my father's. She made the appointment for late afternoon, so we could then pick up my father after work.

The doctor looked like Groucho Marx. He sat me on the table and talked to me a little and then reached into a tray of instruments and produced a thin silver rod with a tiny valentine heart on the end of it. He squeezed the head of my penis from the front and back with his thumb and forefinger, and, before I realized what he was going to do, jammed the rod into it. I had never felt such pain, and it kept hurting with the same intensity so that for hours afterward I insisted that the heart must have broken off inside, driving my mother to such a frenzy that she called the doctor to ask if something could have gone wrong. He said no. It was called being "boojeed," an operation for urinary blockage they don't do anymore. The Groucho Marx doctor gave me a piece of gauze to hold on my penis to catch the bleeding. I went out of his office crying, and cried and screamed the whole time my mother and I waited in the car for my father to get out of work. It hurt so much. I would lift away the gauze pad and a drop of blood would form at the hole in my penis. I'd touch it with the pad, then there'd be another one. I begged her to do something, to take me home, and she agonized about it, but she finally couldn't bring herself to go without my father, so we sat there for what in memory seems like hours.

Apparently, sexual molestation often causes such urinary blockages in children, though it's unclear whether the cause is physiological or psychological. I certainly had no other way of telling my parents what had happened to me. Two years later, after we had moved to Florida, the bad little girl next door who had been caught fellating her sixteen-year-old brother talked me into going into the crawl space under an abandoned house (where her brother had taken her sometimes) to show her mine while she showed me hers. I went home crying and, sitting in the bathtub, I told my mother what I had done, and she took me to confession that afternoon to tell the priest I had committed an act of impurity with another. The penance he gave me was nothing extraordinary—five Our Fathers and five Hail Marys—but I believed the only way I would be forgiven was to say prayers continuously to myself, which I did, the Hail Mary in particular going silently and rapidly through my brain during every waking moment for approximately a year. I sometimes varied it with one-liners such as "My Jesus, mercy!" that we were taught to use when we didn't have time for a longer prayer. The nuns, without irony, called these one-liners Ejaculations. Our Lady of Sorrows, pray for us. Wounds of Jesus, heal us. I learned all of them.

The bad little girl next door was named Betty Short. She was one of seven children (all of them short), but she was the only fat one and all the neighborhood kids called her a piglet; the name we used as often as Betty, in her presence and in direct address, was Piglet. Her brother was sent away to boarding school after her parents discovered them one night in his bedroom. She told me about this night herself on the front stoop of her house, although his being sent away for this reason was somehow already general knowledge among the neighborhood kids. She initiated sexual games among us—a group of six of us, boys and girls, seven years old and younger, played touching tongues and would spin in circles after our tongues touched sending crazy shivers through us. Betty Short also could talk dirty and smile evilly and she was doing this with me on the stoop so that I became stiff.

"Let's go up to the old house," she said, and I knew what she meant. I asked her why she wanted to see mine when she had already seen her brother's. She said, "Because I want to see a little boy's."

She told me all about her brother, but I didn't tell her about Bob

Stoller. She was making me feel the way I had with him, the dream feeling, wanting to go with her and not wanting to go but going. It was in Groveland, in a neighborhood of white stucco houses, when the oranges and grapefruits in everyone's backyard were so plentiful they fell off the trees and rotted on the ground and we would throw them at one another like snowballs. The houses had no basements because the water table is so near the earth's surface, so they are all built on foundations that create a crawl space in which animals go to bear their young or to die. Our dog Topsy had her puppies under our house, and my father had to slither on his stomach with a flashlight and bring them out one at a time while the neighborhood kids cheered. The old house up the block no one lived in was set on a downslope, and its crawl space heightened enough toward the back for a child to stand upright. Betty Short went first and I hung back. The sun was bright and there was plenty of light.

She had on a white pinafore with puffy short sleeves. With her back to me, she dropped her underpants and held the hem of her dress up between her teeth and turned around in a sort of half-squat, pulling her labia open with both hands. It looked red and raw, like a bad scrape. She was grinning and wheezing, her face flushed. It was about the most horrifying thing I'd ever seen—not what was between her legs (I hardly looked) but the maniacal expression on her fat red face, wheezing and laughing clench-mouthed with the hem of the pinafore between her teeth. She skillfully held this difficult, balanced half-squatting pose until I said I had seen enough.

Then it was my turn. I wanted to welch out of it. We exchanged places, but this time I made her turn her back while I fished for it and poked it out through my zipper. When I said okay, she turned around and I immediately pushed it back inside my fly and zipped up again. She complained that she hardly got a look at it, but I was unsympathetic. "Tough," I said. I had fulfilled my part of the bargain and wanted nothing but to get out of there.

We went to a neighbor's yard where there was a swing set and little kids. As we walked together, Betty Short began saying dirty words, one after another, in sentences and sometimes without syntax. Although I had heard such words, I never used them, but by the time we got to the neighbor's yard, I picked it up.

"Fucking cunty prick shit," Betty Short said.

"Shit poop fuck shit," I answered. We both laughed uproariously. It felt crazy. I just wanted to say crazy things and be crazy.

The little kids soon picked it up, too, and before long we were all swinging and running around yelling dirty words, tackling each other and saying them right into one another's faces and spitting. Someone got tackled too hard and started to cry and then there was a woman screaming at me and Betty Short to get out of her yard and never come back, calling us filthy, filthy children.

I started to run, but Betty Short grabbed me. She would go, but at her own sweet pace.

"Don't worry about her," Betty Short said. "She's just an old bitch."

As we strolled back toward our houses, Betty Short hooked my arm. "Now you're my boyfriend," she said.

That was all I could take. I went right into my house and burst into tears. Sitting in the bathtub, I told my mother. She said Betty Short was a bad girl and I would not be allowed to play with her anymore. This was fine with me—I didn't like her one bit. It was all her fault. If I confessed my sin, my mother said, I would be forgiven. After I dried off and got dressed, she drove me to church.

The next day Betty Short knocked on our back door. I called my mother and hid in the shadows of the kitchen while she told Betty Short she couldn't play with me anymore.

Thus began the feud with the Short family. Their house was about fifteen feet from ours. They were the only other Catholic family on the block at a time when there was a great deal of anti-Catholic prejudice in Florida. Koons, Kikes, and Katholics—in that order—were the triple-K targets of the Ku Klux Klan. But we had little regard for the Shorts. The father was a stubby man with a nasty temper and a greasy black lock of hair that fell into his eyes. The mother wore stained aprons. With seven kids, their house and yard were always a mess, toys and rakes strewn all over. But Betty Short was exactly my age and in my second-grade class at school. We had been friendly.

She screamed at me at recess for snitching on her, calling me dirty names. I said she was a fat piglet and she should try to do something about it. What she did about it happened a couple of days later. She had two younger brothers, one year and two years younger than she, which meant they were five and six. I was in my yard the next Saturday morning, punctiliously not crossing the imaginary line that was the border of our property. Her youngest brother was alone in their yard and called to me to come see something he had found. I had no quarrel with him. We had been friendly, too. We met at the imaginary line and he held out a handful of dirt for me to see. When I looked, he threw it into my eyes, yelled "Shitty stool pigeon," and took off. I ran after him down the border between our houses. He took a sharp right around the front of his. I followed, stretching to collar him, but the moment I turned the corner, his older brother hit me flush in the face with the flat bottom of a toy gas station.

It was made of tin and cut me under the eye, but the shock of their hatred is much more powerful in my memory. I didn't know what hit me, and suddenly Betty Short appeared standing over me with her two brothers, the one who had smacked me brandishing the gas station like a baseball bat, cocking it menacingly for another smack. I scrambled home as quickly as I could, them yelling taunts and warnings to stay off their property, me vaulting onto our porch and slamming the screen door behind me and wailing my bloody face off. There were conferences between parents who were themselves angry, and truces drawn. The families agreed to have nothing to do with each other. During the whole business, on our side, much was said about bad Betty Short and the sexual perversion in the Short household as a way of invoking our obvious moral superiority. I was so glad I hadn't told Betty Short or anyone else about Bob Stoller, but I knew I was as bad as she was, or even worse. I had made my first Holy Communion the previous year with this unspeakable sin on my soul. I had been dressed in white—white suit, shoes, shirt, and tie—and carried a white Holy Missal between my folded hands, while my soul inside me was rotten and black and festering. It had now been about a week since I had gone with Betty Short under the old house, a week since I had been to confession. The whole time my family talked about what to do about the Shorts, I was saying silent Hail Marys to myself.

THE GOAT-LAMP

My earliest memory of my father is the happiest. I'm lying on my back on a big bed and he's changing my diaper. Just when he gets the fresh one underneath me, and is bending over to pin it up, I let go and pee full-force straight into his face. He jumps back surprised, and I lie there giggling as the stream arcs down and splashes on me, warm and tickling. I'm so pleased, I think it's the funniest thing that ever happened. Then he starts laughing, too, and we have this great joke together.

Is this a memory or a family story? He was the storyteller in our family, the jokester, the crooner. He could play the guitar, the violin, and—my favorite because the songs and the instrument itself were clearly silly—the ukulele. He's cradling it in the photos of a picnic with my mother and their friends in the twenties—the gay blade: blade-thin, wire-rim glasses, black hair slicked straight back, white shirt, white ducks, white bucks. He would sing his parodies of ukulele songs when we drove the forty back-road miles from Milwaukee to Bellflower, Wisconsin, where his mother had a forty-acre farm.

Ain't she sweet?
Just smell her stinky feet.

Now I ask you very con-fi-den-tially,
Ain't she sweet?

Ain't she nice?
Just ignore the lice . . .

Not exactly stand-up material, but hilarious to a five-year-old, and these trips to Bellflower, where the cars were parked angled to the curb in front of a country store that sold flour and molasses from barrels, were our only family trips, so the tunes of these songs are still charged for me with an incongruous sweetness.

The route took us over a long bridge over a big river, and, before we got to it, my father would always pull onto the gravel shoulder and walk around the front and get in on the passenger side, and my mother would slide over and drive. Once across the bridge, she'd stop the car again, he'd get out and the process would be reversed. All they'd say to explain this odd ritual was that Daddy didn't like to drive over bridges. I saw him drive over only one, on a busy four-lane highway with no shoulder when he didn't know the bridge was coming and he couldn't get out of the traffic. His knuckles whitened on the wheel and the sweat soaked his shirt so his sleeveless undershirt showed through. He pulled over as soon as he could, then walked around by himself for fifteen minutes wiping his face with a handkerchief. He couldn't drive for the rest of the day.

Years later I read in a book about alcoholism that this phobia is sometimes one of its advanced symptoms: a fear that the bridge is going to fly out from under you. The alcoholic can cross bridges, but can't drive over them. I had forgotten what we thought of then as an embarrassing quirk, so when I saw it in the book, it came back in a rush, implying that my father's disease was already advanced during my early childhood. I don't have a memory of knowing he was drunk until I was twelve or thirteen, after we had moved for the third and last time, to Steeltown, PA. I remember very early occasionally thinking something about him was odd, or off, but I didn't know what, and because I had done the terrible thing with Bob Stoller, I thought people were like that, not quite present, not quite available, buried inside themselves in some hidden way. I knew I was.

Every day of his life, when he came home from work, he did exactly the same things in the same order no matter how drunk he was: take off his suit and hang the pants meticulously on a hanger on the bedroom doorknob for my mother to press after dinner; unknot his tie and drape it on the overloaded tie rack in his closet; enshrine his gold cuff links and tie clip in his jewelry box on the dresser, rolling his French cuffs above his forearms as he walked to the bed in his boxer shorts and gartered black socks; sit down on the bed and take off his shoes and stuff them with the varnished-wood-and-blue-steel shoe forms he kept underneath it, and, if I was dumb enough to be standing there, hand me the shoes to shine; and, finally, walk back to his closet and put on a pair of brown sport slacks and slippers. In Milwaukee he would then go sit in his overstuffed chair in the living room and read the paper under the halo of the floor lamp until my mother called us for dinner. Maybe he'd have a drink, or a bottle of beer, but I don't remember it. He stashed a handgrip exerciser in the slot between the armrest and the seat cushion, a shiny spring with two red wooden handles, an upside-down V with a little circle at the top. He'd switch it from hand to hand as he read, a hundred right-handed, a hundred left-handed, again and again, never missing a beat of the two-note squeak of the spring. Often, certainly knowing I couldn't do it, he'd insist I try it; with both hands I couldn't budge the handles. My hands stretched to the limit hardly spanned the distance between them. During the day, hoping one day to astonish him, I'd sneak into the living room and dig it out of the crack and try it, but with no more success.

My father claimed that men judged each other by their handshakes, so that it was a very important ingredient of personal success to have a firm one. He said that on occasion he had met someone who would try to hurt him by squeezing his hand too hard, but such a person had always gotten a surprise from him. He had a handshake that could bring a man to his knees.

He liked to demonstrate on me. He'd call me over to his chair and grab both my wrists in one hand and squeeze until I knelt down before him. The idea, he said, was to see how long I could keep standing, to see how tough I was. The first time I lasted about three seconds and it probably would have been less had I not been so surprised I was being hurt. I screeched for him to stop, which he did after I fell at his feet with my face in the rug. I could smell the dust in it and the leather of his slippers. I was crying, my face was hot with tears, but he wasn't about to console me. He said I better get much tougher if I wanted to be a man, that as I grew up there was going to be plenty of pain, this was nothing. He told me how supremely important this lesson was, that he wasn't punishing me but teaching me to be strong.

Of course, a child's world is *the* world to him. At least it was to me. The world I lived in, split as it was, was the whole world. Even so, it seemed strange that my father would hurt me when I hadn't done anything bad. For a couple of days I avoided being alone with him in the living room. In memory, I sit on the couch as he reads the paper or watches John Cameron Swayze recite the news on the tiny crackly screen of our new Philco. He says "Give 'em hell, Harry" whenever President Truman appears saying something clipped and sharp. After he switches the TV off or folds up the paper, he calls me over. I make him promise he won't squeeze my wrists, and he laughs and says he won't. When I get close enough, his hand shoots out and pulls me onto his lap. And that's it. He lets me sit there. His face is big and the light reflects off the lenses of his wire-rims and I smell the Vitalis he uses to slick back his jet black hair. I like being there with him, just me and him. I don't remember smelling liquor on his breath.

But the next time I'm on his lap, he suddenly chafes my face with his whiskers until it burns, or says "How about a Dutch rub?" (his knuckles on my scalp), or he holds my wrists in one hand and tickles me with the other until I fly off onto the floor with his fingers digging under my ribs. This is called roughhousing, only sissies don't like it, we're playing these games that are going to help me to be strong.

They're interspersed with gentleness and affection, or indifference—
some days he doesn't seem to know I'm there—so it's impossible to
guess what he's going to do when he calls me over. I want to play, but
I'm afraid. If I make him promise not to squeeze my wrists, he might
say "OK, forget it" and ignore me. The negotiation becomes part of
the game, what I can get him to agree not to do, though I know he
may trick me, and sometimes he promises not to squeeze my wrists
and just squeezes them anyway.

Once he got me over by telling me he'd show me how to "milk the
mouse." I know you can't milk a mouse, but I like the funny words.
Does he have a real mouse over there? I stand to his right, next to his
chair, my chest pressed into the fat padded armrest, trying to see into
the folds of his lap. He takes my hand in his lap, telling me he's got a
mouse right here he's going to milk. I'm squeamish and giggly. He
wedges the tip and knuckle of my pinky between his thumb and forefinger and squeezes. The pain's amazing. I scream, and he says,
"There's the mouse squeaking. You hear the mouse? You hear the
mouse?" I screech louder for him to stop, but he wants me to tell him
if I hear the mouse. When I yell "Yesyesyes" and end up on the floor
again, he says, "See, you're the mouse."

I don't remember how many times he hurt me like this, over how
many months or years, but he did it only in Milwaukee, only in the living room after he came home from work, and only when we were
alone. If I had to guess, I'd say ten to fifteen times over the course of
one year, and, although it would be an incredible coincidence, I'd say
he did it during the same year I was sexually molested, and about the
same number of times. But this seems impossibly symmetrical, and,
whether or not they happened simultaneously, or the same number of
times, the memories of being molested by Bob Stoller and of being
hurt by my father simply will not merge. They are so separate they
seem to have happened to different little boys, neither of which is me,
both of which are me.

I also can only guess why my father, drunk or not, did this to me. I
have no indication that he didn't believe it was healthy good fun, part

of a boy's proper education. He spanked all three of his children, usually bare-assed, sometimes with his belt, more often threatening with
his belt by unbuckling it and beginning to slide it out through the loops
of his pants—or sliding it all the way out and then doubling it, grasping
its buckle and tip in his fist, then slapping it slowly on the palm of his
left hand. And once, before I was born, he punched my brother flush
in the face when my brother, age seven, was kneeling on the chest of
my sister, age three, and strangling her. However, my father didn't take
pleasure in these spankings; he didn't beat his children, or ever hit his
wife, so by the standards of the era and according to his own upbring-
ing, he was a normal disciplining father. In any case, none of this ex-
plains the games—which were "not punishment"—he played with me,
and apparently only with me, the youngest son. It seems impersonal,
accidental, to have been unrelated to my character, my self, like getting hit by a bus, like being sexually molested, though that's my understanding talking many years after the fact and not the way I felt then
and for most of my life afterward—that he did it because something's
terribly wrong with me, something I can't ever grasp.

In 1951, the year I was five, the dress company my father worked for
went out of business. There was a recession, and jobs were hard to get.
For a month or two, he did the books for a used-car dealership, but it
was a shady operation—probably double bookkeeping for tax fraud—
and he quit. A difficult decision under the circumstances, and much
was made by my mother of his integrity and honesty. Having gone
through the Depression (he was twenty in 1929, and supposedly supported his parents working fifty hours a week while he earned his bachelor's degree at night and ate a handful of peanuts every day for lunch);
having supposedly given up being first violin in the Milwaukee
Philharmonic to support them; having certainly worried and complained about money his entire life; having a wife and three kids (five,
nine, and thirteen in 1951)—when he lost his job during generally
hard times, he no doubt felt the bottom drop out. It may have been the
first time he thought of himself as a failure. When he found another

job, my mother made his favorite cake to celebrate: angel food. I never liked it.

He had days of good cheer, and what I loved most about him was his liveliness, but, after I was old enough to characterize another person's state of mind, he always seemed unhappy. To him, as to every addict, the world was a hostile place. All of his stories reflected this. In all of them, he was unjustly attacked and defended himself heroically. He had been very short and scrawny, the smallest kid in the class (he looked twelve when he was eighteen), and for this reason, as he told it, the natural prey of bullies. But he always prevailed, sometimes by superior ingenuity, sometimes by sheer courage. To survive you had to be smart and you had to be tough. Both. Neither by itself was enough. By the age of five I knew this, his central idea about life.

I'm sure it was because he liked numbers that by age five I had learned arithmetic. On Saturday mornings my sister would teach me what she had learned that week in school. Then we'd go from door to door in the neighborhood offering to do multiplications in my head. After we performed—my sister requesting from the "audience" any single digit by single digit, single digit by double digit and, ta-taa, double-digit by double-digit numbers (almost everyone asked for 99 times 99, and I had memorized that answer, 9,801, but would wait a beat before saying it as if I were multiplying)—we collected our reward. Remarkably, we were never turned away, although eventually some of the neighbors probably saw us coming and didn't answer the door. I have a very vague, bizarre, perhaps dream memory of standing on Bob Stoller's front porch doing multiplications for his mother. Bob Stoller has already moved away. My sister asks me if I want to skip their house. But we're ringing every doorbell on the block and getting cookies and money for our act, and I don't let on that to me this house is different from any other. Bob Stoller's mother answers the door, and suddenly standing there before her are my sister and me. What a blast of dread and guilt must have rushed through her body. Is this the moment of reckoning? Then where are the parents? There's one step up to enter the house, so we hardly reach the level of her waist. She opens the screen door and looks down at us. My sister says, "Mrs. Stoller, Mikey can do multiplications in his head."

I had never been on Bob Stoller's front porch—I always snuck in through the back. When his mother opens the door, I smell the inside of the house. I remember her giving us money, change from a purse, silver. What did she feel as we toddled down the steps to the sidewalk, when she closed the door and was back alone inside her house?

You had to be smart and you had to be tough. Both. I'm sure it was also for my father's love that I claimed to be the toughest kid on the block and fought anyone who disputed it. I fully believed I was the smartest and toughest boy who had ever lived, that I would be a millionaire, and that God had chosen me for a special mission, like He had chosen the archangel Michael to drive Satan and the bad angels from heaven with a flaming sword. One day a big kid whom I'd never seen before appeared in front of our house to offer to fight me with one hand behind his back. He said he heard I had been bragging about how tough I was. All the neighborhood kids were gathered around us. He was a head taller than me but I was invincible.

We set the bout for that afternoon. I took my punching bag out to the sidewalk. It was mounted on a flexible rod welded onto a tin plate you stood on, so when you punched the bag, it came back at you at an unexpected, evasive angle, ducking and bobbing, just like your opponent's head. I had recently graduated to this superior equipment from an inflatable clown with sand in its bottom whose red nose squeaked when punched, and I was very happy I could display my new professional training methods. The spectators were impressed, and agreed that I would make short work of the big kid.

He showed up when he said he would. The neighborhood kids made a circle, and he waited inside it, impatient and bored, while I did a few fancy final minutes of shadowboxing outside the periphery. Then the circle parted and I stepped inside.

"You can only use one hand, right?" I said, and put up both my dukes. I was invincible, but why take chances?

"Right," he answered. In one motion he locked his right arm behind his back, stepped forward, and popped me in the eye with a straight left. That ended the fight. I fell down and cried at being hit in the face; my previous bouts had consisted of wrestling and punches in the stomach. This was real fighting. I spent the rest of the day in bed with an ice bag on my eye, which nevertheless swelled shut from the one punch. With a jab like that, the kid had a future; the fortunately few times I ran into him afterward, his friends pointed at me and hooted there's the toughest kid in the neighborhood and howled for a rematch.

My father laughed, too, though he seemed secretly proud of me. He sat on the edge of my bed and lifted off the ice bag to inspect my eye. In my memory I slept in my own room upstairs by myself, but in fact—my mother told me—I slept in my parents' bedroom downstairs the whole time we lived in Milwaukee, until I was seven. She may as well have told me I grew up in Tunisia: I *remember* sleeping upstairs in a room by myself. At bedtime, when my mother tucked me in and turned out the lights, an octopus would grow underneath my bed, and touch its suctioned tentacles along the bedstead looking for any part of my body that was protruding over the edge, so they installed a nightlight, but only after much pleading and pestering. This was their bedroom. Until I found that out, it never made sense why they didn't want to.

In that eerie dim light my father told me bedtime stories about the Greenies. The Greenies were a race of tiny people—three feet tall—who lived inside the earth. My father had discovered them when he was my age exploring caves in the Ozarks, where he grew up on a dirt farm. His parents didn't have money for toys like I had, so he'd entertain himself climbing deep down in the dark, among bats and stalagmites and stalactites, farther down than anyone had ever gone. One day he saw an odd light coming through a crack above a ledge high up in the cave wall, almost hidden by rocks. He climbed up, and by moving the rocks he saw an opening just large enough for him to squeeze through. It was lucky he was small. A bigger boy couldn't have made it.

There was a ledge on the other side, too, and there in the great cavern beneath him, in a shining city made of emeralds, diamonds, platinum, and gold, he saw the Greenies, all scurrying this way and that like ants. It was terrifically hot and damp; the stones around him radiated heat. When he climbed down closer, he could see their pale green skin tough as rhinoceros hide and their corkscrew-tipped heads that could drill through granite. There was a gorgeous Greenie princess who was in love with my father (gorgeous, I guess, despite her corkscrew-tipped head), a good king, bad Greenies who had left the city and threatened it with raids, and assorted natural cataclysms and fantastic monsters—the basic stuff of the Old Testament, Buck Rogers, and H. Rider Haggard (*King Solomon's Mines*), my father's favorite author.

The detail I remember best was incidental to the big battles and epic struggle for racial survival. After my father had helped the Greenies and been accepted and honored by them, he was given full access to their kingdom, permission never before granted to an outsider. He could roam about wherever he wanted and treat whatever they had as his own—the latter privilege he didn't exercise except for the three modest, perfect diamonds he took for his mother, for the woman he would someday marry (this diamond could be found in my mother's engagement ring), and for himself (here was his, in the ring on his right hand; he said someday, when he was dead, it would be mine). One quiet day in the kingdom, happy and content with these harmonious, gentle people, he was exploring its outer reaches by himself and, in a grotto on the other side of a stream, he came upon a goat with a head exactly like the lampshade on the floor lamp next to my bed—narrow at the top and opening out—and, behind the goat, emerging from the shadows, the most beautiful woman he had ever seen, completely naked. Then the grotto began pulsing with a strange light. They stared at him, woman and goat. He knew if he crossed the stream his life would be changed. He'd never see his parents again, or maybe even the Greenies. The woman smiled invitingly, but the goat hissed and out of its lampshade skull came poison smoke. My father turned and ran, on to the next wonder and adventure. Although I'm sure I asked about them, they never appeared in the stories again.

After that I couldn't look at the lamp without seeing the goat. It had two simultaneous beings. In the daylight, it was the lamp *and* the goat or the goat functioning as a lamp, and at night when the light was turned out, it became the goat, perfectly still, an immobile outline permanently suspended in the instant before it would start to move and spume poison smoke. It sent a chill through me from toes to scalp, an awful thrill that was finally too much, and made me feel like I was spinning wildly in outer space. But when my father was sitting on the edge of the bed with his elbows on his knees, I could see his white shirt in the dark, I could feel the pressure of his hips, and that contact grounded me enough so that no matter how scared or crazy I became I wanted him to keep telling me the stories.

He didn't tell them often—each time had to be a special treat. And each time, before he would begin, he'd ask me if I believed in the Greenies. I had to say yes to get a story, to say I believed that this fabulous world was going on inside the earth even as he spoke. I didn't believe it, then I said I did, and as the word left my mouth, I believed and didn't believe at the same time, like the goat-lamp, like Bob Stoller's room in the attic. It was secret life. It was my father's secret life.

One night during a story I shrieked out loud and my mother opened the door into the dim room and said to my father: "Why are you telling him those stories when you know they're not true? You're scaring him to death." My father sat there for a moment without arguing, then without finishing the story got up and left. My mother stayed with me. I didn't protest. I *was* scared, and I was pleased my father had been caught doing something bad to me, and I played the injured role for all it was worth.

It was only worth until I fell asleep. No one mentioned it the next day. My father acted like nothing had happened. Weeks went by without his offering to tell me about the Greenies. When I finally brought it up, saying that he could give me a story and I wouldn't yell again, he said, "You don't believe in the Greenies."

This surprised me. It wasn't that he had done something bad by scaring me, but that I didn't believe, and that's why I wasn't getting the stories anymore.

"Mommy says they're not true," I said to defend myself.

"It doesn't matter what Mommy says," he replied. "I promised the Greenies I wouldn't tell anyone who didn't believe. And you don't. I know you don't."

And he never told me a story about the Greenies again. Ever. Once, when I was a teenager, the whole family kidded him about his insistence that the Greenie stories were true, but, bizarre as it sounds, he acted hurt then, too, and left the room, and would not admit they weren't. We were living in Steeltown by then. It was evening, and he had had a few drinks. There was not a single evening during those last years when he was not first tipsy and then drunk, and toward the end of his life he would go straight to drunk. He would throw down four or five straight shots and then pour himself his first drink of the night, pretending the previous five shots didn't count. I came upon him once with his head tipped back sucking straight out of the bottle. When he realized I was there, he wiped his mouth with the back of his hand, and looked at me with a terrible fury, daring me to say something.

He died when I was eighteen. My sister went away to college when I was thirteen, and my brother, who is nine years older than I, had a job in Wyoming, about as far away as he could get. So for the last five years it was mostly just my mother, my father, and me. The weight of his illness doubled and redoubled from year to year and finally from month to month, so by the end we were living in a madhouse. My father became two people: at breakfast every day, until noon on Saturday, and often until dinner on Sunday, he was sober, silent, and remote. He would hardly speak, even if addressed. He looked angry. No doubt he felt sick, hungover, maybe remembering some horror from the previous night. Over breakfast my mother and I would rush whatever business we had with him, whatever we needed permission for, whatever practical things had to be decided or discussed, because he was still the paramount authority (my mother wouldn't have it any other way), and because by the time he came home from work, or shortly there-after, he was the other person. This one was split, too: while tipsy, he was voluble, lively, playful, affectionate—mildly manic, but rarely with the manic's dangerous, disturbing edge; then, without warning, he'd pass over into drunk—staggering, slurring, bitter, paranoic, violent, totally unpredictable, completely nuts. It wasn't possible to enjoy him in the first state because it always led to the second. It implied the second, it contained the second, and, when he was in a tipsy good mood, my mother and I would use the moments of apparent closeness to beg him not to drink any more that night. But he wouldn't stop, and if we begged too much, it turned his sweet mood sour, and he'd accuse us of wrecking even the nice time we had together. In the early sixties, alcoholism was generally thought of less as a disease than as a weakness of character; "alcoholic" was just a fancy word for a drunk. Not knowing I could do nothing, I tried everything to stop him from drinking, from promising to wash the car and mow the lawn to screaming insults and emptying his quarts of whiskey down the kitchen sink.

My father's day began in the bathroom—throwing up into the toilet and then sitting on it, sometimes for forty minutes. When he got off, it would be filled with blood. If he woke up in the morning still drunk, which happened more often during his last year, he might show me and cry and say something was broken inside him. Something was, I knew, but the blood came from hemorrhoids, a vicious case surgically removed three separate times, exacerbated by sitting on the toilet too long, which he wouldn't stop doing no matter what it did to him. Then, hanging his pajama top on the doorknob, he'd shave with the door open, ghostly white but remarkably steady-handed, his big pot-belly pushed halfway into the sink as he leaned close to the mirror to see without his glasses. Then he'd shake his barbershop-size bottle of Vitalis into a little pool in his palm for the obligatory ninety-second scalp massage, after which, reeking of it, he'd comb his still perfectly black hair straight back, as he always wore it, and part it precisely on the left (where I part mine) with the rat-end tip of a finetooth silver-metal comb, locking his hair in place for the rest of the day. (It didn't budge until his head hit the pillow that night, even when he was puking in the kitchen sink or taking a swing at me.) Then he'd get dressed, meticulously, and come to the breakfast table composed, looking like any one of a million particularly well-groomed mid-level business executives. For breakfast, every morning, he ate bacon and two eggs over-easy fried in the grease, white toast with plenty of butter, coffee, and tomato juice or, on occasion, V-8 with pepper in it. After he finished eating, he'd line up the day's pills (more than twenty of them, four or five different shapes and colors for hypertension and angina), swallow the first round with a fat red multivitamin, and scoop the rest of them off the table into a little gold pillbox, on the lid of which was a golfer following through on a drive, with a diamond chip for a golf ball. My father never played golf.

He was fifty-five when he died, his third heart attack. He went to the doctor every other Tuesday and came home with blood pressure readings of 240 over 160 and up. Besides the eggs in the morning, he ate steaks and chops for both lunch and dinner. He smoked two packs of Pall Malls and drank about a fifth of whiskey every day. I never saw him do a moment of exercise, except with his grip-strengthener, which he had also given up by the time we moved to Steeltown. He couldn't walk up two flights of stairs without catching his breath for a few minutes on the middle landing. It must be awful to live in a body like this, sick every morning, dragging until lunch when he'd have two or three Manhattans, enough to dull the edges and lighten the heaviness until five o'clock, when the serious drinking began.

On the way home he'd usually stop for a couple of belts at the Keystone. The Keystone was a private neighborhood social club. It had a long oval bar, shuffleboard and darts, a few tables and chairs in front of a tiny bandstand, and a backroom with a continuous poker game. It was really an old speakeasy. For your annual dues you got a laminated card that buzzed and unlocked the door when you stuck it into the slot. It was built like a bunker out of concrete blocks. There were no windows and only the one entrance. When the heavy door banged shut behind you, the atmosphere was like another planet's, dim-lit honky-tonk, refrigerated air thick with liquor and cigarette smoke. I was never there at night, only on Saturdays or during my father's vacation after an afternoon of chores and errands. Money, his anxiety about it, tormented him; he exhorted, threatened, and complained about our spending too much (which we didn't), fantasized about hitting the jackpot with new inventions (which he never invented), never risked a dime, never cheated on his taxes or anyplace else, and spent every single penny of what he made after living expenses and never before them on liquor and life insurance. I didn't feel poor, but I always felt strapped, as if any minute the world was going to crash like a tidal wave through the walls of our house and sweep us into poverty.

But as soon as we walked into the Keystone, everything changed. Suddenly, I could have anything I wanted: endless bags of nuts, potato chips, beef jerky, Cheez Doodles, Cokes until I drowned in them, an infinite supply of quarters for the pinball machines. He would buy a roll of quarters with his first drink, and break it in half on the edge of the bar. They'd lie there spilled from the torn wrapper next to the change from a twenty (he always paid for his first drink with a twenty), and I could take a handful when I needed it—I didn't even have to ask. Sometimes we'd play the shuffleboard bowling game, zinging that heavy silver disc for strikes and spares amid the smell of booze and wax dust, the lights flashing, the bells ringing. Time didn't exist, nor the intruding world. I was meant to enjoy myself, and I did. It was the most fun I had with him. But eventually he'd go back to his barstool, and I'd get bored and start pestering him to leave. That irritated him. If I was going to be that kind of guy, I shouldn't come along in the first place. Rather than go through this, I'd walk the six blocks home by myself, a lonely walk, back out in the glaring sunlit world of lawns and boxlike houses. As I grew older, being at the Keystone held less appeal for me. Being with my father had less appeal. By the time I was in high school, I just stopped going.

My father once said if the Russians dropped an atom bomb on us we would all be safe at the Keystone. I hooted and asked what would we live on, beef jerky and beer nuts? My mother said she'd rather die. This was at the time of the Cuban Missile Crisis, after he started spending most nights at the Keystone because, he said, we were bugging him too much about drinking. After dinner he'd say he was going out for a pack of cigarettes and not come back until midnight. After an hour or two, my mother would worry out loud about his having had an accident. Then she'd call him at the Keystone, until the bartender began telling her he wasn't there. So she'd ask me to try—maybe a man's voice would bring him to the phone. I was fourteen and hadn't reached puberty, but I tried to deepen my voice. The first time, incredibly, it worked, and, humiliated at having been caught, he came home furious, refusing to speak. After that, nothing could bring him to the phone at the Keystone. When he said he was going out for a pack of cigarettes, I'd scream "Liar! Liar! Liar!" at the top of my lungs. I'd grab his arm, I'd hide his car keys. My mother, who encouraged my every effort, would then step in and insist I tell him where the keys were, that my father was a free adult who had to make his own choices. After he left, she'd sit at the dining-room table and cry, her face uncovered and shoulders shaking.

Once, instead of crying with her, I went right to the phone and left a message with the bartender for Jack Ryan to call home as soon as he came in. It was an emergency.

My mother said I shouldn't have done that, but we both waited for the phone to ring, still at the dining-room table with the dirty dishes, the steak fat and gristle on my father's plate (he ate steak almost every night; even when the rest of us had meat loaf, my mother broiled him a steak). Fifteen minutes, twenty minutes—the Keystone was six blocks away, and he was driving—thirty minutes: nothing. I went to the phone.

"Is Jack Ryan there?" I asked.

"He hasn't come in."

"It's an emergency," I repeated.

"I'm sorry," the bartender said (but he seemed to hesitate). "I'll give him the message."

It made me crazy. I put on my coat to ride my bike over there and drag him out, but my mother stopped me. I dialed the Keystone again. When the bartender answered, I tried to disguise my voice.

"Put Ryan on," I growled.

"He's not here," the bartender said, obviously startled.

"Goddamn you," I yelled. "I know he's there. Put him on the phone."

There was a silence at the other end. I was sure I'd be hearing my father's voice next, and I had no idea what I was going to say. But it was the bartender again.

"Son," he said, "I don't know what to tell you. Your father's not here."

And he wasn't. That night he had gone to another bar somewhere so he wouldn't have to deal with our calling him. Maybe after that night they told him they'd revoke his Keystone membership unless he made us stop calling him. He said if I ever did that again he would beat me until I couldn't walk. At fourteen, I was five feet two and chubby and he was still stronger than me, but I said that in that case he would have to, and, while he was at it, he might as well kill me dead because otherwise I would be calling him at the Keystone every single night from now on. My mother stood between us, alternately begging him not to hit me and warning me to remember his heart condition. We were in the kitchen, which was narrow enough for her to block us. She had just washed the dishes, her back was to me, and I noticed the butcher knife drying on the sink. I saw myself plunging it into his neck, so I didn't pick it up.

Instead, we reached a truce. My father would tell us where he was going and what time he'd probably be back so we wouldn't worry about him and, if we'd stop bugging him about his drinking (he enjoyed drinking, he said), he'd stay home. I didn't think this was such a great deal, but my mother immediately agreed and insisted that I agree, too. My father and I shook hands on it. We tried acting like friends.

But we lived in a very small three-bedroom ranch house. It was all on one floor, the TV was in the living room, and he kept his liquor in a cabinet next to the kitchen sink (and also, I found out later, in various closets). There was no place in the house he could drink in privacy, and he hated drinking in front of us.

He came up with two solutions to this problem, one temporary and one permanent. The temporary one was beer. His drink was whiskey—in the last three years of his life, as he drank more of it, he bought cheaper and cheaper blends, cases of Imperial, finally, at four dollars a quart. But when I was fourteen, his brand was Canadian Club, and he would even go to the trouble to fix himself Manhattans in a heavy crystal glass with Vermouth and a maraschino cherry (which he always offered to me when he finished the drink, its cloying sweetness soaked with bitter liquor), or sometimes he'd mix himself a "highball," whiskey and club soda or ginger ale. Beer wasn't really drinking. He didn't mind us seeing him with a can of beer. He'd bring home sixpacks of sixteen-ounce Budweisers—"tallboys" he called them—and he'd pop a tallboy right after dinner and stretch out on the living-room couch in front of the TV. By eight o'clock, after only two of them, crushing the cans one-handed when they were empty, he was drunk. It was hard to understand how he could get so drunk so quickly on beer. My mother said it was his heart medicine. Of course, he was drinking whiskey from a secret stash.

But he hated us for making him sneak around—that must be how he experienced it, not as his own projected shame—so he thought of a permanent solution: he would build his own bar in the basement. It was by far the most ambitious, sustained project of his life, at least that I ever witnessed. He had two weeks' vacation every summer, but— with one exception, a visit to his mother who had retired to Florida— we never left Steeltown. He'd sleep late and put on a "sport shirt" to do little repairs around the house, work on the lawn, run errands, get his weekly haircut, and close out the afternoon at the Keystone. But this summer, when I was fourteen, he ordered all the material from hardware stores and lumberyards and piled it in the basement; he rented drills, electric sanders, staple guns, and was downstairs banging away by 9 A.M.

He called it the Playroom, and I think to him it must have represented success. Only big shots had playrooms in their houses. He had just gotten a big raise. It had been a stated ambition of his to make ten thousand dollars a year, and, in this year, 1960, he made it. He measured all the dimensions of the basement, and after dinner sat at the kitchen table scribbling on blueprints and expense sheets. He even brought home an adding machine from the office, which chugged and unrolled its paper spool when he hit the keys. One of the first things he decided was the colors. It would be all black and pink: black and pink floor tiles alternating like a checkerboard, black and pink laminated plywood for the partition that would separate the Playroom from the unfinished half of the basement, pink paint for the concrete walls and black paint for the steel foundation post and overhead heating duct, padded pink-leather chromium-plated barstools, a black Naugahyde reclining rocker, pink plastic furniture. The bar itself he built into the far corner, on a diagonal, fronted with the black and pink laminated plywood (to match the partition) and topped with pink Formica. He sank brackets with a concrete drill and ran glass shelves along the two walls that met behind the bar. He filled the shelves with bottles of exotic liqueurs—crème de menthe, crème de cacao, crème de whatever—then, within six months, after he had drunk all the liqueurs on the nights he had already drunk everything else in the house, the shelves were filled with the empty bottles, topped with novelty corks someone had brought him from Germany: a donkey whose mouth opened when you pulled its tail, a mountaineer in lederhosen and feathered cap who threw up his arms when you pushed down his head. There were also highball glasses with cartoons and dirty jokes painted on them. The one I remember showed a honeymoon couple, the man carrying luggage into a cabin in the background, the woman bending into the trunk of the car with a "Just Married" sign on it, while a red-nosed deer sniffed her cartoon-exaggerated ass. She's saying, "Be patient, dear." I guess the deer-dear pun was supposed to be the joke, but I remember it instead of the others because of the woman's short tight skirt and the promise of sex, what I imagined they were going to do when they got inside the cabin. My father said it wasn't dirty because the couple was married.

After the Playroom was finished, and the TV relocated from the living room, my father would go downstairs as soon as he had changed his clothes after work. Before long, he was eating dinner off the bar while he watched the news, and spending the rest of the night lying on the couch, even peeing down the drain hole in the unfinished part of the basement rather than walking upstairs to the bathroom (which I also began doing until my mother said we were making the place smell like a subway). Sometimes I'd follow him down before dinner. He'd take a couple of belts while I spun the barstools. They were imported from Germany and built like a Mercedes, with precision ball bearings under the seats, and boy did they spin. The best you could buy. (Probably the only thing my father owned that was the best you could buy.) Each stool must have weighed a hundred pounds. When I was alone down there, I'd lie flat across the seat on my stomach so my outstretched hands and toes barely touched the bar when I spun, pushing myself faster like a playground merry-go-round, sometimes too fast and too hard so that the stool fell over with a crash. I knew he'd kill me if he ever saw me do it. He hated to see me spin them even with my hands.

My mother would be upstairs cooking. It was just my father and me downstairs, facing each other, our elbows on the bar. He'd ask me about school, about the sports I was playing, and he told me what he felt and believed, often waxing philosophical as the whiskey took effect. I responded to his sincerity, but, at the same time, I hated to hear him say stupid things, stupid drunken things. He told me he knew voodoo, that if he really wanted something bad to happen to someone it would, and because I was his son, I had inherited these powers, which I must use responsibly and sparingly, because if I used them too much the powers would turn back on me. He said he loved me the most, I was the most important person on earth to him, bar none, including my mother. Unlike my brother and sister, I could go to college anywhere I wanted and he would pay for it. He said it was important to have fun, to be kind to people, to love your family, and believe in God, whereas he never went to church, had no friends, and never had any fun unless fun was getting drunk by himself. If I pointed out any of these disparities, he turned mean, calling me a hotshot and telling me to wait until I had some goddamn responsibilities if I thought life was easy.

His lecture to me on sex may have been the shortest in the history of the world. I was watching television when he came downstairs. He walked in front of me and turned it off.

"Gonna talk to you about sex," he said.

I said okay. I couldn't imagine what he had in mind, or why he had decided that the time had come that I should know such things. He went behind the bar and expertly poured a shot, the tiny dome of amber liquid arching above the rim, then threw it down in one lightning motion. I turned around in my chair and looked at him.

He said, "When you're with a woman, use a rubber."

That was it. The end. I nodded. He fixed himself a highball.

This was also when I was fourteen. As he got drunk in the basement, he'd tell me stories about his past—about teaching judo to the Marines during World War II, about knife fights in dance halls. It was impossible to tell if even the slightest part of them was true. He'd get furious when I ridiculed them, which I often did, but sometimes I'd let him talk, my stomach churning with disgust at how foolish he was.

A couple of months after his lecture on sex, in the Playroom together before dinner, he said: "I only killed a man once." It was a Friday so he was very drunk already. He was sitting in his usual spot behind the bar.

"Right, Dad," I said.

"I've never told anybody before." He had used this line many times, and it no longer got my attention. "It was when I was exploring caves," he went on. "I knifed a man to death and threw him into a cave where nobody would ever find him."

"What did he do to you?" I asked, humoring him.

"He tried to shove his cock up my ass."

Shove his cock up my ass? I had been playing on playgrounds and sports teams for years, but had never heard of such a thing in such language and, coming out of my father's mouth, it shocked me to the core. I got out of my chair. I was going to go upstairs to my room, my head was spinning, I felt sick and dizzy, I couldn't even scream at him.

Before I was out of hearing, my father said, "You're real bullshit, you know that, buddy? A real punk." I didn't say anything. I didn't turn around.

I told my mother that he was too drunk to eat, at least I wasn't going to eat in the same room with him. I felt like crying, but I couldn't. I didn't know what to do. I went into my bedroom and closed the door and sat down on the bed. I had begun running away for a couple of hours when I was twelve and was still doing it, going out my bedroom window, or leaving the window open and hiding in the hamper in the closet so I could hear them worry about me. Our fights were getting more and more violent. I'd hit him back if I could and yell that he was nothing but a drunk and lock myself in the bathroom screaming as if possessed, my face red and burning, the inside of my chest burning. Until I was sure he had gone downstairs, I'd stay in there, sometimes for over an hour—sitting on the floor, the edge of the bathtub, the toilet with the seat down, doing nothing, making faces in the mirror, holding the sink like the handlebars of a motorcycle and pretending to drive it, trying to pull it out of the wall. One Saturday morning he brought his tool kit up from the basement and took off the bathroom lock. If I screamed at him when he could reach me, he'd knock me down, hitting me in the head with his open hand, but one thing I could always do was outrun him, and I'd fly up the stairs and out the front door and spend the rest of the evening at the bowling alley playing the pinball machines or roam the neighborhood looking into the lit windows of houses hoping to see a woman in her slip. Three or four times I ran up the stairs ahead of him into the kitchen and pulled the butcher knife out of the drawer. He always carried a pocketknife, a switchblade until they were declared illegal, then—by the time we lived in Steeltown—a grapefruit knife with an eight-inch blade he had brought with him from Florida. But he never pulled it out. I'd hold the butcher knife at waist level and scream, "Come on, I'll kill you if you touch me. I'll kill you!" It stopped him. At the time, I thought he was afraid, but maybe he was more afraid of the life we had come to than of being killed. It terrified me, too, and I quit doing it, partially because I was growing and lifting weights and I finally became taller and stronger than he was. The moment I was sure of it, I let him know that if he ever tried to hit me again he was going to pay but good for all the times he had hit me. He screamed that it was the worst sin of all to raise your hand against your father, but he stopped hitting me and, since when he threatened me I laughed in his face and told him he was a miserable old drunk, he stopped threatening me.

As I got taller and stronger, he got sicker and weaker. As his life was ending, I saw mine beginning. During my last year of high school and, though I couldn't know it, his last year alive, I tried to be immune to him, to ignore him as much as I could. There were still flare-ups, arguments, insults—I still couldn't stand to see him or hear him speak—but I could walk away from all of that. What I couldn't walk away from was his despair. It filled the house. We had not had any guests in our house for years—I never invited my friends in because I was ashamed of him—but he reached a new stage of isolation in his last year. Every night it was nothing but drinking and watching TV in the Playroom until he passed out. He used to read bad detective novels and subscribe to *Alfred Hitchcock's Mystery Magazine*. Now he quit reading. The subscription lapsed and he didn't renew it. He used to be in a bowling league. He stopped bowling. He even went to the Keystone less. At the point in our arguments when he used to hit me or threaten me, he'd cry. And he was always trying to touch me. He'd be drunk, and want to give me a hug. He put his hands on my head, my shoulders, my legs. Drunk, stupid, stinking. I couldn't stand it. Once, I called him a homo to get him away from me, and he stumbled up the stairs and cried hysterically in my mother's arms, as if I had finally violated him completely. I would not apologize, though she begged and begged and then wouldn't speak to me herself for days. I finally said okay he wasn't a homo but he should keep his hands off me. When he touched me, my body turned inside out. It was much worse than being hit.

When it rained, he liked to sit on the front step for hours, drinking, watching the rain. I didn't join him there anymore, but he called inside for me to come out, so I did. I had just graduated from high school and won the Monsignor Herman J. Golty Award for Highest Scholastic Average in Social Studies and he had been proud of me. When I was called to the podium, he stood up in the audience to take a picture of me, which came back from the developers a perfect black square. He was on the stoop and I sat down on the milk box. The rain was coming down in sheets.

He said, "I've had a lot of fun in my life."

I said so what and bullshit, but not out loud, only in my head. This was just tedious. I sighed but said nothing.

He said, "I'm going to die soon." It was so theatrical, so full of self-pity, so much like all his drunken remarks. But he had never said this before, and there was a matter-of-fact authority about it as if he just wanted me to know, as if he were saying "It's raining." I didn't believe him, but I didn't say so, and for years afterward I was so glad I had not responded sarcastically.

"If that's true," I said, "there's nothing you can do about it."

A week later, of course, he was dead. I was in Ocean City, New Jersey, with a carful of friends, yelling out the windows at girls to party with us on the beach, mooning the ones who refused, which was just about all of them. "Oh, gross," they'd say. "Grow up." The father of the friend with the car called and told him he had to come home early because he had some emergency work for him to do at their tool-and-die plant. The whole way home I complained and mocked him about letting his father push him around. I had just managed to spend a moon-lit evening on the beach in a covered lifeguard stand with a waitress from Akron, Ohio, about whom we were all gaga. I had already gotten to second base with another night ahead of us. I could hardly believe my good luck, and now it was back to Steeltown. I was going back the next weekend, by myself and on the bus if necessary, but when I saw her again, it was the next summer and she told me that in the intervening year she had gotten married and her husband had died in a motorcycle accident and the guy at the counter she had been talking to when I walked in was his best friend. She was on her break, smoking a Parliament 100, worrying the inside of the recessed filter with the pink stiletto of her thumbnail. I knew as soon as I saw her something had happened. She had changed her hair from soft honey blonde to a hair-sprayed platinum helmet, and she said she was sorry but she felt I had become much too young for her.

THE RYANS

In October 1945, when my mother was five months pregnant with me, her mother died suddenly from a cerebral hemorrhage. She was the person my mother was closest to in the world, whom she modeled herself after and idolized. They lived in the same house and saw each other every day; in 1945, my mother was thirty-six and her mother was sixty, a pure-blood German, trim, pretty, humble, devout, kind, "always giving to others," in perfect health except for a little high blood pressure. *Her* mother, in her eighties and in every way her daughter's opposite, owned the big house in the German section of Milwaukee in which all four generations lived, divided upstairs and downstairs into two separate apartments connected by a speaking tube between the kitchens. The war against Germany was just over. Every house in the neighborhood displayed the American flag. They had to. You couldn't buy sauerkraut without getting funny looks. People threw rocks at dachshunds. My mother's family, Schultzes and Ernsts, had occupied this house since the turn of the century, shifting apartments as the nuclear families grew and shrank. My mother had lived upstairs and downstairs two or three different times. In October 1945, my mother's grandmother, mother, father, and younger sister lived upstairs, and my mother lived downstairs with her husband

and two children (my brother and sister). The night my mother's mother died, they had all—except for my father and my mother's grandmother—just returned from a movie, a benefit for the Sodality of Our Lady, of which my mother was an active member and her mother was the president. It was a fine night, so the two of them decided to walk home. They talked all the way, quietly, about nothing important, while the kids ran circles around them and zigzagged ahead. When they got home, her mother asked her if she'd like to come upstairs for a treat. She said no because she wanted to get the kids into bed and she was, being pregnant, feeling a little sleepy herself. A short time later she heard a big thump upstairs. She called upstairs through the speaking tube, and her father answered that her mother was having a spell. She ran upstairs as fast as her legs would carry her. Her mother had gotten up from bed to go to the bathroom to take something for a headache, and collapsed onto the floor. She never regained consciousness. A doctor was called who gave her a shot—of what, no one recalls or probably was even told at the time. It was just a shot, to make her wake up. She wasn't taken to the hospital, nor was a priest called to administer Extreme Unction. Everyone was standing around her bed when she died in the early hours of the morning—with the exception of the two who had missed the Sodality benefit movie: my mother's grandmother, who was not awakened for her daughter's death, and my father, who stayed out very late that night. The first thing my mother said to him when he finally came home was "Mom's gone."

My mother's mother had been the glue of the family, and things soon started to come apart. My mother's grandmother had closer blood relations than the ones she was left living with. She had a son with a wife and grown children who wanted to live downstairs, and a sister with a husband who would be happy to share the upstairs with her. When the war ended, housing was at a premium. My mother's father had paid his mother-in-law rent for forty years, a small rent but enough to buy the house a couple of times, which in his mind gave him a moral claim on the property. My father was paying rent, too, and of course there was no lease. About eighteen months after my mother's mother died—I was about a year old—my mother's father and my father both received eviction notices on the same day. In the mail. From a lawyer. They thought it was a joke. It was the first they heard that the old woman wanted them to leave. She cleared them out and brought in a whole new set of relatives, upstairs and downstairs.

So, abruptly and with bad feeling, my family left the house they had lived in all their lives. My mother now had to care for an infant, two little children, a husband who was probably already drinking too much, and a father who expected to be cooked for and looked after—a family, according to her mother's example, whose needs she was supposed to serve before her own, which she would thereby hold together the way her mother had done. In the years following, she often wished she could have her mother's advice. In her prayers she talked to her in heaven. She needed her support, and didn't have it.

In the new house, a squat brick cube a few blocks from the old one, there were two bedrooms downstairs—the master bedroom and a smaller one for my sister—and an attic upstairs with a slanted, unfinished ceiling, which was partitioned for my brother and my grandfather. I would sleep in my parents' bedroom—until I was seven. As I've said already, I don't remember sleeping in their room with them. The memory's blocked beyond the physical boundaries of the half-sized bed, which I do remember, and getting out of it once in the middle of the night when I was six or seven because the puppy we had just bought was crying on the back porch. Its name was Topsy, my father's idea, from "topsy-turvy," because it was jumpy and yappy. Its crying made me so sad, I went outside and petted it. Each time I tried to go back to bed, it would start crying again, so I sat with it, just like my mother did with me when I was sick. When I was found there the next morning, everyone praised me for being a good, sweet boy.

That's how my grandfather always thought of me. He was seventy when his wife died, but he was still working as the office manager of American Car & Foundry, a big ironworks on the shore of

Lake Michigan. Only there wasn't a factory anymore, or an office either. By the end of the war, iron in industry had been replaced by steel, and, amid the booming postwar economy, American Car & Foundry shut down. My grandfather had been in charge of a warehouse-sized room full of clerks, and now he sat all day doing the final paperwork for the bankruptcy court at the same desk in the same immense room with no one else but a police dog. The ironworks stood on the lakeshore among the tin and tar-paper shacks called Hooverville because it was during Hoover's administration that so many destitute people came with whatever they had left and built shanties from whatever they could find on whatever space they could squeeze into and defend. Some of them would try to camp inside the factory when it got bonebreaking cold or to bust a window of the deserted office to look for something of value to sell. The only other employees of American Car & Foundry besides my grandfather and the police dog were night watchmen who carried truncheons, lanterns, and guns. If someone ever tried to break in when my grandfather was there, we never heard about it. Unlike my father, he didn't tell stories.

Even after he retired, every morning he would put on a white shirt then snap thick "elastics" onto his arms above each elbow to keep his cuffs out of the wet ink on the ledgers he had written in all day every day of his life. (He called rubber bands "elastics.") He also had a collection of rubber nipples that fit his thumb and forefinger (for flipping through files and stacks of documents), and he automatically put a couple of them in his pocket before he attached to his belt loop the chain to the pocket watch he was awarded for fifty years of service to the company. He put on the rubber nipples when we played rummy so the cards wouldn't slip when he dealt them. His name was Clarence Ernst. He was small-boned and seemed fragile to me. His hair was white and soft and fine, and he wore rimless glasses he took off to read, and he always smelled like talcum and tooth powder. He thought my father was a barbarian for using Vitalis. "Phew," he'd mouth to me, pinching his nose behind my father's back as my father got up from the breakfast table to leave for work. More often, he'd wait until my father had left for work to appear downstairs for his day of puttering. He had the run of the house until my father got home. Then he'd retire to his room, reappearing only once after supper: at 9 P.M. for a cup of Postum and two graham crackers, which he'd balance like wings on the sides of the saucer as he climbed back up the stairs.

What to my father was sour and cheap was to him sober and thrifty. He prided himself on being nobody's fool, which he expressed with a soft, gruff laugh, and which included never paying one penny more than necessary for anything and never buying anything extra, except the comic books he bought for me (Donald Duck and Little Lulu—no scary or violent ones that would be a bad influence on my development). With his arm around me, the two of us wedged into his easy chair, he'd read me the comic books after breakfast, the same ones over and over again, until I could read them myself, or seemed to, because I had them memorized. Like my father, he wanted me to be smart. It was the only feeling about me they had in common, which gave it terrific force, so I wanted to be smart more than anything else. In fact, I not only wanted to be smart, I had to be smart, and not only smart but the smartest boy of all (which stayed with me deep into adulthood—I felt annihilated when I could not delude myself into believing it). Grandpa didn't seem to care if I was tough, so when I was with him, I didn't pretend to be.

With him I was altogether another boy than the boy I was with my father or the boy I was with Bob Stoller, and now it seems that this boy—the good boy, the daylight boy—was the closest I came to being a child. He seemed happy when he saw me and was happy to be loved by me, and I loved him the way a child can love a grandparent, selfishly and unequivocally. Did the time I spent with Bob Stoller cut into the time I spent with him? I have no memory of that, as if what happened to me with my grandfather, my father, and Bob Stoller happened to different children. Imagining my grandfather now—widowed and displaced, retired and unnoticed—and remembering his grumpiness and silence when my father was around, the boy I was with him may have been the greatest pleasure of this time in his life.

Unless it was his car, a 1948 Plymouth. He loved it like a pet. Every day after lunch he drove it around the block, and sometimes I went along. It was a light chocolate color with ivory interior. All the knobs were ivory. I'd roll the window up and down while he double-clutched and shifted the gears on the thick steering column. Then he'd fit the car meticulously into the tiny garage behind the house and wipe it all over with a rag. The wiping took a half hour. The ride took five minutes. It was, literally (slowly, cautiously), around the block, twice if the day was particularly fine, down to Forest Park on Saturdays to feed the ducks with the brown bag of bread crusts he had accumulated all week in his room. He saved the paper bag. The top half had been rolled and crinkled so many times it was as pale and soft as a chamois.

We left him behind when we moved to Florida. He had lived in Milwaukee all his life, but, whether or not he wanted to come with us, he was not asked. I wasn't satisfied with any explanation for why he wasn't coming along that my mother or my father or he himself would give me, and for weeks before we moved I was inconsolable, bringing it up at dinner and making everyone uncomfortable, refusing to accept the lame story the three of them pretended to agree on. I was the pretending expert. I knew when somebody was faking. I knew he felt he had nowhere to go. After we left, he tried living first with my mother's younger sister and her new husband, then with my mother's older brother and his family, then checked into the old folks' home where he died more than ten years later, less than a month after my father. I didn't go to his funeral. By that time I had forgotten the boy I had been with him.

He stayed in our house until the last piece of furniture had been loaded onto the moving van, personally carrying the box of good china which had belonged to his wife, and giving the driver a stern lecture about it. I waved goodbye as he drove off in his Plymouth packed to the ceiling. I didn't see him again for almost two years. After a year in Groveland, Snow Crop was taken over by Minute Maid: my father's job and our well-being were again in jeopardy. There was much fretting and bemoaning our move from Milwaukee. But then it turned out my father would have a job with Minute Maid, an even better one than he had with Snow Crop. We would have to move again, but only a hundred miles or so, to Dunedin, on the west coast of Florida. This was fine with me. I wouldn't have to live next door to Betty Short and her brothers anymore. We rented a tumbledown antebellum mansion on the Gulf of Mexico, eight bathrooms and thirteen bedrooms—for a pittance, because the owner wanted it occupied while he was trying to sell it. It was a wild area, miles from the Catholic school and the Minute Maid plant in Clearwater. The ocean was across the street. The roads were unpaved, half sand, half moist gray dirt. There were almost no houses around, much less other kids—just extravagant vegetation, lolling palmettos and bright red hibiscus with their obscene stamens; chameleons and pelicans; and miles of empty beach pocked with finger holes into which wide waves of fiddler crabs would disappear as I approached. Fiddler crabs are only two inches long, but the males have one large claw as heavy as their bodies. They drop into their holes backward, pulling the claw in last. If trapped, they stand their ground and brandish it menacingly, ludicrously since they can barely lift it and it won't open wide enough to pinch your pinky. For some reason, this behavior offended me, and I'd pick them up and rip their claws off. This would send them scuttling away, helpless, teaching them, I thought, humility they needed to learn. I thought of myself as a god among fiddler crabs, a natural disaster that swept through their world, a world parallel to ours, like the Greenies. I imagined them talking about me at their summit conferences, the great unfathomable god Mike. I knew the claws grew back eventually, so I didn't think I was doing them any harm. I was merely improving their character. In fact, the females reject males without claws and the other males kill them.

To celebrate our luck at living in a mansion, and maybe also to show how well my father was doing, all the relatives from Milwaukee were invited to visit us, with many assurances that there was plenty of room for everyone. Only the grandparents came, but they stayed a couple of weeks. My father's father had died years before I was born. He was an Ozark dirt farmer and had met his wife walking from Arkansas to Canada to chop trees, picking up millwork along the way. She was the daughter of a mill owner in St. Joseph, Missouri, sixteen years old, half her husband's age when she married him. Within a year of his death, she married the man who owned the neighboring farm, which was considerably better than hers, a man with a sweet saw-toothed smile who, like my father, was both devoted to and terrified of her, and, unlike my father, was comic about it. "When that woman calls, you better jump, Mike," Grandpa Jim would say to me, grinning. "Yes, sir. And when she has her mind set on something, you just step aside and let her have the road. I mean the whole road." Maude Allen was her maiden name. She was one-sixteenth Cherokee Indian (which made me, to my pleasure, part Cherokee—sometimes, in telling other kids, as much as one-fourth). She also claimed to be a great-great-granddaughter of Ethan Allen and to have inherited his fighting spirit. This glorious martial lineage meshed with my holy card of St. Michael driving the bad angels from heaven with a flaming sword. My mother's relatives were petty clerks and burghers who ate pigs' knuckles and sauerkraut and sang novelty songs in German at the family outings (*"Ist das nicht ein Schnitzelbank? Ja, das ist ein Schnitzelbank."*). The only one of my father's relatives I ever met was his mother, but I saw her riddle a coffee can lid at twenty-five paces with a .22 rifle and chop the heads off chickens with a hatchet on the blood-stained tree stump next to her back porch. She was also famously emotional, her eyes tearing unexpectedly at a sentimental thought or memory, and, when she was upset, she'd drive everyone from the house with her screaming, so that all the guests at Thanksgiving dinner might end up standing out on the lawn holding their knives and forks with their napkins still tucked beneath their chins.

She and Grandpa Jim loved to fish when they weren't farming. They had a creek on their property where you could catch catfish almost without baiting the hook. I remember once at sunset lying on my stomach on a high bank with the two of them. We were about to call it a day when we were suddenly hit by a school. As soon as we got our hooks into the water, there would be catfish on them, so many and so fast that we ran out of worms. Grandma chopped the last worms into teeny bits with a pocket knife, but the fish kept biting. She said they were hitting on the smell. I was afraid to take the hook out after I caught one, so Grandma did it for me, sometimes wrenching it out of the gullet when the fish swallowed it. She'd dig her fingers all the way down its throat until she could get a hold of the hook and jiggle it back and forth. It made a pocking sound like an empty plastic bottle being squeezed. Catfish, much more than bass or trout, can gill you to ribbons, and she was trying to get the hooks out so quickly her hands were a dripping bloody mess, her own blood and fish blood all the way up her forearms. It didn't bother her, but it scared me, and I was gawking at her.

"Come on, Mike, get your line back in the water. The Lord is sending us some fish."

"Fish fry tonight, Mike," added Jim, to distract me. "Look at this sucker! Three pounds if he's an ounce." Grandpa Jim didn't seem to mind getting sliced up either. I never saw either of them happier.

Now they had come to Florida for some deep-sea fishing. An expedition was arranged on a dayboat that charged a per person fee, but Grandma didn't go because, she said, never in her life had she paid to fish and she wasn't about to start now. The very idea, as she made abundantly clear, appalled her. So the men went—Grandpa Jim, my father and brother and me—all but Grandpa Ernst, who didn't like the stink and the blood. Grandpa Ernst had a funny way of disappearing in a group, especially a group of men. He would just kind of evaporate. He seemed to disapprove of the whole business, whatever the business was. Everyone would be laughing and I'd look at him and he wouldn't be. All the fun I had with him was when we were alone.

The rest of us got up before dawn and ate the ham sandwiches we had brought along as soon as we boarded the boat, my father popping his first Budweiser before we were out of the harbor. He also had a pint of Seagram's peeking out of his back pocket. There were about thirty people on the boat. We chugged out into the middle of the Gulf where the really big ones were. I asked my dad how big a fish I could catch. He told me there were tuna and tarpon that went over a thousand pounds. We weren't going for those, but I might get one that weighed a hundred, easy, maybe more. Wouldn't a fish that big pull me over? He said he'd stay right next to me and grab me around the waist.

The captain finally cut the engines, and we all propped on the rail thick poles with reels the size of salad plates and barbed steel hooks baited with chunks of squid. There was only a light sinker on my line, but we were fishing at such depth that the line was as taut as my father's ukulele strings. We weren't supposed to let the hooks rest on the ocean floor, but to dangle them maybe a foot or so above. It had to be done by feel. I kept pulling mine up because it felt like something had to be on it. Everyone was amused at first, and then became irritated with me because we weren't catching anything. My father yelled at me to quit it. He said if I kept doing it I could put up my pole and go sit inside for the rest of the trip. Then one guy near us felt an enormous pull that almost took him over the rail, at exactly the same moment that a guy on the opposite side of the boat got a big hit. Maybe it was a school of tuna. Everyone stopped to see what sort of monsters could bend deep-sea rods like that. Their lines were tangled underneath the hull—with eight others, as it turned out, including mine. Everyone had to reel in and the tangled lines had to be cut. "I didn't do it," I said. My father just glared. Grandpa Jim said no one thought I did.

We were out there ten hours, and all anyone caught was a few small junk fish. The captain couldn't understand it. He was a Greek who worked out of Tarpon Springs, where the young men dived for the crucifix at Easter. The fishing boats made a circle in the harbor and, after blessing the fleet, the Orthodox priest, in full sacred vestments, standing on a prow, would motor out into the middle of the circle and toss the crucifix into the water, overhand, like a tomahawk. The divers had to be able to hold their breath for up to five minutes. Each boat had its representative and the one who came up with the crucifix would have good fishing all year. This year it had been the captain's son, a slender, liquid-eyed teenager who looked like Sal Mineo. The captain clasped him around the shoulder as he told the story, and the boy smiled with embarrassment. All week the fishing had been so good that the captain still had a hold full of grouper. So he gave us a couple hundred pounds of them, grabbing them under the gills and tossing one after another onto the pier at our feet. (That's how abundant the sea was forty years ago—now it would be a thousand dollars worth of fish.)

Riding back in the car, my father got the idea that we should tell everyone at home that I had caught not only the biggest one of the bunch—a sixty-four-pound grouper—but also that it was the biggest fish caught on the boat that day. I was eight years old and didn't weigh much more than sixty-four pounds myself. Everybody thought it was a great idea and hooted and howled. It picked up our spirits after an exhausting, disappointing day.

The women all ran out to the yard when we pulled in. "Did you have any luck?" they yelled.

"You bet we did," my dad answered. "Look at this!" He showed them a trunkful of fish. "And Mikey caught the biggest one. Look at this monster!" He held it up next to me. He had to use both hands. It was as tall as I was.

"Oh, Mikey, you didn't!" they squealed.

"Mike's the hero," my dad said.

"Mike, how in the world could you pull in such a big fish?" my mother asked, thrilled.

"Well, I had a little help," I said. I proceeded to describe the whole struggle, how all the other fishermen reeled in to watch me land the big one, how Dad and Grandpa Jim had held me by the waist when it looked like I was going overboard, sure I was scared and nervous, but . . . etc. Everything I said the others corroborated, and the more I said, the more I believed that I actually had caught the fish. The words just poured out of my mouth. In the telling it all became true. But Grandpa Ernst wouldn't swallow it.

"This is a fish story," he said.

My father got angry. "Goddamn it, Clarence the boy caught the fish. Can't you even give credit to a child?"

"I give Mike all credit," Grandpa said. "It's just some others who don't tell the truth."

"Mike, did you catch the fish or not?" my dad asked.

"Sure I did." I answered without missing a beat.

My grandpa looked at me (I'll never forget that look) and walked back into the house.

Before we cleaned the fish, my father strung them on a wire clothesline in the yard, and we had our picture taken. In the same drawer as the eight-by-ten glossy of me in my Hopalong Cassidy sweater is a snapshot of me with the sixty-four-pound grouper hanging from a wire clothesline. I'm wearing a straw cowboy hat and look triumphant.

My mom and grandma fried up the grouper, and we ate ourselves into insensibility and froze the rest. My dad had some more beers and kept coming back to how I had caught the big fish. It was past my bedtime, and finally I got my last congratulations from everyone and thanks for the delicious fish dinner and went upstairs. What a wonderful day it had turned out to be. I was coming out of the bathroom after brushing my teeth and bumped smack into my dad. We were alone in the hall.

"Good job," he said, tousling my hair. "You're a great liar." He went into the bathroom and closed the door.

He was right—I knew it. I was a great liar. Even better than he knew. The previous year in Groveland, I came in second in the school Easter egg hunt by claiming to have found nine eggs, whereas I had only four to show. I said I ate the other five. I claimed nine because the winner had found ten and I knew unless I could produce the actual eggs they'd never give me first prize—a stupid china egg I didn't want anyway. But maybe they'd give me second prize: a large chocolate bunny I certainly did want. I was right. They did. Whether or not they believed me, they didn't humiliate me. But when I got home and bit into the chocolate bunny, it was hollow. Even the ears were hollow. I ate it all at once and made myself sick.

And this year, in my third-grade class in Clearwater, we had had a good-deed contest. In Art Hour (the last hour Friday afternoons), we drew snowmen on construction paper; whenever we did a good deed—it didn't have to be anything big, just something nice for one of our classmates, maybe picking up a coat that had fallen off the hook—we were to draw a snowball next to the snowman. It was on the honor system. Nobody would be checking on us. The drawings were tacked up in the back of the room where the coats were, and I'd sweep a few coats off their hooks by accident so I could draw snowballs for picking them up. Then I realized, Why mess with the middleman? and just drew the snowballs, a couple at first, then furiously, whenever I had the chance, even sneaking to the back of the room during lessons to do it. Somebody reported me, but the nun said, "Michael knows that would defeat the purpose. It's the honor system." I was indignant at the accusation. I said, "I did all the deeds, Sister. There's a good deed for every snowball up there." Most of my classmates had a modest triangular pile next to their snowmen. My paper was crammed with snowballs, as if the snowman had fallen backward into an enormous honeycomb. Needless to say, I won the prize hands down: a plastic Jesus with a gate implanted in His chest that opened to reveal a glow-in-the-dark bleeding heart squinched into a crown of thorns. It pulsed on my nightstand, a reminder of my hopelessly evil nature. I kept the gate closed at night, but I could feel the heart throbbing behind it.

I even cheated playing against myself. In Milwaukee, I had developed a set of imaginary friends—Ainchy, Dainchy, and Awainchy—whose main function was to lose to me (or, more accurately, to "Mike") at step ball. Ainchy was the doormat, and Dainchy was not much better, but, unless I was feeling angry and wanted to trounce all three of them, the game would come down to a neck-and-neck life-and-death battle between Awainchy and Mike, Mike miraculously pulling it out at the last moment. I never lost to him, and he must have been a pretty frustrated guy, coming so close to winning about a million times in a row, at a conservative estimate. I'd play by myself every day after school until I got bored with my dominance, then go for a walk alone on the beach, harrowing the fiddler crabs and looking for weird things washed up by the tide. I started having conversations with my imaginary friends during these walks. We'd powwow over my problems. As in my games, Awainchy was the most substantial, the most intelligent and understanding. He'd want to know why I was feeling so sad, and I'd tell him about a kid I didn't like at school or my big brother teasing me or that I was just feeling kind of blah because there was nobody to play with. He was always sympathetic. I never thought he was an actual person. He had no physical characteristics. But he was a presence, a consolation, not-real-but-real while I was talking to him, as if he could almost-but-not-quite appear beside me as I walked alone. The waves broke across the virgin beach with their relentless rhythm and flattened out and withdrew with a hiss, and the water and sand seemed to go on endlessly. I wasn't saying constant Hail Marys and Ejaculations inside my head anymore. I thought I left the bad thing I had done with Betty Short in Groveland, just as I had left the bad thing I had done with Bob Stoller in Milwaukee. Being in a different place made them disappear. I would never see them again. Without the Hail Marys and Ejaculations, there was a kind of emptiness inside my skull like the deserted beach and the water. I started noticing women's breasts, and thinking about them all the time. The bigger they were, the better I liked them. I started drawing them in my room by myself, but I couldn't draw so they came out looking nothing like what I imagined or had seen in the *National Geographic*. Then one day I made a major discovery. If I drew a heart then a short straight line coming up from where the top curves met, and added a pair of shoulders and a neck, it looked like the deep cleavage of a woman in a strapless evening gown. A decapitated woman, but still a woman. It gave me a boner, and I did it every day as soon as I got home from school, before I went out to play. Sometimes I tried to add a face, but it always looked goofy, and if I tried to draw a woman naked without an evening gown it looked like a used tube of tooth-paste with headlights.

So the sexualization of the world that sometimes happens to mo-lested children remained for me internal and secret and compartmen-talized. I went to church on Sundays and holy days, I had been taught by nuns since kindergarten, I said grace aloud for the family before and after every meal and prayers with my mother at bedtime. I pre-tended to be a good boy, but I knew what sin was, sin way beyond the pale, unspeakable, a swirling cesspool of sin. When the nuns told us about being reunited with our loved ones at the Last Judgment, I knew I wouldn't be. The people I loved thought I was someone I wasn't. It's not so much that I lived in two radically different worlds as in the no-man's-land between them. There was no one where I lived and there never would be, in this world or The Next. And here was a place like that, the blank ocean and deserted beach. I spent hours and hours there by myself, and with Topsy, who joyfully joined in barking when I descended in thunder upon the fiddler crabs.

I wonder what would have become of me had I been seduced by an-other child molester. I don't know if I could have been seduced again, but it didn't occur to me as a possibility. It didn't occur to me that other men besides Bob Stoller did such things, although I had been warned to stay away from strangers. (Always strangers because it's hard to face the fact that the molester is almost never a stranger.) Once a stranger did pull up next to me on the street in Milwaukee and said that my mother had told him to bring me home. I had just seen my mother two minutes ago. He threw open the passenger door, and, when I refused to get in, he yelled, "Get in! Get in the car!" and drove alongside me for half a block. I shrieked and cried and ran for my life. When that hap-pened, I did tell my parents, who praised me for doing the right thing (as I knew they would), but I continued to pretend to be completely ig-norant about sex, to pretend not to understand the risqué jokes at the dinner table, to ask purposely naive questions and make everybody laugh at my innocence. In Dunedin, I started having asthma attacks. They came in the middle of the night, and I would wake up choking, unable to breathe, still the most terrifying sensation I've ever had. It's like drowning, but if you inhale hard enough, with all your strength, you can get a teeny, teeny breath of air, enough to keep you alive. Then you have to do it again, and again, and very soon your lungs and chest muscles are excruciatingly sore, so that getting that teeny breath hurts more every time. The more afraid you are, the worse it gets, and the worse it gets, the more afraid you are. I'd wake up knowing I was dying—the punishment I deserved—and my mother would come and comfort me, holding my hand all night, as she always did when I was sick.

This was what I wanted, I guess, but the asthma attacks continued. Nothing helped. They installed a vaporizer in my room and filled it with mentholated water, and before I went to sleep my mother rubbed my chest and back with Vicks Vaporub, gobs of it, cold and sticky, basting me with it. The sheets had to be changed every day. I'd scrub myself in the morning but left for school still smelling like a sinus inhaler. I could smell myself as I sat in my desk, so I knew the other kids could smell me, too. The attacks came only at night, and I began to be afraid to go to sleep.

One day after school I went on a different walk instead of down the beach—down a one-lane sand road with dune grass growing out between the ruts. There was no way to drive it except with a Jeep, but set off to one side was a rusty silver trailer on concrete blocks, and, in front of the trailer, playing next to a washtub and a wringer with a crank, were a boy about my age and a girl in pink terry-cloth shorts. She had rich brown hair, big brown eyes, a pouty mouth. He looked like Tubby in my Little Lulu comics. They both stopped playing and stared at me. I strolled by as casually as I could—ludicrously, since there must have been a passerby on that road approximately once every third millennium, and it dead-ended into a jungle a little farther down, so I had to just turn around and walk by them again.

"Where you think you're goin'?" the boy yelled at me as I passed them the second time. I didn't have an answer for that. I didn't answer. He was obviously the Enemy.

I started walking by every day after school, hoping to catch her without him, but either there was no one or the both of them. It was driving me crazy. Then I knew what I had to do.

The next day I walked right up to them and took the boy aside.

"She your girlfriend?" I asked.

"Yep," he said.

"I'll wrestle you for her," I said.

"Okay," he agreed, without a moment's hesitation, as if this were a natural courtesy extended to all errant knights and samurai warriors and entirely to be expected.

We assumed the grappler's stance, and began circling cagily, but the girl came running over.

"No fighting, no fighting!" she shouted. So we stopped and stood upright. Then, apparently out of curiosity, she asked, "What are you fighting about?"

I looked straight into her eyes. "You," I said.

"Go ahead and fight," she said.

So we did, and I won. He was heavier than me, but pretty slow, and I had superior motivation. I didn't use the fatal judo chop to the windpipe or the pressure points my father had taught me (such as pressing the soft spot behind your opponent's ears until it cut off the blood to his brain and made him faint). Just your basic headlock, trip, and pin with your knees on the guy's shoulders. He gave up pretty easily. I would have fought until my heart stopped.

After that I had a girlfriend. Her name was Ila Lewis. She had a drawl that made me giddy with desire. She'd knock the knocker on the enormous front door of our Doric-columned front porch, and if my mother answered, she'd ask, "Mis-sus Rhine, can Mike come out and feed his daw-wug?" She'd fill the pockets of her shorts with Hartz Mountain Doggy Treats, and hand them to Topsy one delicious slow one at a time as I sat there mooning.

I had a boner constantly whenever we sat on the porch, and she'd bat her eyelids and flirt and make special little movements with that mouth of hers. I never kissed her or touched her except to hold hands, but I quit drawing the decapitated woman in evening gowns and thinking about breasts, probably because Ila herself didn't have any and it surely wasn't a problem. She didn't have a dad, either, and her mom treated me like a visiting pasha when I walked her back to their trailer.

"Mike, are y'all rich?" Ila asked me one day as I was squiring her home.

I said we weren't.

"My mom says y'all must be rich 'cause you live in the big house."

I told my mom about this, and she said I was right, we weren't rich, but when Ila came over the next time, my mom had a conversation with her, and gave her some canned goods to take home to her mom. I carried them, of course. You were supposed to carry a girl's books, so I thought I should carry her cans of peas and succotash. I presented them ceremoniously when we arrived at the trailer.

"Why, whatever is this?" Ila's mom asked. She was a big pale woman with bright yellow hair that my mother said came out of a bottle. Nothing like Ila, whose skin was luxuriously tanned. I'd see her sometimes fishing off the pier in overalls rolled halfway up her thick pink calves.

"My mom says it's for Ila feeding our dog."

"Well, that's real nice. You tell your mom thank you kindly."

After that I carried two cans of vegetables every time I walked Ila home.

My mother must have been thinking about food. My sister wouldn't eat. They tried everything, from making her sit over her plate at the dinner table until 10 P.M. to offering to cook anything she wanted. She wouldn't eat breakfast and threw away her lunch. She was in eighth grade, thirteen, and weighed no more than I did, though I was half a foot shorter. I liked it because it meant, if necessary, I could beat her up. Her best friend in Milwaukee had been a thin blonde girl named Barbara Leber who looked very much like her. As soon as Barbara Leber walked into our house, I'd jump her, whapping her with anything available, baseball gloves, Parcheesi boards, Golden storybooks. It baffled everyone. There was absolutely no provocation, and I felt no

emotion while I did it. My parents spanked me, my sister tried to reason with me, and, as I was smacking her, Barbara Leber would scream,
"Why are you hitting me? Why are you hitting me?" But I could have
as easily explained to our cats why I pulled their tails (fourteen of them
in a row ran away until we finally got Topsy, whose tail, for some reason, I didn't pull). There wasn't any why, at least that I could tell her. I
just didn't want her around. It certainly worked. After I beat her up a
few times, she refused to come over anymore.

On the other hand, I did like my sister. On Saturday mornings she'd
teach me what she had learned in school (she was five grades ahead),
and then told everyone how smart I was. She even bragged to her
teacher, so in Clearwater I was taken out of class and brought to the
eighth grade for a mental multiplication contest against their best
math whiz, which I won. I was an old pro by that time. My sister introduced me to all her classmates at recess. "This is my brother Mike,"
she said proudly. "You sure can multiply," they said. I graciously acknowledged their compliments.

We did a lot together for a brother and sister five grades apart. We
entered talent contests where she performed dramatic mono-
logues (the kind written in booklets for such performances, with
ample opportunity for portraying widely disparate and intense
emotional states: a half-minute of despair, forty-five seconds of love, a
half-minute of rage, etc.); she could weep real tears at will, and saved
this for the climax, bowing to the judges with her eyes swollen and wet.
When I asked her how to do it, she said to think of the saddest thing
that could ever happen. I thought about both my parents dying, but I
still couldn't cry. Luckily, we competed in different age categories. I
imitated Johnny Ray singing "Your Cheatin' Heart," falling on my
knees, slapping the ground, and sobbing histrionically. It got big
laughs.

But she had become a little weird. In Milwaukee, there were the fits
about swallowing pills and the street-crossing when she saw a man.
During the year in Groveland, when she was twelve, she almost doubled her weight. She's small-boned, was less than five feet tall, and

peaked that year at 130. She had to eat almost constantly to do it. My brother, who was sixteen, made up a song about her.

> *Little plump Donna*
> *plop plop*
> *Little plump Donna*
> *plop plop*
>
> *She wiggles in the middle*
> *She wiggles on the top*
> *Little plump Donna*
> *plop plop plop*

He had one for me, too:

> *Little Michaelina*
> *I'm in love with you*

The two lines were the whole song. The first syllable ("Li-") was enough to send me into a howling rage, but when he was torturing my sister with "Little Plump Donna," I eagerly joined in with original choreography. I'd bloat my cheeks and grab my stomach and chest in sequence on "she wiggles in the middle / she wiggles on top," and bounce my hips from one side to the other with each "plop"—demurely for the first "plop plop" refrain and, with grand exaggeration, for the climactic "plop plop plop." Then we'd do it again. And again. And again. If necessary, following her out of the house at a dead run.

Her starving herself made him stop singing "Little Plump Donna." He even apologized. So did I, but she kept starving herself. Nobody had ever heard of the term "eating disorder," much less "anorexia nervosa," but my parents knew something was wrong. Donna maintained she simply wanted to be thin. Her best friend was named Carolyn Cater and she was also thin. They said they had to be thin if they were going to become Vocal Artists (which Carolyn Cater did become, at last report thirty years ago performing in nightclubs in Florida and

Georgia and waiting for the big break). They gave performances in our living room to an audience of my mother and me and Topsy. They did their hair in French twists and dressed up in taffeta gowns with voile lace at the bodices and sang harmonic duets of "In the Cool, Cool, Cool of the Evening," accompanied by the instrumental version on the flip side of the record. I'd do Red Skelton by slapping myself on the side of the head and falling down, an imitation I was developing to add to my act. Dunedin was so far from the TV station in Tampa, all we got was fuzz. As we performed, the wind from the ocean rattled the palms in front of our house and shook the windows in their casings.

My father and brother never attended these performances. My brother commuted a hundred and twenty miles a day to the Jesuit high school in Tampa, and when he wasn't on the bus, he was doing Boy Scouts. It was his obsession. By this time, at seventeen, he was an Eagle Scout and had earned every merit badge there was, including Reptile Husbandry and Survival Cooking. He wore a sash six inches wide and five feet long completely covered with merit badges: varicolored cloth insignia the size of fifty-cent pieces, five to a row, two hundred and forty-something in all. He'd return from the National Boy Scout Jamboree with the entirely credible report that he had more merit badges on his sash than anyone else in the United States. It was against Boy Scout rules to crown a champion Boy Scout, otherwise he probably would have won the title. He had kept cagefuls of live snakes in our basement in Milwaukee (and jars of dead ones in formaldehyde) until one escaped—an eight-foot king snake—and a neighbor nearly stepped on it mowing his lawn before he smashed its head with a two-by-four. Since my brother's snakes were quite famous in the neighborhood, it was then transported dangling stiffly over the two-by-four and deposited on our front porch. That was the end of the snakes in the basement. But Florida was Boy Scout paradise. There was no need to keep dangerous reptiles at home when one could go camping in sulphur pits where they flourished, and one could also go on weekend survival hikes in swamps with nothing but two pieces of flint, a Boy Scout knife, a canteen, and a compass (the canteen and compass to be used only in an emergency). He'd return early Sunday evening famished and bedraggled, eat triple helpings of everything, and pass out until five the next morning when he had to get up to catch the bus to Tampa.

He didn't pay much attention to me, since I was nine years younger than he was, although I joined the Cub Scouts and, in homage to him, earned my Wolf, Lion, and Bear badges with astonishing rapidity, plus enough arrowheads sewn points-down underneath them to cover the front of my shirt below the belt line. Of course, I cheated my brains out to get them. If the task involved something material ("Make a weather station out of a milk carton"), my mother would make me produce the evidence before she signed the certification, but for the ones like "Do a week's household chores for three neighbors" she'd take my word, although we didn't have any neighbors except Ila, and Ila didn't have a house, much less a household. "Now you're sure you really did this," my mother would say, not looking at me as she signed the certification, and I'd say "Yes" knowing she knew I didn't.

BASEBALL

I left Florida wearing a red baseball cap. Except to sleep, wash, and sit in school, I didn't take it off for the next year, and would not have taken it off then if it hadn't disintegrated on my head. The inside lining looked like a mattress pad in a crack house. I had shaped the bill just so, an arch Brunelleschi would have envied, not creasing it like a paper airplane the way the unenlightened did but bending it gently in the middle and at successively minuscule midpoints in both halves so that you could not have discerned a crease with a caliper. The cloth that coated the bill frayed first, revealing the cardboard underneath, and, after drying out from a dip in a mud puddle, the cardboard itself wrinkled sadly into four distinct layers. Still, with mucilage and red Magic Marker, I did not yield. Above the bill the white block-letter "D" was sewn onto the cap. My brother said it stood for "Dipshit" (he hated sports). It turned gray, then peeled off entirely; that looked better, I thought—a dark red shadow "D," the only part of the cap where the color hadn't faded.

It stood for Dunedin, or, more accurately, the Dunedin Chamber of Commerce (whatever commerce there was between a barber shop, grocery store, and gas station), which sponsored a team—my team—in the Clearwater Little League. In Florida they played baseball year-round, but I didn't reach the minimum age of nine until months after we moved to Dunedin. Maybe in sympathy for my asthma, my father said he'd teach me how to pitch, so when I was eligible to play, I could step right up onto the mound, the best position on the team. I was a Ryan, he said, and that meant I should always be the best. Late Saturday afternoons we'd go out back with a ball and two gloves. My mother had just cashed in a bagful of books of S&H Green Stamps for a spanking new first baseman's glove, which served as my father's catcher's mitt, and I used the glove I had been using, five padded fingers with no webbing like the kind in newsreels of Ty Cobb and Babe Ruth, an antique that had belonged to some remote uncle, a Schultz or an Ernst.

My dad allowed how as a young man he had himself been the best semipro corkball pitcher in Milwaukee. Corkball was in fact played on weekends in the public parks in Milwaukee at that time, three players to a team: a pitcher, a catcher, and a fielder who rarely gets the chance to field. It's exactly like stickball—only you get five strikes because the bat is the size of a broomstick, and the ball, an exact replica of a regulation baseball, is the size of a golf ball. Anybody can start a curveball toward third base and break it across the plate, and throw a fastball for which most major-league pitchers would indenture their souls to Beelzebub. By the time I began high school, I thought the game itself was as apocryphal as my father's record strings of strikeouts, but, after an argument in which I shrieked that every story he ever told me was a lie, he tracked down a company that sold corkball equipment and, to my astonishment, there arrived on our doorstep one day a long box with two bats and ten corkballs inside it. We played a couple of times during the next week—after work, when he had already had a few drinks. The solemn concentration on his face while he pitched I had seen before only when he was playing the violin. He'd bend at the waist with both hands behind his back and stare at the strike zone for a full minute between pitches. "Just throw it, for God's sake," I yelled. I hit him all over the lot. He complained he had no zip left. After that the corkballs and corkball bats worked their way deeper into my closet until I found them years later, years after he was dead, and carried them in one armload down to a basement bin stuffed with unused toys and games.

Every pitcher has a different windup and delivery, but the one my father taught me was unique. Whatever their other differences, every pitcher bends his elbow so he can snap his wrist when he releases and get some spin and power on the ball. My father taught me to keep my elbow rigid and throw completely overhand like a catapult. This was his corkball delivery. Since my hand was so small, he said to hold the baseball in my palm instead of with three fingers. It's hard to get any control this way, but he drew a box on the toolshed to represent a strike zone, and I spent so many hours out there practicing that by my ninth birthday I could hit it almost every time. I still mooned over Ila when she came over and I'd go harrow the fiddler crabs with Topsy occasionally, but most days I quit practicing only when it was too dark to see. Had there been a light on the shed, I would have practiced instead of slept.

When the Saturday for spring tryouts came, I was ready. My mom dropped me off in Clearwater at the big municipal park with six baseball diamonds. I was so anxious I got there an hour early. Nine-year-olds had to play in the minors, but the majors were having tryouts, too. I walked around and checked out all the pitchers. The rubber's only forty-six feet away from home plate in Little League, and some of the twelve-year-olds were nearly six feet tall and really zinging it. One big blond southpaw looked like he was about to debut for the Yankees. He was throwing ninety-mile-an-hour fastballs and a slow curve that dropped off the table. I noticed that, when he threw, his right shoulder was way in front of his left, so that he was snapping his whole body when he released the ball and getting his whole weight behind the pitch. Unlike me. My shoulders were square during my medieval catapult delivery. My pitches were slow. The ball didn't move.

I thought I was in trouble, but it was too late to learn how to pitch like the big kid. I thought of going out for first base instead, but heard my dad's voice saying, "Just do what I taught you." When the coach asked me, I admitted to wanting to try out for pitcher. The coach's name was Mr. Crenshaw. He was a mild young guy with an unlit cigar clamped between his teeth, and a spare tire that peeked out from underneath his golf shirt. He was already bald, but he let his hair grow long on one side and parted it just above his ear so he could paste it over the top with Brylcreem. It flapped up like a piece of cardboard when he was excited. One of his own kids was on the team, but he treated him the same as everyone else.

"Are you sure you don't want to play another position?" he asked me. "We could use a good outfielder."

I said no, I wanted to pitch, so he wrote it down, using the top of my head for a desk, and sent me over to where three-quarters of the kids there had paired up throwing to each other. They all wanted to be pitchers. One scrawny kid stood off to the side seeming bewildered. He looked like he belonged in a photo pleading for famine relief. I asked him if he wanted to toss a few with me.

"Sure, but I ain't no pitcher."

I asked him what he was.

"Catcher," he said. It seemed like a divine message. Maybe I was going to be a pitcher after all if God sent me to my catcher. He was the only one on the team trying out for catcher, so he automatically made the starting lineup. His name was Dewey.

"Put it right in here, Mike," Dewey drawled, so slowly the ball would be in his mitt before he finished his exhortation. When he knelt down to receive the pitch, he wasn't much bigger than a flower vase. But he gave you a good target right at the knees.

"That's a real nice pitch, Mike," he'd say, throwing it back. His legs weren't strong enough for him to squat the way catchers were supposed to, so to return the ball he'd hop from his knees to his feet, all at once, like a grasshopper. He could do it fast enough that once in a great while he could catch an exceptionally overweight base runner trying to steal second. For everyone else, a single meant a double. Besides the time it took to hop up, Dewey did not have a clothesline throw to second. It would arrive at the bag on a slow roll. Each time somebody stole on him, Dewey would kick the dust and berate himself mercilessly.

He loved to catch me because I never let anybody on base. My control was impeccable and, as it turned out, nobody could hit me. The rhythm of the catapult delivery was so bizarre that I was in effect and unbeknownst to myself constantly throwing change-ups; the ball was hidden by the stiff-arm windup until I released it, so the batter had less time to pick it up on the way to the plate. Plus, because of the way I held the ball in my whole hand, I threw exclusively palm balls, another oddity. A palm ball's like a knuckler in that the seams of the ball don't rotate. Interminable one-pitch major-league careers are made of a good knuckler because the lack of rotation makes the ball move in radical, unpredictable ways. My palm ball was as straight as the interstate in Kansas, probably because I couldn't throw it hard enough and the distance to homeplate was too short for it to dip. Didn't seem to matter. Whiff, whiff, whiff, one after another. "Mmmm, thanks for the breeze, batter," Dewey would taunt them as they swung. I was the ace of the league, feared, awe-inspiring, legendary.

Little did I suspect that this was the peak of my baseball career. I was talking Big Leagues. Milwaukee Braves. Didn't Bob Feller break in with the Indians when he was sixteen? So I had seven years to hone my skills, an unimaginable eternity to me in any other terms but these. Here I was languishing in the Clearwater Little League *minors*, wasting my talent striking out nine-year-olds and pathetic ten-, eleven-, and twelve-year-olds too uncoordinated to play with kids their own age. It was rare that a nine-year-old was promoted to the majors, but it could happen. Minor-leaguers wore caps and street clothes, jeans and T-shirts and sneakers; major-leaguers got nifty uniforms, complete with black leather baseball shoes with rubber spikes and long tongues that flipped back over the laces. Minor-leaguers played early Saturday mornings and the only people who came were their parents; major-leaguers played to packed grandstands on Saturday afternoons.

Somebody's dad in a borrowed chest protector umpired the minor-league games; the major league had professional umpires in professional umpire uniforms who gestured operatically and shouted "Steee-rike," and even an announcer who called out the opposing lineups over a crackly loudspeaker. I broached the subject to Mr. Crenshaw and he told me to wait a year. Where was my loyalty to the team? We had a pennant to win. He said he'd continue to pitch me every game. Why did I want to go to the majors and sit on the bench? I was grimly silent in response. That was just it, I wouldn't sit on the bench. I'd be a star in the majors, too. I complained to Dewey about it. "We'd sure miss you, Mike," he said.

Since Mr. Crenshaw wouldn't support me, I began going to the major-league coaches behind his back. I told them who I was, I told them my record. They said they had heard of me. I asked for a tryout. They asked me if Mr. Crenshaw knew I was asking for a tryout. Not one of them would give me a tryout, not even the coach of the Orioles—the worst team in the league (with, however, the best uniforms: orange and black, as if eternally celebrating Halloween)— whose pitchers were lucky to reach home plate on a bounce. We'll be happy to see you next year, they all said.

There was no next year. There was in fact no more this year. Before the season was over, my father took a job as assistant manager of the accounting department for Bosch Industrial Machinery in Steeltown, PA. We were moving again. The third year in a row. I wailed my protest. What about my career? My father said I could wail all I wanted, I was still going. Or I could stay in Dunedin by myself if I'd like to take over the lease for the house, quit school, get a job, cook for myself, and convince the police that I should not be put in an orphanage.

My father had had a rough year at Minute Maid. After the takeover, Minute Maid people had been fired to make room for the Snow Crop people like my father brought in from Groveland. The Minute Maid people gave the Snow Crop people the cold shoulder. My father never felt accepted. Plus he had trouble with his new boss, a Minute Maid man. His old boss was named Cliff Broad, and my father had followed

Cliff Broad from Milwaukee to Snow Crop and then to Minute Maid. His new boss had been fired when Cliff Broad came in, then rehired a month later with carte blanche and an ironclad contract when Cliff Broad, who smoked Pall Malls like my father, suddenly retired with emphysema (though he continued to smoke Pall Malls, sucking alternately on the cigarette in one hand and the inhaler in the other). This left my father in what he understatedly called a bad position. From the first day, he was waiting for the ax to drop. His new boss was diabolically shrewd, however; my father was forced to fire all the other Snow Crop people, then all the Minute Maid people suspected of disloyalty, while explicitly representing the firings as the decision of higher-ups. My father couldn't complain publicly and keep his job, plus he knew that after he had fired everyone they wanted to get rid of, he would be fired, too. It was just a matter of time. Every time he had to fire somebody he'd come home raving that he'd quit on the son-of-a-bitch tomorrow if it weren't for us, if it weren't that he had a family to support.

He had only one hope. He asked Cliff Broad to put out the word for him that he was looking for a job. Cliff Broad was a Big Shot and, according to my father, knew other Big Shots all over the country. From my father's description, I imagined the Big Shots as a national fraternity. They lived in big houses with swimming pools and maids in the nicest section of town, whatever town they lived in. They drove Cadillacs and ate steak for dinner every night. In Steeltown they all lived in Fairmont Green. On the Sunday drives during that first summer in Steeltown, my father at the wheel, we would invariably end up in Fairmont Green looking at the mansions. They represented something important to him. "I'll take that one," I'd say from the backseat. "No, that one," my sister countered, "I bet it has air conditioning and a color television." We'd argue the relative merits of our choices, the luxury of their particular features. I'd dispute the fine points like a Jesuit, but I really only had one criterion: size. I picked the biggest. "Now there's the one I like," my mother would say quietly as we passed something shockingly modest but impeccably groomed. "Someday I'll

buy it for you, Mom," I'd say chivalrously. For sure, I was going to be a
Big Shot.

Before we left Florida, to celebrate his new job at Bosch Machinery,
my father bought a brand-new '56 Buick, two-toned, blue and white,
with a 320-horsepower V-8 engine. We tooled about in it proudly.
What a tank it was. It could have driven through a chain-link fence.
Power steering was still a Luxury Option. My father didn't trust it
(what if the power suddenly broke?) and, without it, the car handled
like a backhoe. Parallel parking took the determination of Ahab. My
mother, who weighed about 110, would actually lift herself off the seat
as she tried to turn the wheel with both hands. I took my driver's test in
it seven years later, to the amusement of the state cop as I tried to ne-
gotiate the serpentine part of the course, drubbing the anchored traffic
cones with the bumper (he passed me anyway because he said he
couldn't have gotten that car through himself). By that time the blue
half of the two tone had faded and chipped, so my father had it re-
painted completely white, which made the car look even bigger. I had
to wash it every Saturday, but just driving it around the block got it
dirty. My friends called it "The White Sow."

For our move from Florida to Steeltown, my brother attached a
Confederate flag to the antenna and insisted we honk at cars and
trucks with southern license plates after we crossed the Mason-Dixon
line. He'd strike up conversations with their drivers at rest stops, and
give the Rebel yell out the window as we passed them on the two-lane
highway. They would look at us like we were deranged. My sister was
mortified, and sat staring stonily forward as if she were not part of this
family but unaccountably found herself in the backseat of this strange
car between my brother and me, to whom, it went without saying, she
had not been introduced. I'd pump my arm out the window to get the
trucks to sound their horns, which she maintained was also quite
"puerile."

I have no idea what provoked my brother's fixation on the
Confederacy. When he was twenty-one, he tried to register in
Pennsylvania as a Dixiecrat. He knew all the words to "Dixie," includ-

ing the obscure verses, and owned a trunkful of Confederacy kitsch—beer mugs, plastic place mats, a bicycle license plate—a good part of it purchased at truck stops on our way to Steeltown, with slogans on it like "Save your Confederate money, the South will rise again." The 1954 Supreme Court decision against segregation had brought up all the old sectional rivalry. The belief that they were being victimized again by the North had been palpable among whites in the South. In Florida the Civil War was living history. I had learned in school that the Confederates were the spirited underdogs against the rich, staid, sanctimonious Yankees—which I translated vaguely as my father's side of the family against my mother's. My parents were quiet about the controversy, but that's where their respective sympathies seemed to lie. Not much was said about racism. The Klan was an invisible presence in both Groveland and Clearwater, and I remember one little girl in our neighborhood calling me a nigger-lover when she heard I was Catholic. Since the Klan hated blacks, Catholics, and Jews, it assumed they were in cahoots with one another. The black people, of course, got the brunt of it. The Clearwater Little League, sponsored by the city and played in the municipal park, was completely white. Although it was not explicitly forbidden, no black kid would have dared try out. This would have been "crossing the color line," a phrase I'd hear occasionally. It meant an offense the Klan would punish. Where the black kids played baseball I had no idea. There were none in my school either, the Catholic school. I simply thought it odd that they had to sit in the back of the bus and drink out of their own water fountains. My father told me to always treat them politely and they would do me no harm. Once, in a grocery store, I started to drink out of the Negro water fountain until my brother pulled me away. I would have gotten sick and possibly died, he said.

After we got to Steeltown, my brother and sister would have arguments about Racial Equality. He was working as a keypunch operator at Bosch Machinery, sorting cards with rows of tiny holes that provided the operating instructions to huge, primitive computers. Each computer, less powerful than a laptop, was the size of a mobile home. He was trying to earn enough money to go to Middle Tennessee Valley College and major in "Humanics," a major unique in higher education to that institution. It prepared the degree candidate for a career as an administrator in either the Boy Scouts of America or the Boys Clubs of America, the latter of which my brother disdained because it promoted sports. Though he got him the job, my father wouldn't give him a cent. My father had paid his own way and he thought my brother should, too. It took my brother seven years to work his way through college, as the night clerk at the Greyhound station in Murfreesboro, while he attended classes during the day, coming home to Steeltown for six months at Bosch when he ran out of tuition money. He hated Steeltown. He worked the graveyard shift, slept all day, and went to Boy Scout meetings in the evenings. We shared a room. When I was getting up, he was going to bed. He snored like a potentate, and no alarm clock yet developed by modern Western technology could wake him. He insisted that I wake him when I got home from school, but you could scream at the top of your lungs from two feet away and he wouldn't hear you, and if you tried to shake him, he'd clip you one before he was conscious. So I'd stand outside his reach with a bucket of cold washrags and paste him in the face with one after another. I enjoyed this very much. He'd lunge at me, but I kept a clear path to the door, and landing on the floor would finally wake him. He'd stagger into the dining room for his 4 P.M. breakfast of a half-dozen jelly donuts and three large Cokes—grouchy, inconsolable, but almost harmless. "Good morning, John Junior," I'd say, singsong. He'd grumble, "You're about as funny as a crutch."

He smoked Marsh Wheeling stogies, about thirty a day, clipping the ends with a cigar clipper he wore on his Confederate key chain, and refused to brush his teeth, ever, despite my mother's daily reminders (he said it made his gums bleed—which, of course, it did—that's what happens if you never brush your teeth). Like my father, he drenched his head in the morning with Vitalis. The room we shared reeked of Marsh Wheelings and Vitalis—two unique, omnipotent, incompatible odors in constant warfare for the stray molecule of uncontaminated air—and his pillowcase looked like the newspaper on which my mother drained french fries. When he wasn't in his Boy Scout uniform, he wore string ties and cowboy boots (at a time when nobody in the East wore cowboy boots, much less string ties) and quickly became known locally as A Character. He must have suffered from the isolation, but outwardly his attitude toward anyone who didn't like how he dressed or what he did was Tough Noogie.

My sister on the other hand became Popular. The summer we moved to Steeltown was the summer before she started high school, and my parents were able to convince her that boys wouldn't like her unless she had a Nice Figure. Breasts, in other words, though the word was not spoken. This was, after all, the era of Marilyn Monroe and Jayne Mansfield, even if neither of them was ever mentioned in our household without the Homeric epithet "That Disgusting" ("That Disgusting Jayne Mansfield . . . ; That Disgusting Marilyn Monroe . . . "; their sudden violent deaths were an earthly manifestation of Divine Justice). My sister began to take a little cottage cheese and fruit cocktail for lunch (sans cherries and pear cubes if I got to the open can before she did), and ate an almost normal portion of what the rest of us had for dinner. She still would not allow a potato to cross the heavily patrolled boundaries of her plate, the belief in those days being that what put on weight was Starch. Luckily for her, we ate like everybody else, with plenty of butter on canned or frozen vegetables boiled into a gelatinous green mass, and plenty of chicken and pork chops fried in Crisco. So, by the time school started, she Filled Out. She also let her blonde hair grow and maybe, sinfully, even lightened it a smidgin with lemon. She wore it in a Debbie Reynolds ponytail, pulled back so tight it stretched her eyebrows. Plus she had my father's aquiline nose and distinct features. To relieve the severity of the effect, she contrived an inch of spit curls to grace the hairline precisely above the midpoint of her left eyebrow. The ponytail itself was a masterwork of curling and waving, a cascade of blondeness, very much like the tails of ponies with Bambi eyelashes in Walt Disney cartoons. I was under a strict injunction not to pull it, which I managed nonetheless in the form of the slightest tug as I'd pass behind her chair while she was absorbed in her homework at the dining-room table after dinner. "Mom!" she'd chime out automatically, as if it were a bell tug. She was a Nice Girl and a Good Student, the prom queen and a class officer (she might have been president, but the president was always a boy). She studied hard every night, the thick, stupid textbooks stacked a foot high in front of her—as opposed to me, who never deigned to crack a book until my junior year in high school, when I finally became afraid that unless I raised my grades I'd never get out of Steeltown.

I began fourth grade in Steeltown, the fourth grade in a row at a different school in a different place. This is when I "forgot" Bob Stoller. I "forgot" what I had done with him. (By "forgot" I mean stopped acknowledging; I never completely forgot it.) It was at three re-moves—Milwaukee to Groveland to Dunedin to Steeltown—at the age of nine almost half a lifetime ago. And there was nothing in the atmosphere to remind me. In the 1990s, when sexual abuse is a daily news item and the subject of talk shows and docudramas and has even become a legal defense for murder, it may be hard to imagine a time when the term was never mentioned. Never. By anyone, under any circumstances, public or private, at least within my hearing. We all knew about perverts who preyed on little boys. These were Queers. All Queers liked little boys. They deserved to have the shit kicked out of them, which some of my fellow football players in high school did regularly, one of them luring a Queer into an alley where the rest of them would appear from behind the garbage cans to stomp him and steal his wallet. They would show up at practice the next day with ready cash and skinned knuckles, but once they didn't show up at all because they had picked out a Queer who had a black belt in karate. An impossible anomaly since all Queers were fems. There were also strange men who molested little girls, a different group than Queers, also perverts but at least they were attracted to the right sex (thus was pedophilia understood)—also not anyone we knew. Nor did such things happen to children of our acquaintance (except Betty Short, a bad girl who had brought it on herself). If a child-molester was ever caught and prosecuted, if a father was ever convicted of incest, it didn't make the *Steeltown Beacon*. Such news was not the news fit to print. Teachers, coaches, Boy Scout leaders, ministers, and priests might suddenly resign or be transferred for no apparent reason, but even rumors of sexual abuse, if there were any, did not then reach the ears of nine-year-olds.

And even if they did, I would not have understood they were talking about the same thing that had been done to me by Bob Stoller. He had been my friend. He had been nice to me. He wasn't bad, I was bad. I was the bad one. Like Betty Short but worse because I kept it secret, I made my First Holy Communion while it rotted my soul, I was not who I pretended to be. When I forgot Bob Stoller, I didn't forget how terrible I was, but the feeling burrowed so deeply I couldn't connect it to anything outside, to something that happened to me or something I had done. It was simply there, it was me, it was what it meant to be me.

I did everything I could not to feel it. Baseball was the first organized game I played with other kids, the first game at which I didn't need to cheat. Its importance to me was, to say the least, disproportionate. I never wanted to take off that cap. It told the world who I was (or, more accurately, who I wanted people to think I was, who I wanted to be). Unfortunately, my fame had not reached quite as far north as Steeltown, so I had to enlist myself as my own publicist. Like all publicists, I took the liberty to highlight certain facts about my client and omit others. Such as the trivial fact that my pitching career had been accomplished in the minors, not the majors. In lovingly fine detail, I described the imaginary black-and-red uniform I tragically had to leave behind, the state-of-the-art ballpark, the immense crowds, their adulation. Newspaper stories? There were plenty of them. Just stop over at the house; I'll show them to you (they looked like origami, so creatively clipped were they to delete the phrase "minor league"). I restrained myself from making this offer to the neighborhood kids for at least five minutes after meeting them, five minutes of waiting for them to ask what the "D" on my cap stood for, which led naturally to a synopsis of my scintillating career. "Gee, you're probably the best pitcher who ever lived," one of my listeners said sarcastically. "Yeah," I answered sincerely.

My mother warned me about bragging. She said empty barrels made the loudest noises. But was it bragging if you just told the truth about what you had done? What about Dad's stories? We had a discussion about it at dinner. Dad agreed with both of us. Nobody liked a guy who tooted his own horn. But there was one thing I should always remember. I was a Ryan. Just keep that under my hat. If I ever thought somebody was better than me, I should say to myself this guy puts his pants on one leg at a time, just like me. It was stupid to brag, but technically it wasn't bragging as long as you could back it up. My sister argued that this was still bragging. She went and got the dictionary. My brother asked if there were any more mashed potatoes, or could he have Donna's if she wasn't going to eat them.

Not a week passed before there were no more inquiries about my cap, and a certain pressure began to build in the neighborhood for me to prove the pitching prowess I had so excellently publicized. I wasn't bothered by the latter—I was a great pitcher, wasn't I?—but I was devastated that my cap had no local currency. Locally, the cap of great price was a maroon one with an overlapping double B over the bill— "Bickle Builders"—a dynasty like the Yankees, loved by some, hated by others, but respected by all. Their record was undeniable: the district Knee-Hi Champs for as long as anyone could remember. The breeding ground of high school stars. Its origin was mysterious. No one remembered when the team was formed or even what the name meant, probably some construction company no longer in business. No one had ever met Mr. Bickle. It made the team seem even more a force of nature. To play for Bickle Builders was the height of accomplishment. I'd see them together at the playground, an aura of effortless greatness emanating from their maroon caps. "That's Denny Koch," someone would confide in me about a tall skinny kid sitting on a basketball in the shade. "He led the league in strikeouts. And that real built guy next to him is Bob Cressman, the catcher."

In response, I immediately announced that next season I would be a starting pitcher for Bickle Builders—in fact, probably the ace of the squad. I may as well have said I could climb the Empire State Building wearing a straightjacket. This finally brought home to my listeners the extremity of my self-aggrandizement; even the ones who had been sympathetic, or were at least suspending judgment until they saw me pitch, abandoned my camp. They tried to reason with me. They recited a litany of sluggers. I'd never get past the tryouts. This wasn't Little League (there was no Little League in Steeltown); it was Knee-Hi League, ages ten to thirteen, not nine to twelve. I was nine years old, four feet six and eighty pounds—did I think I was Superboy? Of course not, I answered. But I had done it in Florida—why couldn't I do it in Steeltown? Didn't these guys put their pants on one leg at a time?

A test was hastily arranged. It was late August, the season was over, but a few Bickle Builders were always hanging around the playground. They were recruited to bat against me, with the invitation "This kid says he's going to start next year for Bickle Builders." Bob Cressman chuckled lightly but wouldn't move from under the tree where he was talking to some girls. "A buck a hit, two bucks for a homer," he said. Nobody had that kind of money.

"How about it, ace?" he asked me. "That's the deal. And I pay you ten bucks if you strike me out."

This was a fortune, twenty weeks' allowance, half my savings account. But Cressman's T-shirt was rolled up to exhibit his biceps.

"How about just for fun?" I answered. It was what my mother said when my father, brother, and I wanted to play poker for pennies. We always moaned in response. How could I say something so dumb?

Cressman guffawed deeply. "No fun for me, ace," he said, and turned back to the girls, who were squirming and giggling and had breasts.

But there were a few other Bickle Builders around—Andy Stone, Denny McManus, Louie Eichstadt—younger ones, ten and eleven, not stars and starters yet like Cressman and Koch, but destined to be.

They seemed to know it. They showed it by the way they carried themselves. They'd be a year ahead of me at St. Boniface when school started. Pro bono they were willing to put me in my place.

And they did, handily. Even before they did, something in me said a terrible thing was happening. Warming up, I felt almost dizzy. I could barely reach the plate. All the kids who had gathered behind the backstop hooted and jeered. "This mound's too far away," I yelled, but my throat was dry, my voice a squeak. I was right—the rubber was fifty-four feet from the plate in Knee-Hi, not the forty-six feet of Little League. "I'm not used to this distance," I yelled, and stepped forward and drew a line in the dirt with my heel. The kids behind the backstop shrieked in protest—"Get back there, Ryan; get back there, you cheater"—rattling the wire mesh like monkeys being teased. Louie Eichstadt was in the batter's box loosening up, swinging three bats in one hand. He was already heavily muscled, a natural, later the home-run king of the league.

"Let him stand where he wants," he said, and dug in at the plate. His bat looked like a telephone pole. The kids shouted, "Blast the shit out of it, Louie."

He hit my first pitch not only over the left-field fence but also over the swings on the macadamized playground three hundred feet away. Then he did it twice more, upper-deck blasts, grinning afterward from the sheer physical pleasure of it. The kids went bonkers. Then McManus and Stone each banged a number of what would obviously be solid doubles and triples off the wall. The whole ordeal lasted about twenty minutes, most of which I spent standing on the line I had cut in the dirt waiting for the ball to be retrieved. My unique catapult delivery. I didn't get a strike past any of them.

"He throws bloopers," Stone said, finally dropping his bat at the plate. "Let's go drown kittens or something a little more challenging."

I was still standing there. Maybe I'd wake up and it would all be a bad dream. My face was burning with humiliation, but I was no longer seeing or hearing anything—it was all an indistinct blur and roar. I didn't want to cry and run away, and I thought if I just waited long enough, eventually they'd leave and I could go home. But my lack of response was apparently unsatisfying, and the whole group—it must have been ten or twelve kids—marched out to the mound.

"I said, what about it, Ryan?" It was Stone again, leading the pack. He was a year older than me, just a little taller and a little stronger and a little faster, with a dirty brown burr cut that he fanned up in the front with butch wax.

"What about what?" I asked.

"You got shit in your ears?" Everyone laughed. "I said you can't pitch for shit. Say you can't."

I didn't say anything.

"Dorkface. You couldn't pitch for Bickle Builders in a million years. You're no pitcher. Say it."

"I'm just rusty," I said. "I'll be there next year. You'll see."

This, my original claim, was not received again with enthusiasm. Stone's face turned bright red. He brought his nose to within an inch of mine.

"You're incredible," he said. "You must be nuts. You're the worst pitcher in the United States."

"Punch him, Andy," somebody said.

"I ought to," Stone said, gritting his teeth, still an inch from my nose. "I ought to punch your lights out."

McManus stepped between us. Both he and Stone could have popped out of a Norman Rockwell painting, whereas Eichstadt had thick features and big hands. McManus was blond and freckled, with the same burr cut we all had under his Bickle Builders cap.

"He's not worth it," McManus said to Stone, as if I weren't present.

"All right, all right, all right," Stone answered, and turned away. Then he wheeled around.

"Wait a minute," he said. "I forgot something." He swooped the cap off my head and started walking off with it. Everyone cheered.

"Give me back my cap," I said, predictably enough.

"I'll give it back to you when you learn a little humility," he answered over his shoulder. It must have been something one of his parents said.

"It's mine," I screeched. "Give it to me."

He stopped and turned, his feet set, his fists clenched. "I'll give it to you, all right. Come and get it."

I tackled him as hard as I could, beside myself with fury. Within a minute he was straddling my back, pushing my face into the dirt.

"Say you can't pitch and I'll let you go," he said.

"I'll kill you," I said. I meant it with all my heart.

"Can't pitch. Can't pitch. Can't pitch," Stone chanted, punctuating it by pressing my face into the ground. He held my skull with both hands and performed a little twisting motion, clockwise and counterclockwise, like he was juicing a grapefruit.

After about ten minutes of this, he must have realized I was never going to give in, so he let me up. But as soon as he let me up, I jumped him again. This was repeated three or four times. My mouth was cut and blood was coming out of my nose. I would obviously have to be knocked unconscious before I'd let him walk away with my cap, and he wasn't prepared to do that. Everyone was getting bored.

"Andy, give him back the cap," McManus said wearily.

"Just hold onto him a minute this once after I let him up," Stone said. Two guys grabbed my arms and Eichstadt grasped me around my waist from behind. It took the breath right out of my lungs.

"You want your cap, Ryan?" Stone sneered. He held the bill daintily between his thumb and forefinger and stepped on it, grinding it into the infield dirt first with one foot then the other. Then he picked it up and tossed it into a mud puddle.

"I'll get you for this," I screamed at Stone as they all trooped off. I was screaming at all of them, and they all laughed.

"Oh-wo-wo," Stone said. "I'm really shitting bricks."

When I got home, I told my mother I had fallen off my bike. I had managed to avoid the mud puddle by landing on my face, but my cap had fallen into it. This didn't explain how my exquisitely arched bill had gotten crumpled like a Handi Wipe, but as usual my mother didn't pursue a strict line of questioning. Her approach was rather, Michael's a good boy, Michael doesn't lie, Michael always tells the truth. She left it to me to enforce this standard.

But I wasn't a good boy, and I was ashamed about what happened at the playground not because I had brought it on myself by bragging but because I couldn't back it up. Whether my sister or father was right about the definition, there was nothing, nothing, nothing worse than a braggart who couldn't back it up. I was not the pitcher I thought I was, I was not a very good fighter, I wasn't a good boy—just what was I?

My mother had a basket of clothespins that were made with two pieces of slotted wood and a stiff metal spring. Although they pinched, I liked to clip one on each finger to make two giant claws of my hands, and duck into the hall closet just before my sister came in and hung up her coat—to be greeted by The Claws. It scared the daylights out of her, delightfully every time. My mother handwashed the cap for me in the sink and, with one of the clothespins from her basket, clipped it on the clothesline overnight. The next morning the cloth was almost dry, but the bill wasn't. When I pinched it, water squished up through the cloth from the soaked cardboard inside. At least it didn't look so crumpled anymore. We pressed the bill between two volumes of the *Encyclopaedia Britannica* and placed them on the back steps in the sun. My parents had bought the *Encyclopaedia Britannica* with monthly payments just before the Second World War. The pages were unnumbered, and when my brother was about nine, he went through the sixteen volumes from A to Z and consecutively numbered the pages. (He also read all billboards and road signs aloud during car trips.) His penciled numbers, which terminated somewhere in the five thousands, looked a lot like my early nudes: disproportionate and wobbly. I don't know if while he was numbering he read anything or not, but my primary use of the *Encyclopaedia Britannica* during my childhood was on this occasion, as a kind of extended steam iron. It worked wonderfully. After a few days the bill was as flat as new, and, after it finally dried out completely on the seat of a lawn chair in the backyard (me checking it frequently with a delicate pinch), I was able to bend it again more or less into the arch it had been before. The cap was a little faded was all.

I didn't like the week or so without it. At the playground I was asked frequently in a singsong voice where my cap was. The story had gotten around. When I did return with it looking almost new, it was as if someone had risen from the dead. I pretended to ignore the general astonishment—it was the only revenge I could muster—but then Stone, McManus, Eichstadt, and even some of their acolytes took to snatching it off my head in unguarded moments, sometimes whizzing by on a bike the way purse-snatchers do on their mopeds in Rome. Then they'd play keep-away, or tear into the bathroom inside the school and throw it into a toilet, or just toss it over a fence. This treatment aged the cap pretty drastically, but my mom and I always managed to doctor it back into shape. "You sure are hard on your cap," she observed. "You'd think you'd take better care of something you value."

In the months following, I flirted with giving up the playground and joining the Scouts. It troubled my brother that after we moved to Steeltown I had gotten bored with Cubs. He thought it was because I wasn't getting enough of a challenge. Since he was scoutmaster (at nineteen maybe the youngest in the country), he could bend the rules to allow me to go on a scout hike before I was officially old enough to join. He said he could do it because I had been such a super Cub. The plan was that I'd get an overnight hike under my belt, knock off the other requirements for Second Class before my birthday, and start out a rank ahead, at Second Class instead of Tenderfoot. I'd be on my way. I might get Order of the Arrow even earlier than he had. Who knows, I could be the youngest Eagle ever.

It was December. There was snow on the ground and it was ten degrees outside. We gathered at the church, piling our packs together on the steps, hopping and slapping our sides, blowing frosty breath into cupped gloved hands. Some of the scouts wore only the scout shirt and kerchief and a pair of jeans under their parkas, but most were in full uniform, especially my brother, who, with special permission from national headquarters, had adopted the original scout uniform of Lord

Baden-Powell—the uniform of the British colonial Army at the turn of the century—boots and jodhpurs and a Mountie hat with a leather strap that looped behind his ears and fastened under the bones at the base of his skull. He introduced me to everyone as his little brother Mike. When he was proud, he would press his lips together as if to keep himself from shouting. He did the same thing when he was angry, but his face reddened and his expression was different. Because of the nine years separating us, we had never done much together. He walked twice as fast as I did, and if he took me somewhere, I had to run to keep up. I made him impatient. But I had taken "John" as my confirmation name because it was both my dad's name and his. No kids my age wore glasses with metal frames, but I did because both he and my dad did (they got bent so often playing sports I looked like a Cubist painting). This was a big moment for us. I felt special being his brother. All the scouts looked up to him and treated him with military deference. They all knew I was coming on the hike, since they had heard about it from him for weeks. I shook hands all around, the scout shake, left-handed, two straight fingers up the wrist. When I had asked why left-handed, my brother told me that scouts use the left hand because it's closer to the heart. I shook with his top lieutenants. He introduced them by their rank: Quartermaster Yankovich, First-Classman Skoyles. This was a tough hike I was taking on for my first time out, they observed admiringly. A twenty-mile mountain hike, in winter, with full pack. "It's okay, he's ready," my brother said. I nodded. The tougher the better.

When everyone had arrived, we lined up and my brother called out our last names and we stepped forward and barked "Present! Sir!" and saluted—also with two fingers extended, as in the scout shake (what those talismanic two fingers signify I never found out). Then we all crammed into cars driven by volunteer parents. We were going to the Appalachian Trail, up the Northeast Extension of the Pennsylvania Turnpike, into the Poconos. Spirits were high, scout songs were sung, we begged our driver to pass the other cars in the caravan, which he refused to do, maintaining a dull safe distance from the car in front of us. We wanted to yell and give raspberries and thumb our noses out the window and act quite unscoutlike in general. After a couple of hours, the caravan exited from the turnpike and drove farther up a blacktop and turned onto a gravel road and went about another mile and stopped. Here we were. We all got out. There was nothing in sight except bare trees and snow, snow considerably deeper than in Steeltown. It was also colder. Much colder. Below zero. We were in the mountains. The wind blew in sharp bites and the dark sky looked surly. I don't know what I had been expecting—maybe a donut shop?—but not this arctic waste. Nothing. Anywhere. Then the cars left, their headlights on at midmorning in the icy mist, backing down the road because it was too narrow to turn around. We were on our own. I looked over my shoulder and watched the headlights become pinpoints, then disappear.

The rest of the scouts seemed a little dumbstruck, too. They were moving slowly, as if we had just landed on Mars. But my brother wasn't fazed in the least. He was already at full throttle, checking this and that, peppering instructions, in charge, efficient, focused. "Anybody's who gotta go, better go," he announced, and we all scattered into the woods. I went deeper than the others because I didn't want anybody to be able to see me wee. Underneath an inch of fresh powder, the snow was frozen over into a thick crust, so I had to take baby steps to keep from slipping, and I extended my arms as if I were walking a tightrope. When I unzipped my fly, the cold rushed in and lifted me onto my toes. I leaned my tailbone against a thin tree and whizzed a little zigzag design, Z Z Z, the sign of Zorro, the yellow stream cutting the snow and steaming up in little wisps. Of course, I was the last one to get back to the road. The scouts were all waiting in formation, with their packs on. Waiting, I realized, for me. My brother yelled, "Fall in, Ryan. On the double!" His face was flushed and he was pressing his lips together. My pack sat in the middle of the road by itself where I had dropped it on a pile. Quartermaster Yankovich picked up the pack and held it for me like an overcoat while I stuck my arms through the loops.

We started off snappily, my brother hut-hutting us, setting the pace. He knew exactly how fast we had to march to get to where we were going before sundown, and this was exactly the speed we would march. He wasn't trying to show off or burn anybody out. He was in the front, but he seemed to know everything going on behind him, to have eyes in the back of his head like certain teachers. The moment we started to drag, he'd break into some World War II marching tune, bellowing it into the silent impersonal immensity that encased us:

> *Left my gal in New Orleans*
> *With forty-eight kids and a can of beans*
> *Sound off*
> ONE TWO
> *Sound off*
> THREE FOUR
> *Sound off one two three four*
> THREE FOUR

He knew about a hundred of them, each with a hundred verses. They picked us up. But he couldn't be shouting them constantly, and soon a few of us began to straggle. The road had been plowed, a steady grade uphill that gradually escalated until we were all leaning forward underneath our packs as if into a stiff wind. The scouts on my brother's heels stayed tight, three across with him alone in the front, but the lines lost shape farther back as if he were holding them by the force of his will and it weakened with distance. On the turns I couldn't hear him or see his Mountie hat bouncing above the troop. Only one pudgy Tenderfoot, puffing melodramatically, was farther back than I was. He wanted me to slow up even more so we could walk together, but I wouldn't. I hated his weakness, hated being associated with him. I wanted to punch him, kneel on his chest and punch him. The rest of the troop was well ahead and getting farther ahead. I just couldn't make my legs move that fast without running. My brother kept sending messengers back to warn us to tighten up. We'd double-time until we caught them, but almost immediately fall back again.

Before this, my longest hike had been maybe three miles, in summer, with a Cub Scout canteen strapped to my belt and a backpack containing the sandwiches my mom had made me for lunch. All I could think of now was: Donut shop. Heat. Rest. Hot chocolate. Plump jelly donuts and crullers fresh from the oven, their sugar coating warm and runny. I said it over and over inside my head to keep myself walking: Donut shop, donut shop. "Full pack" was sixteen pounds (I weighed about eighty), plus canteens and sleeping bags and fold-up cookware. With his own money my brother had sent away for a pair of brand-new official scout hiking boots in my size which, kneeling before me, he had laced through their intricate double rows of hooks and eyelets. But they pinched and were heavy and stiff and, despite my woolen official scout socks, my toes became numb. The straps of the green canvas pack—one of his old ones—cut into my shoulders, and my aluminum scout frying pan bounced against my butt. My nose dripped from the cold and the snot froze on my upper lip. The pudgy Tenderfoot kept yelling "Wait up, Ryan, wait up, whydoncha," but I managed to keep ten yards ahead of him. The plan was to hike to a log cabin in Hickory Run State Park, build a fire, fry Spam for dinner, and sleep on the floor in our sleeping bags amid the four hundred and twenty million hibernating spiders awakened by the warmth and voracious for a snack. What fun. I could be home playing tackle football. There was a game every Saturday morning, and I usually got to be quarterback because it was my football and I could throw a spiral. It was great to play in snow because you slid when you hit the ground. The kids I played with thought scouts were dorky, and had mocked me for going on this hike. Cubs was one thing. You did Cubs when you were little, before you went out for team sports. But the only boys who joined Scouts were like the pudgy Tenderfoot, weak and gloppy, whose idea of a good time was to sit around an unheated cabin in the dead of winter and tie exotic knots. Scouts all had stamp collections or coin collections (as opposed to baseball cards, a different matter entirely). Dorky, dorky, dorky. Why hadn't I seen it before? My brother collected both stamps and coins. He was a penpal of scouts throughout the world so he could trade uncanceled stamps with them. He was always getting letters from the Philippines that began "Dear Friend Scout," and he kept bound folios arranged by regions from the British Isles to the Pacific Rim in which he knew all the monetary units and modes of transport (he was thoroughly entertained by the fact that in Tibet they rode yaks, ate yogurt, and lived in yurts). He also had blue cardboard folders with slots filled with pennies and buffalo nickels. For hours at a time he'd sift through the gallon Mason jar we all had to drop our pennies into when we came home, and he'd buy rolls of pennies at the bank to examine and reroll and exchange for others. He recruited me with a fifty-fifty split of untold riches if I found the rare 1911e penny. Sitting across from each other at the dinner table, we must have fruitlessly scrutinized fifty thousand pennies for that teeny *e* under the date (I was going to buy a house in Fairmont Green with a bowling alley in the basement for the family and a cabin cruiser with giant twin Evinrudes for myself). But now the evidence was overwhelming: my brother was a dork. Scouts were dorks. I was about to join the dorks. And if I joined the dorks, I might become a dork. Just being on this hike I was putting myself in mortal danger of becoming one.

At the first rest stop my brother came over and asked how I was holding up.

"Fine," I said.

"You want me to carry your sleeping bag?"

"Nope," I said.

He squatted down to talk to me at eye level and gave me a hard look. I was sitting on an icy boulder I could feel through my pants, but I was too tired to move. The thick lenses of his glasses had steamed up and he had taken them off. They were so heavy they left angry red imprints where the eyepiece pinched his nose. With his gloves off he was cleaning the lenses with what he called his snot-rag, feeling for the one square inch of it that wasn't slimy. His fingernails were bitten down to the white moons. It hurt to see them. My mom bugged him about biting them, like she did about his not brushing his teeth, but he'd say "Nag nag nag" and bite them until they bled. Even here, outdoors in subzero weather, I could smell the Vitalis emanating from his scalp.

"You're dragging your butt, buddyboy," he said, putting his glasses back on. "You pooped out?"

"Nope," I answered again, eloquently. I was furious for getting myself into this. It was all his fault. I considered pretending that I sprained my ankle so he'd have to carry me. He could make a stretcher out of sticks in less than ten minutes.

"How's the boots? How's your toes?"

"Comfy 'n' toasty," I said, with my most exquisitely tuned sarcasm. This was a mistake. It was always a mistake to make him mad, especially now since he was right in my face. He reddened and pressed his lips together. I didn't think he'd pop me one in front of his scouts, but you never knew. He had a temper that could explode in a second.

"Wiseguy. Mr. Wiseguy. That what they teach you at wiseguy sports, Mr. Wiseguy?"

I didn't say anything. It was too dangerous.

"Why do you want to be like that?" he asked—a plea, not a question. It lasted only a second, and I had no idea how to answer. It was like something flying past too fast to catch. I think it surprised him as much as me. He stood up abruptly.

"All right," he bellowed at everyone. "Nap time's over, kiddies. Let's move out." He snatched my sleeping bag. It had been tied onto the top of the pack, and he popped it free with a single motion. At every rest stop he took something else from my pack until all that was left in it by the time we got to the cabin was a can of Spam and a loaf of Wonder bread, and it hung off my back like a bladder.

The cabin was a one-story square box, maybe forty by forty, built of unfinished split logs blackened inside from years of creosote and dirt. It was bare, except for a fireplace in one wall and a picnic table with garbage on it. Someone had broken in and left a bunch of beer bottles and a condom as brittle as a dead leaf that broke into bits when a scout tried to scrape it off the floor with a spatula. I imagined the orgiastic sex that had occurred there as a whirling black blur—vague and evil, a terrible sin. I didn't like the scouts giggling about it. My brother expertly built a fire, tin cans were pried open with scout knives, and dinner was cooked with frying pans whose detachable handles folded out in six-inch segments until they were three feet long. We had each brought our own food, but it was shared freely. My Spam tasted like Chateaubriand.

After dinner two scouts assigned to K.P. wiped the cookware with handfuls of snow, while the others immediately began working on merit badges. I was struck with how occupied everyone suddenly was. Some were indeed learning to tie exotic knots, sailor's loops and double hitches, with a length of rope my brother brought for this purpose. At the picnic table he was teaching a few prospective sea scouts how to read maritime maps, although we were in the mountains in the dead of winter about four hundred miles from the ocean (what Steeltown, Pennsylvania, was doing with a chapter of sea scouts is another one of those unsolved enigmas of childhood). Quartermaster Yankovich offered to go over with me the requirements for Second Class in the scout handbook. He was about fifteen, blond and solemn, Life-going-on-Eagle, second-in-command and my brother's friend (my brother had two friends his own age, but they both still lived in Milwaukee). Yankovich looked like a deacon; he also wore glasses with metal frames, also in homage to my brother. I feigned interest for a half a page, absolutely certain that I'd never be Second Class or even Tenderfoot, for that matter. Rather than go on another hike like this, I'd have my legs amputated. This would be my last adventure in Scouting. But I didn't let him know that. When he asked me how I liked the hike, I said, "Great." He clapped me firmly on the shoulder and said, "Welcome to the Scouts." I nodded off as he was showing me how to make an arm sling out of his scout neckerchief. He poked me awake and said he thought maybe I could use a little shut-eye. I unrolled my sleeping bag near the fire. The floor was hard, and I saw a spider the size of a small pizza stretching lazily in the shadows, clearly eyeing the little midnight snack of my ear, but I could have slept on a bed of ground glass in a boxful of tarantulas. I remember waking in the middle of the night to see my brother rebuilding the fire. I didn't know where I was. It was completely silent. Everyone else was asleep. His back was to me, a dark figure against the quivering firelight. I thought state troopers had come, that something terrible had happened, before I realized it was my brother in his Mountie hat. I guess he put it on because he had gotten cold sitting up by himself. He was so used to working all night and sleeping all day.

My brother knew I had hated the hike. As soon as I got home, I trumpeted about the neighborhood how dorky it was. But against all reason he was still disappointed when my birthday came and I wouldn't sign up for Scouts. He kept bugging me about it. "Nag nag nag," I said. My mother finally said to him, "John, if he doesn't want to join, you can't make him join."

He wouldn't talk to me for a while, then settled into his routine of working, sleeping, and Scouts, in which we hardly talked anyway. And, *mutatis mutandis*, I did the same. I would come home from school, change my clothes, paste him with wet washrags from across the room, and bang out the door, baseball glove or football or basketball under my arm. The transformation from white dress shirt and blue St. Boniface tie to jeans and sneakers took about a nanosecond. I was like a rubber ball hitting the house. My mother begged me to hang up my school clothes, but she didn't understand that it simply took too long, and I knew she'd pick up the puddle I had made of them on my bedroom floor. Whatever the weather or season, I'd be the first at the playground and the last to go home. When it rained, I'd wait in the rain. If no one showed up, I'd go knock on their doors. I'm sure the mothers thought I was wacko. "Intense" was the word the mothers used: "Mike's very intense." I was usually the one who got hurt—two concussions, water on the knee, broken fingers, my body always a fresh bouquet of bruises—because I would run through a brick wall for the opportunity to make a diving catch. I loved diving catches, flying body blocks, jump passes, anything that justified leaving the ground. I wanted to pitch, I wanted to hit, I wanted to tackle, pass, block, run, dribble, shoot, score, score, score. I wanted to do all of them all the time. If there were a sport in which I could have done all of them simultaneously, this would have been the one I played, and I would have played it instead of eating, like the rats with the electrodes implanted in the pleasure center of their brains who push the activating button with their noses all day and all night until they die of starvation. When it got dark and my playmates went home, I'd stay by myself and play against Ainchy, Dainchy, and Awainchy: shooting baskets at the shadow of a rim (knowing only by the thump or swish if I missed it or made it), throwing a baseball straight up into the air and trying to catch it when it appeared out of the black sky six inches from my face. These were lonely, sweet hours. I believed I was different from other kids: more purposeful, more powerful, more courageous—a great hero bound for a great destiny. What life had in store for me I didn't know, but it was certainly spectacular, and I was impatient for it.

ALL BOY
GOOD BOY

My fourth-grade teacher was named Sister Ann Christopher. She was a large young woman, about twenty years old, fresh from the novitiate, sweet and mischievous, with a face like a blossom. It pinched out of the starched white wimple of her habit—the habit of the St. Joseph Order—which began six inches above her head with a white box like an upside-down quart-size take-out carton. Black veils were pinned and draped from the top, yards and yards of them, so all you could see of the box was a white triangle above her forehead. The habit served mainly to conceal everything but the nun's face and hands, to deny the body for the good of the soul. So clean and white were Sister Ann Christopher's face and hands, her soul seemed to glow through them like a 150-watt bulb. She wore no makeup or jewelry, except a heavy black agate rosary around her waist that clacked when she walked and the wedding band on her left hand that signified her marriage to Christ. She told us that this was why she took the name Ann Christopher, so Christ would be within her name, so she would think of Christ when she thought of herself. It touched her to say this. She showed her emotions on her face. When Father Kelly (assistant pastor, football coach, and school heartthrob) visited the classroom to hand out report cards, she would blush and lower her eyes and be so pleased by his gentle banter it seemed she might explode. We didn't dare tease her about it, although in the schoolyard their names were blasphemously conjoined in the durable lyric that begins "[X] and [Y] sitting in a tree, Kay-I-SS-I-N-Gee." Sister Ann Christopher wouldn't reveal what her name had been before she became a nun, but the boys with a crush on her who stayed after school to wash the blackboards managed to find out that she had grown up in Philadelphia in an Irish family with nineteen brothers and sisters, half of whom had entered religious orders—six nuns (including herself), three priests (one a monsignor), and a Trappist monk.

She favored boys. Maybe I reminded her of one of her brothers, or maybe she felt sorry for me because I was starting my fourth new school in four years, but before long I was her pet. I'd show off shamelessly and try to make her laugh, which she loved to do. At opportune moments I'd shout out witticisms in class. I was the only one who could get away with this. She laughed, so the class laughed. Other boys would try it and she'd look at them sourly or sternly. Their jokes hung in the air, unfunny, an embarrassment to us all. It pleased me to the quick. Soon the field was mine alone. I timed my remarks precisely, according to her mood. There were days when she was not in the mood at all, so I kept my mouth shut. She fed my appetite for attention (insatiable, devouring), and I did not ask for it when she was too occupied or preoccupied to give it to me. I could sense exactly where she drew the line. She allowed me to play there, right at it, because I wasn't testing her authority. I was showing her how well I knew her. It was perfect communication. "Look at the cut of him," she said to my mother when she was called to bring a white shirt to school after I had ripped the one I was wearing half off my back playing keep-away at recess. "He's all boy, Mrs. Ryan," Sister said. It made me happy. That's exactly what I wanted to be.

The foundation of our relationship was the profound piety I began, under her influence, to practice. I made sure she knew how devout I was, my deep faith beneath my antics. I wasn't being cynical. I wanted her approval, but this is truly how I felt. I "forgot" Bob Stoller, but I was

furiously driven to save my soul, to somehow make up for the rotten-
ness at the core of my being. Catholicism suited me perfectly. If I were
perfectly good, I would be saved. We were required to put JMJ on
our school papers, to dedicate our work to the Holy Family and the
Holy Crucifix. I put it on every piece of paper I touched, including the
league records I kept for the baseball game I invented using baseball
cards and dice. I joined the altar boys and volunteered for the daily
6 A.M. mass, which the nuns attended as a group, their heads bowed in
prayer, an enormous black square organism filling the front four pews
in the predawn light and shifting at the ringing of the altar bells as if
wafted by a current in the bottom of the ocean. My mother would drive
me to church in the freezing dark, and the sacristy would be so cold
when I was changing into my cassock that I could see my breath. I happily offered it up for the Suffering of Christ. That's what my mother
said when she thought I was complaining too much: "Offer it up." But
I did offer up what was uncomfortable or upsetting—to save my soul
and also to win prizes, sort of like spiritual Green Stamps. If I wanted a
new bike, I'd offer up getting out of bed at five thirty to serve mass. It
wasn't a flawless system. Maybe I'd get the bike, maybe I wouldn't. But
even without the potential prizes, there were aspects of being an altar
boy I liked. I liked being in front of the congregation in my cassock and
surplice and spit-shined shoes. I liked the way the cassock snapped all
the way up the front and unsnapped all at once with one hard pull. I
liked the idea of sacrifice. And I knew I was scoring big points with
Sister Ann Christopher. I would hold the golden tray under her chin as
Father Kelly gently placed the Communion Host on her trembling
pale tongue. Her tongue came within a micrometer of his fingertips,
and her eyes quivered behind her closed eyelids as if she were having a
wild dream. I was a participant in their deepest intimacy. I could feel
the power of it, the power of a sexual act but wholly pure and conse-
crated in God in the sacrament of Holy Communion. Nothing bad.
Nothing wrong. All holy. Hosannah in the highest. I could feel it down
to my toenails. I was joined with them in God's bosom.

I read a story in the *Junior Catholic Messenger* about a boy whose family could not accept his calling to the priesthood. On the same page was a two-panel cartoon of a nun handing a child a daily missal with an embossed crucifix on the cover while next to it a slanty-eyed Communist with a star on his cap was hitting a Chinese kid with a brick. The story was about a boy who is ridiculed for his Vocation by his non-Catholic father; his Catholic mother cannot bring herself to contradict her husband's authority; the boy's older brother owns a sports car and is held up to him as an example of worldly success. After the brother drives his car over a cliff, the father sees God's vengeance, converts to Catholicism, and accepts his youngest son's Vocation. I decided this story was about my family, overlooking the minor disparities that both my parents were born Catholic and my penurious brother not only did not own a sports car but rode the city bus and memorized the schedules even for bus routes he never used. (He was on a first-name basis with all the drivers and always sat in the first seat behind the driver to discuss with him the unique and fascinating characteristics of his particular route.) At dinner one evening I announced with great ceremony that I was going to become a priest. I said it solemnly, using the words of the boy in the story: "Mom and Dad, John Junior and Donna, my dearly beloved family. I have an announcement to make. I have a Vocation. I have decided to enter the priesthood and give my life to God." I then looked up to the ceiling. There was a little network of cracks around the light fixture, like the wrinkles around my mother's eyes. If anybody gave me trouble, I thought God might make it drop, bam, into the middle of the dining-room table.

Both my mother and sister said, "That's wonderful, Mike." My mother added, "That would make me very happy." My father smiled. He looked like he wanted very much to make a joke, but instead he said, "I could use somebody to pray for me every day." My brother, unimpressible as usual, kept a straight face with no perceptible effort. I was disappointed by their lack of resistance. Then dinner continued as if I had not made this momentous announcement. The conversation turned to more earthly concerns, and my Vocation wasn't mentioned again.

But I hinted to Sister Ann Christopher that my family didn't fully accept my religious calling. It wasn't exactly that they would stand in the way, but I didn't feel they could understand the turmoil in my soul, which I did my best to cultivate, using as a model St. Augustine, whom I had read about in the daily missal when I got bored during church. I was being torn from God by the temptations of the world. (Although I couldn't quite imagine what those temptations were, I pictured the nightclub in Tarpon Springs I once waited outside of while my father went inside to buy a pack of cigarettes; there was live mariachi music and flashes of loose-haired women in tight sequined dresses.) Sometimes I grimaced when I prayed, squeezing my eyes shut so tight they hurt. This was like turning blue, which I called squinching, a trick of mine my brother very much appreciated. He'd ask me to perform it for his favorite Boy Scouts when they came to visit him at our house. My mother had forbidden squinching, so we had to go down the alley behind a neighbor's garage where she wouldn't see us. She thought I was doing myself permanent physiological damage. I'd kneel on the gravel and clench my teeth so hard the blood would rush to my face and change the color of my skin to deeper and deeper red. "Blue, blue, blue," my brother would shout the moment the transformation occurred. I'd hold it a few extra seconds, trying to scare him. I had practiced many times in front of a mirror. I was actually more purple than blue, and the longer I held it, the deeper the color became, as if not just my skin but my skull were a solid block of purple. The Boy Scouts were suitably impressed. When I stood up after I squinched, I felt as if I had been inhaling airplane glue. I was rocky and light-headed for a full five minutes. I felt that way after I prayed hard, too, opening my eyes to find myself, impossibly, in the same world I had left, Sister Ann Christopher watching me with tenderness and concern on her face. But how could the world be the same after I had been with God in the darkness inside myself?

One day after school I discussed my Vocation with her. We were the only ones left in the classroom. It was winter and already dark, so the windows reflected the fluorescent lights like black marble. As we spoke, she gathered her papers and books into her black leather book bag, which I carried while she locked the classroom door with a big iron key; then we walked side by side down the corridor and across the street to the convent. I was shorter than her shoulder, and her habit blocked her peripheral vision, so she had to corkscrew her body to look down at me as she walked. She told me a religious vocation was never an easy decision. We were all human, we all have human feelings, human desires. But one human desire was the desire for God, and it was the greatest and most sacred desire. When God made all the souls, He put this desire into the ones He loved the most. At some point He activated it like an electronic magnet. So my Vocation would not finally be my choice. It was God's choice. If God activated the magnet, you'd be drawn to him (I pictured a very large throw switch in the power room of heaven). You had to give up your personal will to obey His Divine Will. I would know when I was older if I were being called. For now, I should simply try to live my life in a way that's pleasing to Him. Obey my parents, do my best in school, follow His commandments, be a good Catholic. At the foot of the steep stone stairs leading to the front door of the convent, I handed her the book bag and she caressed the back of my skull. "You're a good boy, Michael," she said. I walked home suffused with Divine Light. I was in the world, but God was in me.

My piety, and Sister Ann Christopher's favor, were soon recognized by my landslide election to president of the St. Tarcissius Club. Tarcissius, saint and martyr, was a Roman boy stoned to death by Pagan boys as he transported the Sacred Host under his cloak, the whole time never releasing it, not even to put out one hand to break his fall as he fell dead to the pavement. In his death grip he clutched the Sacred Host so tight the Pagan boys couldn't pull it out to desecrate it after they had murdered him. They wanted to jump up and down on it and grind it into the dirt, the way Andy Stone had done to my baseball cap. I dumped St. Augustine. St. Tarcissius became my model. I gave speeches arguing that we, as Catholic boys and girls, should cultivate his courage and fortitude in our devotion to God. We should be willing to die for God. Admittedly, there were not all that many opportunities to die for God in Steeltown PA in 1956. We should think of the Catholic boys and girls living behind the Iron Curtain under communism. They were like the Christians of St. Tarcissius's time. We were so much more fortunate because in America we had Religious Freedom. We weren't persecuted. But we had to be just as devoted and vigilant to save our own souls and convert Protestants and Jews by our example, so they can go to heaven instead of to Limbo. We had to be just as courageous to face down the enemies of Christ. When I said "the enemies of Christ," I pictured mug shots of Stone, McManus, and Eichstadt, despite the fact that they were Catholics, too, and sitting in the classroom next door.

The club, consisting of everyone in the class, met for the last hour on Friday afternoon, right before we went home for the weekend, when everyone was antsy. My best friend, Danny Shea, was vice president and treasurer, and, pinching our red tin St. Tarcissius pins onto our shirt collars, we'd arise simultaneously to stride to Sister's desk at the front of the room to deliver our weekly report. We coordinated our movements with military precision. Since I was president, he'd wait for my signal: eye contact, subtle nod. I'd give it to him as soon as Sister gave it to me. The report consisted mainly of how much money we had collected to buy African mission babies, boys against girls, five dollars per baby, and voting on their names. They had to be official names of saints, to replace the pagan names of the babies when they were baptized into the Catholic church. Nancy Wink always put the girls over the top by giving a whole dollar at the last possible moment, and, like all big political contributors, made very good use of her financial influence. Today there must be many young women in Africa named Nancy (a name not among the saints in *my* missal). Danny and I would think of entertainments to begin the meeting and get people's attention. Sister had to approve these in advance, and, if they didn't contain a religious theme, they at least had to be Educational. I composed lyrics to the tune of Tab Hunter's "Young Love" that listed the forty-eight states by region along with a regional characteristic. Instead of "Young love. First love. Filled with sweet devotion," we sang, "Western states. Western states. Hot all the time." Since there was a verse for every region (central states, mid-Atlantic states, New England states, etc.) the song took about as long to perform as a Wagner opera. Plus the meter never quite fit, but we filled in, also adjusting the pronunciations when necessary: Arizona and Nevada. California. Coloradah. Ha-ah-ah-ah-aht all the time.

Danny was an Elvis fan (I preferred Little Richard for his hyperventilating scream) and consequently affected a slight trembling sneer when he performed. He was a handsome round-faced kid with dark red hair, a pale freckled complexion that flushed easily, and sharp blue eyes. Because of the whiteness of his skin, the colors of his hair and eyes were particularly intense. He was always at the vanguard of fashion—such as his discovery of Elvis even before Elvis had appeared on "The Ed Sullivan Show" and was cut off by the camera at the waist. (The maenadic shrieks Elvis the Pelvis's gyrations provoked caused a doctrinal controversy among the clergy at St. Boniface about whether or not listening to his songs was an Occasion of Sin, and, if so, all songs or only particular ones?) Danny was the first to break the ranks of the burr cut and let his hair grow. I followed soon after. He taught me how to fix swirling waves in front and comb the sides and back into just the suggestion of a DA. At the height of the Elvis craze, DAs were outlawed at Sacred Heart High School, and St. Boniface soon followed. "Only hoods wear them," my sister said. "Do you want to look like a hood?" I argued that Danny's older brother had a DA. "Thomas Shea's a hood," she answered with syllogistic finality.

This was deeply alienating. I thought Tommy was a neat guy. He drove a brand-new bright-red chopped-down '57 Chevy Malibu with "Heartbreak Hotel" in cursive on the front fender. I spent Saturday afternoons at Danny's, and sometimes stayed over, and was thus privileged to witness Tommy's sartorial preparations for Saturday night dates. He let Danny and I study his sculptural technique using three successively smaller fine-tooth rat-tail combs and enough Alberto VO5 to lube Heartbreak Hotel every three thousand miles for the rest of its road life. It must have been how Rilke felt watching Rodin. At the bathroom mirror, Tommy consumed forty-five minutes on his hairdo alone. The rule at Sacred Heart was that there had to be at least an inch of neutral territory down the middle of the back of your head— no bringing the curves together to imply buttocks and certainly no razor-sharp part down the middle to represent their cleavage. Tommy had been pulled from his homeroom one morning by a priest patrolling the halls with a hairbrush. So on Saturday nights he constructed the full-blown DA with a vengeance. He had Danny hold their mom's hand mirror at the back of his head so he could plump the DA with both hands. The finishing touch. Then he put on a starched white dress shirt open a couple of buttons down the front to reveal his black turtleneck jersey (complimenting his black chinos, white socks, and black penny loafers with newly minted dimes in the slots), and topped it all off with a black motorcycle jacket, collar definitively up. A little Elvis sneer-smile in the mirror before going out the door, and off he went into the night, while Danny and I watched Jackie Gleason and played Monopoly with his parents.

Tommy, of course, was the source of Danny's intimacy with the quick pulses of high fashion and popular music, but his parents were also devoted to their two boys in a way that seemed to me luxurious. Danny had the latest 45s as soon as they hit the stores, and "You Ain't Nothin' but a Hound Dog" before I heard it on the radio. As soon as we played one 45, the next dropped down automatically on the record changer—the latest technology on the latest hi-fi system. His parents took me right in because I was Danny's friend, and I spent as much time there as I could.

Steeltown was laid out according to income. There were thirty-two numbered streets intersecting sixty or so with proper names. The poorest families lived on First Street and the richest on Thirty-Second, so your numerical street address was also a financial statement. My family lived at 1650 Trexler Street. The borders of St. Boniface parish were from Sixteenth to Thirty-Second streets: my family was dead center in the middle class of Steeltown and at the poverty line of the parish. There was not one black, Hispanic, or Asian child in the school—about as ethnic as St. Boniface got were a few second-generation Sicilians like Lou Nepi, whose family owned a pizza parlor, and Natalie Moscone, whose father was indicted at least once a year for racketeering (every year on the day the headlines appeared in the *Steeltown Beacon* she'd come to school holding her chin high and tell everyone at recess that the charges were trumped up). The Moscones lived on Thirty-Second Street. The Sheas lived on Twenty-Fourth. Mr. Shea managed a box factory, which put his income close to but not above my father's (parity was very important to Danny and me). The difference was that Mrs. Shea also had a job, as an executive secretary. This was almost unheard of, and much disparaged—a public humiliation to Mr. Shea. But he seemed quite unaware of it. He was a dapper little man whose wife was the same height as he was, and about the same weight. They both drank bourbon on ice out of tumblers while we watched TV, and when the Jackie Gleason show was over, and our stomachs hurt from laughing at Ralph Kramden and Norton and Crazy Guggenheim, they'd put Frank Sinatra on the record player and dance cheek-to-cheek, Mr. Shea smiling and winking at Danny and me over his wife's shoulder as he maneuvered her briskly around the furniture. She was a volatile woman whose hair frequently came unpinned. She'd sometimes break into tears for no reason. Mr. Shea would cover her hand with his and say, "Now, Honeypie," as if he knew the cause of the anguish abruptly overtaking her soul. I'd be embarrassed, and he'd look me squarely in the eyes and say, "It's okay, Mike." And soon it was okay. Mrs. Shea would be back to normal, dry-eyed, brave, cheery. No explanation was ever offered. All they required of me in exchange for their hospitality was that I be a true friend to Danny. "A true friend sticks by his friend when he's in trouble," Mr. Shea said to me once during a commercial when Danny had gone to the bathroom and Mrs. Shea was in the kitchen refilling the snack bowl. There was no preface nor particular occasion for the statement, which might have popped out of a Chinese fortune cookie. He seemed to have been waiting until we were alone to say it. I nodded my understanding and agreement. Was he telling me Danny was in trouble? I took it entirely as a statement of principle. I liked Danny. He was the only kid I knew who tried as hard as I did at sports. He was the guy in Audie Murphy movies who would smother the grenade with his body to save the platoon, and so, I imagined, was I. We valued loyalty and heroism and zeal. Through St. Tarcissius, we somehow managed in our minds to make Roman Catholicism into a martial philosophy. If there had been a Catholic martial art, we would have practiced it with the utmost discipline, using our altar-boy cassocks as karate smocks. Danny was a combination of his mother's passion and his father's loyalty, ideal qualities of the modern warrior. We shared our secret feelings, the girls we thought were sharp, the boys we thought were chicken, and late one afternoon, with our eyes closed, we gently stroked the short hairs on the backs of each other's neck and pretended it was being done by the cutest girls in our class. I got a boner, and I don't remember thinking we had committed a sin, but for some reason we did it only once. "Oh Natalie, Oh Liz," we moaned.

Mr. and Mrs. Shea always treated me as an honored guest, as if whether I could want more potato chips or another Coke were matters of great moment—even when they were both sloshed to the eyebrows, which they most certainly were by the end of Saturday night. They'd freshen their drinks and feign interest in the outcome of our game of Monopoly while Danny and I battled it down to the last capitalist dollar. Then we'd all go to bed, leaving the porch light on for Tommy, whose curfew was an unimaginably liberal 1 A.M. I'd hear him come in after two, having no doubt bathed all night in every forbidden pleasure of the flesh. His parents, unless they were comatose, must have heard him, too. Heartbreak Hotel had a muffler designed to broadcast the music of its chromed fuel-injected 409-horsepower engine to the frontiers of the civilized world. Plus Tommy was a virtuoso of the downshift. As he pulled in, it sounded like the driveway was being strafed.

When our class started having boy-girl parties, Danny's basement quickly became the favorite site, increasingly so as we crossed the misty border between childhood and pubescence. In sixth grade we loved Danny's because of the spanky new game equipment and lavish refreshments, no expense spared—cereal bowls of Milk Duds and a zinc washtub brimming with cases of bottled soda and jagged ice chunks that could be dropped down the back of the blouse of a girl you especially liked. In seventh grade, we loved Danny's even more because Danny's parents never came downstairs. Uniquely, they never even opened the door to the basement to check if the lights were on. At parties at other kids' houses, this was always the first item of business the boys discussed while the girls jitterbugged with one another (self-respecting boys didn't fast-dance). Would the parents be coming downstairs? If not, would they be checking the lights? Elaborate sentry systems were established and shifts assigned. One boy had to stay in the kitchen and stamp on the floor, and another had to dance within an arm's radius of the light switch—the boy in the kitchen preferably diverting the parents with a little Eddie Haskell chatter. But at Danny's no stratagems were necessary. In Danny's basement, when the jitterbugs ended and the slow dancing began, an anonymous hand would reach under the lampshade of the floor lamp and we would be floating inside slow-dance darkness for the rest of the evening. Welcome to pre-teen heaven. Fifteen couples pressing and caressing as if to fuse their nervous systems, and feeling the pressure where their bodies connect travel from hairlines to toe tips. Fifteen beings made of thirty, shoulder to shoulder, radiating heat. There were enough pheromones in that basement to ripen a warehouse of green peaches.

Because of these slow-dance parties, our eighth-grade nun told us we had a reputation as "a fast class." Her name was Sister Caritas. She was approximately half the size of Sister Ann Christopher, and when they stood next to each other, she looked like a toy. But she made up for her size with meanness. She thought our hormonal distractions were responsible for our not doing our homework, so she instituted an innovative pedagogical technique she called Lineup, a marathon bee in every subject all afternoon every day. It made use of our primary concern—how we appeared to one another—to get us to study. When you missed, you had to sit down in the last seat in the last row until the next Lineup, so the last part of each school day was spent shifting desks—except for the desk of Nancy Wink, who missed only once all year, and otherwise occupied the first seat. She knew everything from the date of the Lend-Lease Act and the names of the three diplomats in the XYZ Affair to the exact height of the Matterhorn and the natural boundaries of Tanganyika. She studied so hard she'd arrive at school with her eyes looking like she had spent the night underwater in a chlorine pool. As her turn approached, she'd grasp the blackboard ledge behind her so hard her knuckles turned white. When she answered correctly, she almost collapsed with relief. The one time she missed she rushed to her desk and buried her face in her hands and sobbed inconsolably.

The rest of us didn't want to disgrace ourselves, but it was more important to be Popular, which Nancy Wink certainly wasn't. To be Popular you had to be an athlete or a cheerleader, or at least good-looking and smooth. Our cliquishness infuriated Sister Caritas, and one day she hit Danny with a wooden hanger. Word had gotten out that he was having a party after the official graduation party at school, and only the in crowd was invited. He was hanging up his coat after coming in late from lunch and she told him to sit down immediately in his desk. He said, "I'm hanging up my coat." She flew to the back of the room and snatched the hanger from his hands and began clubbing him with it. She was much shorter than he was, and had to jump to reach the top of his skull. It was breathtaking to everyone, and probably surprised even her when she found herself standing there afterward gripping the hanger like a hatchet. After the first whack on the head, Danny had thrown his hands up as protection, so most of the welts were on his wrists and forearms. He went to his desk still wearing his coat (as she insisted), and sat there in it, flushed scarlet, for the rest of the afternoon. Mr. and Mrs. Shea complained to the principal—itself causing a controversy, because many parents thought Sister Caritas responded properly to Danny's insolence, which they attributed to parental permissiveness. She was never publicly reprimanded and continued teaching our class, although she didn't hit anyone else.

She seemed to despair of us, to realize we were past saving, beyond her control. On graduation day, when we gathered in the room before going to church where all the awards, including General Excellence, would be announced, she told us in a flat voice we were the worst class she had ever taught, that with a few exceptions we were headed straight down the highway to hell. We were all dressed in our best clothes. Nancy Wink burst into tears. Luckily, she wasn't wearing makeup to smear. After much debate, no makeup was allowed for the official graduation party, although the girls who were invited to Danny's after-party brought along mascara and lipstick to put on in the girl's bathroom as soon as the official graduation party was over.

"Sure," Sister Caritas said. "The only one of you who cares is the exception." She went to Nancy Wink's desk and caressed the back of her skull, the way Sister Ann Christopher had done with me in fourth grade. Our hearts sunk: we knew Nancy Wink had won General Excellence. However, she was still not invited to Danny's after-party.

FIRST LOVE

I didn't go to Danny's after-party either. I had the same girlfriend for almost three years, from the beginning of sixth grade until the eighth-grade graduation party, where she broke up with me. I wasn't in the mood for another party that night. The reason she gave for breaking up was that I was "too serious." This was like saying the pope was too Catholic. I was serious, all right. I had no doubt whatsoever that she was my mate for life. I had been in her face constantly—increasingly, as I sensed I was losing her—watching her every move for a sign of disenchantment, a flicker of interest in another boy. When I wasn't with her, I thought about her, picturing the two of us in romantic scenes of the Hallmark-card whispers-on-the-shore variety. I fantasized catastrophes, floods and fires, fiends and rapists, in which I would save her life after suffering a serious but flattering injury, always ending with me in a hospital bed with the pillows plumped and her nursing me back to health. I agonized over whether or not I would in fact die for her, because it meant I didn't really love her if I wouldn't. Being as honest as I could be—really, really honest—I decided that I would. I told her that this was how much I loved her: I would die for her.

While slow-dancing at one of Danny's parties, I came upon the perfect vehicle for expressing to her the depth of my love: singing along

with the record into her ear. I favored mournful ballads, such as
"Tragedy" by the Fleetwoods ("You're gone from me. / Oh, woe.
Tragedy.") and "All I Have to Do Is Dream" by the Everly Brothers,
which I personalized. Her name was Liz, so whenever "Gee whiz" appeared in the lyrics, I crooned "Gee Liz." I must have done this at least
fifty times, as much as five or six times in a single night, jockeying at
the record changer to slip "Tragedy" and "All I Have to Do Is Dream"
yet again into the stack, and not once did she run screaming up the
stairs nor even gently ask me to stop. This was, on her part, true love.
Or true forbearance.

In eighth grade Liz was elected May Queen, which meant she got
to march down the center aisle of the church with a wreath of flowers
on her head and place it on the statue of the Blessed Virgin Mary
while the rest of the school sang "O Mary, we crown thee with blos-
soms today, / Queen of the angels, / Queen of the May." Before we
cast our ballots, Sister Caritas instructed us to pick the girl who most
resembled the Blessed Virgin. She meant morally, and she counted
the votes. She would have liked nothing more than to appoint Nancy
Wink by executive fiat. To us, it was mainly a Beauty and Popularity
contest, and, had it been necessary, I would have campaigned for Liz
like an evangelist, but it wasn't. Every year there was one eighth-grade
girl who was a shoo-in. There could be and were Jesuitical disputes
about the prettiest or the nicest, but well in advance of the actual election everyone knew which girl was the prettiest *and* the nicest (probably because she had formed her personality to fit the ideal). This was
Liz. Queen of the May, Queen of the school.

And she was *my* girlfriend. How proud I was. As she glided down the
aisle at the head of the May procession, her hands piously folded, her
eyes modestly lowered, she shot me the swiftest secret smile that went
kaboom straight into my heart. The wreath of bluebells and cowbells
matched her ash blonde hair and deep blue eyes, which in turn
matched her school uniform, her sleeveless blue jumper and crisp
white blouse. Despite the uniform, I pictured our wedding as she approached the altar. Here came my bride, to join me forever in the

Holy Sacrament of Matrimony: "Elizabeth, will you take Michael from this day forward . . ." I described my vision the following Saturday night while we were dancing, whispering into her ear the words of our vows. I asked her to repeat them after me, which, without noticeable reluctance, she did. I felt we were married. I knew we were only in eighth grade, that we had many years before us, that we'd both be going to college maybe in different states, etc. But as far as I was concerned, we were married. Our parents might have a different idea about it, other eighth-grade couples might not feel this way (which in my mind put us at the top of the moral hierarchy), but that's how I felt in my heart of hearts, and I needed her to tell me, approximately every twenty minutes, that this is how she felt, too.

Her reputation, impeccable as it was, I nonetheless guarded like Lancelot. Among the boys, in my hearing, her name was sacred, and death to the infidel. The first article of the athletic chivalric code was not to insult a girl in front of her boyfriend. I saw it violated only once, in high school. It resulted in the bloodiest fight I ever witnessed, on the railroad tracks behind the football practice field, utilizing the wooden ties, steel rails, and the gravel railroad bed. In Steeltown PA in 1960, when mothers told their daughters that the most valuable thing they had in the world was their reputation, they were telling the truth, at least about the social world. Any girl who became known as a slut was finished. She was approached for one reason, over and over again, often by complete strangers who had heard about her, and any boy who granted her the dignity of actually asking her out on a date was laughed out of the locker room. In the school corridors, on the playground, on the street, these girls were humiliated—especially one girl, after a spectacular episode involving multiple partners in the parking lot during a high school dance, the word of what was happening outside traveling through the knots of boys around the dance floor like a bolt of electricity you could almost smell.

In eighth grade, stories of this kind hovered at the periphery of our consciousness, beyond the pale, but we also had our own hormones to deal with. The St. Boniface Cougars were undefeated in football and basketball, and there was a party every Saturday night, in celebration of our victory that afternoon, and the smaller the party, the sexier it was. Most of these parties were at Danny's, for which the guest list became increasingly more exclusive, finally restricted to ten in couples of long-standing for the graduation after-party—certainly out of cruel childish snobbery, but also because the prohibition against sex was so strong it could only be tested by a unified group. This produced behavior more characteristic of a resistance cadre during wartime than of a bunch of eighth-graders in Steeltown PA in 1960. Our cohesion was absolute, our loyalty fierce, our emotions unfettered—and expressed strictly according to stereotyped gender roles. When Stephanie Blair's mother made her break up with Lou Nepi because they were "too serious," Stephanie wouldn't eat and wept bitterly for days, and Lou shattered his hand punching a brick column on his front porch. Stephanie was a cheerleader and Lou was a tackle. It sidelined him for two weeks, then he wrapped the cast in foam rubber and used it as a club, incapacitating any number of opposing linemen, provoking protests from their coaches. So extreme was Stephanie's grief that her mother finally relented, with the stipulation that Stephanie could see Lou outside of school only on Saturday (the game in the morning and the party at night), a stipulation the other cheerleaders immediately conspired to circumvent by covering for her.

Liz lived twenty miles outside of town, so the only time I ever saw her outside of school was on Saturday, my mother driving me after dinner in the yet two-toned blue-and-white '56 Buick to pick her up for the party, while my father, already loaded from his afternoon at the Keystone, stayed home and drank tallboys and watched TV Sometimes he'd want to drive me, but I insisted my mother do it, and he always gave in without the battle such a dispute would become in another year or two. Liz probably saw him no more than a couple of times during the three years she was my girlfriend. I never told her or anyone else about his drinking. Her own father had been killed during the War, before she was born, and her mother had not remarried, so she was used to fathers being something you could only imagine. I'd hold the car door for her, and she'd slide across the front seat between my mother and me, her tartan skirt over her knees, making expertly polite conversation of the kind bright children learned to have with adults. She would always inquire first about my sister, whom she idolized, a former May Queen who had just begun her first year on a full scholarship at Marymount College, then about my father, and finally about my brother, whom she had never met. My mother made the expected replies about how well everyone was doing. I let them talk together without interruption (that's how I experienced it—*letting* them talk), approving Liz's rapport with my mother, knowing their relationship had me at its unspoken center, the feminine tones of their voices part of the solace I felt as I watched the passing countryside of gentle hills and red barns festooned with white six-pointed hex signs the Pennsylvania Dutch painted to keep out the devil. I didn't hold Liz's hand while we rode, and would never have touched her in front of my mother. In fact, I never touched her except when we were slow-dancing in the dark surrounded by our friends. I assumed—wrongly, as it turned out—that this was the only time any of the couples touched each other. If the music stopped or the lights went on, Liz and I would disengage immediately, though we'd continue to hold hands. I think part of me pretended we were "just dancing." When I could no longer deny we were also doing something else, I agonized over it, praying novenas and the Stations of the Cross and asking the Holy Spirit for guidance. The feeling of her body against mine was overwhelming. I had never experienced anything like it. I almost wept at its intensity. I was completely transported, wanting to die like this, with her, here, inside the music and the darkness. I needed her so much. She was everything to me. At just such a moment, if the song was right, I would be inspired to express my feelings by singing "All I Have to Do Is Dream" or "Tragedy" along with the record, into her ear.

But was I condemning our souls to hell? Since I was the man, I assumed full responsibility. Worse, if I were sinning with her, would God punish me now? Would He make her stop loving me? Or kill her in an auto accident on the long drive to or from school? (That year her cousin was crushed to death underneath a tractor.) My anxiety made me a moral pit bull. Some of the boys, nonchalant about the consequences, were beginning to kiss their girlfriends on the lips. Danny was kissing Natalie Moscone until their lips blistered. I alone stood against this. During the annual retreat, with the girls in a separate room being lectured by Mother Superior, Father Kelly told the boys that kissing on the lips for more than three seconds was a mortal sin. When he was pressed about the time limit—for example, what if you didn't *know* it was lasting more than three seconds? were you supposed to count one one thousand two one thousand three one thousand?— he said it meant any kiss you wouldn't give your mother or sister. I never kissed my mother or sister on the lips at all. Unilaterally, I declared lips off limits until Liz and I were in high school. Everyone in the in crowd was acutely aware of "how far" each couple was "going," but my declaration of principle had no effect whatsoever on slowing any of the other couples down. Nonetheless, I held to it rigorously the entire year. It seemed somewhat arbitrary even to Liz. Periodically, she would ask me to review aloud the dogma behind my thinking, but she did agree with the fundamental idea that sin would corrupt our love, and finally demurred to my masculine moral authority.

Luckily, this left to our delectation every other square micrometer of skin above the collarbones—ears, necks, eyelids, cheeks, jawlines— and the embraces and caresses that turned our bodies to mucilage. Thigh to thigh, her breasts rising and falling against my chest, we'd breathe together to the music, swaying a little but not moving our feet, kissing everywhere our mouths could reach except the other's mouth, kissing, kissing, kissing. Once, at Danny's, someone got an emergency phone call during the thick of the evening. Suddenly, the overhead lights clicked on, and Mrs. Shea summoned Danny upstairs. Liz was flushed scarlet. It startled me. I looked at her with concern, and felt her forehead with the palm of my hand. "Gee, you're hot," I observed. "Do you have a temperature?"

I had no idea what was happening to me either. I didn't feel desire in general, only desire for her, fueled by love. One was the vehicle of the other. One was impossible without the other. Or so I thought, even when Terri Burr enrolled at St. Boniface. Terri was from the South, and had a voice like dark syrup, and darker eyes with a knowing look. She was also "stacked." This was the definitive judgment—arrived at by a rapid plebiscite of the boys at recess the very first day Terri showed up in eighth grade. We had already developed considerable expertise in this subject, masterfully distinguishing between who was really stacked and who was padding them—Annette Funicello, the Mouseketeer, being the standard against which all judgments were made. Terri was not unaware of the furor she was causing. She looked a little like Annette, with the same black curls but without the heavy black eyebrows whose single inclination was to join above the nose like two colliding caterpillars. Terri was in every way Liz's opposite—flirtatious where Liz was friendly, selfish where Liz was solicitous, chummy with the boys and saccharine with the girls. Sister Caritas despised her immediately, hectoring her daily about her uniform, the length of its hemline and its tightness at the bust ("Just what am I supposed to do about *that?*" Terri would ask you, throwing back her shoulders). Everyone but Sister Caritas was nice to her at first, until it emerged that when she was nice to you it was because she wanted something. Her voice would become more syrupy, and, coupled with what she did with her eyes, she usually got what she wanted if she were talking to a boy. All she wanted that first week was information—about the star halfback, Randy Lelong, who had modeled his body language and facial expressions after James Dean. Also like James Dean, he was blond and quiet and explosive and appeared to bear a deep wound that he wished only to be left alone to nurse. By the end of the week Terri had stolen him from his long-standing girlfriend, Carol Schaeffer, cocaptain of the cheerleaders, thus breaking up the central in couple of our class.

It was all anyone could talk about, but Terri was calm at the eye of the hurricane, smiling and nodding as the turmoil roiled about her. In the schoolyard, the boys and girls had always voluntarily remained seg-regated. Since none of the girls would speak to her, she marched right up to the group of boys in which Randy stood and took him off into a corner. Unheard-of behavior. Nobody went within ten feet of them. In the crowded school yard, it was as if they were surrounded by a moat. They spent all the recesses and lunch periods in that same corner, Randy lounging James Dean–like against the fence, Terri inclin-ing toward but not touching him (Sister Caritas would have put a stop to that) except every once in a while to surreptitiously hook one index finger in the front pocket of his pants and give it a suggestive tug.

This went on for a couple of weeks, while Randy continued to gain three hundred or more yards a game. He had great balance and com-plete abandon. You'd hit him with a very good shot and he'd come off it acrobatically, spinning and dodging. He had learned to run low, so unless you got underneath him and tackled his legs, you couldn't bring him down. This skill, along with his apparent disdain for his looks, gave him great social cachet, greater than the general oppro-brium for his dropping Carol (which was blamed on Terri anyway), and it wasn't long before Randy-and-Carol was replaced at our parties by Randy-and-Terri.

I knew how I felt about that: outraged. Morally outraged. This was a threat to the moral order. But I had to be careful about expressing it. The piety that had gotten me elected president of the St. Tarcissius Club in fourth grade came off in eighth grade as priggishness (which it was). Of course, I wanted to do unspeakable things to Terri, although I had no idea what things or even that I wanted to do them. Some of the boys thought she was prettier than Liz, which made me fume. I thought my classmates resented my moral super-iority, so I displayed it all the more resolutely, but subtly, I thought, as an example.

I needed to take the high ground somewhere. Everybody else was growing, but I wasn't. I had to stretch to the full height of my flattop to be as tall as Liz, who was five one. I had been the only sixth-grader starter on the football team, when I had won her heart, but in two years I had gone from being one of the biggest boys to one of the smallest. This made me all the more reckless at practice. I would have tackled a speeding bread truck, and blamed myself if I didn't stop it cold. Even off the field my body yearned for this contact. After dinner I practiced my forearm smash on my chest of drawers. Until I was in college, slamming somebody as hard as I could seemed almost an affectionate gesture.

It was Lelong himself I was trying to tackle when I got the concussion (my third) that put me out for the season. The drill was end sweeps. Two tacklers, one behind the other, waited for two blockers sweeping to their right with a ball carrier behind them. The first tackler was supposed to take out the blocking and the second was to bring down the ball carrier. I was the first tackler. Lelong was really unstoppable in this drill. At the first contact he'd cut by with remarkable acceleration. But I was not only going to take out the blocking; I was going to bring him down by myself. As they thundered toward me, instead of meeting the blockers, I knifed between them. One hit my legs at the exact moment the other's helmet collided with mine. Lelong waltzed by untouched. I spent the next three days in the hospital. The doctor told my parents the next concussion could kill me. That was it for football.

My mother consoled me, my sister consoled me, Liz consoled me. My dad bought me a pool table—with a wood base instead of slate, almost regulation size, used. A real one, with a slate base, was just too expensive. He set up the pool table in the basement next to the washer and dryer. Within three months the wood base warped and it became impossible to level. A ball traveling slowly would curve unpredictably. The felt wrinkled and the bumpers went dead. He bought a dehumidifier, which cost as much as the pool table, but it was too late. Before the year was out, my mother was using it to fold laundry.

I was touched by his buying me the pool table, but what I wanted was to play football and I couldn't, and I couldn't accept that I couldn't. I went to the games in my street clothes and letter jacket and watched from the sideline. Each game we won just made it worse. I wasn't needed. I sulked and brooded and wept in solitude, but unlike Stephanie Blair, I ate more not less and, without football practice, I started to get chubby.

About this time, tryouts were announced for the school musical. I had never taken part because it always conflicted with football and therefore only sissyish boys and unpopular noncheerleading girls like Nancy Wink were in it. Not an in crowd activity at all. Still, I had won talent shows, with my imitation of Johnny Ray singing "Your Cheatin' Heart" and, more recently, of the Diamonds singing "Little Darlin'" (doing all four voices); in second grade I had soloed in the choir and had sung at the top of my lungs out my bedroom window every day after school in case a Hollywood talent scout happened to be walking down my block in Groveland, Florida, hoping to hear an eight-year-old singing at the top of his lungs out his bedroom window (the neighbors up the street told my mother I had a very nice voice). And of course I knew how to act. But I wanted to be talked into trying out, so my mother and sister and Liz did just that. When the word got around that I was going to be in the play, my friends on the football team said I must be turning queer.

It didn't occur to me that I wouldn't be given the lead ("You're a Ryan, you're the best"), so I wasn't surprised when I was. It meant a lot of lines to learn, which my mother and sister drilled me on in the evenings. I also practiced in front of the bathroom mirror a moving solo rendition of "Pennies from Heaven," which I addressed to Liz in the audience, locking my gaze into hers and gesturing toward her like Frank Sinatra with my hand made into a pistol. In fact, the play wasn't a musical. It was a regular play for Catholic schools with a few songs thrown in at not entirely logical moments. The play involved a moral lesson. A boy named Seaweed who is always tardy learns how to be responsible after being hit by a bus. I was not Seaweed. He was skinny and impish. I played his conscientious older brother, who fretted continuously about Seaweed's character. At the climactic moment in the play, I was to be pouring myself a glass of milk while I waited for him to come home after school (we were latchkey children, hence my poignant sense of responsibility). The door opens, but it's not Seaweed, it's one of our friends.

"Where's Seaweed?" I ask him, milk in hand.

"That Seaweed," he answers, shaking his head ruefully. "He'll probably be late for his own funeral." (The Tragic Irony being that at this moment offstage Seaweed is lying under the bus.)

I can't remember my next line, nor could I remember it then. There we were, in front of the footlights in the school auditorium, before our parents and classmates and priests and nuns. Just about everyone I knew in the world. I had already sung my solo and wowed Liz, pointing right at her in the audience on the line "Don't *you* know each cloud contains (gesture toward ceiling and fingers fluttering downward) pennies from heaven?" I had imagined I saw her in the darkness blush with pride and pleasure. Now we were in the final act, only a few minutes to go. I was standing there holding the glass of milk when my mind went blank. I felt only surprise at first. The next line just wasn't there. I put the milk down on the table. Still nothing. Then the panic hit, which took me right out of my body. My body was still on the stage, but I wasn't. For lack of anything better to do, I poured a second glass of milk and picked it up.

"Where's Seaweed?" I asked again, my voice coming out of somewhere.

This startled my fellow actor. He blinked as if unsure he had heard what he had heard, then, before missing a full beat, he answered the same way: "That Seaweed," he said, shaking his head ruefully. "He'll probably be late for his own funeral."

This brought us back to where we had been before. I heard a few titters from the audience. I became resolute. Forcefully, I put down the second glass of milk beside the first, and poured yet another one. There were three of them on the table now. I picked up the third one and held it firmly, as if this, by God, were the one glass of milk I had been intending to pour all along.

"Where's Seaweed?" I asked angrily.

The other boy, flustered, hesitated this time, then answered almost inaudibly, "I don't know."

This was too much for the audience. The scattered nervous titters became unanimous full-throated laughter. Two full glasses of milk on the table and I was standing there holding the third, unable to move. The music nun was in the wings going bananas. "Say the next line!" she hissed. This was like shouting at a psychotic to talk sense. If I could have said the next line, it wasn't likely I'd be asking "Where's Seaweed?" over and over again and inexplicably pouring glasses of milk. But I had reached an impasse. All I could do was stand there silently, milk in hand. The nun pushed somebody onto the stage. He didn't bother entering through the door of the set at stage rear, where the other boy was standing, so to the audience it was as if he had popped out of the wall.

"Seaweed's been hit by a bus," he shouted.

The audience loved that, too. The big tragic line of the play turned into a howler. It also cut out about five minutes of the final act, but we all remembered the rest of our lines and got through to the end.

So culminated my theatrical career. After the play everyone complimented me on my solo. They said what a socko voice and professional delivery I had. No one mentioned my forgetting my lines. The next day at school my classmates were surprisingly gentle. But nobody forgot it. Weeks later, in the schoolyard, at parties in the pause between records, my friends would ask me, "Where's Seaweed?" It began to seem funny even to me. And years later, in high school, at a lull in some conversation, apropos of nothing, someone would turn to me and say, "I was just wondering, Mike, where *is* Seaweed?" "Dead," I'd answer. "Skull crushed horribly by a bus."

I thought the play was dumb anyway, and probably improved by its transformation into a farce. In any case, I shouldn't have been messing around with this dorky stuff. It was only two weeks to the first scheduled basketball game, but we were without a coach, Father Kelly having been suddenly transferred to a poor parish in South Philadelphia whose pastor had keeled over saying mass. Other schools were scrimmaging and playing exhibitions; their teams had been practicing together for a month. The whole season was already practically down the drain. The officers of the Knights of Columbus met to choose a new coach. My father was not a member of the Knights of Columbus—by this time, he was sleeping off his hangover until midafternoon on Sunday and skipping mass—but Mr. Shea was, and Danny told me, in the utmost confidence, that we would be hearing something soon.

A couple of days later Mother Superior announced through the loudspeaker that hung above the blackboard and under the crucifix in every classroom that all boys who wanted to try out for the basketball team should report to the gym. We jumped out of our seats and cheered, and bolted for the cloakroom, where we kept the packed-and-ready purple-and-gold leatherette Cougar gym bags we had been bringing to school for weeks. Sister Caritas immediately sat us back down, and, as punishment for this outburst, made us wait until all the bus routes had been called and the classroom was emptied of everyone not trying out for the team. There were about eight of us left, scattered throughout the room according to our performance in that day's Lineup. She had us sit there for a full five minutes in silence as she surveyed the pathetic spectacle of our souls, her arms folded and her hands inside her sleeves like a mandarin judge. Then we were allowed, in an orderly and civilized fashion, to walk like gentlemen, not heathen savages, to the gym. Who was the new coach waiting for us there? We had no idea, but at this point we would have been happy to play for Attila the Hun.

As we filed into the gym, he stood at center court, at parade rest, inside a circle he had made on the floor with five basketballs: George

"Casey" Connor. My heart sunk when I saw him. I thought I was done with him forever. He was the coach of Bickle Builders. I had played third base for him the previous summer, after he had returned from a three-year stint in the paratroopers and took over the team again. He showed up for the first Bickle Builder practice in his dress combat uniform, spit-shined boots, and spats. Pointing to the red number one on his sleeve, he told us it stood for his outfit, the Big Red One, *the* elite outfit in all of the military, tougher than the Marines. The Big Red One stood for pride and discipline, and if we didn't know what those words meant, we would be learning soon enough. ("Want to see my big red one?" McManus asked us, cupping his crotch when Connor was out of hearing. "It stands for pride and discipline.")

Everything about Connor was snappy and sharp. His trunk was a wedge, the planes of his skull accentuated by military bristles. You could shave a ham on his cheekbones. His eyes were the color of ice. He had a spine-chilling vulpine smile, and when his face muscles relaxed into their natural expression, he looked like he was plotting something. His voice went right to your motor nerves; you found yourself doing what he had barked at you to do before you had thought about it. Some of his players hated him and even his pets admitted he was a slave driver, but there was no denying the effectiveness of his methods: he built championship teams. Drill, drill, drill until you could do it in your sleep. When he finished with you, you knew how to play baseball. And, what was even more important to me, you had earned the privilege of wearing the maroon Bickle Builder cap and satin Bickle Builder jacket.

I had started every game for Bickle Builders, though just barely, batting at the bottom of the order. Connor rode me hard all season. There seemed to be an instinctive antipathy between us, bad chemistry, magnetic Scotties. I could have punched my head through a brick wall and not impressed him. Connor loved to say: "Give me an ounce of natural ability, and I'll make you a pound of baseball player." I thought that was it. He favored the naturals, boys who moved with grace and had a textbook swing. I had a hitch in mine, which I copied from Stan Musial (my father's favorite player). But nobody who played for Connor swung with a hitch. It was a matter of principle. No Bickle Builder had bad fundamentals. Either it went or I went, he said. It went and my average dropped two hundred points. My timing was a mess. In the middle of the season, I went one for twenty-three. I kept starting at third base only because of my fielding. After my pitching dreams fell apart, I had practiced so many hours at stepball I had developed fast reflexes. I didn't have much of an arm (the vestige of my catapult delivery), but if I set up in front of the bag, I could knock down most of the balls hit my way and still make the throw to first. Connor suddenly decided I should play very deep, behind the bag, for no reason he would divulge. I had to throw a pop-up to reach first. I couldn't throw out a paraplegic. I made him mad arguing about it, but I wouldn't yield on this one. I had nothing to lose. I was about to be benched anyway. He finally agreed to a test: I could position myself where I wanted to if he could hit me grounders as hard as he wanted to. We would see just how well I could play third base. With the whole team watching, he smacked grounders at me for twenty minutes, really whacking them, once in a while intentionally hitting a line drive that nearly took off my face. But I handled everything without an error. I was ecstatic. There was enough adrenaline in me to fly. My teammates congratulated me, after practice, behind his back. It just made him hate me more. A couple of days later, ostensibly to prevent the bunt, he devised a special infield shift in which I had to stand twenty feet from the plate, and he actually used it during our next game—for only one batter, as it turned out, for the purpose of terrifying me, which it did. Had the batter pulled one down the line, I would have been decapitated. But the kid struck out, three massive cuts, after pointing the tip of the bat at me between each pitch (it seemed about three inches from my nose) while his teammates and their parents crowded the third-base line—as close as the umpire would let them get to me—and screamed witty imprecations of their own devising such as "Hey, Four-Eyes" and "Knock it down his throat," red-faced, at the top of their lungs. Every time the kid swung, my stomach jumped into my mouth.

It was really Connor they hated, not me. Around the league he was infamous for his ruthless tactics. "Sure they hate Casey Connor," he said of himself. "He beats them." He liked to refer to himself in the third person. It was rumored that he had given himself his nickname. Casey Connor also liked surprises and tricks, because of the "edge" they gave; for the big games, without exception, he had a plan, which provided a reasonable explanation of why we were going to win. This had great power, we all believed it, and, despite what we thought of as his quirks, we believed in him. The power was that of community, of working together toward the same end. Every athlete knows how it feels—the feeling of being on a team, redoubled when it's a championship team, and redoubled exponentially when it's a championship team of boys aged ten to thirteen. Our belief was total. Connor was our coach. "Winning's not the most important thing. It's the only thing," he'd say, as if he had made it up. If we did what he told us, we won, and everything in our lives told us that's what mattered. That's what life, and being a man, was about.

But Connor's quirks weren't just quirks. Although it was the last thing anyone suspected at the time, he was a child molester. In retrospect, it's clear how his character was shaped by it, his denial of it: the constant suppressed anxiety of keeping it secret, which he took out on us through dominance and violence and abuse. Many years later he was sent to prison for molesting a boy and was beaten to death by a group of inmates for having "short eyes." None of us suspected Connor, because to molest little boys was to be queer and to be queer was to be effeminate and no one could have been more "masculine" than Connor. He was also shrewd. By contrast, there was an old pot-bellied guy named Roy who wore a golf hat and had bad teeth and hung around the playground during the day and the bowling alley at night, watching us play pinball machines. He *looked* like a pervert as well as acted like it, telling incredibly dumb dirty jokes with a leering grin ("Why are Ryan's pants like the Holiday Inn? No ballroom"). Every once in a while, Roy would invite somebody out to his car to look at the photos he kept in his glove compartment of Virginia DingDong Bell and her forty-fours, and try to get the kid to wank it for him right there. Everyone was on to Roy. Connor did nothing like this, though his "quirks" would now be obvious signs of pedophilia. His chiding was filled with sexual references, about being lazy because we pulled our puds too much, about being so horny we couldn't see straight, etc. He instituted "jock checks"—as if he were reviewing his troops, he went down the line and we each had to pull down our pants to show him we were wearing a jock. He made his favorite players massage his neck and sit on his lap, especially one pretty little boy with long eyelashes who was also gifted with extraordinary grace and coordination and covered center field like Willie Mays. "Come here, Barry," Connor would say, and the boy would sit on Connor's lap with his back to him while they watched infield drills. I don't know what anybody else thought. All I thought was that Connor liked Barry and didn't like me. Barry was a natural and I wasn't.

Connor lived with his parents and didn't go out on dates and didn't have a job. I'd see him sometimes downtown or in church, in civilian clothes, without his Bickle Builder uniform or cap. He looked smaller, thinner, paler—like George, not Casey. He was always alone, except with his mother in church. I never saw him with anyone his own age, of either sex. He told us what he wanted to do was coach high school, but the school district wouldn't hire him because he didn't have a teaching credential; he criticized all the high school coaches as "dodos" who didn't know their asses from their elbows. He was more careful about what he said about Father Kelly, but implied that he, Connor, could do a better job, especially at basketball, in which St. Boniface had never won the championship.

There was only one incident that caused everyone to agree that he had a screw loose. It was play-off time, August, at the end of an all-day practice. He had been pushing us hard on one of the hottest days of the summer, and our execution had become a little ragged. When he finally allowed us to get a drink, we starting spitting water at each other and horsing around. He sat the whole team down and lectured us about how soft we were, how anyone in his outfit, the Big Red One, was worth any three of us. Whenever Connor mentioned the Big Red One, it was impossible not to picture McManus cupping his crotch, and, on this day it produced more perceptible suppressions of hilarity than usual—pretending to cough, elbowing, etc.—which Connor misinterpreted. He said since we thought this was a funny idea he himself would take on any three of us right there and then to prove it. It silenced us immediately. We knew he was serious. Nobody responded, but he kept hectoring, going down the bench lambasting us individually ("How about you, Ryan, you're a tough guy")—even his stars and pets. He had had it up to here with the whole lot of us, and now he didn't give a flying shit, he was going to teach us a lesson. He wouldn't let it go. He really intended to fight. He really intended to fight boys on his own team, thirteen-year-old boys. Some of us were embarrassed for him, but all of us were fed up and wanted to see *him* taught the lesson. Eichstadt alone was as big as Connor, and could probably almost take him by himself. With Stone and McManus, it was a sure thing. They were all-stars, in their final weeks of playing for him. Knowing he couldn't win the championship without them, they had become openly defiant, talking back to him under their breath, so he couldn't hear what they said but knew that they had said something, which they would then deny. First one of us then another began encouraging the three of them to go ahead and take him on, until it became a chorus. A few rules were haggled out— no this, no that: it would be essentially a wrestling match—then they got up together and faced him. Connor stripped off his shirt—thick sandy hair covered his chest and shoulders and back—and the three boys began circling him like dogs. He tackled Eichstadt hard, trying to pin him fast, which by the rules meant Eichstadt would then have to sit out. Had it worked, Connor would have won. But McManus and Stone pried him off, and put their weight on him, then Eichstadt grabbed his legs and held them until Connor was helplessly trying to flip himself loose like a fish in a rowboat. After a few minutes of this, it was clear they could pin him if only McManus and Stone were a little heavier or a little stronger. Eichstadt switched places with Stone and in the process took a knee in the nose. The four of them rolled in the dirt for a few more minutes, then Connor ended up on his back again, with that much less strength, with Stone on one leg and McManus on the other and Eichstadt up top handling the coup de grace, his biceps bulging. He dug his elbow into Connor's adam's apple, choking him (maybe not entirely by accident), and was about to put him away when Connor started biting—real biting—clamping onto Eichstadt's forearm like a pit bull. Eichstadt bellowed and tried to punch him away with his free hand—real punches, flush in the face. When he finally got his arm loose, it was bleeding through the teeth marks around a big blue bruise, which he held up to us as if he needed our confirmation to believe it himself. "Look at this!" he said. "He bit me! The son-of-a-bitch bit me!" It stopped the fight. They let Connor up and he tried to shake hands with them. Stone yelled: "You're nuts, Connor. I'm not fucking shaking hands with you. Don't touch me, don't you touch me." Connor said that you don't pull punches when you're taking out sentries behind enemy lines, but he was obviously embarrassed and quickly trying to calculate the consequences this incident might have.

It had hardly any. Connor had to meet with the parents and apologize, but the three boys finished the season, and, as I said, we won the championship. Unlike most of my classmates, I would be fourteen before the next season started, so it was my last year, too. I missed the cut-off date by a couple of months and felt cheated by fate. I didn't tell my parents about the fight in case they might make me quit the team, but when McManus, Stone, and Eichstadt said they were glad it was their last year, they wouldn't play for Connor again for a million bucks, I realized I was glad I was ineligible. I wouldn't ever have to play for him again either.

But here he was at center court, the new basketball coach. I thought, Oh no, not Connor. My parents advised me to adopt a positive attitude and do my best, which I did, but by the time the season began, I was one of the subs—not sixth man as I was under Father Kelly, but ninth or tenth man, a benchwarmer who gets in the game only after it's overwhelmingly won or lost. And we won, game after game—as in football, without me—heading for a possible CYO basketball championship for the first time in St. Boniface's history. Everybody was thrilled. Connor was celebrated. Nobody wanted to hear my complaints, which didn't stop me from complaining. How could I argue with his benching me? He was putting the best team on the floor. He was obviously right, indisputably right. I didn't deserve to play. He adapted the same coaching methods he used for baseball: drill drill drill. Father Kelly's practices had been low-key and fun. A few demonstrations of fundamentals and then a scrimmage, maybe we'd run the bleachers afterward, maybe we wouldn't. He often canceled practice or left in the middle because he was called to a priestly duty—somebody was dying and needed Extreme Unction— and practices weren't scheduled that often in the first place. Connor had practice every day after school and all day Saturday. We didn't get home until seven o'clock. In answer to parental protests, he explained that we had to have double practices because we started the season so late. We had drills to improve our fundamentals and calisthenics to build our stamina. We learned to execute plays and box out and run backward to prevent fast breaks. He tied a length of rubber hose around our ankles so we would shuffle our feet on defense instead of crossing them, keeping our eyes on the belly button of the player we were guarding ("He can fake with his head, but where his belly button goes, he goes"). We had offensive plays and defensive zones designed to exploit the weaknesses and offset the strengths of our next opponent, whom he had thoroughly scouted. Before we had ever seen them, we knew the names of the best players on the next team we faced, their physical characteristics, their bad habits. If their center dribbled with his back to the basket after he caught a pass in the post, we'd have a guard there to steal the ball before he turned and shot. If their guard was clumsy with his left hand, we'd overplay him to his right. If they had one gunner who carried the team, we'd play a box-and-one, a four-man zone with man-to-man on the star; we'd keep him from getting the ball, much less shooting it. All strategies hitherto unknown to Steeltown Catholic Youth Organization elementary school basketball.

As much as he knew about opposing teams, Connor knew more about us—our families, our girlfriends, how smart we were in school, how we liked our teachers, who were our enemies and who were our friends. Bickle Builders were comprised of kids from St. Boniface and Trexler Junior High; as large as Connor was in our lives during the summer baseball season, he wasn't part of our school life. There had been at least that much distance. Now there was none. He forgot the kids from Trexler. McManus, Stone, Eichstadt, and their class had graduated from St. Boniface and gone to Sacred Heart High School. He fixated on us, our group of eighth-graders, the athletes and cheerleaders. He knew about our parties, that the hot ones were at Danny's, and complained jokingly about not being invited to them. It was as if he were there anyway, standing in a dark corner of Danny's basement, watching us. It was as if he were inside us. Most eerily, he could accurately characterize people in our lives whom he had never met. "How's Donna doing at Marymount?" he'd ask me. How did he even know my sister's name, much less where she was going to college? He spoke respectfully of her, as everyone did, but he did riffs on my brother. My brother was Connor's age, and to Scouts what Connor was to sports, and justifiably hated it when people compared him to Connor. Anytime the subject of Boy Scouts arose, Connor would start in on how weird my brother was, his merit-badge sash, his Mountie hat, his cowboy boots and string ties. Invariably it got the whole team laughing, and when I laughed along, I felt like Judas, and when I didn't, I didn't know what to do with my face. Connor knew my father worked at Bosch Machinery and went to the Keystone and never went to church. And he knew all about my love for Liz and that I felt married to her and even what I said to her when we were dancing. Except about my brother, he didn't use any of this knowledge to humiliate me, but I always knew he could humiliate me whenever he wanted to.

Every day when school was over, he was waiting for us in the locker room. He decorated it with slogans, white cardboard strips he cut out himself and printed in beautiful script with black Magic Marker. "Quitters Never Win and Winners Never Quit," "When the Going Gets Tough the Tough Get Going," and his favorite, the plagiarism from Vince Lombardi: "Winning's Not the Most Important Thing. It's the Only Thing." He did the same things with our names on smaller strips and taped each of these to a locker that was then our own. He set up a card table in the corner, which he called his office. The table was piled with plays, scouting reports, and notes. He still had jock checks—at any moment during practice he'd have us line up and pull down our gym shorts—although he could see from his "office" who was putting one on and who wasn't. His jokes got more anatomically specific, about who needed an extralarge jock and who needed only a peanut shell and a rubber band, who had a bush and who didn't. Whether or not any of the other boys told their parents about this, I don't know. I didn't. I didn't tell them about his mocking my brother. I didn't tell them anything.

As the play-offs approached, we were undefeated, but we would face some tough opponents, especially St. Paul's, last year's champion, with their star center, Ricky Wetzel. Connor decided that if we hoped to win, certain key players needed one-on-one private coaching sessions. There was just so much he could do coaching us as a team. He would spend a whole Saturday afternoon honing the skills of one of us at a time, concentrating especially on what we'd have to do to beat St. Paul's. What went on during these sessions would be a matter of utmost secrecy, since St. Paul's might have spies afoot. But if we listened to him, goddamnit, we'd walk away with the CYO championship, no matter what they threw at us.

Each week he announced the name of the boy he'd be working with the following Saturday. It was a great honor. It showed how much you meant to the team, how important you were to the championship effort. Each week my name was not the one he called. He went through the starting lineup and down the bench, eight or nine boys in all, including Bernie Barker and my best friend Danny, both of whom I thought played behind me. I was never called. I never had a private session. Bernie Barker quit the team after his private session. It was a scandal—not about Connor, but about Bernie. Bernie was like his name—loyal, courageous, kind, deliberate, and relentlessly conscientious. He was the only boy who did his homework every night and consequently was the top boy in Lineup after Nancy Wink, Liz, and a few other expert girls. He was elected captain of the patrol boys, which suited him perfectly. He would spread his arms at a crosswalk to stop traffic, holding them steady for a count of three after the last child had stepped onto the curb. No one could fathom how he could quit just before the play-offs. It was completely out of character, and Bernie wouldn't discuss it.

According to Connor, what had happened was this. Because he, Connor, wanted to help the guy, he had shown him how to squeeze his zits. (Bernie had bad acne.) Bernie told his dad, and Mr. Barker had gotten mad about it—he thought it might leave scars—and made Bernie quit the team. Well, Connor said, it won't leave scars if you do it right. The day after Bernie quit, Connor brought in a wash basin and some rubbing alcohol. He cleared his card table and moved it to the middle of the locker room. He filled the wash basin with warm water and held his hands tips-up like a surgeon and scrubbed his face vigorously and wiped it with a hand towel. Then with the index finger of each hand, he showed us the proper way to squeeze a pimple (he happened to have one on his chin), and immediately applied alcohol to the spot with a cotton ball. His movements were all exaggerated for emphasis, like a flight attendant explaining safety measures. Using this method, he told us, you'll get rid of your pimples and will most definitely not leave scars, despite what Mr. Barker may think.

A pimple—Bernie quit over a pimple. What a dork, we said. Eichstadt hadn't quit, Stone and McManus hadn't quit; you just did not quit the team, much less over a pimple. But no matter how much we mocked him and pestered him and tried sincerely to reason with him, Bernie would tell us nothing. He wouldn't confirm or deny the pimple story. All he would say was his dad made him quit. Okay, we said, the hell with him. He wasn't a starter. We didn't really need him anyway— he seemed to have to consider every move before he did it, on the court as well as off. He even dribbled ponderously. As far as I was concerned, it was one less guy who might get into the game ahead of me.

Bernie was the only one who quit, and whether or not this means Connor molested almost everyone else on the team during his private sessions, or tried to molest some and not others, I don't know. The only one I know about is Danny. He did molest Danny—and it contin- ued through high school and into college. They shared an apartment in Pittsburgh. During college, at Thanksgiving and Christmas vaca- tions, our old group from St. Boniface would meet again and play foot- ball—tackle without equipment, characteristically enough, which usually resulted in somebody breaking something and a trip to the hos- pital emergency room. Danny showed up once after missing a few years. He still played with the same abandon we shared as kids, and it made me feel close to him again. After the game I asked him if he was dating anybody in Pittsburgh. "A little redhead," he said. When I heard about him and Connor years later, I realized he had made an obscene joke. An angry joke.

After Bernie quit, Connor said as a team we just had to put it behind us. Yes, it was selfish and inconsiderate, a distraction as we were head- ing into the play-offs, but the great teams were great because they faced adversity and came out stronger than before. There would be no more private coaching sessions. He said he had done all he could do and now it was up to us. All of us. Everybody on the team was impor- tant. This would be a team effort. This was when they separated the men from the boys.

But we knew who was important and who wasn't. Since I wasn't, with the St. Paul's game only a week away, I was surprised when

Connor asked me to stay after practice. Everyone else filed off the court into the locker room, tired but in high spirits. We were at our peak as a team and we knew it. I watched their backs, happy despite myself to be part of it. Connor hadn't spoken to me individually all season. Was I getting kicked off the team or something? Connor sat down next to me on the bench and didn't say anything for a minute, and then just looked at me. It made me uncomfortable. Whatever he wanted to say to me, it couldn't be good.

"You must hate me, Ryan," he said.

It startled me out of my sneakers.

"Why do you say that, Case?" I asked, stalling. What was this about?

"Don't give me that shit," he answered. "You know as well as I do you would have started for Father Kelly. Then I come along. It's your last year of basketball, and here you are riding the bench. We've never liked each other much. You must hate my guts."

I had no idea what to say. I was completely disoriented. What did he want from me?

"It's okay, you don't have to admit it," he said, when he realized I couldn't speak. "I just wanted to tell you you're going to get your chance. You're starting against St. Paul's."

I couldn't believe it. I almost burst into tears. The frustrations of Bickle Builders, sitting out my final year of football, the eighth-grade play, Father Kelly leaving—none of it mattered now. I was starting the championship game! It was too good to be true. I immediately told everyone I knew, starting with my teammates in the locker room. They didn't believe it either, in a way that wasn't completely flattering. I had no more perspicacity than modesty. I didn't understand that my good news might be somebody else's bad news, and that such an inexplicable, sudden change might cause a general disturbance among the team.

Connor explained it to the team the next day. It was part of his secret plan. St. Paul's would be throwing a 2-1-2 zone defense at us, with their star center, Wetzel, in the middle. He had been in foul trouble in their last five games, and the only reason he never fouled out was they knew how to collapse the zone around him. Now what we do is this (he said, diagramming the play on a blackboard): the first two times we have the ball, we hit Ryan with a pass in the paint, Wetzel picks him up, Ryan drives on him and throws up that double pump underhand layup of his (I had a layup like my batting swing) and bang-bang, two fouls on Wetzel in the first minute of the game. Ryan comes out, Bauer you're back in as usual. But we don't forget about Wetzel. We don't let him go. We're crowding the paint, we're roughing him up. He's already got two fouls on him, minimum. He's neutralized. It's either free lunch in there or we foul him out. That's it. They can't win without him. They can't beat us.

Every day thereafter, we ran the two opening plays. I practiced with the starting team, taking the pass and drawing the foul from our substitute center (who was playing the role of Wetzel). Connor told me not to worry about making the layups, that was secondary. He showed me how to lean my shoulder in to force contact and how to come down off-balance and fall down as if I had been really hatcheted. To do, as he said, a little acting. ("And this time, Ryan, don't forget your lines.") After we finished running the plays, I practiced with the subs, as usual. I had been right. It was too good to be true. I would be starting—for about one minute. But it was better than nothing. I was a key player, sort of.

Connor swore us all to secrecy. He didn't care if St. Paul's found out I was starting. They couldn't have a book on me. I hadn't played enough. They wouldn't know what we were throwing at them. It would just make them nervous. But under no circumstances were we to divulge to anyone—animal, vegetable, or mineral—the specifics of the plan. "Zip up your lips," Connor said.

So everyone knew I was starting, but not that I was coming out after two plays. Including Liz. She said, "I hear you're starting the big game. That's pretty good." Although I knew she wouldn't tell anybody, I couldn't bring myself to say, "Yeah, but I'm coming out after two plays." So all I said was "Yeah," as if it were no big deal. I wanted her to be impressed with me, to be proud of me. My fear of losing her, which was increasing daily, I experienced as anger. I gave her lectures on what I expected of my future wife, with particular emphasis on single-minded devotion to her husband, and compared her to this standard, complimenting her on her piety, intelligence, beauty, manners, and good grooming, and criticizing her for not focusing her attention exclusively on me every second. In order to deserve this attention and devotion—my part of the bargain—I expected to conquer the world. I did not feel anxiety about this. I would be among the smartest, strongest, and richest men in the world. In other words, a Big Shot. We would have three children, two boys and a girl, and a large dog.

Problem was, the world was not right then acknowledging my eminence. That was okay. Just wait, I'll show them, I said to myself about 400 zillion times a day. And sometimes to Liz, too, as a promise to her, what she was going to get from me.

I smiled at her when we took the floor for the opening tip-off. We ran the two plays as we had practiced. Wetzel blocked one of my shots, fouled me on neither of them, and, when Connor pulled me out after fifty seconds, we were down four zip and Wetzel was in no more foul trouble than when he got up and brushed his teeth that morning. We won anyway, and carried Connor into the locker room on our shoulders, as he had instructed us to before the game if we won. He didn't put me in the rest of the game. At Danny's party that night, Liz was upset. Why had I taken those two shots? Everybody thought Connor had pulled me because I was gunning.

This was the beginning of the end. Danny had broken up with Natalie Moscone and started dating Carol Schaeffer, Randy Lelong's former girlfriend. They were in the corner, practically undressing each other. Lelong was dry-humping Terri Burr on the couch. Rumor was the four of them had spent the afternoon at Danny's when his parents weren't home, and Terri had let Randy take her bra off. French-kissing was old stuff. Everything was out of control. Just because we had won the championship, I was not going to lose my soul. That's what I told Liz, and then I told everyone else. Lelong told me to mind my own business unless I would like to have my teeth handed to me, and Danny said I was becoming a real square.

Then Liz broke up with me at the graduation dance. She was distant beforehand when I presented her with her wristlet corsage, and wouldn't hold hands with me as we walked into the gym. She informed me that she wanted to dance with other boys, just once or twice, because this was the last party and all. Unthinkable. We argued about it. She admitted she had already promised to dance with Tommy Bauer, the starting guard, the boy who went in when Connor pulled me out. I was crushed. How could she be doing this? I demanded. She wouldn't speak, she wouldn't look at me when we were dancing, she wouldn't dance with me cheek-to-cheek. This had to be a dream, a nightmare. And in her prom gown she had never looked more beautiful.

Her best friend came over to me between dances. I was standing with a group of boys, and she took me aside.

"Liz doesn't like you anymore," she said.

A trap door opened and I slid down the black chute into hell. The worst thing that could ever happen. I ran over to Liz and confronted her. We started dancing—I didn't want anybody to know anything—but she kept turning her head and pretended to look around, at other couples, at the decorations on the ceiling, streamers and balloons. I was screaming in whispers, trying to control myself, accusing her of this inconceivable betrayal—I, Michael, who loved her so much I would die for her. Still, she wouldn't speak.

"Just tell me if it's true," I said finally.

She looked at me with fury and vengeance.

"Yes," she hissed.

"You don't like me anymore. I have to hear you say it."

"I don't like you anymore," she said.

I ran into the bathroom and cried, wailing—as I was told later—so loud I was heard by everyone at the dance. I didn't come out until the dance was over and everyone had left. I didn't go to Danny's after-party.

The next day was the graduation picnic at Bishop Park. I didn't want to go, but I didn't want not to go, to give Liz that satisfaction. The boys took their girlfriends on rides and won stuffed animals throwing softballs at bowling pins weighted with lead, which collapsed with a sick thud. Every time Liz went on a ride with another boy, someone would run over to me and report it: "She's on the roller coaster again with Tommy Bauer." I pretended not to care. Since all my friends were with their girlfriends, and all the prettiest girls were taken, I spent hours by myself in the penny arcade, punching the punching-bag strength test, testing my courage on the electric shocker ("Are You a Man or a Mouse?"). The electric shocker was an upside-down handgrip like the one my father used. When you squeezed it, it sent a shock up your arm. The idea was to hold it until the thermometer painted on the console registered Superman! I did it again and again and again. A bunch of seventh-grade girls were having fortunes told by Madame Rosa, a glass-encased puppet head wearing a babushka and hoop earrings that spit a card down a slot when you put in a quarter. I went over to the cutest one, Judy Pinella, a cheerleader. She was dark-haired and dark-skinned, and had big black eyes and breasts like tennis balls. I had never spoken a word to her before. Without so much as a howdy-do, I asked her to go with me into the Old Mill. She had heard about me and Liz breaking up. She said okay, she guessed so.

We were both nervous as we stood in line waiting for the boat. The boat was attached to a cable underneath the water that pulled it gradually uphill through a tunnel for about five minutes, and down a little ramp at the end, so it landed where it started with a splash. It was a boring ride, but it gave you five minutes in the dark.

She said, "You're just after revenge, aren't you?"

"No, I've seen you before," I answered. It was a line from a James Dean movie.

As soon as the boat pulled into the tunnel, I put my arm around her and kissed her on the lips. Neither of us knew how to do it, so we just sort of pressed our mouths against each other. Hers was open. It was like kissing the mouth of a glass bottle—probably for her, too. I didn't feel anything. When the ride was over, she went back to her friends and I went back to the penny arcade. I never spoke to her again.

T O P S Y

Later that summer I was standing on tiptoes in the five-foot area of the swimming pool at Rodeo Beach when someone's hand rubbed the front of my trunks. Rodeo Beach was the public pool for the West Side, the higher street addresses, St. Boniface parish; it was, of course, the nicest public pool in Steeltown. The five-foot area was where the going-to-ninth-graders gathered, boys and girls chatting and splashing in the rumble of pool noise punctuated every few seconds by a lifeguard's whistle or a child's delighted shriek. Some boys had already reached their full height and could stand flat-footed, but others—like me—were still children, five one and pudgy, bobbing on tiptoes to keep their chins above water, trying to look nonchalant, worldly, and six inches taller. After Liz broke up with me, something changed inside me, I didn't know what. I was humiliated, not only publicly but also within myself. I couldn't forgive myself. I lost her because I wasn't good enough to keep her. Then I'd bounce to the opposite explanation: I was fine, I was great. It was her fault. How could she break up with me for being "too serious"? Wasn't love serious? She must have done it for some other reason—because I was too short or too fat or couldn't play football anymore or screwed up in the championship game against St. Paul's. I hated her—she was stuck-up and a prude like some guys said after she dumped me (as if this were a consolation). I hated her.

She had been my consolation, the thought I went to when my life at home or school wasn't what I wanted it to be. At idle moments I'd project in my mind a little movie of our blissful future with our three children and large dog. Now I started thinking about sex, with almost every premenopausal woman I saw—neighbors, customers on my paper route, women on the street—imagining them in the clutches of slathering, uncontrollable desires, panting and drooling, barely able to keep themselves from ripping off their blouses. I watched them for signals (a wink, a look, a password), I fantasized unleashing their hidden passions with aphrodisiacs (Spanish fly, powdered Asian rhinoceros horn) and Proven Seduction Techniques advertised in the back of forbidden magazines (subliminal suggestion, X-ray glasses, hypnotism: "You are very sleepy. Take off your bra."). Nonetheless, this touch underwater was a shock. I had been floating, daydreaming, buoying myself a little by spreading my arms. I didn't know where it had come from, much less who did it.

She surfaced a few feet in front of me, in one motion sweeping the water from her eyes and slicking back her hair: Corky Kellogg, Cougar cheerleader, bony and freckled, bitchy and prissy, bored and sharp-tongued. Her characteristic gesture was an exasperated sigh, as if she were a princess-in-exile, or (as we put it) Thought She Was. She was nobody's girlfriend, but would occasionally show up at Danny's parties with someone who was between girlfriends and make out with him like they had been going together for years. I had never looked at her twice. I didn't approve of her, I didn't like her, and I thought she wasn't pretty enough to be my girlfriend. Liz was the prettiest girl in the class, or at least tied for first with the raven-haired Terri Burr. Anything less would be to admit defeat. Corky Kellogg, I thought, was not in my league.

She no sooner surfaced than she dived and rubbed me again, and dived and did it yet again. The third time was necessary because I was so stunned I hadn't moved, though by that time—despite balancing *en pointe* to keep my chin above the water line—I had a boner. She must have felt it. She smiled mischievously and splashed an ounce of water gently at my face. "Bet you can't catch me," she said, and swam off. When I caught her, from behind, my hands on her waist, she grasped both my wrists and slid them up her rib cage. Her swimming suit was made of some sort of knit, silky and knotty. I'll never forget its texture, or its color (black), or the sensation of cupping her breasts inside it like baby mice: a force like concentrated light shot from my hands into my body and filled it, changing me into an exposed nerve. I pressed against her like that for a minute, against her little bud of a butt, cupping her tiny breasts, almost not knowing where I was anymore. I could smell the chlorine in her wet hair. Neither of us spoke a word. Then I panicked. What if someone were watching us? What was I doing, with Corky Kellogg? I had to get out of there. I swam away as fast as I could, leaving her to wonder what had happened, and climbed out of the pool. My knees were shaking. I walked back to the grass where I had left my towel, where some of the other kids were playing cards and blasting their transistor radios. One of them said, "We saw you with Corky Kellogg." I looked back at the pool. She was just pulling herself up the ladder, the freckles on her shoulders distinct and shiny, the water rushing off her skinny girl's body. "We weren't doing anything," I said. "Sure you weren't," they said. "Ha, ha, ha."

I didn't go into the pool for the rest of the afternoon, but I didn't want to leave either. I didn't want it to seem like I was leaving for a reason. I hung around on the grass, playing catch with a tennis ball, pretending to nap with one sweat sock over each eye. Late in the afternoon Corky Kellogg roused me with a flick on the arm. We were alone. Everybody else had gone in for the last dip of the day. "Why aren't you going in?" she asked. "I don't feel like it," I answered. "You chicken," she sneered, and ran toward the pool. "Eat shit, Corky," I called after her, hoping everybody heard me.

When I got home, I went into the bathroom, sat down on the terry-cloth-covered toilet lid, dropped my swimming trunks, and tried to wank it. My mother was making dinner. In the small one-story ranch house in which we lived, the kitchen shared a wall and plumbing with the bathroom. I could hear the noise of pots and faucets. I looked down at my boner, the mesh built-in of the swimming trunks a net between my ankles. I screwed my eyes tight the way I did when I prayed, and tried to feel what I had just felt, Corky's hand on me and my hands on her, blocking out the kitchen noise, blocking out the facts of my swimming away and the other kids seeing us and her calling me chicken. I pulled until it hurt, but all that would come out was a drop or two of clear fluid like tears.

Corky went off to prep school somewhere in Connecticut, and, as with Judy Pinella, I never talked to her again—except once, years later, when we were about to start college. We happened to be at the same party during summer vacation. She was smoking cigarettes with a holder. We engaged in witty repartee. The time in the swimming pool was all I could think of while we were pretending together that it had been a droll childhood experience not worthy of mention, way beneath our collegiate level of sexual sophistication. She was the first girl I touched like this, and the first one who touched me, the whole incident lasting no more than five minutes yet every sensation etched indelibly into my brain. The swimming pool became completely eroticized. But I also hated being there because I hated to take off my shirt. I always stood hunched over as if I had a stomachache, my arms folded and my hands covering the flab at my waist while trying to press my thumbs under my biceps to make them look bigger. I listened like a horseplayer for tips—about which girls would let you feel them up while dunking them. When one of them actually let me do it, I stretched these moments into minutes replaying them on the toilet, merging them into fantasies about the housewives on my paper route who, according to Freddy DeLuca, were Dying For It.

Freddy DeLuca lived next door and was my mentor in these matters. He had been tutoring me in how to wank it, counseling patience. He said it was only a matter of time before I'd start creaming. He was two years older than me, already going into his junior year at Sacred Heart, but was short and scrawny and walked with his arms stiff at his sides like Richard Nixon, who was campaigning for president that summer against handsome John Kennedy, our Catholic hero. Freddy's mother was a dead ringer for the Queen of Hearts in *Alice in Wonderland*. She had the same temperament ("Off with their heads!"). Her hair was the color and texture of brass. She wore it clipped and straight, very unusual in those days of pink plastic rollers and Toni permanents. His father's name was Tony—Anthony DeLuca. He was a low-level officer in the garment worker's union, and wasn't much taller than Freddy and me but was heavier than both of us put together. My father called him Two-Ton Tony. Because he was Italian and a union officer, my father believed he worked for the Mafia, but made me vow never to say so to Freddy. The DeLucas did seem suspiciously more prosperous than we were. They took an annual vacation to the Poconos. They bought the lot between our houses and built an enormous redwood swimming pool entirely aboveground, obliging their neighbors to discuss frequently and at length the DeLuca's ostentation and bad taste. They had a pedigreed boxer, with signed papers, a beautifully muscled two-year-old male with a shining brown coat, which they bought for two hundred dollars. Nobody else in the neighborhood paid money for a dog. Its name was King, the self-avowed love of Mrs. DeLuca's life. She would feed it from the table with her fork and grasp it firmly under the chin and kiss it smack on its rubbery black lips. She said a dog's mouth was cleaner than a human's, and laughed at me if I made a face when she did it. The DeLucas also had two cars: Mrs. DeLuca's ancient green Studebaker and Mr. DeLuca's black Lincoln Continental, which must have been twenty feet long. Despite all these luxuries, they fought frequently and loudly, their shrieks and wails echoing through the neighborhood during the summer when everybody's windows were open, Mr. DeLuca's skyward imprecations often delivered in the original Italian.

He was a charter subscriber to *Playboy*, and stored the back issues in the basement where Freddy, of course, found them. Early in our acquaintance, Freddy casually invited me over to look at them some afternoon when the rest of the family was out. I didn't take him up on it until the summer after eighth grade. We had been neighbors for two years, but I had snubbed him. My family looked down on the DeLucas. They were crass and uneducated and, as my mother put it, "subject to their emotions." Freddy seemed a little creepy and, even if he wasn't creepy, he was certainly a loser. He wasn't involved in any school activities at Sacred Heart, he got mediocre grades, he couldn't get a date, he wasn't popular, he wasn't good at sports, and he was probably headed for the Navy or a job on the assembly line at General Electric or, with his father's pull, foreman of a sweatshop. This did not seem to him a bad fate. Freddy told me such foremen got plenty from their workers, who were all women and illegal aliens anxious to keep their jobs. "It's like being the rooster in a henhouse," he said.

This kind of talk just confirmed my negative opinion of him, until the summer after eighth grade, when it began to have a subterranean appeal. I was hanging around the neighborhood a lot more. Being fourteen and ineligible, I no longer had Bickle Builder practice every day, and that's where my classmates were spending their summer after triumphant football and basketball seasons at St. Boniface that were anything but triumphs for me. I tried out for the next level in the city baseball league, and made the only team I could make, the worst team in the poorest white section of town. I rode the city bus to practice and rode the bench during games until we were down by twenty-five runs in the ninth inning and I'd get stuck into right field. I don't play right field, I declared to the coach, I play third base. He nodded and told me to go play third base in right field. I quit after a routine single went through my legs and became an inside-the-park home run, and the coach chewed me out in front of everybody although we had already been losing 28 to 2. I told him to go fuck himself, which was language I had just started using that summer, but never in my parents' hearing. I was still the good boy at home. Instead of real baseball with the Bickle Builders, and the snap and discipline of Casey Connor, I was reduced to Wiffle ball with Freddy DeLuca and the neighborhood kids. One of these was Happy Dale, a twenty-five-year-old hydrocephalic who always wore a baseball cap, Bermuda shorts, oxblood shoes, and argyle socks, rode a twenty-four-inch bicycle, and thought he was eight. He was known as Happy Dale, because, besides being retarded, he suffered from Tourette's syndrome, and would suddenly for no apparent reason spume enraged obscenities, a two-minute string of them climaxed by a laugh that went huh-huhhuhhuhhuh-yeah-uh. We had no idea what was wrong with him, and simply thought he was crazy, but he never hit anybody during his sputtering, scarlet-faced rages so we let him play with us. In right field.

I enjoyed these games, forgetting myself as I always did playing sports, except when I thought of how far I had fallen. I felt sorry for myself: if only I would grow, if only Liz hadn't broken up with me, if only my dad would stop drinking, if only something. I would show everyone, just wait. The shitheads. I started to like Freddy's sense of humor. It was nihilistic and cynical, and when he smiled, he showed his gums really repulsively. Like my father, he parodied songs, but his lyrics were gratifyingly more obscene. Coincidentally, one of his favorites was "All I Have to Do Is Dream," which Liz and I had regarded as Our Song, the song I had personalized and sung repeatedly into her ear while slow-dancing only weeks before. Freddy's parody was entitled "Cream": "Whenever I want you, all I have to do, Is cree-ee-ee-ee-eam. Cream, cream, cream." I got giddy every time he'd sing it; thus encouraged, he sang it many times. I didn't try to tell him what it meant. It was an act of blasphemy that nobody understood but me. Nothing was sacred, anything could happen. The idea was weirdly exhilarating. I thought, Could this be what life was? Could it possibly turn upside down like this? It could. It had.

Mrs. DeLuca frequently declared that her favorite children were, in this order: King, the dog; Freddy's little brother, Cosmo; and Freddy, who, on her list, sunk to fourth behind her Studebaker when it was not in the shop for repairs. Like many jokes, this one spoke an unspeakable truth for the teller. She openly favored Cosmo and said she would have believed that Freddy had been left on her doorstep had she not witnessed him coming out of her own body. Mr. DeLuca likewise never laid a finger on Cosmo but at the dinner table was given to smacking Freddy upside the head without warning, in one casual motion, as if he were raising his hand to speak. It would lift Freddy right out of his chair. During their family battles, he would come bolting out of the house, running like Richard Nixon walked, with his arms rigid at his sides, and pace up and down the alley within his father's sight but not his grasp while he bellowed traditional Italian curses. Sometimes I'd meet Freddy after one of these episodes when I was also running away from my father and we'd go down to the bowling alley and play pinball machines, or walk around the neighborhood and peek into windows.

Freddy not only knew where the good-looking women lived ("Ooolala," he'd say. "What a dish"); he also knew which windows were their bedroom windows, and who left a crack between their curtains (intentionally, in his opinion) when they undressed for bed. This was one bonus of his friendship. Mr. DeLuca's *Playboys* in the basement was another. Yes, it was a mortal sin, but what had God done for me lately? Anyway, as long as you didn't die with the mortal sin on your soul, you were okay. The nuns had a story about a boy who thought this way—who thought he could sin all week and just confess it every Saturday—and sure enough crossing the street to the church he was run over by a bread truck. I had been mocking that one for years, performing my Red Skelton pratfall to mime the impact of the bread truck, but I still felt guilty when I committed a sin, and Freddy and I began enacting the very story I mocked, going to confession together every Saturday evening, often after looking at his father's *Playboys* the very same afternoon. No matter what I said, I couldn't shake the feeling that God was going to punish me. Freddy took a less apocalyptic view. He thought there was no harm in a little insurance.

This was the summer my father built the Playroom in our basement. The DeLucas' basement had already been converted by a professional contractor, who had (suspiciously) done it as a favor at cost. It looked like a seraglio. There was no bar or TV, only a sea of cushions and pillows, and couches so soft they swallowed you when you sat down on them. It was unclear what anyone would do there except sleep or stare blankly into space. According to Mr. DeLuca, it was designed for relaxation. He called it the relaxation room.

Freddy called it the rack-off room. The day of my first visit was hot and bright outside, but it was pitch dark in the rack-off room. Freddy switched on one of the blue lightbulbs in the floor lamp. I sank into a soft chair, and, as carefully as a rare-book librarian, he placed the first volume of *Playboy* on the floor next to me—twelve issues arranged by month with the first month on top. "See if you find anything there you like," he grinned, showing his gums. He retired to his usual spot across the room with the current issue. I found quite a lot I liked. I had seen photos of naked women before, but not in such concentrated abundance or in such a private setting. And these were beautiful women with jumbo breasts, staring right into my eyes and pouting their lips as if the next pulsation of their hearts depended upon whether or not I would deign to favor them with my fourteen-year-old weenie. Others smiled teasingly as if to say "You naughty boy" before they initiated me into the delights of their pneumatic pink-toned flesh. I completely forgot myself. It was like being in the pool with Corky Kellogg, only I didn't have to worry about anybody seeing what I was doing. There was just Freddy. I looked up from the magazine, and through the dimness across the room I saw that he was whacking it, furiously, as if he were pounding chuck steak. His dick was the size of a ham bone. Simply immense. He noticed my surprise.

"We didn't come down here to play Ping-Pong," he said. "Whip it out if you feel like it."

That first time I just watched. As Freddy pounded it, the expression on his face got angrier and angrier until he climaxed, at which moment he shouted, "Whoa." Just like that, once, as if to stop a horse.

Afterward, wiping himself with a Kleenex, he always made a wise-crack—"Builds strong bones twelve ways," he'd say, or "Makes you crazy and blind"—and grin at me, showing his gums really repulsively.

The next time, I did take it out, and performed fruitlessly on myself under Freddy's expert eye. That's when he said it was only a matter of time before I'd start creaming. He said I had a good solid set of balls, I didn't need to worry. Once he offered to rack it for me, and wanted me to do it for him. "It won't bite you," he said, though it surely looked like it would. After two or three mutual strokes, sitting on the floor and facing the same direction as if watching a movie, I felt creepy so I stopped. I said I didn't like it, and indeed I didn't. This was agreeable to him—he wasn't too disappointed. Though he suggested it again once or twice, we never tried it again. It wasn't what he really wanted from me. What he really wanted was my friendship. He had no other friends, zero, before I started hanging out with him or after I quit. For both of us, our friendship meant doing these forbidden things together and knowing there was another person in the world who thought about sex all the time. Freddy argued that in fact everybody thought about sex all the time. I wasn't so sure. Girls didn't seem to. My mother certainly didn't, except to condemn it. When a sexy woman came on TV, like Edie Adams on "The Ernie Kovacs Show" or Abbe Lane with the Xavier Cugat band, my mother would hop in front of the screen and fan out her skirt, dancing and laughing, while my father and I (and my brother, when he was home) yelled at her to get out of the way. "Oh, you men," she'd say. My father was bawdy in the basement with me, but never upstairs in front of my mother. I couldn't figure out what he actually thought about sex, because I didn't trust what he said when he was drunk and he didn't mention it at all when he was sober. He told me the most beautiful thing in the world was when two people in love came at the same time, but I had no idea what he was talking about, and, like his story about killing the man who tried to shove his cock up his ass, it made me feel weird and scared. With other boys I made the usual boyish jokes, but other boys didn't seem to be quite the way I was, and I didn't let anyone but Freddy know I was this way, either then or for a long time afterward.

But I also thought Freddy was a little crazy, and that I was not exactly like him either. He had taught King to lick him when he was about to climax ("Watch this," he said, as offhandedly as if he were going to show me how he had taught his pooch to sit up and beg). We were in the rack-off room, but I was still shocked. Freddy must have sensed this, because he never did it again in front of me. But I knew he was doing it, and it was all I could see afterward every time Mrs. DeLuca kissed the dog. It was as if there were no limits to Freddy's anger, no limits to what he'd do as long as he could get away with it. He believed his parents hated him, and would say so, as a simple statement, in a flat voice. I didn't believe my parents hated me. My father smacked me around when he was drunk, and said crazy things to me, and hurt my feelings so deeply it made me dizzy, but he also said he loved me more than anyone else in the world. He didn't think I was going to be a nobody. Quite the opposite. I was a Ryan, he told me, I was special. Indeed, I was the most special Ryan of all. That's why he had to be hard on me. That's why he expected so much. I would be rich and famous. Many doors were open to me that were bolted shut in Freddy's face. I was smarter, handsomer, a better athlete. I thought I was better than Freddy, and not just better: a lot better. Freddy was a loser. I was a winner.

This idea was also encouraged by my mother in her own way. She had a habit of reading newspaper stories about prodigies aloud, then asking me, "Why don't *you* get out there?"—"out there" being the greater world of glory and accomplishment. She particularly favored articles about math and science prodigies—children who built nuclear reactors at home out of ordinary kitchen utensils and were admitted to MIT at the age of nine. Not coincidentally, math was my best subject, and my learning how to multiply in my head when I was five and competing against kids five grades ahead of me led us all to believe I was a sort of prodigy myself, if of the local variety. This view was gradually modified as I got older, but at fourteen I was still the bearer of my parents' hopes and expectations. My brother was an oddball and my sister was a girl. It was up to me. I could do it. In our family I would be the one.

But it wasn't so much that Freddy wasn't as good as I was that my mother didn't like me hanging around with him. She felt sorry for him, but he gave her a funny feeling; she couldn't put her finger on it—he seemed sneaky. Though she was mollified (and puzzled) by the weekly pilgrimage to confession, and knew I had recently undergone a series of crushing failures, and didn't want to deprive me of any sort of solace or entertainment, she still didn't like me hanging around with him. Had she known what we were doing, she would have liked it even less. One time he and I camped out together in a tent in his backyard, and my mom made us breakfast the next morning.

"What do you guys do out there?" she asked, trying to sound nonchalant as she served up our eggs. (All moms take the detective course at Mom School, but mine made Gracie Allen look like Sherlock Holmes.)

I thought of what we actually had been doing before I realized I had to make something up, but Freddy answered her without missing a beat.

"Oh, he tells me his life story and I tell him mine."

I remember the exact words because his skill was so striking. I saw that this is how to lie. You have to be ready every moment.

What we had been doing was what we usually did. Only this time, without the aid of the *Playboys*, we were telling each other our fantasies. Mine were elaborate and detailed, involving selected women on my newspaper route coming to the door wearing a bathrobe with nothing underneath, making the excuse that they had been taking a shower, and would I like to sit down on the couch and have a nice cold lemonade? I made a little screenplay out of it, complete with dialogue ("Ouch, I have a sudden cramp in my leg. Would you mind rubbing it for me, honey? Mmmm, that's good. No, higher"). Freddy's fantasies were blunt. He had one story, which he maintained was true, about walking in the poor white section of town and seeing an older girl on a porch with her dress hiked up. When he passed, she didn't seem to mind his looking, so he walked up to her and said, "How about it?" She took him inside and they did it. Afterward, she paid him a compliment. She said, "You've got a lot for a little guy." That was it. That was the whole story. I was interested by the idea that sex could be had so easily, but I found the story itself about as erotic as colliding with a fireplug. My fantasies all involved pretending one thing and doing another, and the woman's uncontrollable, slathering desire directed, of course, at me.

Freddy seemed unable to believe in such a possibility, even in fantasy. Sex, and life in general, was to him just a matter of luck. His was usually bad and he didn't expect it to be better. I questioned him once about why he wasn't going to college. "Join the Navy, see the world," he said, with his usual irony. But I pressed him on it. "Get serious," he said. "My old man would never pay tuition. I don't have the grades for a scholarship, or even to get in, probably. I'll go swab decks for a couple of years, then who knows?"

No doubt our friendship would have ended when he left for the Navy, if it had not ended, more dramatically, before that. There were fewer opportunities to visit the rack-off room after summer was over and school started again. Both of Freddy's parents and Cosmo had to be gone on a Saturday, which was rare. Sunday was out. Since confession was offered only on Saturday, we would have had to carry the mortal sin on our souls for a whole week. Plus it seemed doubly sinful to rack off on the Lord's Day. I'd get randy during Sunday mass ogling the girls in their crisp dresses, but if I did rack off afterward, I felt particularly guilty about it. I'd try to wait as close to the next Saturday as I could; in other words, until Monday.

But one Saturday, Mr. and Mrs. DeLuca took Cosmo with them to the Poconos and left Freddy at home. They drove off in Mr. DeLuca's Lincoln. What they didn't know was that Freddy had stolen the spare key to his mother's Studebaker, had it copied, and put it back before she noticed it was missing. Freddy was almost seventeen, and they wouldn't let him get his license. They said he had to show them more responsibility and maturity. Fine, he said. Your car, your decision. He enjoyed the idea of them wondering why he didn't argue about it.

We spent a satisfying afternoon in the rack-off room with Mr. DeLuca's *Playboys*, and I ate dinner at home, my father as usual on Saturday already loaded and trying to provoke a fight, criticizing the way I had mowed the lawn or washed the car that morning. If I was smart, I didn't answer, but that irked him, too, and he had a genius for finding the insult I would not suffer in silence. He was particularly surly that night, but I got out the door clean, because this was the night Freddy was going to let me drive.

With Freddy at the wheel of the Studebaker, we headed for church. He was an excellent driver, having taught himself in snatches at every opportunity for over a year. Confession was from four to six. We always went as late as possible, because then we didn't have to wait in line, and the pastor, Father McSwain, was on duty the last hour. Father McSwain was renowned for his speedy absolutions, light penances, and not recognizing you by your voice. One kid was the same as another to him. It was dusk when we arrived at the church and, yet again, we did not get hit by a bread truck crossing the street. I loved the inside of the church at dusk, the smell of incense and candles, the echoing cavern empty except for a solitary man or a woman in a babushka kneeling in prayer among rows of empty dark wooden pews. Was God here? I guessed so, it was spooky enough. The confessional box was also made of dark wood, and it was pitch black inside. There were three compartments: one on each side with a kneeler for those confessing and one in the middle where the priest sat facing forward, head bowed, two fingers pressed to his temple. You whispered through a screen right into his ear. It wasn't until the little door that covered the screen slid back that you started your confession. When you first knelt down in the box, the little door was closed and the confession on the other side was underway. You were not supposed

to listen; you were supposed to use that time to examine your conscience. If it was a long confession, the question was whether it was
juicy enough to make up for the discomfort of kneeling in that
cramped box. I generally thought it wasn't, and when we went to
confession as a class before major holy days, I'd jockey for a place in
line that would put me in the box with one of the nice girls who
wouldn't have a long list of sins.

Mine usually went about like this:

> Bless me, Father, for I have sinned. It has been one week since my last
> confession. I disobeyed my parents five times, I used the name of the
> Lord in vain nine times, I had impure thoughts twelve times, and I
> committed an act of impurity by myself four times. For these and all
> the sins of my past life, I am sorry.

Except for the acts of impurity by myself, I never actually kept track;
I'd halve that number and vary the others to make them sound credible but not too appalling. After the confession of sins and before the
Act of Contrition, the priest is supposed to ask, Do you sincerely re-
solve not to commit these sins again? But Father McSwain's hurry-up
version was more like "Commit these sins again?"—to which I could
have sincerely answered yes. But he didn't wait for my answer before
he growled "Say a good Act of Contrition" and banged the sliding door
across the screen.

Freddy always went after me into the confessional, because even
with Father McSwain he took a while. I never asked him if he confessed about King. I'd wait in the vestibule, reading the list of movies
rated C (Condemned) by the Legion of Decency. It was a mortal sin
to see these movies. The titles were spicy and evoked sexy images.
None of them ever came to Steeltown, except Brigitte Bardot's *And
God Created Woman*, which did great business at the Art Theater for
over a year. Just her name, the sound of it, evoked a sexy image:
BridgeEat BarDoe: those yummy, fat lips. But the title that fascinated
me most was *The Moon Is Blue*. It was on the list for years. I couldn't

guess what the moon being blue had to do with anything sinful or even what it meant. It made me feel there was so much "out there" in the larger world I didn't know or understand.

After confession that evening, I slid into the driver's seat of Mrs. DeLuca's Studebaker. The driver's seat. It felt great. I put one hand on the wheel and turned the key in the ignition. The engine started with a roar. This was going to be fun. With Freddy patiently giving me instructions in the simple sentences and measured tones of an air traffic controller bringing in a child at the controls ("Okay, now gently, *gently*, press down on the accelerator"), I promptly ran the first stop sign and drew the attention of a cruiser, to which I responded by swerving from one side of the street to the other, nearly sideswiping two parked cars, one on each side. This resulted in our being also quite promptly arrested. I had driven a total of four blocks. We had been in church less than five minutes before.

When the cops pulled me over, Freddy tried to switch places with me, but they saw him. He jumped out of the car and began fast-talking them, how he had left his license and the registration at home, that I almost had my learner's permit, that we had just been to church, etc. They bought none of it. When he saw it wasn't going to work, he tried to get me off, saying okay this was his mom's car, he didn't actually have a license, but why not just let his friend go, he'd take the rap. No dice, said the cops. We were instructed to put our hands on the roof of our vehicle and spread 'em. They radioed for a paddy wagon and off we went. It happened very fast. The paddy wagon took us down the main street of Steeltown, past the library where I had earned reading club certificates, only now I was looking at it through bars. I had been crying since the cops pulled us over, answering their questions through my sobs, and I continued to cry the whole way to the station. Freddy kept saying, "Take it easy. What are they gonna do, give us the chair?" He said it was all his fault, he should never have let me drive where there might be cops, he took the blame and did his best to console me. I did not think of him for a nanosecond. What I thought about was me. It seemed like I had fallen into a black abyss. I was in the back of a paddy wagon on the way to the police station, my life was ruined, God help me I knew I shouldn't have looked at those *Playboys*. Forget the bread truck. This was God's punishment. Freddy didn't shed a tear. "Take it easy," he kept saying. Only once, in that flat voice he used when speaking of his parents, he said, "My old man is going to put my nuts in a wringer."

My mom came and got me by herself. Luckily, when the police called, my dad was already, as she put it, "asleep" (passed out for the night), and she agreed not to tell him until the next day. Freddy's parents were en route home from the Poconos, so he had to wait at the station until the police could reach them. "I'll be fine," he said, waving goodbye woodenly as if he were wiping a windshield. He was sitting on a straight-backed metal chair next to a detective's green metal desk. To him, it was just bad luck, to be expected in the course of things. We had to appear in court together the following Monday, which consisted of our standing up in our places while the judge assigned each of us to a juvenile officer we had to report to twice a week for the next three months.

My parents were shocked by what I had done. My dad didn't beat me for it immediately, though he did remind me for the next couple of years that he had never been arrested in his entire life and what the hell did I think I was doing breaking the law? "You don't break the law. Period," he said. What kind of a dufus was I? Both my parents were eager for an explanation, and the explanation they settled on, with my help, was the bad influence of Freddy. I was forbidden to see Freddy again. This insulted all the DeLucas, but did not cause the kind of feud we had with the Shorts in Florida. Both families just pretended the other was invisible. If they were in their yard or swimming pool, fetching their newspaper, or getting into their car, we simply didn't see them and they didn't see us.

I told no one at school about my being arrested. Twice a week, after school, I'd sneak down to the police station to report to my juvenile officer, praying no one I knew would see me go in or come out. I soon exhausted the plausible excuses why I wasn't taking the bus home with everyone else, but as far as I know, no one ever found me out. It was winter, during my freshman year. The year had started off pretty well. Sacred Heart had a tracking system, thus explicitly presenting you with the official view of your intellectual capability during those first anxious days of high school when everyone was categorizing one another and trying to find a safe niche for themselves. I was placed in the Advanced Classes, which I relished, never imagining the feelings of those assigned to a lower track, much less to the lowest track of all, physically mature men and women carrying around elementary school textbooks they could barely read. One of these was a six-foot-three, 240-pound miner's son named James Bozowski. The first week of school had not passed before those in the lowest track became known as the Bozos.

Humiliation, in a thousand forms, was a fact of daily life. Who was (and who wasn't) the best-looking, the best athlete, the toughest, the smartest? Who was sharp and who was dorky? Judgment, ranking, pecking orders. I participated wholeheartedly. Some kids knew how to take their triumphs modestly, and were canny enough to diminish them publicly, whatever they really felt about them. Not me. I felt obliged to remind everyone that, unlike everyone else in the Advanced Classes, *I* never studied. I wanted it understood immediately that I was the smartest. I would no doubt be valedictorian without ever cracking a book, not to mention president of the National Honor Society and the Student Council, and, if I'd only grow a little bit, captain of the basketball team and king of the Junior Prom. Eat your heart out, Liz.

The freshman class consisted of over five hundred boys and girls, but being in the Advanced Classes meant you went from class to class with essentially the same group of thirty students—one of whom was Liz herself. All day every school day I watched her walk, sit, smile, laugh demurely (covering her mouth with her delicately tapered fingers), listen alertly with her sharp blue eyes, crinkle her brow quizzically, stand up with her shoulders back and answer questions with the voice that had once whispered I love you into my ear in the dark. Now we didn't speak to each other at all, not even hello. She looked so beautiful I was startled by it every time I saw her, even if I had glanced away from her for only a second. Her body was perfect. I stared at it when I thought she wasn't looking (which she kindly pretended not to notice), torturing myself, knowing I'd never hold her in my arms again. When I got into trouble for disturbing class with my smirking commentary, I could read the disdain on her face. I disgusted her. She already had another boyfriend, a boy from one of the poorer parishes whose announced intention was to better his economic status in the world and adjust his speed according to weather conditions when he got his driver's license. What a weenie. He and I were in the same homeroom, and I rode him at every opportunity for wearing polished oxfords and clip-on ties and not being in the Advanced Classes with his girlfriend and me. His name was Bill, but I called him Willie because it irritated him. "Just a little slow upstairs, eh, Willie?" I'd say when we got our scores back from one of the inevitable barrage of standardized intelligence tests that predicted our futures. "Got to get ahead, Willie. Got to go to *college*. Study hard, Willie. Study, study, study." I'd clap him on the shoulder in mock encouragement and he'd slap my hand away. He'd threaten and glower, but I knew he wouldn't punch me because he didn't want it on his record. Just as my father had with me, I had a genius for spotting other people's vulnerability. Handling it compassionately, especially by a parent, is a sacred responsibility and an act of love. I'd get a little knife in there and twist it relentlessly—not just with Bill, but with many other classmates, yet was truly puzzled when they didn't seem to like me. Here I was: the smartest, the handsomest (I looked like a flesh-colored beach ball with a flattop and glasses), and the wittiest, making hilarious jokes at everyone's expense. Why wasn't I elected class president? I specialized in physical defects (because I hated my own body so much). I humorously pointed out Ed Kinkle's Pepsodent Smile (his teeth were the color of chicken skin), Johnny Rosario's Breathmint Breath (his mother was Italian and cooked with garlic), and Sam Steinke's Clearasil Complexion (his acne blanketed his face and neck with green and yellow pustules)—as if I were the only one who noticed such things and had been appointed to enter them into the public discourse. At election time I walked behind Bill, smiling like Miss Universe. Up and down the halls between classes, in the cafeteria, I parodied him, saying, "Hihihi VoteforWillie VoteforWillie." It worked. He was elected to Student Council. I voted for myself, the only vote I got.

I had somehow lost the connection between how I treated people and what they thought of me, between my behavior and its consequences—if I had ever had it. I believed winning was the only thing: dominance, strength, getting what I wanted. That was what it meant to be a man. If I was taught anything else, it went right by me. Nothing in life was free, you had to take it. It was you or the other guy. Dog eat dog. You had to be the best. You had to do whatever it took. You had to make people think of you what you wanted them to think. But I couldn't. Now it would be obvious to some teachers that I was disturbed, but in 1960 a child pretty much had to murder his family in their beds and burn down the house to be diagnosed with a psychological problem. The nuns talked to me in the ways they knew how, encouraging me to study and behave, warning me of the consequences for The Future, in this world and The Next. To them I was a boy wasting his God-given talents—not as bad as some of the poor boys on the road to hell (for most of them, as it turned out, in Vietnam), but a major annoyance in the Advanced Classes, where the boys behaved impeccably and did extra homework. Like the prodigies in my mother's newspaper stories, these boys built neutron gas chambers for science projects and calculated the astrophysics of orbiting bodies for leisure-time entertainment. They wore soft plastic pocket protectors in their breast pockets (with a proper selection of pens) and leather slide-rule cases on their belts, the dorkiness of which I unhesitatingly pointed out to them. I let them know what hopeless weenies they were. And I let everyone else know I wasn't one of them. I was masculine. I picked fights, about twelve or so my freshman year—and lost them all. I'd choose an opponent I was sure I could beat and walk into his round-houses with my hands down. I couldn't see even the most telegraphed punch without my glasses, but that didn't deter me. If I bloodied my white shirt, or ripped it, I'd throw it away before I got home, and buy another with my newspaper money. I was once swung by my school tie into a brick building. Many times I was punched flush in the face, stunned and momentarily blinded, flailing my arms in front of me until another punch from nowhere knocked me to the ground. At the end of the day the principal announced detentions over the loudspeaker: a litany of names of the same bad boys day after day. Mine was soon one of them. Once you got on the list, it was hard to get off. If there was smoking in the lavatory, a fight in the locker room, commotion in the cafeteria, an obscenity carved into a desk—anything a teacher could not pin on another culprit—one of these boys, if he happened to be in the vicinity, would get the detention. When this injustice befell me, I howled in protest. One younger nun, weary with me, answered, "Michael, if you really didn't do it, just think of it as punishment for something you got away with." The nuns all carried pads of pink detention slips in their bottomless pockets and would write you one on the spot, scripting your name across the top with their perfect Palmer penmanship, one copy for you, one copy for the principal, and one copy for your parents. Sometimes I'd get two or three a day.

This was the life I quickly made for myself at school. I had no idea what I was doing to myself or why I did it. I wanted to be something. I wanted all the boys to admire me, I wanted all the girls to desire me, and I wanted everybody to like me—though I wasn't about to compromise. They would just have to see how great I was. If they didn't, it was their problem, not mine. I still couldn't play football because of my concussions. I went out for basketball and didn't make the first cut. Then I was arrested with Freddy and had to sneak down to the police station after school. My grades were sinking. I couldn't keep up with the kids in the Advanced Classes, who turned out to be as smart as I was, or smarter, and did all their assignments. My nickname freshman year was "Menu," because I had so many food fights in the cafeteria you could usually tell what was being served that day by looking at my shirt. Girls avoided me. Boys who had been friends and teammates at

St. Boniface avoided me. Nobody wanted to expose themselves to my mockery, or even listen to it. Nobody wanted to hear my bragging. I was not invited to a party all year. In the spring, class schedules were issued for sophomore year. When I saw mine, I got a shock. I was no longer in the Advanced Classes. I had been bumped down into the general throng.

Without friends, without studying, and without an organized sport, I had a lot of time on my hands. I got a chance to buy the paper route adjoining mine, so I did. This meant I was delivering about 140 papers every morning, which on the days the paper was thick (Thursday and Friday) meant doubling back to the drop-off and refilling my two green canvas *Beacon* bags, the straps crisscrossed bandolier style across my chest and cutting into my shoulders, the heavy bags thudding against the sides of my knees as I walked. The route took almost two hours, from about five to seven every morning, a little less and a little later on Sunday, because my mom drove me in the Buick. At 5 A.M. it was pitch dark. I'd carry a flashlight in my bag with a pair of wire cutters for the newspaper bundles. I didn't like waking up, especially in winter, but once I was out on my route—if my bags weren't too heavy—I enjoyed it, the dark houses and unpeopled streets, the predawn, the sky gradually becoming light as my load became lighter, the feeling of a burden lifting. Being alone like this was a solace to me. I had perfected the fold and flip, and could usually bull's-eye a newspaper from the sidewalk into a storm door with a satisfying bang, a frisbee toss of fifteen yards, really whacking it against the doors of the people who stiffed me at collection time, lofting it noiselessly onto the doormats of the women who answered the door in their bathrobes.

There were in fact a couple of these. One woman who was shaped like a pear actually did offer me a lemonade and sat me down on her living room couch and questioned me first about the doings of my family and then about my girlfriends, and feigned incomprehension that I didn't have any girlfriends (*"C'est impossible,"* she said). Although I had fantasized this very scenario about 6 billion times, I found myself blushing and stumbling. This happened in the summer after my fresh-man year. She was wearing gray Bermuda shorts that were as wide as an elephant's forehead and a strapless halter with rigid half-cups that kept slipping down, which she apologized for repeatedly and tugged back up, pinching the cups at the tops. To my surprise, I wanted more than anything to get the hell out of there, although as soon as I got home, I wanked it and began plotting what I would do the next time she invited me in, which she never did. I blamed myself repeatedly for blowing a golden opportunity. This was not one of the women I had fantasized about, or was in the least attracted to, but to me that was irrelevant. As Freddy would have said, she was Dying For It. What a stupid klutz you are, I said to my face in the bathroom mirror. Look at how stupid you are. It was what my father said to me.

The other incident of this kind occurred with a young woman I had indeed fantasized about and was indeed attracted to. It was one of the strangest things that ever happened to me. Laura was her name. ("Luscious Laura," Freddy had called her. "Ooolala, what a dish.") A raven-haired, pale-skinned beauty, curvaceous in the Terri Burr–Annette Funicello mode. She was eighteen, three years older than I, which meant she had just graduated from high school that summer, the summer after my freshman year. I had never spoken to her, or imagined I could speak to her, except in the fantasies in which she slavishly begged me to give it to her as I sat on my toilet ("Oh Mike, Oh Mike," she panted). She was never home when I collected, no doubt out doing glamorous things in convertibles with dashing playboys and heirs to local fortunes. I usually collected on Saturday or at dinnertime (and even then some people would close their blinds and not answer the doorbell), but sometimes if I wanted pocket money I'd do a few houses. I liked the feeling of being able to get money anytime I wanted. This was a summer weekday afternoon, when very few people were home. The blinds were shut, but I rang the bell anyway. When the door opened, it was so dark behind the screen door I couldn't tell who was standing there. It was Laura. In fact, it was Laura wearing a black one-piece bathing suit, black fishnet stockings, and black spike-heeled pumps. In her living room. With the lights out. At about two on a weekday summer afternoon.

"Paperboy," I said, my voice a squeak.

"We already got our paper today," she answered.

"I'm collecting," I explained.

"Collecting what?" she asked, moving up out of the darkness. She bumped the screen door with her hip. Her swimsuit had a scoop neckline.

"For the paper," I managed to answer.

"You're funny," she said, tasting her index fingertip.

I didn't know what to say to that.

"So what do you want?" she asked.

I did know what to say to that, but I couldn't say it. I just blushed.

"You're funny," she said again. "I'll see if I can find the card. Don't you punch the card? Maybe you're not really the paperboy. Maybe you're an impersonator. Impersonating a paperboy is a serious crime. Show me your puncher."

I held up my puncher.

"Come on in," she said. I stepped inside. She held out her hand for the puncher and I gave it to her.

"Punch, punch," she said, squeezing it, and handing it back and touching my fingers. I laughed, the sound like someone next to me clearing his throat. What should I do? Don't blow it you idiot, I said to myself. She sashayed across the room to the secretary, swaying her hips. I was riveted. Fishnet stockings, spike-heeled pumps. I watched her walk back to me holding out the card, and I didn't know anybody else was in the room until her mother spoke.

"You like Laura, don't you, Mike?" her mother asked. She was a large red-haired woman who usually wore a lot of eyeshadow, but here she was only a darker shape in the darkness, on the couch, against the far wall. She had been sitting there the whole time. I was too startled to answer.

"Of course you do," she said. "What a stupid question. How utterly stupid of me. But, tell me, Mike: don't you think Laura's very attractive?"

"I do," I whispered.

"Of course you do. Give him a nice tip, Laura. Mike's such a nice boy."

I took the bills, and popped the change from the three-cylinder changer I wore on my belt (nickels, dimes, and quarters). Laura told me to keep the change. I shakily fit the coins back into the slots. I punched the card, catching the cardboard punched-out dates in my palm so they didn't fall on the customer's rug, the way they had taught us at the Saturday morning *Beacon* paperboy clinic. Then I didn't know what to do or what to say. I handed the card back to Laura.

"Bye, Mike," she said.

I stepped outside into the daylight. Before I turned around, Laura had already closed the front door. "Bye," I said to it.

I never told anybody about this. I had nobody to tell now that Freddy and I weren't friends anymore. It seemed too bizarre for the boys at school. Plus I hoped it, or something like it, would happen again, and maybe it would if I kept it a secret. But as always it didn't. I thought this was my fault. I should learn how to make it happen. I cursed my inexperience, my clumsiness, my lack of cool. On the toilet I had Laura answering the door in all manner of negligees, my imagination remodeling her living room to include a fireplace and a bearskin rug (as featured in *Playboy*) and vaporizing her mother right out of the picture. I rubbed myself against my bedsheets screaming LauraLauraLaura into my pillow, flipping onto my back at the last possible moment to climax into a hydrangea-size wad of toilet paper.

Sophomore year, I started skipping school, partially to wank it more, partially because I couldn't stand being at school, who I was there, what everyone thought of me. I had always made up mocking nicknames for people, and, in return, someone found one, a real beauty, for me: Pork. Pork rind, Pork Ryan. Menu hadn't bothered me. But Pork did, a lot, and I couldn't keep it from showing on my face, so it stuck. Everybody in my class was calling me Pork, even the girls. I'd go back to bed after I finished my paper route, and when my mother told me to get up and get ready for school, I'd say I was sick. After about the fiftieth time she started not believing me. My father would march into my room with a thermometer and, without a word, stick it under my tongue. As soon as he left, I'd switch on the light over my bed and hold the tip of the thermometer against the light bulb until the mercury shot up to 105, then shake it down to a low grade fever, around a hundred, not enough to call the doctor, but too much to ignore. Both parents would apologize for doubting me, which I would gallantly accept. "I told you I was sick," I'd say in a weak, wounded voice.

This worked until late spring, when my father hid behind the door and spied what I was doing through the crack above the hinges. Until then, for almost half of the school days of that year, I had the house to myself. Although my father vehemently opposed his wife working, my mother had begun teaching fourth grade at St. Boniface when I was in sixth grade. (I hated her being at my school, and sided with him during their arguments about it. The nuns, when they yelled at me, would exclaim, "And your good mother is a saint!" and sometimes send me to her classroom, which made her angry at them.) When I was in high school, until she got home at four, the house would be empty, except for Topsy, our rat terrier. After they left in the morning, the front door closing with an authoritative slam, I'd wait fifteen minutes in bed in case they doubled back and were spying on me through the windows. Then I'd get up and make myself a nice breakfast and read the newspaper I had just delivered, already feeling a little throbbing of anticipation, a little thickening of my tongue. I liked the silence in the house: it was palpable, specific. My father was proud of the house. He had chosen the design and bought the lot and had it built. When we moved in, he glued a brass plate with "The Ryans" etched on it above the doorbell. It was a prefab ranch, with small rooms and flimsy walls and a thin green wall-to-wall carpet. The least sound traveled through the heat ducts. Silence made the house into a very different place than when my parents were there. The objects, the furniture, all seemed to vibrate imperceptibly. Sometimes when I was alone, I would just stop and stand in the silence for a few seconds. It seemed like I was on another planet. The same house, another planet. I had been picked up and deposited there, and outside the door was black empty space.

After I finished breakfast, Topsy would beg to lick the plate, and I'd place it on the kitchen floor next to her dog dish. Then I headed for my parents' bedroom. There was a big circular mirror at the end of the hall next to their doorway, and I'd see myself approaching it, getting larger and larger. Who was this boy? What was he doing? I didn't look, or, conversely, I'd put my nose up to the mirror and make a gargoyle face, sticking my tongue out as far as it would go and holding it until I gagged.

My parents' bedroom consisted of a double bed, a dresser, a closet, a vanity table, and a nightstand. By this time they were already at work, but I held my breath and listened for noises of their sudden return (the car's engine in the driveway, the key in the front door), my heart pounding, my skin tingling, my nerves buzzing. I had examined every square inch of the closet and the drawers, and I knew where to find what I was looking for: my father's detective novels, under the nightstand. I had combed them all for the dirty parts, and memorized the page numbers. Plus a couple of them had lurid covers. My favorite was a pouting brunette in a diaphanous peignoir and powder-puff sandals and painted toenails, sitting on the edge of a bed, her legs crossed, pressing a black automatic pistol flat against her bare thigh. I'd gather the four or five paperbacks that had either a dirty part or a dirty cover or both, along with any recent acquisitions that needed to be researched, and retire to my own bed with a wad of toilet paper. This was my morning. I'd wank it three or four times, with time out for a snack in between and maybe a game show on TV, each time with increasingly less pleasure.

Then I got the idea, no doubt from Freddy, of including Topsy. It never occurred to me that King was a two-year-old male and Topsy a ten-year-old female who had been spayed for the last eight years and maybe wouldn't be interested. She was a scrappy, yappy little dog, piebald black and white like a pinto pony, extremely aggressive to strangers and affectionate to the family. She had to be tied up outside because, even at age ten, she'd fight other dogs and nip pedestrians. My father said she was a good watchdog, she had the Ryan spirit. She had been with us since I was five and she had cried the first night we brought her home and I had sat with her until dawn on the back porch. She had moved with us from Milwaukee to Florida to Steeltown. I had spent more time alone with her than with anyone in the family, especially in Florida when I had no playmates and we harrowed fiddler crabs on the beach. Petting her was a comfort to me. Because I was the youngest child, she became more or less my dog, but I no longer paid as much attention to her as I had as a little boy, hardly any attention at all.

She came eagerly when I called her to my bed, leaping up onto it and licking my face, excited, happy. I didn't contemplate the idea beforehand. It was as if I were in a trance. Like all dogs, she liked her stomach rubbed, and would roll on her back and spread her hind legs when you did it; if you rubbed with a stocking foot, she would move down on it and try to straddle it. I put one arm around her in bed as if she were a girl—she was about two feet long—and rubbed her stomach with my other hand. She gladly spread her legs. When I went lower and lower, she got an alert look in her eyes and licked her chops nervously. I picked her up so she straddled me, balancing her back paws on my thighs and her front paws on my stomach, and rubbed myself against her genitals, which were external and black and small as a rosebud—not trying to put myself inside (which didn't occur to me), just rubbing against her. I only took a minute, but each second she got more nervous, and began shaking violently. When I climaxed, she leapt off the bed and ran out of the room.

After a minute I went looking for her. She was hiding between the stove and the refrigerator among a bunch of mops. I tried to pet her, and she let me, but she was still shaking, as she did once after she had tried to nip the wheels of a moving car and had nearly been crushed.

That made me feel strange, but not enough to stop it. I did it again—

twice, on two different days, both times knowing I was going to do it when I was pressing the thermometer against the light bulb before my parents left for the day. I was as crazy as Freddy. Crazier. I hated everybody. No, I didn't, but they hated me. It was as if those hours from tricking my parents into believing I was sick until I did this to Topsy were a deep black groove that I could slide automatically down. Time didn't exist. I didn't exist.

The third and last time I did it, Topsy wouldn't come when I called her, and I had to pull her from under the mops and carry her to my room. She growled the whole time. When I tried to make her straddle me, she showed her teeth and snapped at my face. I never thought she would try to bite me. She almost took off my nose. It scared me and made me angry. I threw her from my bed, across the room, and she ran away as fast as she could, her nails skittering on the hardwood floor. When I went into the kitchen to make myself something to eat, she started growling at me again. I screamed at her to shut up. I picked up a mop. She growled and snapped, ready to defend herself. I wanted to hit her with the mop, hit her and hit her. But I didn't. I put the mop down and went back to my room and closed the door. What in God's name was I doing? What had I done? I vowed not to do it again. Maybe if I didn't do it again, it would be as if I had never done it.

When my mother came home that day, she noticed that Topsy wouldn't stay in the same room with me. If I came into the kitchen, she ran out of the kitchen. Freddy DeLuca had had the opposite problem. King followed him around continuously, scratching at his bedroom door, trying to hump his leg under the dinner table while the family was enjoying their evening meal.

My mother asked me, "Why is Topsy running away from you?"

"I have no idea." I answered the way Freddy had, without missing a beat.

"Well, there must be a reason," my mother said.

"Topsy is a dog, Mother," I answered haughtily. "Dogs don't reason."

But I felt terrible. In my own home, in all the hours there alone or with my parents, no matter what was going on or what was on my mind, I was reminded how awful I was every time I saw my dog. I was awful. I had to hide it. Nobody knew me or would ever know me: exactly how I felt when I was five years old, although I didn't think of that, or of Bob Stoller.

I tried to make it up to Topsy. I bought a box of Hartz Mountain Doggy Treats with my newspaper money and put a handful in her dog dish while she skirted me, watching. I did it every day, but it was weeks before she would eat a Doggy Treat out of my hand and I could stop worrying about someone somehow finding out what I had done.

F O O T S I E

A few weeks later my father caught me pressing the thermometer to the lightbulb. He burst into my room like a SWAT team and began smacking me before I could scramble out of bed. I didn't know what hit me. I crossed my forearms in front of my face and the thermometer went flying, splintering against the wall. Everybody was screaming: my father at me, me at him, my mother at both of us (while hanging on his arm). Topsy began barking, as she always did when there was yelling in the house. Then, in mid-swing, my father just stopped.

"You've got five minutes to get ready for school. I'm driving you myself."

"You didn't have to hit me!" I screamed, red-faced and crying, after he walked out of the room. My mother told me to remember his heart condition. I yelled at her to please just leave so I could get dressed. Topsy was still barking. Topsy always kept barking after the yelling was over until somebody bent down, scratched her behind her ears, and told her in a soothing voice that everything was all right. Today I wasn't going to be the one to do it. She would probably run away from me anyway.

I wolfed a bowl of cereal while my parents put on their coats. Nobody said anything. We were all too embarrassed to speak. Nothing compared to how embarrassed we would have been had they known what I had actually been doing. My mother was still teary when we dropped her off at St. Boniface, giving me one last sad look as if I were being strapped into the electric chair and might, after all, deserve it. My father and I both stared straight ahead through the windshield. After a few more blocks of excruciating silence, he told me he was concerned about me screwing up. First there was my getting arrested by the police and now this skipping school. Was I a fuckup? He thought he might ask, because I was sure acting like one.

He turned the Buick onto the shortcut to Sacred Heart, past the bowling alley, down a long street without stop signs where the railroad used to run, the tracks overgrown with weeds, the warehouses abandoned, the overhangs of their tin roofs bitten by rust, every window smashed. Although there was no traffic, my father always kept both hands on the wheel and his eyes on the road, so he spoke without looking at me. But I was looking at him: his sharp profile, his black slicked-back hair and glinting gold-rimmed glasses, that stern expression he had in the morning before he went to work, now sterner than ever. You are a great mystery to me, he told me. What in God's name did I think I was doing? What was the big idea? Was I stupid? He knew I wasn't stupid. If I was stupid, that would be another thing. He knew I had a good head on my shoulders. It was way past time to start using it. "Time to get on the stick, my friend," he said.

I knew he was right. I had dug myself into a deep hole at school. I was still picking fights and getting punched around. I rarely got through a week without a detention, my name a regular feature of the principal's loudspeaker litany that ended each day. My primary modes of social interaction were mocking and bragging. I had become a clown. I'd do anything for a laugh. I put my shirt and tie on backward and wore a Dixie Cup on top of my head to the class following lunch period, which earned me a detention not for disruptive behavior but for violating the dress code (and I crowed about how ridiculous *that* was). I led a vigilante campaign to stomp bag lunches: any brown bag on any flat surface was subject to stomping, and would be left like a cow pie where it had been stomped. It was the rage of the school for about a week. There was no logic to it (I brought a brown-bag lunch myself) except the Absurdity Principle. It was something to do. Plus I had the satisfaction of having invented it. I was so bored during my classes I felt like exploding. My favorite class was geometry, partially because it was taught by the only young female lay teacher (a big-boned six-footer who wore a bullet bra that almost punched through her blouses), but mostly because I got to sit next to Kathy Keene.

Kathy Keene was the shortest cheerleader, the one most tossed and flipped, her skirt also flying up when she leaped, splayed, skipped, and somersaulted, which, in the context of regulation school uniforms that covered the kneecap, made her famous. She would have been famous anyway. She had an auburn pixie cut and doe brown eyes, and was generally regarded as one of the superboss sophomores, quite a bit out of my range. I spent my time in geometry inventing ways to amuse her. During tests I would pass her the answers I knew, which weren't many, since I never bothered to memorize any of the theorems or corollaries and was nearly flunking myself. By April, when my father caught me pressing the thermometer against the lightbulb, I had made her like me. She thought I was A Riot. There was also something else. My desk was near the front in the row against the wall, so, ostensibly to face the teacher, I could justifiably sit sideways and prop my feet across the aisle under the same desk Kathy propped hers under. I'd pry off my penny loafers and rub her foot and stare at her legs where they disappeared under her uniform and the lacy black border of her slip. She'd smile at me when I did it, a flash of sharp little teeth, and immediately I'd have a boner and be more inside my trance than in the classroom, the droning about trapezoids and isosceles triangles transformed into a kind of benign mantric hum. Sometimes I'd get snapped out of it by the teacher asking me or Kathy a question—boom, down came the feet and I was back in geometry class, 1962, Sacred Heart High School: Pork Ryan, This Is Your Life. I would have no idea what page we were on or what we had been talking about. More often, I'd be snapped back because Kathy would simply move her foot away. But if

I left mine there, before the class was over she'd put hers back, snuggling it under, as if we were holding hands. It made me happy. When the bell rang to end the class, our feet were always touching. This was our understanding.

Neither of us ever acknowledged it. I'd see her at the Friday night dances in the old gym. She got asked every dance by popular juniors and seniors, tall athletes and class officers, who would drape their right arms over her left shoulder while she wrapped her left arm around their waists. She danced that way with me, too, although I was almost as short as she was. I'd put my lips next to her ear and work my thigh between her legs, mashing my engorged weenie against her pelvic bone. But without warning she'd pull back and start chatting—it was like her taking away her foot. The rule, I induced, was that I had to act like we weren't doing anything. Okay, I'd kid and chat and make a joke, and after a half-minute she'd come back close and we'd finish the dance the way we'd begun, in which you couldn't have slipped a microchip between our abdomens. Then she'd go back to her girlfriends and dance with the upperclassmen. I could still smell the way she smelled underneath her perfume. I might get one or two more dances with her before the night was over, but I wasn't supposed to ask her too often. If I made myself a pest, I'd wreck everything.

I asked her out only once. She had dates all the time, and would joke about them, imitating the duh-duh star fullback, and I got the feeling that I was the guy she wanted to tell about her dates, not go out with. Except there was the secret thing we did under the desk, like the sexy black slip peeking out from under her Catholic blue uniform. For my part, I didn't want her to be my girlfriend anyway. I didn't want a girlfriend. I just wanted to have sex with her—a vague idea to me, since I still had not even French-kissed a girl much less touched one outside the confines of a swimming pool, with mutual consent and open acknowledgment. But she had come to me in her black slip many times while I was sitting on the toilet or humping my bedsheets, so right before school was out for the summer, I asked her to go on a picnic, hoping there would be a chance to get her off into the woods.

The picnic was organized by a group of boys from the public high school whom I had met while bowling in the Police Athletic League on Saturday mornings. They were a year older than me and had driver's licenses, a prestigious mark of maturity, when you could take out girls without your parents driving you or you could ride around all night with your friends drinking six-packs and throwing the empty beer cans onto strangers' lawns. I had been friendly with one of these boys before. His name was Chuck Holstein. We had adjoining paper routes. We fooled around at the *Beacon* newsboy clinics, mocking the peppy salesmanship techniques and substituting obscene dialogue during the instructional films whenever the Norman Rockwell newsboy talked to a Norman Rockwell housewife, who was invariably wearing an apron and had invariably been baking a pie. The newsboy listed the advantages of home delivery, how economical and convenient it was, how you got back ten times the price of the newspaper just by clipping the grocery-store coupons, which we turned into his presentation of various sexual options to the happy housewife. Chuck was one of those people everybody likes, sandy-haired and clean-cut, with a ready smile. He could and did strike up a conversation with anyone—gas-station attendants, convenience-store clerks, middle-aged waitresses. He'd get the life story of the shoe salesman whenever he bought a pair of shoes. We went to different schools and had traveled in different circles. His group of friends had an established identity at Steeltown High: they were smart but not dorky, they weren't varsity athletes but played sports, they dated cute girls but not the cutest, and they liked to drink and party but appreciated the Absurdity Principle—i.e., my slapstick antics and cynical remarks. About eight of them bowled in PAL. They seemed comfortable with themselves and generous with one another. One had the driest wit, one looked old enough to buy beer, a third had smooth moves with girls, and so on: each had a distinct talent that functioned for the group. Their individual foibles were sources of amusement, not mockery. They kidded one another continuously, but it seemed affectionate when they did it—which was new to me.

After the PAL league bowling in the morning, we'd bowl for money, at first just a few guys, then teams. There were other boys from Sacred Heart, including Danny (whose best friend was no longer me but Casey Connor, who would sometimes come to watch him bowl). The teams became the Catholics against the Protestants—an ironic way of admitting the difference between us. Chuck and his friends thought the Catholic prohibitions and rituals were strange and entertaining, and loved my imitations of weird nuns. Gradually, I picked up on the unwounding way they bantered. They represented a fresh start, a new social life. They had parties I might be invited to. I could be somebody different with them than I was at Sacred Heart. They called me Mike, not Pork. I told Kathy all about them, what neat guys they were.

The picnic was the first of their social affairs I was invited to. After PAL on Saturday morning, they were going to take dates to Lake Wallenpaupack, not far from where I went on the Scout hike with my brother. The girls were supposed to provide the lunches and the boys would bring the refreshments. There would be boating and swimming. We could check out the girls in their swimsuits. We wouldn't come back until after dark. There would be plenty of chances to get our dates off into the woods, plus we could make out in the car on the drive back, a good hour and a half on a dark highway. First we'd loosen them up with a few beers, then God knows what would happen.

I was ecstatic when Kathy agreed to go with me. Her being a prominent cheerleader, and Sacred Heart having an intense basketball rivalry with Steeltown High, she was not unknown at the public school, where she had been tossed and flipped at center court in the steamy deafening auditorium, and had also leaped, splayed, skipped, and somersaulted. I could see my stock rising the Saturday I announced she would be my date. A couple of the guys punched me on the shoulder.

They weren't disappointed when we picked her up, nor was I. She had on a pair of short shorts that could have been made of paint, which, when she wanted to take them off would certainly have to be removed surgically by epidermal peel. I rolled my eyes at the guys in the backseat as I held the front passenger-side door for her, so she got into a car full of strangers to a chorus of guffaws. There were seven people in Chuck's 1951 Packard: two couples in the back; Chuck, Kathy, and me in the front. Chuck's date finked out at the last minute, but he had already committed himself to driving and we needed his car. He was the only one without a date. He was good-humored about it and we were consoling. "It's okay," he said. "I'll just get totally shit-faced and we'll have a head-on collision on the way home."

Within minutes we were sailing up the turnpike in high spirits. I had planned out the whole day. I'd make a couple of subtle moves on the drive up to the lake, so that Kathy knew the way things were going to go now that we were dating. What subtle moves, I hadn't quite decided. I'd just play it by ear. By the time we got there, we'd be arm in arm, nuzzling, feeding each other the cold fried chicken she had lovingly prepared, and mooning into each other's eyes. I wouldn't have to push it. I'd let nature take its course. We'd naturally want to be by ourselves before the day was over, and what better way than a little romantic walk in the woods at dusk? I even brought along an extra blanket in case we wanted to lie down and look at the stars.

The front seat of the Packard could comfortably accommodate three full-grown gorillas, but I thought I'd seize the advantage of sitting next to Kathy by pressing my knee against hers. She moved her knee away as if mine were dry ice. She actually seemed irritated with me. I asked her a few questions and got monosyllabic responses. I tried making jokes, which she didn't seem to hear. In fact, as we drove, she was looking at Chuck a lot more than at me, and asking him about his neat old car and did he fix it up himself, etc., so that I was quickly acquiring an expert topographical knowledge of the back of her head. The longer she ignored me and paid attention to him, the more panic I felt. My plan called for a subtle move within the first twenty miles on the turnpike. We were already past that. It was time to do something. After scratching my head with my left hand for about five minutes, I snaked my left arm across the top of the seat. She didn't seem to notice. I left it there for another minute, then casually dropped my hand onto her shoulder. It was there less than a second. She reached up with her right hand and, using her thumb and middle finger as tongs, grasped my left wrist and lifted my hand back onto the top of the seat, without so much as a blip in her enthusiastic conversation with Chuck. The two couples in the back snickered.

That was it for me. I pushed myself as close to the door as I could and fumed. We stopped at a root-beer stand to buy more food because Kathy had forgotten to lovingly prepare fried chicken or indeed any lunch whatsoever. She sat down next to Chuck at the counter and I sat at the far end. I announced that I wasn't paying for any food since Kathy was supposed to bring it. She said she didn't have any money. Chuck said he'd pay, and the others offered to chip in. I did not. While we were waiting, I pulled all the paper napkins out of the holder and dipped them into my water glass and squeezed them into balls and began pelting Kathy and Chuck with them until the manager told me to stop. There was a big keg over the counter, the symbol of the establishment, from which was drawn an everlasting supply of delicious frothy root beer into frosty frozen mugs. I said I might just take a hot piss right into it. The manager glared homicidally at me for a full minute, then apparently decided it wouldn't be worth the life sentence and walked away.

"God, you're gross," Kathy said to me.

"Yeah, well, I won't tell you what you are," I responded.

And so it went for the rest of the day. I wouldn't eat anything when the others did, but when they went swimming, I devoured everything that was left, including cold French fries and sodden onion rings from the root-beer stand. I hadn't brought a swimming suit because I was still ashamed to take off my shirt in public. Everybody else was jumping off a dock and dunking each other and giggling. Some of the couples were having chicken fights in the shallow water, the girls riding the boys' shoulders, Kathy up on Chuck, straddling his neck and shrieking, his steadying hands on her firm bronzed thighs. In her black swimming suit, she looked like one million bucks. I hoped she would fall off, break her neck, and drown. I made bitter remarks about her until everyone was tired of hearing them. The walk in the woods at dusk I took by myself. I threw rocks at birds and whatever other cute woodland creatures happened within range, but I missed them all. I considered getting lost and making the others find me, but I figured they'd probably just leave. That's what I would have done to myself if I were them. I rode home in the backseat with the other two couples, the girls on the boys' laps. I scrunched myself into the corner while they made out. I didn't say a word the whole way home. The only sound was the tires on the highway and their kissing and breathing.

Kathy and Chuck went steady all summer. He apologized for scooping her at the picnic, but I didn't blame him. I blamed her. I was her date. She owed me that respect. I was quite self-righteous about it, declaiming the rules of fidelity within the time limits of the agreed-upon date as a contract of honor between the two parties. I didn't tell him what I did with her in geometry class. That was a secret between Kathy and me, dirty and sexy, a much deeper bond and promise than a date. But to her it had obviously meant nothing. Was I the one who was weird? That was what she said at the picnic after I had insulted her for the hundredth time—"You're weird, Mike"—in a tone that embodied her secret knowledge of me. It shut me up. I was afraid she was going to say something more, but she didn't. The memory of it made me feel dizzy and short of breath. Is that why she didn't like me, because I was "weird"? Or was it why she liked me at all? I couldn't let myself think about it. There were all too many obvious reasons why no girl would like me: I was too short and too fat and had hardly any hair under my arms. I hated buying pants because I had to get the "husky" size and couldn't stand seeing myself in a full-length mirror. I tried to avoid plate-glass storefronts, instead sometimes spending fifteen minutes in front of the bathroom mirror admiring how handsome my face was from different angles and testing sexy, roguish come-hither looks. I would do this when I locked myself in the bathroom during fights with my father, holding the sides of the porcelain sink like handlebars. He was enraged that I was becoming a loser. My physical presence, the money I cost him, the food I ate, the space my body occupied—everything I was or did seemed to irritate him. As I got weaker in the world, he was smacking me more, for my own good, to wake me up to life's demands and responsibilities—a couple of times without warning, the way Mr. DeLuca did to Freddy, ostensibly for something I had done hours or days before. When we watched TV together in the Playroom, he'd lie on the couch drinking tallboys, his belt unbuckled and pants undone and his potbelly sticking up like a burial mound. I'd flinch if he got up suddenly. Ninety-nine times out of a hundred he was only going to fetch a beer or pee in the drain hole. "What's with you, hot-shot?" he'd ask innocently, as if he didn't know, or, if he was feeling nasty: "I'd be nervous, too, if I was a frigging punk like you." I learned how not to flinch while tensing my muscles to duck and run. I became expert in calibrating his moods and discerning the signs of an imminent eruption, sometimes goading him to it with back talk, preferring slapping and screaming to the ugly tension and slurred insults. When he exploded, I could *move*; until he exploded, I was waiting for it to happen, even on the nights it didn't happen, which was the majority of them.

Chuck and I managed to stay friends by not mentioning Kathy's name, nor his mentioning that he knew I was slandering her every chance I got. I let it be known how at Sacred Heart she was known as a stupid, conceited bitch. You'll see, I said to Chuck's friends. She thinks she's God's gift to men. Over the summer, they started to arrive at the same opinion. One by one, they confided in me: yes, at a party she had said this, on a double date she had done that. She expected Chuck to take her out every night. Very demanding. She said she'd never go steady with a guy who didn't have his own car. How shallow. Whatever the subject, she had something pedestrian to say about it, and the less she was listened to, the more insistently she expressed her opinion. Bore-ing, they said: yak yak yak. I nodded sagely, the prophet vindicated.

Chuck picked up on what his friends thought. Nobody disputed her looks, but was it worth it to have to listen to her yammer about shopping and the dopey records she liked? Plus the word was she wouldn't put out for him. Nothing below the waist. They were having arguments. He was sick of her making the rules. She said he didn't respect her. He accused her of being selfish. She told him she could get any guy she wanted and he was no big prize. At the end of the summer she dumped him for a bodybuilder with a chopped-down Ford. Chuck told me I had been right about her. There's only one person in the universe Kathy loves, Chuck said: Kathy herself.

Though I was thus eventually vindicated, I was not a big hit at the picnic. The girls didn't like some of the language I used. There were more parties during the summer, but I wasn't invited. That was all right with me. You had to bring a date, and I couldn't get one. Shortly after the picnic another bowling buddy with his own car asked me to double with him, and I called up fourteen girls before one agreed to go. One after another: no no no. Some without bothering with an excuse: just plain no—click. The fourteenth girl was named Olga Schnick. She had just emigrated from Lithuania. She sewed her own clothes: ankle-length taffeta skirts and blouses with frilly bodices. Her mother cut her hair and fastened it behind her ears with ornate barrettes. My buddy's date looked like the young Sophia Loren. Her name was Bonnie and his name was Dick. When we picked up Olga, I went inside while Bonnie and Dick stayed in the car and got started. Olga's father inspected me warily as he shook my hand, as if he might read on my face my dishonorable intentions toward his daughter. Olga's mother asked if my friends would like to come in for a piece of ladke. I said I didn't think so. She insisted I eat a piece of ladke, which I did, whatever it was, the four of us sitting stiffly at the dining-room table. Olga's parents inquired about my father's occupation, my parents' parish activities, and my own career plans. I told them I wanted to become a professional bowler. They looked at each other as if this were an American idiom they hoped the other understood. "Bowlink, Mother," Olga explained, swinging her arm. "Oh yes," her parents answered, but still looked puzzled. Olga was their oldest child and this was the first time she had ever gone out unsupervised with a boy in a car—her first American date. Her father acted like he was being forced to trust his life savings to an imbecile, which of course he was. As we said goodbye, he told me I was to have her back by ten-thirty.

We went bowling, which somehow didn't impede Dick and Bonnie's lubricious foreplay. It seemed they had their hands on each other even when one of them was rolling the ball down the lane and the other was sitting at the scorer's table twenty feet away. Bonnie had on a pair of pedal pushers and a sleeveless red blouse whose tails she tied into a knot above her navel. Olga kept hitting her ankle-length taffeta skirt on the backswing, and the ball clonked into the gutter. "I make the gutter ball," she said.

I was embarrassed she had to be home by ten-thirty, but Dick and Bonnie didn't mind at all. After they dropped me off, they would stay out as long as their bodily fluids lasted. On the way to Olga's, on the same shortcut to school I had driven with my father, I slipped my arm across the back of the seat like I had with Kathy, and let my hand drop to her shoulder. Unlike Kathy, Olga snuggled closer to me and looked up expectantly. I kissed her on the lips, for maybe fifteen seconds. She whispered, "I hope you don't think I'm cheap." When we got to her house, she asked that I see her in and speak to her father. She was very worried because it was almost ten-forty. Her father admonished me, but gently. He was relieved she had come home in one piece, her clothes apparently not having been ripped from her body by a horde of marauding cossacks. "Next time you be on time," he said, clapping me on the shoulder as I left. Righto, I thought.

In the car Dick and Bonnie hooted when I told them Olga's line, imitating her whisper and earnest intonation. The whole night for them had been simply too rich. This was the capper. I was sitting in the front seat by the door and they each had a hand on the other's inner thigh. I knew Bonnie thought I was funny. It was more fun with just the three of us. I wanted to drive around with them forever and forget my rotten life. I asked Dick if they wanted to go to the Charcoal for cheese steaks. "Ohhhh, I don't think so," he said in a funny voice, and they both laughed. I laughed, too, as if I had only been kidding.

I was also not kidding when I told the Schnicks I wanted to become a professional bowler. I was in four adult leagues that summer, my averages ranging from the low 180s at the Hula Bowl where the lanes were new and heavily waxed to almost 200 at the old Cassandra Lanes across town where the lanes were soft. The latter was the more relaxed summer version of the Steeltown All-Stars, the best league in the city, by invitation only. I was tearing them up for Industrial Vend-O-Mat. I was talking to people about turning pro after high school, discussing the ins and outs, getting a sponsor to bankroll me for the tour, to pay tournament fees and front the money for a camper in which I would sleep in the bowling-alley parking lots. Could I make the pros? The great bowlers didn't choke, they thrived on pressure. You either had steel cajones or you didn't. In a big tournament sometimes I choked, my heart rising to my throat and my hands sweating so the ball slipped, but sometimes I came through. The jury was still out on me. I'd have to raise my average twenty or thirty pins a game, and as you got better it was harder to improve, but I told myself I had plenty of time to do it and still become the youngest national champion in history.

My father humored my ambition, but I believe he thought I'd grow out of it. I argued with my sister about it when she came home from college. She thought professional bowling did not contribute to the good of society. She was wearing black turtlenecks at the time, and had brought home Ahmad Jamal albums and walked around the house quoting T. S. Eliot's "The Hollow Men" in mournful ominous cadences ("We are the hollow men, we are the stuffed men"). My father supported me in these arguments, saying it was more important to do something you enjoy than something that contributes to the good of society—which had a powerful authority behind it because we knew he didn't do something he enjoyed and we thought it was the reason he drank. I certainly enjoyed bowling, everything about it: the feel of the ball, the sound of a strike, the smell of the lanes, the paraphernalia, grit, and lingo. It was its own world, and I could be alone in it. I didn't need anyone else or depend on anyone else. If I was good, it would be right there in my score, an objective indisputable fact. And I had gotten good—as a sophomore probably the best high school bowler in Steeltown. I should have been. I put in more hours of practice than a concert pianist. My right thumb was half again as wide as my left one, the knuckle had swollen from so much bowling (thirty bowlingless years later it's still noticeably larger). The Hula Bowl was only a few blocks from my house. When I stayed home pretending to be sick, I'd sneak down there for a quick three lines between three o'clock (when school was out) and four (when my mother came home), tearing up the driveway on my bike and changing back into my pajamas as she unlocked the door. I'd practice my delivery in front of the same hall mirror where I made gargoyle faces before gathering my father's detective novels from under the nightstand in my parents' bedroom. I'd perform my five-step approach toward the mirror as if I were on the lane, the last step sliding on the throw rug as I delivered yet another imaginary strike, looking good, perfect balance and follow-through, the pins exploding as I pulled the string on them with a little underhand jerk of my arm, kaboom. Kaboom, kaboom, kaboom. Over and over and over again. I'd bowl the cue ball on the warped pool table in the basement, using ten numbered balls as ersatz pins, or bowl all the balls into a far pocket, sometimes for hours until I had broken my previous record for how many I could do in a row. I'd lie in my bed with my bowling ball on my stomach before I went to sleep, comforted by its weight. I'd caress its perfect roundness the way Sister Ann Christopher had cupped the back of my head. The summer after Liz broke up with me, when I couldn't play team baseball or football or basketball anymore, I had bought the bowling ball with my newspaper money—custom-fitted and dyno-balanced, with a bowling bag and matching shoes (the best you could buy, fashioned of fine soft leather the color of breast milk). The bag had two zippered compartments, one underneath for the shoes, where I also stored my Sure-Grip and Tuff-Skin and bowling glove and funky hand towel (bad luck to wash it), which smelled quintessentially like Bowling. Bowling carried no prestige at school, and the real athletes thought it was dorky and so was I for taking it seriously. This didn't stop me from bowling, but, as much as I loved it, I would have dropped it in a minute if I could have played a varsity sport. I still played pickup games of baseball, basketball, and football, and even managed a few desperate weeks against doctor's orders on the junior varsity football team, but the only sport I was really good at was bowling, and I wanted more than anything else to be good.

The idea of bowling is to do exactly the same thing every time, which certainly suited my temperament. Before each roll I'd touch the sole of my left shoe and blow on my fingers. I'd pick up the ball with both hands and slide my left toe onto my mark on the approach. Tenderly, I'd press the ball into the dimple of my chin, almost kissing it as I inserted my fingers into the holes; then I'd lower the ball to my chest, recalling its familiar weight and balance. I'd find my spot on the lane, the exact one-inch-wide board my ball would travel over before it dug in and curved into the pocket, chiding myself to hit the spot hit the spot hit the fucking spot you miserable-piece-of-shit asshole. I'd concentrate on the spot until it shone like the Grail, until I had become it, until there was no me only it, and even the chiding voice faded into silence. Then, at peace, calm, slowly as syrup, I'd begin my approach, guiding the ball down into my grooved arm swing, picking up speed and momentum with each step, and finish by sliding to the line low and square, in one liquid motion releasing and lifting and following through: kaboom. Kaboom, kaboom, kaboom.

Bowling was my father's favorite sport—the only one he watched on TV and the only one he played since his corkball days in Milwaukee. His first job was as a pinboy at a nickel a game and tips. It was a rough job in a rough neighborhood with rough boys. Yes, there were fights, pinboys in the pits behind the lanes, struggles to the death with switchblades and stilettos. Sure, he carried a switchblade. You had to. And you had to know how to use it, particularly if you were a small boy like he was. Some of those characters packed brass knuckles and zip guns. They'd watch to see who was making money that night, and jump you on your way home. And he made the most money. He was the top pinboy, the one the pros asked for, because he was quick and nimble. Just as he would never have been able to fit through the crack in the cave to the land of the Greenies had he not been so small, his size was an advantage for a pinboy. He could move faster and tuck himself tighter into a corner of the pit ledge to avoid getting cracked by flying pins, though of course he did get cracked all the time, some real beauties, but you couldn't let it slow you down—you just jumped into the pit and set 'em up again. It was no job for crybabies. He had met the great bowlers of his time, and the really great ones, without exception, were real gentlemen and good tippers. My mother liked tennis, so tennis was okay, if somewhat effeminate and finally frivolous compared to bowling. Tennis etiquette called for polite silence and white-gloved pitter-pattery applause. Bowling was loud and smoky and profane; the air was thick with oaths and the smell of sweat and beer and cigars. Bowling was for men, and not just men, a certain kind of man, a real man, a man's man.

Every Tuesday, after dinner, my father would change into his sport slacks and bowling shirt (blue, with "Jack" over the pocket in white script, and the Bosch Machinery pit bull imprinted on the back). He'd dig his bowling bag out of the hall closet and carry it outside to the trunk of the Buick, already staggering a little, a Pall Mall dangling from the corner of his mouth, one eye squinting from the smoke. Sometimes I'd carry his bowling bag for him; I had begun doing this when I wasn't much bigger than it was, to show him I was strong, hefting it in both arms like a bag of groceries. We wanted him to have his bowling night. We wanted him to have fun. He hated his boss at Bosch as much as the one at Minute Maid, and complained about being in the pressure cooker at work. We never went on vacations. He said we couldn't afford them. He claimed to have friends at the office, but no one ever came to our house and we never went to anyone else's. My parents rarely went out for dinner or a movie. He said it was because he ate lunch every day in restaurants (and drank three Manhattans) and there was plenty to watch on TV (he could drink while watching TV). He'd drink while he was bowling and drink more afterward and come home drunk, but we knew where he was and didn't worry about him, except for the drive home; my mother always worried about him driving home (though, remarkably, he never did have an accident and was never arrested). On bowling night at least he was doing something besides drinking, or in addition to it. He had taught me how to bowl when I was little, and we had bowled together during my boyhood, not so many times but more than anything else we did together. Bowling was still something we could talk about. At breakfast the morning after his bowling night, I'd ask him what he had bowled. He was often vague and uncomfortable when I asked. I thought it was because his scores weren't as high as mine. It never occurred to me that he probably didn't remember.

When I bowled after school, I'd get home about the same time he got home from work, and I'd join him downstairs in the Playroom while my mother prepared dinner. This is when we'd talk, when he was having his first few drinks of the evening. At first, he was rushed and cranky and brusque, listening with one ear and a skeptical frown; but after three or four straight shots, expertly poured, belted down with his head thrown back, he'd fix himself a double highball and settle in behind the bar on his imported German padded-pink-leather barstool and start to relax. I could see his mood change. The muscles of his face visibly slackened. It would happen in a single moment, like a comedian doing celebrity imitations who turns around and becomes somebody else. This is when my dad was fun to be with. He forgot the troubles he had brought home from the office, how lousy he had felt all day. I'd tell him my bowling scores, inflated by my customary practices of not beginning to keep score until I rolled a strike and of discounting certain frames when I had obviously been robbed. These scores were astronomically higher than his, but in his relaxed mood he didn't care, nor did he call me to account on the difference between my practice scores and tournament performances, nor let on that he knew I was cheating and bragging. He'd tell me the best joke he had heard that day at work. This was a ritual for us. It was invariably a dirty joke, and I would try not to laugh. If I laughed despite myself, he'd giggle with glee and say "I got you on that one." I was still pretending at home I didn't use such language or approve of such topics, although in the basement alone with me he had already talked about sex many times in that bewildering variety of ways, including cautionary tales about certain kinds of women who flirted with him at office parties and tried to get him to go with them into the storeroom, the point of these tales being that he had never been unfaithful to my mother and never would be. It was nonetheless clear that it was important to him to be attractive to women. He dressed well, groomed impeccably, and was very proud of his full head of jet black hair without a gray one in it. He thought a man should have a strong handshake and clean fingernails—the strong handshake for men and the clean fingernails for women and both for your own self-respect. He believed women should be treated chivalrously. You opened doors for them; you offered them the crook of your arm when you walked together on public streets, always staying between them and the traffic; you did not suffer filthy language to be used in their presence, much less use it yourself. My mother maintained that once, before they were engaged, he actually put his coat over a puddle so she could walk on it and not get her feet wet. He told me he was a ladies' man, a lover not a fighter (despite his stories about fighting)—although, in this dog-eat-dog world, you had to be a man's man, too (hence his stories about fighting). I understood that sex was something men talked about, that sex was very different for men and women, that some women were tramps but the good ones were virginal and pure like my mother and my sister, and you did not share with them these basement feelings about sex or even let them know you had them. I understood he was showing me a part of himself he never showed my mother, and, as a consequence, I thought I knew him better than she did—not differently, *better*. But I still couldn't let myself go. I had been hiding who I was since I was five years old. I knew if he knew who I really was, the things I had done and thought about doing, he would have been shocked out of his shoes. He spoke to me about fidelity, integrity, honesty, and honor—holding your head high, being able to look yourself in the eye in the mirror in the morning. I knew he believed what he said and that he tried to live by it. I respected him. Yet

I also saw the façade at the breakfast table in a fresh-pressed suit after I had just watched him bleed into the toilet and shave bleary-eyed in his sleeveless undershirt and boxer shorts with his belly hanging into the sink. I saw the split between the daylight respectability we presented to the world and the nights of insanity inside our house, between his mania for mowed lawns, washed cars, clean shirts, and shined shoes when he was sober, and puking in the kitchen sink and fouling himself when he was drunk, between what he believed and what he did. Something inside him made a mockery of his ideals. It came out of his mouth like an enormous worm as he got drunker and uglier and raved about how bitter his life was and what a disappointment I was, when he was about as chivalrous to my mother and sister as an invading army of Visigoths. It came out when he was drunk but it was there coiled inside him all the time, and as I got older, I saw it had something to do with sex—I couldn't tell what, except I knew it was in me, too.

I saw him act it out sexually only once—with one of my sister's friends. He was drunk, of course. We all saw it, and after a few days of aftershock we never mentioned it again. This was the only way we could deal with the unspeakable: don't speak it.

My sister's friend was named Sharon. She was short and sexy and very buxom, with a pixie cut like Kathy Keene's, only blonde, and pale skin and freckles and devilish green eyes. She was, in the argot of the time, a flirt. She had all the equipment for it, which she found ingenious ways to display within the conventions of modesty: bending over in loose blouses, stretching languidly in sweaters, etc. I was gaga in her presence. She was always giving me a kiss or a hug or offering to massage my neck and asking me to massage hers. Once, I was massaging her neck standing behind her chair at the dining room table and, when my sister left the room for a minute, she grabbed my wrists and pulled me down and kissed me under the chin while my fingertips brushed her breasts. "You're such a cutie," she said. I was fourteen or fifteen, when I could easily have been mistaken for the flesh-colored beach ball with a flattop. To say this incident attached me to her would be a profound understatement. When she visited my sister, I followed them from room to room the way King followed Freddy DeLuca, hoping she'd do something like this again, trying to think of an excuse to put my hands on her. The only one I could think of was the one she used: massages, lots of massages, massages galore. If it had been up to me, her entire visit would have been one continuous massage. My mother and sister started giving me strange looks when I offered to give Sharon yet another massage, and Sharon started politely turning me down. But whenever we sat at a table, she'd play footsie with me underneath it. When she snaked her toes up my ankle, I felt like my head was going to pop off my neck like a champagne cork. I believe she introduced me to footsie (my father's term—I first heard the word from his mouth), but the memory of the first time is as blank as the night of the day Bob Stoller's mother caught us in his basement, and I have no idea how I knew the first time that she was deliberately touching me. Once, after we had been playing footsie at breakfast (as when she kissed me under the chin, we were suddenly alone), she asked me to come talk to her while she got dressed. And that's what I did. I talked to her while she got dressed. We went into my sister's room, and she closed the door. I sat on the bed. She took off her robe. She had on a white slip underneath, and bent over to fold the robe carefully on the bed, revealing to me her remarkable bosom. She held up selected items of apparel and pressed them against the contours of her body, asking whether she should wear this sundress or that halter top, then bending over again in her slip to fold them meticulously and arrange them tidily in her little red overnight case. After I had expressed my trenchant fashion opinions about most of her wardrobe, she wiggled into her skirt and buttoned her blouse and gave me a little peck on the cheek and opened the door and left. I sat there for a minute on my sister's bed, dazed, before I proceeded with my normal day. I replayed this scene with the predictably revised climax about 42 million times, sitting on the toilet and humping my bedsheets (Sharon was the featured star of my fantasies for years hence). I would also have excoriated myself as usual for blowing a golden opportunity except my mother and sister were in the house the whole time. I remember exactly where they were: in the basement doing laundry, almost directly under where I was sitting on my sister's bed. I could hear them chatting through the heat vent. They could have walked in on us at any moment. Sharon may have known what she was going to say if they walked in on us, but I didn't. I was so nervous I didn't get aroused. Afterward, my knees felt like Jell-O for an hour, and the physical world seemed to be behind glass.

Sharon was the only one outside of our family who really knew about my father's drinking, and we trusted her with that secret. During these years, my first two years of high school and the summers between, when my father's drinking started to get really bad, she was the only one outside of our family who stayed in our house overnight. She kissed everyone whenever she arrived. She kissed me, my mother, and my sister on the cheek, and my father on the lips. My mother complained to him about it once or twice, but he pooh-poohed her. Sharon was just affectionate, he said. Sure they flirted, but it was only in fun. Sharon was part of the family. But when he was loaded, he would hug her and put his arm around her and be very touchy-feely in ways that disturbed us all. I'll never forget his bizarre scene with her, but I can't remember exactly when it happened. It had to have been after I was arrested and forbidden to associate with Freddy DeLuca (because I don't remember talking about Sharon with him, and I certainly would have). It was during the summer, probably before my sophomore year, the summer before staying home from school and Topsy and my dates with Kathy Keene and Olga Schnick—which would make Sharon nineteen. Four of us—my mother, my sister, Sharon, and me (playing footsie)—were sitting at the dining room table, talking. We may have just finished playing cards or a board game. It was dark, it must have been late, on one of the nights Sharon was going to sleep over. She was wearing cutoff jeans and a loose red top with a snowflake pattern and a black zipper up the front which I had been gazing down goggle-eyed all evening. The Buick pulled into the carport and my father came through the front door. I could see he was very drunk. It was always frightening when he was this drunk, and especially so when Sharon was there. He greeted us all, and said to Sharon, "Hey, don't I get a little hello kiss?"

She hopped out of her chair and bounced over to him. They were near my chair, not two feet away. I could smell the alcohol exuding from him. He put his arms around her and kissed her. And kissed her. And kept kissing her. Sharon began to struggle to pull away.

"Jack?" my mother said.

But still he held her—surely for less than a minute, maybe for less than half a minute, but during those seconds he was really kissing her, seriously, sexually. It wasn't a friendly hello kiss at all. He had her bent over backward, pressing his body against her.

We all began yelling—my mother, my sister, and me—"Let her go! Let her go, Daddy! Let her go!" He did, finally, and she broke away. We were all standing up by now.

"My God, Jack," my mother said.

"Aaahh, goddamn bullshit," he said, and staggered toward the bathroom.

None of us knew what to do or say after he left the room. We were all shaking. I believe my mother offered to drive Sharon home.

She said, "It's all right, Mrs. Ryan. I know he's been drinking."

Somehow we managed to go to bed and go to sleep.

But over the next few days, against all reason, and against what our eyes had witnessed, my mother and I ended up blaming Sharon. My sister argued with us. I said Sharon had been flirting with me, too. She flirted with my sister's boyfriends. She flirted with my brother whenever he was home. As my mother put it, she flirted with everything in pants. She really flirted with Daddy. I didn't tell about her kissing me or us playing footsie or me watching her dress. I just said she flirted. My sister called Sharon right then and told her what I said, and Sharon apologized and said she wouldn't flirt with me anymore and she was sorry if she had made me uncomfortable. This blasted the foundation of my sister's defense and settled the argument: Daddy was so drunk he didn't know what he was doing, but Sharon was a flirt. She did know what she was doing. It didn't break up her friendship with my sister, but she came to our house less and less often, and when she did, she was very subdued. No bounce and no bubble. No massages. No footsie anymore.

Our survival didn't depend on Sharon. We were loyal to my father, he was our father (my mother still refers to him as "our Daddy"). We had to find some way to keep living with him. But he was sinking deeper, a black hole sucking in everything, including himself—all his intelligence, ingenuity, will, and power devoted to preserving what was killing him. He simply would not admit he was doing anything to us. He enjoyed drinking, he said. This was his house. He paid the bills. He was the boss. Nobody on this planet—certainly not me, my mother, or my sister—was going to dictate to him what he could and could not do, and if we thought we were going to we were sadly mistaken. "There are only two things in this life I've got to do," he said. "Die and pay taxes."

I don't know if my mother ever talked to him about kissing Sharon. I don't know if he even remembered it the next day. We never mentioned it in his presence, nor did I ever talk about it with anyone else. How could I? Even if I could bring myself to speak about it, I had been sexual with her, too. To speak meant to hide that secret, to lie— which I did arguing with my sister, pretending I didn't like Sharon's flirtation, not to mention the other stuff, the dirty stuff, when I not only liked it, I loved it, it made my tongue thick and my throat dry. I wanted to kiss her, too, just like my father did, only more. I wanted to grab her breasts, I wanted to rub her all over. I was playing footsie with her when she hopped up to kiss him. I was sexual with the same girl my father was sexual with. It was too weird to imagine, much less to talk about. And so was I. It was like two wires crossed in my brain. It was like the veil of reality had been ripped apart, and there was the horrible truth behind it: my father kissing Sharon. Kissing her kissing her kissing her. The image was branded in my head. All I could do was not think of it.

So I didn't think of it. As much as I loved footsie and massages and seeing Sharon in her slip, I loved my father more. I cared what he thought of me. I was disappointing him and failing myself. I was screwing up, as he put it, royally. But not at bowling. I just got better and better. For hours a day while I was bowling, time would evaporate. I'd think about my approach, my backswing, the angle of my thumb when I released the ball, whether or not I was getting enough finger lift. Was I rushing the line? Should I move over a board on the three-ten split? I was coming up tight on the pocket: maybe I should slow down the ball and try to go more outside in. Maybe I should switch to a semifingertip instead of my conventional offset: I could get more roll. Fine-tune, adjust, read the lane. That's what makes the great ones, as well as steel cajones. They don't make mistakes. They aren't stupid. I'd chide myself in one sentence and encourage myself in the next. Follow through, you dipshit. You're the best, Mike, you're the best.

My father never invited me along on his bowling night. He said nobody else brought their kids. It was fine, it was his night—though I wasn't a kid when it came to bowling. I was in four adult leagues. I showboated in PAL once in a while. Okay, I showboated a lot. I had a little dance-and-jump I'd do when I released the ball and knew it was going to be a strike, so I'd be in midair when the ball hit the pocket. Or salaaming at the foul line like a Muslim. Or sliding on my knees, eight lanes to the right, after my patented run-and-slide, kaboom. But I knew how to act on the lanes when I wanted to—better than he did when he was drunk and stumbling in front of the people bowling next to him, yelling something stupid, even falling down. I didn't like to bowl with him anymore anyway.

So I thought. But one Tuesday when he invited me to substitute on his team, I was thrilled. Two guys were on vacation; unless they got a sub, the team had to forfeit. My father thought of me. He had already cleared it with the rest of his team, the captain of the opposing team, and the league president. I would be the youngest person ever to bowl in the Bosch Machinery company league. They had given him the green light. It was a go if I wanted to do it. Did I ever. I was at the peak of my form. This was my chance to show him what I was made of, and in front of his friends. There would be a little wagering, friendly side bets, a beer frame every game in which the loser bought the drinks for the team. This would apply to me, too. I didn't need to worry about it— my father would stake me. I was an official member of the team, for that night anyway. My score would count, there was no doubt about that. He admitted he had fibbed a little about my average. The guy I was subbing for was a 150 bowler. Did I think I could top that? Har, har, I said. Well, don't get too cocky, my father said. You might regret it.

I was filled with questions. I wanted to know the technical stuff. I wanted to know about the lanes. How often were they refinished? How many coats of wax? Were they soft? Did they give you a high hit? Did they like a big ball or a tight line? My father got a little irritated. I was showing off, it was true. I wanted to display my expertise. I wanted to wear my PAL bowling shirt with the 600 Club patch on one shoulder and the 250 Club patch on the other. He said I had to wear street clothes. I should bowl, be polite, and keep my mouth shut. Just don't disgrace me, he said.

My mother gave us a big send-off. She fried a chicken and cheered us out the door. "Go Bosch Machinery," she said, kidding, but it really made her happy to see us go bowling together. We had been fighting so much. My father was already a little loaded, as usual on bowling night, and when we got to the club, he popped a couple of doubles first thing, before we had even taken our warm-ups. The club was dingy and old, in a basement downtown; you entered from an alley with a laminated card that made the door buzz, like the Keystone. It was a different kind of place than the Hula Bowl or Cassandra Lanes. There were no windows and nothing on the walls. The ceiling was lined with cork that had absorbed fifty years of beer fumes and cigar smoke. Your eyes had to adjust to shadowy dimness instead of the fluorescent blast that greets you when you enter a public bowling alley. There were only twelve lanes. There were back rooms for gambling and who knows what else. There was only a few feet of space between the dark wood bar and the bench where you sat while you waited for your turn to bowl, so you could reach your drinks almost without getting up and the orders were made by shouting. A gallon jar of pickled eggs in a grayish brine squatted on one end of the bar. There were no women, no families, no kids, no snack machines. This was a men's club, and the men could act up a little if they felt like it. My father said that's what it was for: a place you could go and not be bothered. A sanctuary. You could rent a back room for an hour and just sit in it. Yes, he had done that once in the middle of the afternoon. I could picture him doing it, sitting at a poker table in a dark room alone. It made me think of how much I didn't know about him, the troubles he had taking care of us, when what he really wanted was to play the violin and invent things and live on a desert island in the South Pacific. I was happy to be here with him, and excited.

The club filled up fast, bald men and fat men and young tough-looking men in bright bowling shirts with their first names stitched in cursive over the pockets, skinny old men and hairy powerful middle-aged men with arms as thick as my thighs—welders and pipe fitters and foremen, assembly-line workers who tightened the same five bolts with the same wrench all day long, only a handful of white-collar workers and virtually no other executives like my dad who got a weekly salary not an hourly union wage—laughing, ragging one another, beer bottles clinking, the air already dense with smoke from their cigarettes and cigars. My father introduced me around. Everybody was friendly. "Jack's son," they called me. "Oh, a ringer, eh?" a couple of them laughed. I smiled to myself. Little did they know.

I took a couple of practice balls. These were old lanes. They hadn't been refinished for years, and the ball hooked like crazy. It dug in two feet after you released it. The pin action was incredible. My mouth started to water. Cream puffs. These lanes were cream puffs. I could roll 150 blindfolded with my left hand. The opposing team was giving me side glances—at my expensive bag and shoes, my bowling glove, my eyeshadow-sized jar of Sure-Grip, and the two strikes I threw in practice. "Fucking kid *is* a ringer," one of them said.

Then the bowling started. I bowled and kept my mouth shut, like my father told me to. No showboating. I smiled and nodded at a compliment, answered politely when addressed, and complimented others in masculine monosyllables on a good shot. Otherwise, I said nothing. Team bowling is on two lanes, switching each frame. You can find the strike line on one lane but not the other. These two lanes were very different, as old lanes are that aren't carefully maintained. I was laying my ball out almost to the gutter on the right lane and it would still come up high on the headpin. I rolled a one-ninety something nonetheless. I wasn't pleased, but tried not to show it. One ninety was way beneath what I could bowl here. At least I hadn't embarrassed myself. My father had warned me not to tell what my real average was. There were a few good-natured grumbles from the opposing team about my high score. "I'm dreaming," I answered. "I'm way over my head." "Listen to this sandbagger," they said. They knew I was a bowler. Everyone was saying nice things about me to my father, what a good kid I was. Modest. A hell of a delivery. I could overhear them, and, if nobody could see my face, I beamed. I left my father alone. He was drinking fast, and staggering on his approach, and bitching when he missed. But he wasn't the only one. I was the only one not drinking in the whole place. A lot of liquor was going down, heavy traffic in the narrow aisle between the lanes and the bar, trays spilling with highballs and boilermakers, four long-necks in hands the size of hams. Liquor and smoke—my father's smells. The place recked of it.

I concentrated on my bowling. The second game I settled down and broke 200—210 or so—nothing spectacular, but a high score for that league. More important, at the end of the game I found my line on the right lane. I almost smacked myself for not seeing it sooner: what I needed to do was not throw it wider for a wider curve, but speed up a little more and keep a tighter line. It meant speeding up my approach and threatening my timing, but at the end of the game I was hitting the pocket with remarkable power, really cleaning the pins, kaboom. The compliments abounded. Nobody was complaining anymore, even good-naturedly. They knew I was the real article. They were happy to see me bowl well. Everybody was on my side. My dad took me behind the bench and draped his arm around me and asked me how I felt. I said I felt great. He was loaded and slurring and his breath stank. "You've got a nice series going," he said. "Don't blow it." I said I wasn't going to blow it. Why did he always have to say stuff like that? But I could see how proud of me he was. He was just being hard on me because he was proud. Everybody was saying "Jack's son" this and "Jack's son" that.

I started the third game with a strike, and followed that one with eight more in a row. When I stood up for my turn in the seventh frame, everybody in the place stopped bowling and crowded behind my lane. Twelve strikes make a perfect 300 game—one in each of the first nine frames, then three in the tenth. For the seventh, eighth, and ninth frames, I was hardly in my body anymore. Somehow, it still did what it knew how to do. It was in a deep groove, and I was flying. Seven strikes, eight: the place buzzed. Everyone stopped talking to me, they became superstitious. They made a little space for me on the bench so my shoulders wouldn't have to touch anyone else's. They didn't want to wreck it for me. But they were gathered around my father. I hadn't spoken to him the whole game. I could see he was trying to keep his cool, not cheer too loud or anything, not make a big fuss about it because I was his son. I could also see he was blind drunk. He led off for our team and I was second, and when he was bowling, somebody yelled at him, "Hey, Jack, get off of there so the good Ryan can bowl." My father glowered. He did not like being kidded when he was this drunk. It was the end of the night. Half the men there were loaded. They were noisy, having a good time. But when I stood up for the ninth frame, they became as silent as the dead. I took a deep breath, and caressed my ball, just like in practice, just like in bed. Hit the spot, I said to myself, as I always did. Everything is the same as always, just hit the fucking spot. I started my approach. When I released the ball at the line, everybody screamed at the top of their lungs. When I got the strike, kaboom, they went crazy. They jumped in the air and spilled their drinks. They slapped my father on the back so hard he nearly fell on his face. Tenth frame coming up. Three more strikes for a perfect game. Un-fucking-believable.

It was too much for me. Everybody was looking at me now. I could hardly breathe in that air. I didn't want to stand up for the tenth frame. But it was coming and there was nothing I could do about it. The moment of truth. Each bowler finishing his turn brought it closer. None of the other teams were bowling at all now. The whole place had stopped completely except for our two lanes. I wanted to tell them to keep bowling, to act like nothing was happening, but I couldn't say anything or look at anybody. I knew I was going to blow it.

Then my father got up to bowl. I was next. He didn't look at me. His expression was solemn, as when he played the violin. He missed the headpin entirely. He was so drunk he slipped when he released the ball. He looked at the sole of his shoe as if it were the shoe's fault. There were a couple of good-natured boos. He didn't acknowledge them, nor did his expression change. He seemed determined to make the spare, a difficult one, a 1-2-4-7 rail, and he did make it, punching with his arm when the ball struck the pins, to a smattering of ironic applause. He had another roll coming, and he took it as quickly as he could and finished with one forty-something and got off the lane. He, too, seemed very aware that everyone was watching him and he didn't want to make a fool of himself. I don't remember if he said anything to me. I wouldn't have heard him anyway. All I knew was that I had to get up there for the tenth frame. When I stood up, my knees almost collapsed. I was shaking uncontrollably. My hands were clammy. I knew I wouldn't throw a strike. I just wanted to hit the headpin. I did everything I always did on the approach, as I had done in the ninth frame, but it didn't calm me or console me. I was simply gone. I wanted to sit down for another minute, to sit by myself in a back room, but I felt I couldn't. Everyone would know then. Taking that first step of my approach toward the line was like jumping off a ledge: just get it over with. Then it was too late to stop. I knew as soon as I released the ball that I had pulled it across the headpin. I was so terrified that I'd miss the headpin, I pulled my hand across my body, compensating at the last moment with a stupid velocity, as if I could knock everything down if I just threw hard enough. The ball hooked over to the Brooklyn side and smacked the 1-2 pocket with a thud, leaving a solid tenpin. Everybody groaned.

It was over: no 300. But I didn't feel any relief. I was still nervous and everybody was still watching. I could pick up the spare and then get good wood on the last ball for a maximum 279. The tenpin is the toughest spare for a right-hander, especially on a lane hooking like this one. I managed to convert it most of the time, but this time I didn't come close. I threw the ball in the gutter. Total score: 267.

Everyone seemed embarrassed. The silence was different than before. Some people were looking down at their feet, making thin lines of their lips, shaking their heads, grumbling. They made comments out of the side of their mouths. But this only lasted a minute or two. Then they started congratulating me. Hell, how old was I, sixteen? It was the highest score ever bowled in that league, by anybody of any age. It was a hell of a score. They started to celebrate what I had done, not what I failed to do. Thirty or forty men shook my hand and grabbed my shoulder and slapped me on the back. Someone handed me a cold Coke. "Hey, great game," they said. "Don't worry, you'll get a bushel of three hundreds before you're finished." "See you on TV, kid."

"You've got some bowler there, Jack," they said to my dad as we made our way to the car. By that time I was feeling pretty good again. I had done great. Everybody liked me. They invited me to sub again anytime, though they'd have to give me a handicap based on my real average, ha ha. As my dad and I drove away, I waved to guys in the lot putting their bowling bags in their trunks. Yeah, I had done great. I had broken the league record, even if it couldn't be listed officially because I wasn't an official member of the league. That was okay. I had rolled a 267—my highest game of all time, including my longest string of strikes, nine in a row!—and a 674 for the three games, my highest series, an average of almost 225 per game (I was already doing the statistics in my head), the average of a top-notch professional. I replayed each one of the nine strikes. I had in fact gotten a couple of breaks on a couple of balls, but six or seven of those babies were solid hits. I had done great.

I looked over at my father. He still hadn't said anything to me, not even "Good game." Although he had been friendly when people were giving me compliments, his expression changed the moment we were alone in the car. Something was wrong. What had I done?

"What's the matter, Dad?" I asked.

He turned his head toward me, which he never did when he was driving.

"You choked," he said.

Oh God, I thought. I started to cry. It made him angrier.

"You choked," he repeated. "You choked. You choked. You couldn't stand the pressure, could you? You're a frigging loser. You're shit. You disgraced me."

I didn't answer him. I didn't have any answer. He was right. I had choked. I cried all the way home, and when I got there, I ran into the house and told my mother what had happened and what he had said, and she said she was sure he didn't mean it. My father said he goddamn well did mean it, and not only was I a choker, I was a crybaby, running to my mother. He went downstairs to the Playroom and drank more whiskey by himself and passed out on the couch still wearing his bowling shirt. He was so hungover the next day, he skipped work, a rarity for him. He puked all morning in the toilet. Good, I hope he dies, I thought. I didn't speak to him for a week. I don't remember if he apologized. If he did, I didn't forgive him. I never cried in front of him again. Within a few weeks I decided I didn't want to become a professional bowler after all.

HELPLESS
BABY ANIMALS

Instead, I would go to college, probably MIT or one of the Ivys. Never mind that my grades were abysmal, and that I showed up for the first day of school junior year to find I had been demoted to an even lower track—in one course, American history, to the lowliest track of all: the Bozos. I was a Bozo. I was assigned to the desk right next to James Bozowski. He could barely squeeze into his. He weighed about 240. I had played linebacker against his offensive tackle in junior varsity scrimmages. He had knocked me aside as if I were made of Styrofoam. "Never thought I'd see you in here, Ryan," he said, smiling. "Now I got somebody to copy from."

The teacher was named Sister Michael Margaret. She had taught American history for almost forty years and was still interested in it, illustrating the fat, numbing textbook with anecdotes that transformed the names and dates into characters and stories. She had a square, mannish face, and, behind rimless glasses, lively eyes that would flatten with disappointment. Every neglected assignment seemed to hurt her personally. She also had what she called "an Irish temper," exploding in frustration at our laziness and disregard, her face inflating like a blowfish and testing the elasticity of her habit. Her face was unambiguously grim as she surveyed our class, virtually all of whom were convinced of their stupidity after years as Bozos. The girls, for the most part, had become pathologically mute and never volunteered an answer; the boys were either as quiet and self-protective as the girls, taking their pleasure from solitary hobbies like hunting or rebuilding old cars, or they were in open rebellion and ran in packs—loud, crude, poor boys with greaser haircuts and heavy motorcycle boots, headed for the Army, a factory, or jail. At the beginning of junior year, each student had to choose one of three programs: Academic, Business, or Vocational. Almost everyone from St. Boniface, west of Sixteenth Street, enrolled in the Academic course; almost everyone else enrolled in Business (girls) or Vocational (boys). There were exceptions like Liz's boyfriend, Bill, but they only proved the rule. Everyone still had to take English, history, math, and religion; but when the Academic students went to physics and Latin, the Business students went to typing and home economics, and the Vocational students went to shop.

I was the only Academic, male or female, in Bozo history. All the girls were Business and all the boys were Vocational. When I inquired about this apparent mistake in scheduling, Sister Michael Margaret said, on the contrary, there had been no mistake. Indeed, my placement had been quite carefully considered. She said I might respond to this fact in one of two ways, and she thought I was bright enough to figure out what those were. She said I could return to my seat now, if I didn't mind, so we could begin class.

Since some of the boys were Behavior Problems (like me), she arranged the boys in the front desks, and the girls behind them. I was in the last boys' desk in the middle row; in the first girls' desk, directly behind me, sat Sheila Jerome. She wasn't a heartthrob like Kathy Keene, but she had acquired a certain prominence because of her Reputation. She was from a poor parish and a crazy family whose arguments often spilled out into the street and were settled by the cops. Sometimes her father beat her up and kicked her out of the house, and she was seen downtown getting into strangers' cars, and at Bishop Park riding into the Old Mill with older men. Someone claimed he saw her at Bishop Park with a guy who must have been forty, who for sure wasn't her dad. She was thin and vampy and had delicate high cheekbones and eyes like a starved deer; she poufed her short black hair on top and parted it above her forehead into bangs, and wore thick black mascara that made her look like she was staring out of a pit. And she would stare. She would fix you with those eyes, and stare until they burned pinholes into your brain stem.

This practice, which appealed to me very much, had caused us both some embarrassment during our freshman year. The incident occurred in the cafeteria. The cafeteria was half as big as a football field; the boys sat on one side and the girls on the other—at picnic tables and benches, ten to a table, five to a bench—divided by a heavily trafficked aisle that led to food counters at the front and garbage cans at the back. Every day, Sheila Jerome sat at the end of a bench closest to the aisle with her uniform hiked above her thighs. She had beautiful legs. She spoke to no one at her table as she ate her lunch, but would cross and uncross her legs and sometimes even tilt her pelvis so you could see her panties. I sat four tables down, closer to the garbage. All ten boys at my table knew what she was doing ("Sheila's hiking it up"), and some of us would jockey to sit at the end of the bench facing her for the best view. The view was the advantage of sitting at the end of the bench. The disadvantage was that the other four guys on the bench, at a predetermined silent signal, would slide into you like a battering ram, and you would find yourself suddenly sitting in the aisle. I had learned how to steel myself against being banged off the bench while simultaneously concentrating on Sheila Jerome. I'd rush to the cafeteria to buy my milk to drink with my bologna sandwiches, or choke them down without milk, and thus managed to claim the prime seat almost every day—an inequity duly noted at table. Years of experience pass-blocking enabled me to frustrate any number of attempts by the human battering ram to bang me off the bench once and for all.

On the fatal occasion, however, I let my guard down. It was different than the other occasions because, although I usually stared quite shamelessly, this time Sheila happened to stare back, while she crossed and uncrossed her legs and tilted her pelvis, seeming to invite me to look at her instead of pretending she wasn't aware of it. Furthermore, when she finally finished her lunch and stood up to carry her tray to the garbage, she looked me right in the eyes and kept looking right in my eyes as she walked toward me. I was mesmerized. When she was at my shoulder, two feet away, at the moment we broke eye contact, the battering ram struck, and I went flying across the aisle still in a sitting position, taking her legs out from under her with a spectacular cross body block. Her tray went straight up in the air and came down on us lying in the aisle in a tangle. The entire cafeteria stood up and pointed at us and laughed. I mean everybody in the whole place, as in an anxiety dream. Sheila was furious and I was dumbstruck. It had happened so fast I didn't know how it had happened, although I figured it out pretty fast. Sheila disentangled herself and got to her feet, brushing garbage from the front of her uniform. "You jerk," she said to me.

She never spoke to me after that, and she wouldn't look at me again. I stopped sitting at the end of the bench. We had never been in class together, but here I was two years later in the desk in front of her. She didn't seem unfriendly. Girls in general no longer seemed unfriendly, which I ascribed to my growing half a foot over the summer and lifting weights and acquiring a smart new Kennedy cut instead of my old flat-top. I hated them for it—although I evaluated them primarily on their looks and firmly believed that, no matter how smart any particular girl was in school, girls were by definition stupid, an alien species with alien emotions and fundamentally idiotic concerns. I spent the first few classes in American history dropping my pencil so I could bend over and look (upside down) under Sheila's uniform. When I walked into the room, she'd smile, a rarity for her, and say hi. I'd say hi back. I didn't know what else to say to her, so this was our entire conversation, repeated daily. Hi. Hi. The End.

Being put with the Bozos scared me. I saw myself stuck in Steeltown forever, to me a fate worse than death, working at Bosch Machinery and bowling in the company league with my father. I made some resolutions. No more fistfights. No more clowning. No more mocking and bragging. It was time to start thinking about College. SAT scores. Extracurricular activities. And grades. I was going to get good grades. The best grades. I was going to start studying, doing all my homework every night. Suddenly, junior year, what mattered most was not being a tough guy or great athlete, but your Future Prospects: whether you were going to college and, if you were going, where you were going. Girls started to like the boys with Future Prospects. And here I was with the Bozos. It was way past time to show that I was, as the nuns put it, College Material. It was way past time, as my father put it, to get on the stick.

So I'd retire to my room every night after dinner and actually read my assignments and do my homework. It was also a way to stay away from my father. I could not be criticized for doing homework, or even legitimately interrupted, and behind my closed door I'd hear him rummaging in the refrigerator or flushing the toilet before returning to the Playroom to lie on the couch and watch TV with his belt unbuckled and a tallboy propped on his stomach. In class I had never been shy about volunteering an answer and tried to fake it if I didn't know it. Now that I actually knew the answers, my hand was up all the time. Plus I was in slow classes across the board, in which most of the students were afraid to speak, so I was answering as much as the other students put together—especially in history class—and acing all the exams. Sister Michael Margaret tried to draw everyone into the discussion, with no success whatsoever. Question. Silence. Question rephrased. Silence. Exhortation to speak. Silence. "You're like a field of stones," she'd say wearily, with an expression of grief. She'd give up and call on me. I knew all the answers and was eager to show it. After the first few weeks the class turned into a dialogue between the two of us. I not only knew the facts, I could interpret them. I found ironic twists in the XYZ Affair. I treated the class to a disquisition about the conflict of ideas of the fledgling democracy embodied in the duel between Hamilton and Burr. I explained how the timing of the Emancipation Proclamation revealed its political and military purpose, which was not to suggest it was not also a courageous moral act ("You sure can sling the shit," whispered Bozowski admiringly). I won Sister Michael Margaret's heart. She clearly enjoyed our discussions (and so did I). She didn't give up teaching the other students in the class, but, as far as response went, I was it, and she came to depend more and more on me.

At the same time, things were heating up with Sheila Jerome in just the way I liked. One day, retrieving my pencil, I noticed she had moved forward a little in her desk and that, with her legs crossed, her upper knee was pretty close to my seat. I sat up straight, sliding my butt as far back as I could into the space between my seat and the first rung of my chair back. Sure enough, it met her knee. And instead of moving her knee away, she began moving it up and down, slowly. Oh-kay.

Thereafter, after I said hi, I'd take a moment to straighten our desks before I sat down, pushing them as close together as they would go, so she had approximately the legroom of the backseat of a Yugo. She'd give me a knowing look, and sometimes thank me, almost laughing out loud. She'd rub her knee on my butt the whole class. And that wasn't all. I'd hook my right arm over my chair back and she'd make slow little circles on my triceps with her fingernail. Somehow I even managed to get my left leg into a sort of straddle around the aisle side of my desk, so she could touch my calf with her toe and make slow little circles on it, too. This was my version of the Rosemary Wood stretch—butt pushed back, right arm hooked over the chair back, left foot straining backward—the upper half of my body twisted one way and the lower half the other, *contraposto molto strano*. It's a miracle I didn't cripple myself permanently. Further, to accompany my extraordinarily slippery pencil, I developed a chronic itch on my left calf. Scratching it, I'd grasp Sheila's foot and rub my thumb where her toes snuggled into her pointy red Capezio—only for a second or two, so I wouldn't get caught by Sister Michael Margaret or noticed by the other students. It seems impossible that I was never noticed. Sister Michael Margaret, who usually stood directly in front of me no more than five feet away, must have thought my posture idiosyncratic, to say the least, but she apparently never perceived its purpose. In any case, she never mentioned it. Nor did anyone else, not even an innuendo.

It put me in a bizarre, exhilarated state of mind. I was completely attuned to what was being discussed in class, even hyperaware, while simultaneously transported, gonzo, completely aroused. I felt superhuman. It was as if the secret sex made me sharper. I loved it and loved getting away with it. I wanted it constantly and got it constantly—for that one hour each day. Some days Sister Michael Margaret would show us an instructional film—costume dramatizations of the signing of the Declaration of Independence, a story about two brothers who fought on opposite sides of the Civil War coming home after the war had ended to Missouri and finally, tearfully becoming reconciled. I knew we were having a film when I walked into the classroom and saw the green metal Bell & Howell 16mm projector balanced on the last desk in the middle row in the back of the room. My heart would start pounding in anticipation. The entire middle row of desks had to be moved over, so the beam of the projector would be unobstructed by our heads. I chivalrously moved Sheila's desk for her, and then my own, straightening them both, of course, very carefully. Bozowski pulled down the movie screen from above the blackboard, and the shades over the windows, and the lights were turned out, and the film would start. Bye bye, everything and everyone. By this time I could hardly breathe. I'd drop my left hand to find Sheila's foot waiting for it, and for the duration of the movie I'd rub up and down her silky nylon-clad foot and ankle and calf, squeezing and patting and plumping, stopping only when I was about to ejaculate in my pants, the evidence of which I knew I couldn't conceal. It was difficult enough concealing my erection, which was constant, since, *de rigueur*, my pants were pegged tight as tourniquets and Sister Michael Margaret made us stand when we answered a question. When I stood up, I'd hold my hands in front of my genitals like Adam being expelled from Eden—and I stood up to answer at least ten times a class. Unlike the secret touching with the lights on, touching Sheila during the movies was almost too much for me. It was as if the boundaries of myself were the boundaries of what I could get away with sexually, and in the dark there weren't any. Since we couldn't be seen, I became no one. I became what I was doing, pure sex, totally absorbed and totally diffused. I no longer knew what I could do and what I couldn't. Although I might have found a way to do more than rub her calf, I never tried. I couldn't guess what would happen if we were caught. I couldn't guess how we could be caught with the lights out, but I was afraid it would happen suddenly, just as I had found myself lying tangled up with her in the cafeteria aisle: boom, and everybody would be screaming at me, or pointing and laughing. They'd know how weird I was.

Sheila knew it. We were alike in this dark way. We continued to stare at each other—that articulate, locked gaze—before and after class, in the halls, at assemblies. Just looking at her made me hot. Sheila often smiled at me on these occasions—as I said, a rarity for her. She had no friends, male or female, and sat in the cafeteria and walked the halls alone. Now that I was on the stick, I made some friends at Sacred Heart, but the wounds I had inflicted with my mockery were deep, and the collective memory of them powerful, and my self-proclaimed transformation was generally viewed at school with let's-wait-and-see skepticism. I was still called Pork, though less frequently, and was still a ferret of phoniness, à la Holden Caulfield, especially phoniness that resulted in the Popularity I wanted and believed I was too Honest to get. I mostly hung out with Chuck and his friends from Steeltown High instead of my classmates. They had the unheard-of habit of reading books they didn't have to read for school (the first one of these, for me, was *Catcher in the Rye*—three times in a row, finishing the last page and immediately starting the book again). They introduced me to existentialism and we had earnest discussions about the meaning of life as we swigged quarts of Budweiser in parked cars, even in winter, running the engine for the heater when we started to see our breath, getting out to piss together in the snow. I got my driver's license, and my dad let me borrow the White Sow one night a weekend if I washed it and performed my household chores and kept my grades up. There were two dances every weekend: on Friday night at Sacred Heart (where I had danced with Kathy Keene) and on Saturday night at the Hub Club (where I met girls from all the public schools in the area). I was suddenly able to get all the dates I wanted. And I wanted all of them, at least all the dates that fulfilled two criteria: is she good-looking and does she Put Out. Nothing else mattered. By Put Out, I meant French-kissing and petting with clothes on. Despite what I did with Sheila, the idea of going further than that scared me.

This is one reason I never asked her for a date. The other was that she was a poor girl from the poor side of town, a Bozo, a slut, a pig, not the kind of girl you go out with. Dating was a public act, involving prestige. Sheila was secret life. I'd often get home from school before my mother did, and, after I had my school clothes off and before I put my play clothes on, I'd lie down on my bed and masturbate, imagining that instead of being alone in my bed I had walked Sheila home and she invited me in, saying her parents didn't get off work until five. Did we ever do it then, wild and passionate, right there on the floor: Oh oh oh Sheila yes. At school people started to notice how we stared at each other, and I started getting teased about it: Hey, Ryan, you asking Sheila to the prom? You gonna take her home to meet your mother? Etc. Every time I came close to asking her out, it stopped me.

The only time I ever saw her outside of school hours was one night at the Friday dance. I went almost every Friday, specializing in slow dancing, as I did with Kathy Keene, working my leg between whomever's thighs, mashing my engorged weenie against whomever's pelvic bone (or more often, since I was now five-ten, their stomachs). Sheila never went to these dances—or any other school event, social or athletic—but this Friday, to everyone's surprise, she showed up. She stood in a shadowy corner by herself, trying to look bored. Immediately, I started getting teased: Sheila's looking at you, Ryan. Sheila wants to dance with you, Ryan. Sheila's waiting for you, Ryan.

I didn't ask her to dance, but I couldn't keep myself from staring at her, even when I was dancing with other girls. She stared back, and smiled, even when she was dancing with other boys—boys in the Vocational course with long greasy hair and clunky motorcycle boots. We had been touching each other in history for months, and we still had not spoken a word to each other except the one: Hi. I wished everyone would disappear so I could go over and crush her against my body and do it with her on the floor, but every time I resolved to ask her to dance, my heart started racing and my face started burning and the distance I would have to walk to her with everyone watching me seemed infinite. Only when the night was almost over, the thought of not having asked her to dance seemed worse than just asking her, so, despite the hooting of the guys, I finally did.

"Took you long enough," she said.

I didn't say anything. I just held her. She pressed her body into me. She was so thin I could have fit two of her into the compass of my arm. She felt like she weighed one pound. I was too nervous to get aroused. The knot of guys I had been standing with were jumping up and down and waving their arms.

"What's with those guys?" Sheila asked.

"Don't mind them," I answered.

"What a bunch of jerks," she said.

We danced another minute, but with everyone watching it wasn't fun. I pulled back to speak to her.

"You don't come to these dances very often, Sheila," I said.

"Call me Bunny," she said.

"Bunny?" I asked.

"My friends call me Bunny," she said. She was chewing gum, popping it inside her mouth as she spoke. "Yeah," she continued, "I don't ever come to these dances. I only came tonight because there's a guy comes here I want to go out with. I want to go out with this guy in the worst way."

"Anybody I know?" I asked.

She laughed. "Oh, you know him, all right. You know him real well."

I didn't say anything.

"Hold me close again," she said. I did. We danced cheek to cheek. She started to make slow little circles on my neck with her fingernail.

"I don't know what he's waiting for," she whispered.

Then the music ended. I said thanks for the dance and went back to the guys I had been standing with, and she went back to her corner. "She's got the hots for you, Ryan," somebody said. I said, "She wants me to call her Bunny," and everybody howled. I looked over and saw she was watching. I couldn't look at her after that.

I danced the last dance with another girl, closing my eyes so I wouldn't see Bunny or anyone else. As soon as it was over, I headed for the door. I was almost out of there, when I noticed that she was the person walking next to me.

"Don't say hi or anything," she said petulantly.

"Okay, I won't," I said, without thinking. The words just came out of my mouth.

She gave me a long, appraising look.

"So that's the way it is," she said.

"I guess so," I answered. I really wasn't sure. I had no idea what way was the way it is. When we got outside, she turned up the street and was gone.

When I walked into class the following Monday, she didn't say hi and she didn't look at me. Absurdly, I pushed my butt back to meet her knee and her knee wasn't there. I hooked my right arm over the chair back as usual: nothing. No slow little circles. I dropped my pencil. Her legs were tucked under as far as they would go. She wouldn't look at me. She never looked at me again. I didn't know what to say to her, any more than I knew what to say before. Even less. So, as before, I said nothing. A guy in my homeroom took her to the Junior Prom, and told me that afterward she had given him a hand job. I think that was the last word anybody ever said to me about her. Since we stopped staring at each other, I stopped getting teased. That, at least, was a relief.

But I had blown it again. Bunny had been Dying For It. Almost every day in my bedroom after school, I still had passionate sex with her before her parents came home from work, switching to Sharon bending over in her slip to Luscious Laura with her mother airbrushed out of her living room to whomever I saw on the street in a tight skirt or sweater and back again to Bunny writhing and foaming underneath me. Outside of that I put my sexual energy into dating, sometimes two different girls a weekend—dances, parties, the rare successful pickup at Bishop Park, writhing in the weeds under the roller coaster—cajoling, kissing, groping, dry-humping, making our clothes wrinkled and sweaty (in parked cars, their windows steaming up), more than happy to ejaculate in my pants, then stop abruptly and suggest we hit the Charcoal for a cheese steak. I would never say why I stopped so abruptly, although if they noticed the smear near my zipper, they probably guessed. The purpose of the whole date, as I saw it, was to go parking afterward, and the purpose of parking was for me to go off in my pants. With few exceptions, I took these girls out once or twice or three times, max, and didn't call them again. It wasn't long before I had a Reputation for being Fast. A girl automatically compromised her Reputation by accepting a date with me. One spunky girl, declining my invitation, said, "I hear you take out girls for what you can get." It shouldn't have shocked me, but it did (so much that I remember the exact words and the sound of her voice). I felt unmasked. With the parents, I was a real Eddie Haskell, complimenting the mother on the color coordinates of her living room, then rumpling her daughter on some dirt road outside of town. I was College Material. My mother taught at St. Boniface. I was a nice boy and an excellent student. I had Future Prospects. "What lovely drapes, Mrs. Brown. They go so nicely with your couch." "Why, thank you, Michael. Linda will be down in just a minute." When her daughter returned after our date, needing a brisk shower and a dry cleaner, her mother would say, "That Michael Ryan is such a nice boy."

My sister graduated from Marymount at the end of my junior year of high school. She moved back into her old room and, in the fall, began teaching fourth grade in the Steeltown public schools. It shifted the relationships in the household. I now had a strong ally against my father. It was two against one instead of me against him, my mother as before wandering shell-shocked in the demilitarized zone between, not knowing which side she was on, not knowing what to do. My sister certainly knew. She had been out of patience with my father at least since the Sharon episode, and set the force of her considerable will against whatever lunacy he might spring on us. Nothing he did could shock her. When he got mean and tried to start something, she would dismiss him as beneath contempt, calling him "a miserable old sot" (she had just earned an A in The British Novel). It was an effective tactic, coupled with my superior brawn. I was now bigger and stronger than he was, and informed him that if he ever tried to hit me again he was going to pay but good for all the times he had hit me before. He screamed that it was the worst sin of all to raise your hand against your father, but he stopped hitting me and, since when he threatened me I laughed in his face and called him a miserable old sot, he stopped threatening me.

But there was a way in which defeating him was worse for me. He started sinking fast, as if bullying me had been propping him up. He seemed to give up entirely. He quit his bowling league; he stopped reading, even his soft-core detective novels; he canceled his subscription to *Alfred Hitchcock's Mystery Magazine*. When I asked him why he didn't try reading good books (like me), he said he had read them all already. He had often barbecued ribs on a Saturday, popping his first tallboy at 11 A.M., sitting in a lawn chair at eye level with the grill, smoking a Pall Mall, his elbow propped on his knee and his thumbnail slotted between his two front teeth. He'd soak hickory chips he had ordered from North Carolina while he concocted his secret special sauce, and he'd paint those ribs for eight hours over a fire so low it barely warmed your hand, squirting it with a water pistol when it flared, getting drunker and drunker as the day went on. More than once, he delivered the heaping platter of ribs to the dining-room table, then fell flat on his face on the floor, passed out, mission accomplished. (They are still the best ribs I've ever tasted.) Now he quit barbecuing. He hadn't touched his ukulele since I had broken the strings pounding on it when I was about twelve, but now he also quit playing his violin and guitar. He never sang anymore. He puttered around in his basement workshop less and less. He'd get his hair cut every other Saturday, and would stop at the Keystone on the way home, but essentially he quit going anywhere or doing anything except drinking and watching TV and paying the bills once a month. He even quit yelling about how much money we were spending. He began going to the doctor every Tuesday instead of every other Tuesday, and came home with blood pressure readings of 240 over 160 and up. He had already had two heart attacks. My mother went to see his doctor herself: What could we do to make him stop drinking and smoking? Nothing, the doctor said.

The house, with its one story and thin walls, was exponentially more crowded with my sister there. My father became a denizen of the Playroom, living underneath us like a troll. He bought a minirefrigerator for under the bar, so he wouldn't have to come upstairs even for his tallboys. He took his dinner at the bar while he watched Huntley Brinkley, cursing the politicians. He ate breakfast at the dining-room table and slept in his bedroom at night (unless he passed out on the couch), but that was it for his life upstairs. Still, we'd bump into him. And we could never forget he was there, the black hole. My mother constantly fretted about his health. I stayed as far away from him as I could—out of the house whenever possible. I could drive, I had friends, I had dates, I always had somewhere else to be and something to do. It was easier during the summer, when I didn't have to be home at night studying. I'd come home for a shower after work and go out again. My summer job started at 7 A.M., before anyone else was up. Sometimes leaving the house in the dawn light, I'd find sheets of his graph paper on the dining-room table covered with his signature: John H. Ryan   John H. Ryan   John H. Ryan—hundreds of times in neat columns. And doodles and drawings, mostly of svelte women with arched eyebrows in the style of fashion illustration of the twenties, sometimes sketches of horses or dogs. There they'd be, with a whiskey bottle or beer can and an ashtray full of butts, evidence of his having sat up for hours drunk and alone.

My summer job was in a concrete-block factory, stacking onto pallets bricks and blocks, some of them fifty pounds each, which shot out of an oven onto a conveyer belt. It made me even bigger and stronger. I was still growing and reveled in my physicality, the hormonal surge of power. For every inch I grew he seemed to shrink. Every ounce I gained seemed to have been sucked off him. In his pale blue boxer shorts, his legs looked like twigs. His facial expressions, especially when he was drunk, became wilder. He'd bug his eyes and make crazy faces, and not when he was trying to be funny. Sometimes, apropos of nothing, he'd begin imitating a gorilla, grunting and scratching— again, not as a joke. My sister came home to a dark house one night thinking no one was home, and found him in the basement in the dark hanging by his hands from a crossbeam. When she switched on the light and asked what in God's name he was doing, he said, "Exercises." We tried to get him to see a psychiatrist, but in Steeltown in 1963 it was an insult to tell someone to see a psychiatrist, and in truth most of the times I suggested it I was yelling, "You miserable old sot, you should see a psychiatrist." My mother thought it was his heart medicine. She wondered if she should try to get him to change doctors. She felt helpless and hopeless. She fretted and cried. She told me to pray, which I had quit doing years before, after Liz broke up with me. I had stopped going to mass on Sunday. I'd pretend to go to late mass by myself, and drive to one of my make-out spots in Fairmont Green and read existential tracts about the meaninglessness and absurdity of life.

Late in the summer between my junior and senior years, my father did something completely out of character. He bought a new car. And not just a new car, a convertible: a 1963 Buick Skylark, jet black, with a white imitation leather top and white imitation leather bucket seats and white imitation leather interior. In those days nobody in Steeltown drove sporty cars. Bucket seats were unheard of. People on the street stopped and stared at it, children waved (and so did cars full of girls). Nor was it just the car, but the way he bought it: on a Saturday afternoon without telling anyone in advance or even mentioning he was considering buying a new car, much less this one. We thought he had gone to get a haircut. He drove off in the White Sow and a couple of hours later pulled into the driveway in the Skylark.

Of course, I was ecstatic. He tooted and tooted and we all went outside to see what was going on. He was sitting in the carport in this jazzy convertible with the top down, one arm draped over the wheel and the other across the top of the passenger's bucket seat. It had to be a trick. We couldn't believe this car was really ours. He said he got a great deal. It was a demonstrator. He had knocked the salesman down a couple thousand bucks from the sticker price, which was never you mind how much. It was time to retire the old Buick anyway. I felt sort of funny that I'd never see the White Sow again, that it had just disappeared. But I got over that feeling fast. I begged him to let me drive the Skylark around the block, and he did, sitting in the passenger seat and warning me not to gun it, saying if he ever caught me driving this car crazy or in any way abusing it, that was it—from then on I'd be a pedestrian.

It was all we talked about at home that night. Chuck and his friends (now also my friends) came over after dinner and looked at it, walking around it, petting the fender and the interior, sitting in it, admiring the spiffy little engine. Few of them had previously met my father. It was dusk. He sat in the shadows on the porch with a tallboy and a cigarette, answering their questions. They were truly wowed. They thought any dad who would buy a car like this must be some kind of guy. I let them think it. Maybe he was some kind of guy, in his own way, after all.

After they left, and I was alone with him on the porch, he told me he had bought the car for me. He didn't mean it was my car, but that he had bought it because of me, because he knew I'd like it. I was going into my last year of high school, I had gotten on the stick, I had straightened up my act. Hell, he said, life was short. This was my reward, to make my last year at home more fun. There had already been lots of jokes about how many girls I was going to get now, that I'd better watch it at stoplights because girls on the street would be diving into the bucket seat, etc. My father said he had told the salesman that he had a son going into his senior year of high school, and that the salesman had said, "That boy's got himself a real cuntcar."

I didn't respond. He knew I had a lot of dates, but he didn't know what I did with them, and I was not about to tell him. He always told me to treat girls the way I'd want my mother or sister to be treated, but then there were those contradictions. I knew perfectly well that girls would like the car, and I couldn't wait to use it, top down, in some farmer's field in the moonlight. He said I could use it as much as the old Buick—one weekend night a week—as long as I treated it responsibly.

But at first this turned out not to be true. He was much more reluctant to let me drive the Skylark by myself. The fact that I wanted it more seemed to make him give it to me less. I'd do everything he told me to all week: I'd wash the car and mow the lawn and clean up my room and take out the garbage, and he'd be drunk on a Saturday night and simply refuse to turn over the keys. "Why the hell should I give that car to you?" he'd ask, as if it were an outrageous idea. No amount of reminding him what he had said or agreed to had any effect. Once, I had a date who was baby-sitting in some remote farmhouse, and she had let me know if I arrived after she put the toddler to bed I was in for one hot time. I had never been in a bed with a girl. She made a very complicated, precise map for me and told me she would have a surprise waiting for me when she answered the door. When my father, at the last minute, wouldn't give me the car keys, I almost murdered him. He was lying on the basement couch, and I could have crushed his skull with one of his solid-chrome, pink-padded imported German barstools or knelt on his chest and pummeled his face into mush. I knew I could beat the shit out of him. But I didn't, then or at any other time. I never hit him, although I threatened to, the way he had threatened me.

When school started in the fall, I was placed in the Advanced Classes again. The other students—the core group of about thirty— had been going from class to class together for three years, academically insulated from the rest of the school, and they knew one another like a family. I was the prodigal, returning after spilling my seed and wasting my inheritance and ending up on the pig farm. Except I was not repentant. Some of the boys, still wearing clip-on bow ties and soft plastic pocket protectors and leather slide-rule cases on their belts, were understandably wary. To them, I was a Wild Guy, the unpredictable element in a daily routine that had become comfortable as long as they did their homework, paid attention to the teacher, stood up straight, and spoke clearly and concisely. Even if my behavior was no longer openly disruptive, what was I thinking about them? How would I hurt them? These were the pimply skinny fat flabby uncoordinated boys: eggheads dorks weenies pathetic in gym class, grotesquely misshapen in their white shorts and T-shirts, hyperventilating red-faced for a single pull-up or push-up. The coaches, for the two hours a week they had them in their gym dominion, rode them mercilessly. To the best of my ability, I had fashioned myself according to an idea of Masculinity that was for them a torment. I no longer blared it into their faces, but I submitted the weakest ones to my not-so-subtly-tuned sarcasms—anybody who, in my existential judgment, was a brown-noser or a Phony.

This wasn't everybody, of course. Some of the brightest boys were also athletes and class officers who glowed with confidence. They were well groomed and had neatly trimmed haircuts. They were generous and self-effacing. They weren't threatened by me at all. One boy told me he hoped my return would stir things up, it had been pretty dull in the Advanced Classes without me. The course material, especially in math, was considerably more sophisticated than what I had been studying for the last two years: advanced calculus and, before the year was out, a sampling of mathematical arcana such as imaginary numbers and topology. He offered to help me catch up—and he wasn't the only one. A number of students, boys and girls, offered to fill me in on anything I had missed. They were remarkably welcoming and kind.

None of the girls in the Advanced Classes were good-looking enough for me to favor with my attention—except for Liz. Here she was again, at seventeen more beautiful than ever, and smart, having been in the Advanced Classes all along. She was still my ideal, although I could not admit it to myself, much less to her. We were on speaking terms now, polite repartee. I took great pleasure in nailing her when I thought she was being prissy, and she didn't hesitate pointing out my vanity and arrogance with keen sarcasm. But there was affection in it, too, on both sides. She knew me and I knew her. I dismissed what had happened between us as the doings of children. I didn't forgive her, but I dismissed it. She was still going faithfully with Bill, her earnest boyfriend—for three years, longer than she went with me—but, word had it, she still wasn't Putting Out for him. Just kissy-face, that was it. This consoled me. When I got bored during class, I'd undress her and submit her pristine body to all manner of ravishments until she was Dying For It. But I didn't get bored very often. There had been a big change in the curriculum this year. The Advanced Classes had become Advanced Placement Classes. They were designed so we select few could take Advanced Placement tests and receive college credit in those subjects.

This was lucky for me, since it broke continuity with the previous three years, and the material was new to everybody else, too. The chemistry course represented the most radical departure. There was no textbook. It was all lab and experiment, with the theory provided in college-type lectures by the nun, Sister Ursula, who, like Sister Michael Margaret, had been teaching for forty years and was still interested in it, but, unlike Sister Michael Margaret, took a particular dislike to me (bad chemistry). Sister Ursula suffered no nonsense whatsoever, and worshiped a God that made the God of the Old Testament seem like Mr. Rogers. As far as Sister Ursula was concerned, there were only two commandments: Rigor and Discipline. Anybody's nose that was not to the grindstone got bopped. On the rare occasions when she laughed (invariably at something I thought sentimental or obvious), her face shattered into wrinkles like shards of glass, and her laugh sounded like a smoker's cough (heh heh heh)—for one second, possibly two, then it was back to business.

Early in the term I made the mistake of trying to endear myself to her during a session when we were supposed to brainstorm creatively about the chemistry of everyday life. I asked her to explain the chemistry of getting drunk. The class tittered and her face went stern with impatience. She said becoming intoxicated was a physical response. It had nothing to do with chemistry. Next question, she said, and not a frivolous one like Mr. Ryan's.

I knew she was wrong, that there was no such thing as a physical response in the body that was not also chemical, and I also knew she didn't know the answer, and that she hated me for it. For all her Rigor and Discipline, she was a Phony. Further, like most Phonies, she was vulnerable to flattery. The worst brown-noser in the class had her wrapped around his finger. His name was Bob Gruber. He was handsome in the Pat Boone mode, bright-eyed and big-smiled, with smarmy country-club manners. He was not among the smartest but had managed to stay in the Advanced Classes all four years solely (in my opinion) by sucking up to the nuns. With Sister Ursula he was particularly shameless. She was the head of the Science Department, with (as she informed us) many important matters to attend to, so she sometimes arrived at our class late. We met in the lab, which was always locked, so we had to wait in the hall. Gruber wore a very expensive slide rule in a buffed leather case on his belt, and I would stick my unsheathed $1.98 slide rule between my belt and pants and challenge him to a showdown, saying this class was not big enough for both of us, square root of seventy-seven, draw! It was funny maybe the first twelve times. Once, after we had been waiting a long time outside the lab, Sister Ursula appeared at the end of the hall, wearily toting her black book bag. Gruber sprinted down the hall to carry her bag to the classroom for her. She handed it to him, with one of her shattered-glass smiles. When they reached the door where we were standing, I patted him on the shoulder and said, "Good boy, Bobby." Sister Ursula went bonzo. She was so furious she sputtered. Words to describe my irredeemable character failed her. "Michael Ryan, you are nothing but a . . . big . . . sloppy . . . baby." My friends called me Big Sloppy Baby for a number of weeks. I fancied myself a folk hero, the only one with the kabongs to take on Sister Ursula.

Sister Ursula's be-all-and-end-all was the Annual Science Fair. Each school had its own science fair to select the best individual student projects, which would then compete with those of students from all area high schools in the Annual Science Fair. There were prizes for each grade level in each of the three sciences (biology, physics, and chemistry), and an overall grand prize winner. The basketball court of the host school was filled with row after row of displays that explained the principles of the experiments, the winners often featuring a button to push that would demonstrate the principle before your very eyes, turning on a homemade TV or illuminating a cloud chamber or lifting a little door that would start a mouse through a maze. According to Sister Ursula, the Annual Science Fair was the main opportunity for Sacred Heart to prove its academic superiority to the public schools— but, although we always made a good showing, the grand prize had unaccountably eluded us for the last five years. Since we were the senior advanced science class, it was up to us to bring the grand prize home. One of us, she said (narrowing her eyes), was going to be the Grand Prize Winner. Doing a science project was optional for other students, but mandatory for our class. Furthermore, we were required to write up our projects, with photographs, data, and proof, and enter them in the Westinghouse Science Talent Search, a prestigious national competition that awarded college scholarships to the winners.

This did not make my juices bubble. Math and science were still my best subjects (I thought)—they were the masculine ones, the practical ones, the ones society depended on. I planned to apply to college in engineering, without having the slightest idea what engineering was. My father thought this was a good plan, that I'd get a good job and make a good salary. Sounded fine to me. Engineering it would be. But in fact I had the scientific curiosity of a mollusk. I had no desire to please Sister Ursula, much less to bring glory to the school. And, unlike the boys in the Advanced Classes who in their leisure time discovered unclassified species of beetles, I had no idea what to do a science project on. To those uninspired ones like me, Sister Ursula suggested going to the public library (the one I had gazed at out of the back of the paddy wagon after I had been arrested with Freddy DeLuca) and researching back issues of *Scientific American* for an idea. After putting it off as long as I could, with Sister Ursula breathing down my neck for the preliminary description of the project, that's what I did. I got my idea from the first article in the first *Scientific American* I picked up. My research took a total of six minutes.

The article was entitled "The Immunological Role of the Thymus Gland," which became the title of my project. Somebody had just discovered that the thymus gland is 2 percent of body weight at birth and two ten-thousandths of 1 percent in a mature adult. This little curiosity might be explained by the thymus gland playing a major immunological role in a newborn and withering away after it has performed its role, the functions of immunology being adopted by other glands. Not much was known about it, how or why it should work this way. Nobody had paid much attention to the thymus gland before.

Eureka. Here was my project, made to order, fun and easy. What I'd do is get some baby mice. Half of them I'd leave alone. I'd cut out the thymus glands of the other half. Then I'd inject them all with a virus. When the half without the thymus glands sickened and died, voilà! Q.E.D.: proof of the immunological role of the thymus gland.

Nobody, including Sister Ursula, tried to dissuade me from this boneheaded Frankensteinian experiment. Everybody just nodded and smiled when I told them what I had in mind. Full speed ahead I went. Getting the baby mice was the first problem. I needed real babies, the fresher the better. I tracked down a lab in Tennessee (probably the same one that built the atom bomb) that sold research mice; the youngest ones I could get were three days old. I ordered a dozen. They arrived via UPS in a box with wire-mesh–covered airholes. I opened it on the dining-room table. They were about as big as a finger joint, curled up, sleepy, with pink microdots for noses. They weighed about a tenth of an ounce each, sweet little puffs of fluff. Topsy kept barking and snarling and jumping up trying to bite the box. I carried it in both hands like a pizza down to my surgical theater: the Playroom. My father's pink Formica bar was the operating table. I had cadged a scalpel and some ether from somewhere. I soaked a cotton ball in the ether and put it in a Mason jar. Then I selected a hardy-looking mouse, dropped it into the jar, screwed on the lid, and waited a minute. I unscrewed the lid and dumped out the mouse: dead as a chunk of pig iron. I killed five of them this way. They say anesthesia is the riskiest part of most operations, and this was certainly true in my (brief) surgical career. I finally figured out that screwing the lid back on was sending them over. The sixth mouse I dropped into the jar, shook the jar up a little, and dumped it right out onto the bar—asleep but breathing. Of course, I couldn't predict for how long.

I had to work fast. The thymus gland is located under the breast bone in humans. Needless to say, I neglected to find out where it's located in mice, or if mice even have a thymus gland. It didn't occur to me that they might not have one. I flipped the baby mouse onto its back, splayed its spidery-thin legs as best I could, and made the incision, down the middle and across the top and bottom (like a capital *I*), so I could open its chest like a dollhouse cupboard. Remarkably, there wasn't any blood. I had made the incision at precisely the right depth to simply peel back the skin. The mouse did indeed have a breastbone. Peeking out of the top of it was a white lump of something. This, in my expert medical opinion, had to be the thymus gland. (It was probably fat.) I poked around a little with my scalpel and dug the sucker right out of there. It detached easily. I picked it out with the tweezers my sister used to pluck her eyebrows, and put it into a tiny jar that had once held a holiday sampler of Amish jam. Then I stitched up the mouse with my mother's needle and thread, and returned it to the box to recuperate. It was still asleep and still alive. I ran upstairs with the thymus gland to show my mother and sister. I held the tiny jar up to their noses. They both made the same face and said, "Ugh." My mother told me to move the box of mice out of the Playroom before my father got home from work.

I decided this would do it for the surgery. One mouse would be my sample group. No way was I going to cut up any more mice. I had already bought a hypodermic needle at the drugstore. Now I had to get a virus. I figured I could pick up the virus at Steeltown Hospital the next day on my way home from school. I had worked so efficiently, it wasn't yet 5 P.M. I called up the hospital and was connected to the doctor in charge of medical research, who was apparently about to lock up and go home. I told him who I was—a senior in the advanced placement science class at Sacred Heart—and explained my project in detail, including the theory behind it, emphasizing how much I'd appreciate his cooperation and advice. I spoke clearly and concisely, saving my request for the virus for last, adding that I could pick it up the next day, if that would be convenient, which I hoped it was, time being of the essence for this experiment, which I was sure he understood. I took his silence at the other end for consideration. I hadn't thought too much about the virus; I imagined it as a squiggly little line, like a strand of DNA, or maybe a teeny bug. What kind of container would it come in? The doctor was probably figuring out how best to effect the transfer. Finally, he spoke, in a tone of voice that did not quite reflect the gratitude of a scientist who has just been presented with the opportunity to make a historical contribution to groundbreaking research.

"We're not going to give you a *virus*," he said.

"Pardon me?" I asked, surprised.

"We're not going to give you a *virus*," he repeated. "What in God's name would make you think we would release a virus into the environment? Do you want to start an epidemic? For one thing, it's against the law. For another, you're a *high school student*. You don't know how to handle a virus. What could you possibly be thinking of?"

I couldn't really answer that one. He had said *high school student* with what I thought was a rather uncalled-for disdain. It wasn't my fault I was a high school student. I told him I was just hoping to do a good science project, which was a requirement for my class, it was already half done, I had gotten these baby mice from Tennessee and everything, and I had paid for them out of my own money. He said that was too bad. I asked what he thought I should do now. He said maybe a different project, one that was a little safer and didn't involve cutting up helpless baby animals. I said it was too late for that. He said he was sorry. If it would help he'd write a note to my teacher who, in his opinion, ought to know better anyway. I should tell her from him not to be sending students out into the world looking for viruses. "We don't hand them out like popcorn," he said.

I was pretty dispirited when I hung up the phone. I was in the kitchen and Mom asked me what was the matter. She had started dinner and there were pots and pans on all the burners. I said Steeltown Hospital wouldn't give me a virus. She said she thought I might have trouble with that one. I asked her why she didn't mention it before. She said I had acted like I knew what I was doing.

I trudged back downstairs to the Playroom. I had a cold and wasn't feeling that good anyway—in my sophomore year I would have used it as an excuse to stay home from school for a week. I was still carrying the tiny jar with the mouse's thymus gland (fat lump) in it. I had just performed this successful operation, and now the whole project was wrecked. What was I going to do? The box of mice was still on the bar where my father always poured his first shot of the night. I opened it up. The mice were all running around. I couldn't tell which one I had operated on. Then I saw the black thread hanging from its chest. The mouse had completely recovered, and was even nibbling the crumbles of Velveeta I had dropped into the box.

Then I had another inspiration. The mouse seemed fine. I could get this stupid project over with right now. I couldn't get a virus, but I already had a cold. Right here. In my nose. I was really stuffed up. Weren't colds caused by a virus? Or something. Germs, in any case. I was loaded with germs.

Not to put too fine a description on it, what I did was inject the mouse with snot. I honked my snot into a plastic cup and mixed it with some warm water and drew it into the hypodermic; I pinched the skin of the mouse I had operated on and injected it. Unfortunately, it squirmed and I did accidentally prick its spine with the needle. It began running around in a circle on the top of the bar, dragging its hind legs, which were paralyzed. I thought this was just about enough science for the day. I put the mouse back into the box, and actually said a prayer for it. (I couldn't pray for my father, but I did pray for the mouse.) I carried the box into the other part of the basement, left it on the warped pool table in the dark, and went upstairs for dinner. I was rattled. I didn't tell anybody what happened. I just hoped somehow the mouse would be okay. My father came home, changed his clothes, and took his plate downstairs to eat, as usual, on the same spot on the bar that had just served as my operating table. I ate with my mother and sister upstairs, as usual. When my mother asked me what I was going to do about the virus, I told her I had already thought of something.

After dinner I snuck downstairs and checked the mouse. It was kind of huddling in a corner of the box. It had had a trying day. I flicked it lightly with my finger, and it scurried to another corner of the box and looked up at me as if to say, What next? It wasn't paralyzed anymore! A miracle! As far as I was concerned, this concluded my science project. No more injections, no more operations, no nothing: The End. The Sacred Heart Science Fair was two weeks away. I displayed the thymus gland (fat lump) in the sample jelly jar. Over the two weeks, it had dried up, turned yellow, and shrunk to the size of a sesame seed. I put the six unmolested mice in one plastic container, and the one very molested mouse, with my mother's black thread still hanging from its chest, in another container by itself: it had survived the operation and snot injection and paralyzation with absolutely no ill effects. The project should have been called "The Remarkable Resilience of a Mouse." I developed a deep affection for it, and gave it extra crumbles of Velveeta. In my project description, I claimed that five mice, all with thymus glands removed, had died from the "viral agent" I had injected into their systems. (Out of good taste, I did not display their corpses.) This, I explained, was the one surviving mouse from this group. You could tell I had operated on it because of my mother's thread. I diagrammed the incision and showed the steps of the operation on white poster board. I made up a bunch of data for the two groups about milligrams of daily weight loss, temperature, appetite, blood count, symptoms, etc. I plotted it all on my father's graph paper, using different-colored Magic Markers for the two groups. It was still a pretty boring display. I tried to figure out how to hook up a push button that would make the mice do something (maybe a nice electric shock?), but I couldn't think of anything remotely related to the immunological role of the thymus gland. So the mice just sat there, and people strolled by without pausing to read about my project.

Sister Ursula was not impressed. My project wasn't chosen to compete in the Annual Science Fair. I got a B for it. I thought I shouldn't have to write it up for the Westinghouse Science Talent Search. If it wasn't good enough to enter the local competition, it certainly wasn't going to win the national one. I presented this logic to Sister Ursula in class. Narrowing her eyes, she said that everyone, without exception, whether or not chosen for the Annual Science Fair, was required to write up his project for the Westinghouse Science Talent Search. Including Mr. Ryan. (Big Sloppy Baby.)

So I wrote it up. I may have embellished the data a little more. Okay, I embellished it a lot more. I used a plasticine binder that actually made the whole thing look pretty scientific. There were graphs and charts and photos of the survivor mouse (Say "cheese") and a photo of the dried-up thymus gland (fat lump). Then I forgot about it.

Nobody would take the mice. Topsy still wanted to eat them, and we were all tired of being vigilant about keeping her upstairs and the door between the kitchen and basement tightly closed. I couldn't bring myself to offer them to the lab at Steeltown Hospital, or even to talk to the director, though I'm sure he would have enjoyed hearing about the "viral agent" I used. On the warmest day of the winter I released the mice into a field, where they survived for maybe twenty minutes. My favorite had managed to chew out most of my mother's black thread. A few wisps remained, still apparently the only distinguishing effects of its ordeal. I felt terrible when I dumped it out of the box into the underbrush. I told myself if it could survive what I had done to it, it could survive anything.

In the spring I started getting strange letters. Two or three a day. I'd come home from school, and there would be these letters from colleges I hadn't applied to offering me scholarships—science-oriented schools such as Case Western Reserve and Rensselaer Polytechnic Institute—and not just scholarships, but full scholarships: tuition, board, books, a free ride. They all began "Congratulations on your Honorable Mention in the Westinghouse Science Talent Search." I really did think it was a joke. But it wasn't. My project, "The Immunological Role of the Thymus Gland," won an Honorable Mention in the 1964 Westinghouse Science Talent Search, one of two winners from Sacred Heart and one of five in the area. There was an article in the *Beacon*. I had to describe my project to a reporter over the phone. I had to have my picture taken with the other winner from Sacred Heart, the two of us flanking Sister Ursula wearing her shattered-glass smile. She did not say a word to me about the project, although she must have known I had fabricated the data, and I didn't tell the reporter that she had not chosen it to compete in the Annual Science Fair. I regarded this as an unspoken deal we had. Luckily, there was no ceremony or presentation. But all spring the letters kept coming. About twenty schools offered me scholarships.

The day the picture was published in the *Beacon*, I got an anonymous call from a girl telling me I was cute. She said I must be real smart, too. She said she heard I was a make-out—how would I like to make out with her? Cars full of girls I didn't know drove by my house at midnight and yelled for me to come outside. This happened three times. My mom went out onto the lawn in her robe and chased them away. A mash note under the windshield wiper of the Skylark was waiting for me when I came out of the Hula Bowl after a doubles tournament. (Danny was my partner, and Casey Connor watched us in the finals, standing with his arms folded in the crowd behind the lane.) The phone call, the mash note, the carful of girls yelling for me to come outside turned out to be the same four girls, who were a couple of years younger than me and bowled in PAL. Two were moderately good-looking. I took each of them parking on successive weekends. I drove the Skylark into a farmer's field, and stuck my hand into their pants and masturbated them while they masturbated me. Then I didn't call them anymore. This is what I did my senior year—probably with thirty different girls. Another thirty or more would not Put Out on the first date, and I'd argue with them about it and get mad and take them home. I really believed they ought to do it. They knew about me, they knew my Reputation. Why the hell were they going out with me if they didn't want to make out? Some said they were afraid I wouldn't respect them. What a cliché, I said. Some of them said they'd just like to get to know me better. I said, so after another two or three dates maybe then? Forget it, I said: now or never. Some of them let me talk them into it. These I would usually take out a few more times. As long as they understood there was no way I was going steady with them or anybody else.

Sister Michael Margaret continued to be my champion at school. She taught the senior advanced social studies class—current events— and made sure I was in it. Before my sister moved home after college, we had subscribed to *Reader's Digest*, *National Geographic*, and *Alfred Hitchcock's Mystery Magazine* (until my father canceled it); my sister bought a subscription to *Time*, and I read it each week cover-to-cover. I thought it was intellectual. I liked its snappy style. I imagined the writers as sharp young men in sharp white shirts, their ties unnotched and their sleeves rolled up as they tatted out those sharp sentences on their typewriters. I used the most arcane information I got from it to win debates in current events class. "Yes," I'd say, concerning the efficacy of socialism in underdeveloped countries, "but what about the economic chaos in Burma?" My opponent would have to admit he did not know anything about the economic chaos in Burma, which I would then explain in minute detail from the article I had just read in *Time*. I also read a number of books like *Thirty Days to a More Powerful Vocabulary*, and would, whenever possible, use big words no one else understood, often in combinations never found in speech (like someone who teaches himself a foreign language from a text): "That's a disingenuous ostentation," was one of my favorite ripostes. I had a dictionary beside me whenever I read, and I began reading a lot. We had to give book reports in current events class. I gave one every couple of days. If someone else was absent or unprepared, I'd step right in. On one occasion, as an act of bravado, I gave two reports back-to-back on books by James Baldwin, neither of which I had read. I improvised on the titles. I knew nobody else in the class had read them either. As Bozowski once said, I could really sling the shit.

It gave me a charge like sex. I could dominate the Advanced Class just as I had the Bozos. It was fun. My classmates were so pinched and solemn, so worried about getting the right answer. I loved needling them. I could run verbal circles around most of them and was exhilarated by my prowess. I liked to argue and make jokes and Sister Michael Margaret liked me.

Still, I was as surprised as everybody else at graduation when my name was announced as the winner of the Monsignor Herman J. Golty Award for Highest Scholastic Average in Social Studies. There were over five hundred students in the graduating class, and only seven awards, including Valedictorian and Salutatorian. I got rotten grades my freshman and sophomore years and was a Bozo my junior year. I didn't have the Highest Scholastic Average in anything.

Of course, it was Sister Michael Margaret's doing. All seven awards went to students in the Advanced Classes. She chose the winner in social studies, and she had chosen me. When I thanked her, she said I deserved it. Her lively eyes became wet at the edges. She said I had come a long way. She said I should use my talent to do good. She said she was sure I would someday.

When I walked to the stage to get the award (from Monsignor Herman J. Golty himself, the retired principal of the school), my father stood up in the bleachers and took my picture as I was being handed the scrolled citation tied with a blue ribbon—the picture that came back from the developers a perfect black square. After he died, my mother told me that when my name was called she had said she was surprised and he had responded, "I'm not." She told me this to confirm that my father had believed in me, that he thought I was special.

I knew that. In the last months of his life, he told me all the time. He was sending me to Notre Dame at his expense. He didn't pay a penny for my brother's or my sister's college expenses, and Notre Dame cost a lot more than the schools they went to. He didn't make me accept one of the scholarships I was offered for the Westinghouse Science Talent Search competition. I could go anywhere I wanted. He was proud of me. He bought the Skylark for me, which, as the year went on, he let me use more and more (as he went out less and less). When he was drunk, instead of insulting me, he'd want to touch me. He'd say sentimental, stupid things. He'd want to give me a hug. He'd put his hands on my head, my shoulders, my legs. Drunk, stupid, stinking. I couldn't stand it. This is when I called him a homo to keep him away from me, and he stumbled upstairs and cried in my mother's arms.

It was not long after this that he told me he was going to die soon and I said, "If that's true, there's nothing you can do about it." What else could I have done? I had learned how to protect myself from his violence, but not from his love. There was no way to protect myself from that.

TRUE KABONGS

After the three-day round of graduation parties and celebrations, I left for a week in Ocean City, New Jersey. Ocean City was our Fort Lauderdale. Atlantic City (precasino) was for families, Wildwood was for greasers, and Ocean City was for college students and high school students pretending to be. We grew up with its lore of wild parties and easy sex, motel rooms with cold beer in the bathtubs and hot coeds in the beds, bonfires on the beach and taut, tanned, bikini-clad beauties undulating to Caribbean rhythms (New Jersey, in my imagination, being transfigured into an island somewhere near Jamaica). On summer weekends, Ocean City was packed with kids wearing T-shirts of prestigious eastern universities they did not attend scoping one another on the beach, on the street, in cars, in bars, and in the hamburger-and-fries restaurant everybody went to (the Chatterbox)—the hub of the gridlocked blocks we trudged up and down trying to pick up girls. We had been doing this two or three weekends a summer since we were sixteen, with no success whatsoever. We didn't look old enough to fake our way into the bars; nobody had a fancy convertible to cruise in (even after my father bought the Skylark, I couldn't take it to Ocean City—it was the family car); so we pounded the pavement. For hours. After dinner we'd split into pairs (because most of the girls traveled in pairs) and regroup at a predesignated hour at the Chatterbox to narrate our nonadventures and share our woe. The Chatterbox was aptly named. It was deafening, overlit, and painted bright pink inside and out—the same shade of pink as the Playroom, a color that seemed to have been put on this earth to hurt my eyes. The waitresses, all dispiritingly cute and cheery, wore pink uniforms. Even the Naugahyde in the booths was pink. We'd hunch in Maoist self-criticism over our cherry, vanilla, lime, and chocolate Cokes trying to figure out what we were doing wrong. We had smiled, we had said "Hi," we had walked and walked and walked and looked and looked and looked, passing the same girls again and again and again. It was exhausting. It used more energy on a hot summer day than New York City. Of course, we had our standards. It was bad enough to get no girl, but it was worse to get an ugly girl. We had to get pretty girls, very pretty girls, girls at least as pretty as the ones we dated at home, preferably the prettiest girls in Ocean City—babes foxes knockouts—who were invariably pinned to a lifeguard who was also a three-sport all-American athlete and president of his fraternity at Harvard, Yale, and MIT (simultaneously). We were terrified of getting shot down by these girls—with good reason, because that's exactly what happened when we approached them. Bluntly or politely, they told us to buzz off. We blamed ourselves for not being older or cooler or better-looking. We knew the cool guys in Ocean City were having a wild time at that very moment. If we couldn't get the babes, it was because they didn't go for guys like us. So most nights we approached no girls at all. Oddly, this didn't stop us from trudging the streets every night, or from ending up in despair at the end of every night, lamenting like Hittites on our way back to the motel room two of us rented and the rest of us shared in a chaos of erupting suitcases, empty beer cans, greasy potato chip bags, and wet sandy clothes.

But this trip was going to be different. I had given it a lot of thought. We were older. Instead of pretending to be in college, we actually were—at least we would be next fall. We had fake ID that wouldn't get us into bars but would work just fine in package stores. I made sure we brought a cooler. My plan was to buy rum and Coke (many girls

wouldn't drink beer) and invite girls to beach parties. No more trudging the streets. No more lame offers of a cherry Coke at the Chatterbox
or a warm beer in a hellish motel room or a walk on the beach when
they had been trudging the streets themselves for the last six hours. In
my analysis, which I presented on the trip down in my best Monsignor
Herman J. Golty Award–winning rhetoric to the other five guys
smashed into my friend's mother's Corvair, what had been wrong was
we didn't have a good offer. We had to have a concrete, attractive invitation, something fun and collegiate: rum and Coke—a beach party.

Of course, this didn't work either. We'd drive up to a group of girls
on a street corner and yell, "Hey, want to go to a beach party?" It was
inexplicable to us that they said no. Hadn't they just been waiting for
an opportunity to put their well-being into the hands of a carful of un-
ruly, tipsy, ravenous teenage boys they had never met? Remarkably,
some of them initially entertained the possibility, and inquired into
the particulars of the beach party. We tried to present the impression
that this was a large, well-established gala, indeed the hot ticket in
Ocean City that evening. We advertised the abundance of free rum
and Coke. A few of them wavered slightly before they were able to in-
tuit that, in point of fact, the only people at this beach party would be
them and us. There would be no music, except for my pocket transistor AM radio that couldn't be heard outside a radius of two feet and
made the popular songs of the day sound like they were being sung by
a housefly. Maybe we'd build a bonfire if we could find some drift-
wood, but everybody knew it was illegal to party on the beach after
dark, and a bonfire would attract the cops and we'd all be arrested for
underage drinking. What a concrete, attractive invitation, fun and collegiate: a weekend in the slammer, with a collect long-distance call to
your parents for bail money. When the girls said no, we'd yell something charming as we drove away, like "Fuck you" or "You're ugly anyway," and moon them for good measure, packing the car's window
frames with our bare asses. "Oh, gross," they'd say. "Grow up."

So it was that kind of week, the kind we always had in Ocean City.
My friends joined in my lamentations, but they didn't seem as de-

pressed by our failure. It really depressed me. I had to get one of those pretty girls. Each one I saw was a recrimination, a reminder of what I wasn't. Never mind that none of my friends got one either. Secretly, I believed I was better than my friends: not exactly better-looking, or smarter, or stronger—just better. If I tried harder, or something, I could get one. I *should* get one. I had to get one. Ocean City was the only time away from my parents, my big chance, and I was blowing it. I don't think my friends knew how I felt, because I would play every situation for the joke in it, never really talking to the girls we approached but to my friends overhearing me talking to the girls we approached. I would say crude, rude, insulting things. I couldn't get what I wanted, so I acted like I didn't care, that it was the girls' fault because they were shallow, boring, timid, and hadn't read enough existentialism to realize that we were all going to die and be sucked into The Abyss and therefore they should without any further hesitation take a Kierkegaardian leap into the backseat of our car.

This was my state of mind the day before we were to return to Steeltown—a Saturday—particularly depressing since we had nothing lined up for our last Saturday night in Ocean City but our usual fruitless routine. I had decided I was just going to stay in the motel room and get drunk. I had had it. There were plenty of girls in Steeltown. This was my last trip ever to Ocean City. I wasn't going to cruise around; I wasn't going near the boardwalk or the Chatterbox. I was going to buy a quart of rum and two quarts of Coke and drink it all by myself. On the way back to our motel, we passed a tiny out-of-the-way Italian-American restaurant we hadn't noticed before and decided to try it. It had only three booths and four tables and one waitress—the prettiest girl in Ocean City. She had soft honey blonde hair and blue eyes and a perfect little nose—a *Playboy* Playmate face, with a body to match. We crushed ourselves into the corner booth and went gaga. I sat on the end, as in the freshman cafeteria, with a view of her every voluptuousness as she dipped gracefully to serve armfuls of plates heaped with spaghetti and tomato sauce and trays of pizzas and Cokes. I was transported. Here was the one. We managed to find out that she came from Akron, Ohio, had herself just graduated from high school, and was working in Ocean City all summer. This made her exotic. We didn't know anybody from Ohio. We thought she must be pretty neat to travel all this way on her own and get a job. She knew we were gaga, and responded to our questions and smiled at our jokes, but that was it. The place was packed and she was busy. She didn't have time to talk, and we didn't ask her to. But all during dinner we discussed nothing else among ourselves, noting all her charms (in fairly reverential terms: this was Beauty), sighing at her obvious inaccessibility to us maggots. At my insistence, we left her a stupidly large tip.

When we got outside, we punched each other and fainted and screamed that we had to have her. I ran a block on top of parked cars, trunk to hood to trunk to hood, and leaped onto the pavement and lay there on my back spread-eagled. She had told us her name was Dusty. "Dusty Dusty Dusty," I screamed. "I worship you! You are a goddess!"

I declared that I was going to ask her for a date that night. "Get out of here," my friends said. "Saturday night? Get out of here." I said I didn't care what the chances were. I had to give it a shot. She was just too beautiful. Back in the motel room the argument continued. Nobody else thought it was even worth trying. Forget whether or not she'd consider going out with me under even the best of circumstances. This was Saturday night in Ocean City. No way did she not have a date. That wasn't the point, I countered. I wasn't saying I was going to *get* a date with her. Just that I had to try. I couldn't live with myself if I didn't. Nobody quite got the distinction—intellectually, they got it, but why try something that was obviously impossible? Why not try swimming to England wearing ankle weights? What was the sense of getting shot down? That was it, I said. With this one—this Dusty, this goddess of Beauty—I'd rather get shot down.

I waited a little while in the motel, to bolster my courage and let the restaurant clear out. I changed into the best clean clothes I had left (which were none too clean)—khakis and my favorite madras sportshirt—slapped on my usual predate half-pint of English Leather, and recombed my Kennedy cut so it swept devilishly across my fore-head. Everybody said they'd wait there until I got back with the report. I said if she turned me down I'd have an excuse to get good and loaded. They said they'd have the first drink ready when I got back.

When I walked into the restaurant, it was miraculously empty. Dusty was sitting in a booth by herself, taking a break.

"Hi," she said. "Forget something?"

"I did," I said, and slid into the booth, across from her. My heart was pounding. But I had to do it. "Would you go out with me tonight?" I blurted.

"Go out with you?" she asked. She seemed genuinely surprised. I nodded gravely. She looked down at the table and smiled. It really was an absurd idea, I knew. Just look at her. Look at those lips, look at those eyelashes. "I'm not off work until nine," she said.

As I recounted it to my friends back in the motel room, I responded, "Nine? Nine at night? Oh well, in that case, forget it." They couldn't believe she accepted and I couldn't believe she accepted, but she accepted. I had a date on Saturday night with the prettiest girl in Ocean City—no, the prettiest girl anywhere, the prettiest girl I had ever seen. We all celebrated. Nobody was jealous. It was a group victory. They toasted my kabongs and said I deserved it. True kabongs, they said. I acknowledged their compliments modestly, but thought they're right, I've got what it takes, I have true kabongs. My friend gave me his mother's Corvair for the night. There were five of my friends and only one of me, but they gave me the car, the only condition being that I bring Dusty into the Chatterbox at midnight, where they would be oc-cupying our usual booth in our usual state of despair.

At midnight, as promised, I walked in holding hands with her. I was more than happy to show her off to my pals and to everyone else in there. We had been to a movie. She was wearing a blue-and-white pin-striped blouse and white shorts, and had piled her fluffs of blondeness on top of her head, which showed off her delicate cheekbones and ex-quisite neck. I told her my friends and I thought she was the goddess of Beauty. She said we were pretty silly.

I remember nothing about her personality. I didn't really care about her personality or expect her to have one. After displaying her at the Chatterbox, I drove out onto the highway outside of town to a deserted part of the beach where we could walk. She knew about this place, I didn't. We parked the car, took off our shoes, and walked the surf in the moonlight. I held her hand, I put my arm around her, the heft of her breast against the inside of my wrist. I got what I wanted and it felt great. Wait until I tell my friends about this, I thought. It already seemed like a story, that it wasn't really happening, even as it happened. There was a covered lifeguard stand up ahead. She knew it was there. Obviously, she had been here before, maybe many times, with different guys. I didn't care. We climbed into the lifeguard stand and made out. I didn't try very much, I didn't even unbutton her blouse. This was a girl I wanted to see again. We kissed and petted and watched the waves break white in the moonlight and rocket along the shoreline. I lamented that I had to leave for Steeltown the next day — but not until evening. We could have brunch. And I would be back the next weekend to see her, even if I had to come by bus. She was surprisingly noncommittal about it. Girls always seemed more concerned about the next date than the one we were on, but she wasn't. "We're here now," she said. "Kiss me some more." It was after 3 A.M. when I dropped her off at her room. This was the sort of thing that happened in the movies, with budding starlets who looked a lot like her. I thought this must be what love is. My lips were still tingling as I cleared a space to sleep amid the garbage and beer-breathing bodies on the motel room floor. Dusty Dusty Dusty, I said in my head.

Very early the next morning my friend who had driven us in his mother's Corvair got a call from his father to come home immediately. His name was Timmy Flaherty. He was fair-skinned and light-haired, and looked as Irish as his name. He was going to Boston College in the fall. I had known him since fourth grade, we had played together for the St. Boniface Cougars and the Bickle Builders, and he had started in the Advanced Classes with me freshman year at Sacred Heart and had been similarly demoted. But he did not mock and brag and make everyone hate him. He was a star pitcher and class officer, one of the Popular crowd, and our friendship had waxed and waned over the years—according to my fortunes, I thought. When I was up, he was close; when I was down, he was distant, afraid to besmirch his reputation by associating with a heedless fellow like me. Or so I believed, and was bitter about it. By the time we graduated from high school, he had become wilder, to share my conviction that reputation was a façade and appearances a joke, but in my opinion he was still too mindful of other people's opinions, especially his father's, and I often needled him about it. On this occasion, since I couldn't have my farewell brunch with Dusty, I needled him all the way back to Steeltown. He took it like St. Tarcissius. He said his father had some unexpected work for him at the family tool-and-die plant. He didn't say his father had told him on the phone that my father was dead. He suffered me for six hours on a hot day in a cramped car without revealing the real reason we had to go home early.

I remember vividly his dropping me off. We were all tired and sandy and cranky. We had left Ocean City before 8 A.M. I had slept only a couple of hours, on the floor, using a bunch of filthy towels for a pillow. I had to tape a note canceling our brunch on the locked front door of Dusty's boardinghouse. Besides fretting about whether or not she'd be mad at me, or ever go out with me again, or even get my note, I had spent the trip when I wasn't needling Timmy rhapsodizing about her, describing her silky kisses and divine attributes in meticulous detail, and had exhausted everyone else's interest in the subject before we crossed the border into Pennsylvania. As we drove up Trexler Street, a carful of nuns was pulling away from my house.

"Nuns!" I said. "My mother's becoming a fucking nun."

I didn't think anything else about it. My mother still taught fourth grade at St. Boniface, though it was unusual for the nuns to visit her at our house. If she had to meet with them during the summer, she went to the convent.

I walked through the front door carrying my bag. All the curtains were closed, and it was dark inside on a bright sunny Sunday afternoon. My mother and my sister and my sister's boyfriend were sitting at the dining room table. Something was wrong.

"What's going on?" I said.

"Donna, will you tell him?" my mother said (which later seemed strange to me: why didn't she tell me herself?).

My sister took me into my room, and told me to sit down on my bed. She sat down with me. She took both my hands in hers.

"Michael, our daddy's dead," she said.

"Oh no," I said. "Oh no oh no oh no." I buried my face in my pillow. My sister rubbed my back and neck as I cried.

He had died of a heart attack at 6 A.M. that morning. It woke him up. He stood up, then he lay back down, it hit him and he died. He didn't say anything. My mother ran and woke up my sister, but by the time they got back, he was dead. There wasn't even time to call an ambulance, although they did call an ambulance, and a doctor, and a priest, who administered Extreme Unction posthumously, anointing each of the five sinning senses with holy oil: with a drop of oil on the tip of his thumb, the priest applied a tiny sign of the cross to my father's eyes, ears, lips, hands, and feet.

The body had already been taken to the funeral home. I walked into my parents' bedroom anyway and stared at his side of the bed, where he had died. I don't know what I expected to see. His absence? Everything was the same. The furniture was solid and silent, the way it was when I stayed home from school and snuck in here to steal his detective novels, which were still stuffed under the nightstand. He would never read any of them again. He would never sleep in this bed again. He would never barbecue a rib or drink a tallboy or go to the Keystone or sing a song or tell another joke or story. He was dead. It seemed impossible.

All the funeral arrangements had already been made. There would be a wake Monday night, the funeral Tuesday morning, and on Wednesday we were all flying to Milwaukee for another wake and funeral, and that's where he'd be buried. Milwaukee was his home. That's where his family and friends were, where my mother's family and friends were, where my mother and father had been married. They had lived there forty years. My mother sometimes said we should never have left Milwaukee, that that's when our troubles began (she meant his drinking). She probably would have said this more often if she didn't believe such talk did no good. In Florida and Steeltown they just didn't have the support of community and family they had had in Milwaukee. She thought he would have wanted to be buried in Milwaukee, despite the extra expense, but she wanted to know what I thought.

I didn't understand why she was asking me. I thought it was fine. It made sense to me. Whatever she wanted. I felt sorry for her. She didn't have a husband anymore. She was a widow. She was being brave and strong, but this was a terrible blow, all her fears come true. His blood pressure, his heart condition: It had filled the air in our house. It was a warning, but it had been more a way of saying something else, some-thing terrible that was happening all along to all of us, not just what might happen in the future to him. It certainly hadn't prepared us for this.

The wake and funeral in Steeltown were dignified and solemn. His casket was lined with padded white satin and he lay in it in a business suit with his eyes closed and a rosary entwined through his fingers. I hadn't seen him holding a rosary since we had lived in Milwaukee and knelt around the radio on Sunday evenings to pray the family rosary with Bishop Fulton J. Sheen. My father's skin had always been pale, but now it was so pale it seemed translucent, and his jet black hair looked even blacker. He wasn't wearing his glasses. He always wore his glasses. He didn't look like himself without them. It's all right he doesn't look like himself, I thought. He's not himself. He's dead.

The family knelt on a kneeler next to the casket during the offering of prayers. I knelt at his face, less than a foot away. Up close, it looked doughy, dusted with a faint white powder like flour. If I poked his cheek, my finger would sink all the way in. I stared at him, unmoving and unbreathing, while the meaningless prayers rumbled in accompa-niment. When they were over and we stood up, my mother grasped his hand, which didn't tear off at the wrist like bread, but hung in hers limply, a dead weight. It sent chills through me when she did it.

Everybody said how sad it was that he died. He looked so young. Nobody mentioned his drinking. My friends all came with their parents to offer condolences. So did a couple of girls I had gone out with, though I had stopped calling them after the usual two or three dates. After the wake my brother, who had stepped off the plane from Wyoming in a Stetson, a string tie, and boots, did a breathy imitation of one of them saying to me, "If there's *anything* I can do for you, Michael, *please* let me know." My brother said she was just as cute as a bug. A real babe.

He was not in particularly low spirits, although he, too, felt sorry for my mother and did his best to console her. She wanted somebody to take charge, and he liked to be busy, to be doing and organizing. He was the eldest son. I was pretty useless. Everything was going too fast for me. It seemed I had just been in the lifeguard stand with Dusty the Babe of All Time, and now we were about to fly to Milwaukee with my father's casket in the cargo hold. I asked my brother what the hurry was, and he said the casket was going to be open in Milwaukee, too, "and you don't want the corpse getting too ripe." "Why the hell wait around anyway?" he added. I couldn't give him a reason. It just seemed too fast.

My electric shaver was being repaired, and I drove the Skylark to the appliance shop to pick it up right before we were to leave for the airport. The shop was on a busy street. I pulled up in front, planning to just run in and run out. I opened the car door and it ripped out of my hand with a crash. A passing car had hit it, nearly taking off my hand in the bargain. The driver screeched to a stop, and all the traffic halted for a moment before slowly starting up again. My door hung by one hinge, crumpled into folds like an accordion; the window had shattered and sprinkled onto the street; the inside panels had sprung out, multicolored wires sprouted in every direction. I hadn't checked the rearview mirror before opening the car door into traffic. My father was dead two days and I had already smashed up the Skylark. Thank God he wasn't there to see it, I thought. He would have gone nuts. I held the door with one hand and steered with the other on the way home. The accident—exchanging license numbers and insurance and the rest of it—made me late. Everybody was waiting for me on the front porch, bags packed, the cab running its meter, my brother pressing his lips together as he did when he was very angry. "Oh, neat," he said when I got out of the car. We left it in the driveway with the door hanging off. "It doesn't matter, Michael," my mother said. "We'll deal with it when we get home." My father would have never said that. How different things were already.

The wake in Milwaukee was not like the wake in Steeltown. The wake in Milwaukee was in a big funeral home with four different wakes going on in four different rooms. I thought this was demeaning—as if my father's death were only one of four, and, by implication, one of a zillion. We arrived early. A blonde receptionist in a black dress met us at the door and asked, "Which party are you?"—as if this were a restaurant, the kind of restaurant where the waiters tell you their first names. She had a svelte figure, and when she turned her back, my brother caught my eye and moved his eyebrows up and down like Groucho Marx. I didn't care what she looked like. I was furious. As she led us down a long corridor to parlor number four, I glanced into the other rooms, my hostile glare startling some of the mourners. Parlor number four was a huge room, eighty by fifty feet, empty except for my father's casket, which was set up near the entrance between two large wreaths of flowers on easels. My mother headed for it, and the rest of us followed. Here he was again, exactly as he was the last time I had seen him at the funeral in Steeltown. It struck me as odd: boom, he's gone; boom, he pops up again, a thousand miles away, wearing the same suit and tie and nonexpression on his face, lying in the same box of padded white satin. I was ready for it to be buried, in one place, under the ground, and never see him again. My mother grabbed his hand first thing, just as she had the last time. Her hand looked bruised by comparison, the veins puffy and blue. I was staring at her without knowing it, and she noticed me.

"Touch him, Michael," she said, her eyes welling with tears. "No," I answered, and walked away. I would have rather died myself.

My grandmother (my father's mother) arrived, with her sister and Grandpa Jim and two of his relatives, all country people, retired farmers in their seventies and eighties, the survivors of the last generation, the generation before my father's, their fingers gnarled from farming accidents, their faces etched with deep grooves by a life in the sun from dawn to dark. All five of them had on their mourning clothes— old homespun suits and dresses made of scratchy black wool (on a sweltering June day in Milwaukee). It was the first time my grandmother saw my father's body. She whooped when she saw it and her knees buckled, so Grandpa Jim had to hold her up by the elbows. "My son. My boy," she wailed. "Whoo," she whooped—as loud as a train, with long pauses between whoops to take a deep, deep breath, and push it out from her toes: "Whooooo." She continued whooping and wailing, making the rest of us edgy at such a raw show of emotion. She could certainly be heard in the other rooms. It was primitive, and she looked primitive in her big broken body and the black dress that was probably half a century old. Grandpa Jim sat her down in the chair nearest the casket and put his arm around her and held one of her hands while her sister held the other.

Gradually, the rest of the Ryan Party began arriving: my mother's more restrained side of the family, pure-blood Germans, Schultzes and Ernsts—her sister and brother and cousins and aunts and uncles and nieces and nephews—and her father, my grandpa, my father's old antagonist, who had lived with us in Milwaukee and still lived here in a nursing home. He was in his eighties and desiccated and frail, in high contrast to my father's mother. She could have picked him up in one hand and bitten off his head like a carrot. He was wearing slippers and moved with tiny, sliding steps as if he were walking on ice, the soles of his feet flat on the ground. I don't know if he even looked at my father. It would have taken him ten minutes to get over to the casket, and he didn't make even a token move in that direction. He said hello to everyone and smiled wanly, and his daughters and granddaughters kissed him on the cheek, leaving lipstick smears on his dry, papery skin. We shook hands. "Hello, Mike," he said. "You're all grown up." After a little while he said he was tired and wanted to go back to the home, and was escorted out at his own excruciating pace.

By that time the room, big as it was, was almost filled. The obituary notice had been published that morning in the *Milwaukee Sentinel,* and friends my mother had not seen since we had moved from Milwaukee showed up. As they arrived, they paid their respects at the casket, but then they stood around talking to each other. It started to get loud. There were occasional bursts of laughter. There was a ten-to-fifteen-foot space between my father and where the party began — as if to avoid him. They acted like he wasn't there. Except my grandmother and her relatives: they were still huddled in the corner nearest the casket, weeping. I wanted to scream at everyone else, My father is dead! Shut the fuck up! Get the fuck out of here! I looked for my mother. She was talking to people I had never seen before. Who were these people? She was actually smiling at them. How dare she. How dare them all.

I fumed about it the next day through the funeral and the burial, where my grandmother tried to throw herself onto the casket as they lowered it into the ground. Although I was glad my mother wouldn't do such a thing, I thought this was what she should feel: wild, inconsolable, unanswerable grief. I wanted to chew her out but good for the way she behaved at the wake, at allowing it to turn into some sort of reunion party. I complained about it to my brother and sister, who seemed to have hardly noticed. They told me not to say anything to mom, which I didn't. Even so, she sensed my anger at her, through her grief and worry about what would happen next to her family.

What happened next was we were suddenly richer than we had ever been. My father had said many times we would be better off when he was dead. It was another in the litany of self-pitying, drunken remarks I had learned to ignore. He kept his financial papers in the locked steel strongbox he hauled out once a month when he paid the bills, and hadn't told anybody exactly what he was doing, even my mother. He had been buying insurance that paid off the funeral, the car, and the mortgage on the house, and, in addition to that, upon his death by natural causes, presented us with a lump sum check of fifty thousand dollars (big bucks in 1964). Plus settlements of his pension fund and Social Security, including a hundred dollars a month for any child under twenty-one enrolled as a full-time student at an accredited college (me). When my mother found out what he had done, she cried and said it proved how much he loved us. I cried with her. I didn't forget his drunken rants about money ("We can't afford snacks!" "If you're hungry, eat a piece of bread!" "I'm the boss, I pay the bills, I own you!"), but it made me believe he was a sort of martyr. He had spent every available penny on liquor (to kill himself) and life insurance (to make us rich after he died). He had tormented us about money, but money had tormented him. He hated his job, but was terrified of losing it. I never felt poor, but I had always felt strapped, as if a tidal wave could hit our house at any moment and sweep us into poverty. Now the tidal wave *had* hit our house, but it was made of money, and he had been building it every month of his life when he sat at the bar in the Playroom and wrote the payment checks. It must have been like bleeding. Such deep secret love for us underneath the craziness: it overwhelmed me.

My mother kept teaching at St. Boniface and supplemented her salary with the interest on the fifty thousand dollar cushion. Our standard of living didn't change, but there would be no more ranting or agonizing or even discussions about money. Fifty thousand dollars: unimaginable. Notre Dame was going to be no problem. She said the hundred a month from Social Security was mine, for books and expenses (and dates!). She would have hardly any expenses herself. My sister would continue living at home and she was teaching, too. The house was suddenly paid for. The Skylark was suddenly paid for. And it was suddenly my mother's car. The cuntcar. It was too ironic. She looked funny driving it. Although you could do a U-turn with one finger, she drove it like she drove the White Sow, hunched forward with both hands white-knuckling the wheel.

It was weird to come home to its mangled body in the carport. It

seemed Symbolic (one of my current words-of-the-month). It represented something to my father, even if it was only a tipsy impulse on a
Saturday afternoon, a wish for himself he gave up almost immediately
but passed on to me forever. Now he was dead and the Skylark was
mangled and I had done it. And look at what he had done for me:
Notre Dame, his insurance money, the Skylark itself. He was right. I
was better off with him dead, and this made me feel worse. I hadn't appreciated him enough. Sure he drank, but the world had made him
drink: working at a shit job from nine to five, having to support us, not
being able to do what he wanted. I had to make up for it somehow. I
would make up for it, by God. I was never ever even for one moment
going to do anything I didn't want to do. The world had defeated him,
but it wasn't going to defeat me. To everyone else in the family the
Skylark was just a car with a broken door.

My brother left for Wyoming before it came back from the body
shop. He always got antsy in Steeltown. "There's nothing to *do* here,"
he complained. He didn't know anyone in Steeltown anymore. He
hung around the house, playing solitaire at the dining-room table with
country-and-western music on the radio (he called it "hillbilly"),
smoking Marsh Wheeling stogies and drinking Cokes and reading
plane schedules (he plotted about forty alternate routes back to
Laramie). My mother expected me to entertain him. She gave me a
lecture about "including" him with my friends—inviting him to go
along to movies, etc. She said this is what "a nice guy" would do. But I
knew her real motive. She just wanted him not to be bored so he
would stay home longer. No way was I inviting him to go to movies
with my friends. That wasn't what he wanted anyway. He wanted me
to fix him up with dates. No girl I knew (except Bunny) would go out
with a twenty-seven-year-old man, much less my brother. Even if I
could dig up one who would, I wasn't about to put myself through a
double-date with him in the backseat of the Skylark, the air inside the
car reeking of Vitalis, wondering what embarrassing thing he would
say or do next. "You're too old for girls my age," I said to him.
"Everybody does it in Wyoming," he countered. "Legal age fourteen."

Sometimes I couldn't tell if he was kidding. He loved to be outrageous, and would laugh in short, loud bursts like a tommy gun.

My sister did get him a date with one of her friends (the homeliest one), and, with my sister's boyfriend (a mild, handsome guy she broke up with soon afterward), they doubled to a movie. My brother put a good face on it when he got home. But to me in private he made the thumbs-down sign with both hands and a farting noise with his lips and said it had gone over like a lead balloon. "A good-night kiss on the cheek," he said. "Big deal." We were sharing a room again while he was home. He wanted me to fix him up instead of my sister because he couldn't tell her what he really wanted was a little lovey-dovey. He complained that her friends were all prudes (except Sharon, who had come to my father's funeral clutching her new fiancé). He offered to fix me up in return if I visited him in Wyoming. He wanted to know what I got off that chicky who came to the wake, but I didn't tell him. It would have been nearly telling him who I was, and I couldn't tell anybody in my family who I was. Not telling him was also a way to keep the upper hand. He was amazed by the girls I had, and sometimes seemed to be asking me, his younger brother, for advice. I wanted to say, Try brushing your teeth once a month for starters. We had fun sometimes when we were alone; though he was bossy and bragged (like me), he was also generous and guileless and loved to laugh. If he was in a good mood, he tried to make everyone around him feel good. But he didn't have a clue about girls. Not like me. I knew about girls. I was getting all the girls I wanted. And not just girls. Babes. Foxes. Knockouts.

We had stayed in Milwaukee the weekend after my father's funeral, the weekend I had planned to take the bus to Ocean City to see Dusty; and the next weekend I stayed home in Steeltown, as I did the following weekend and the weekend after that. It seemed too complicated to take one bus to Philadelphia, another to Atlantic City, and a third to Ocean City—thirteen hours in all (even my brother couldn't plot a faster route with his archive of bus schedules)—just to end up in Ocean City without a car. After the last trip I couldn't talk any of my friends into driving. Dusty probably had four or five new boyfriends by this time. She was probably mad at me for standing her up when I had pledged, promised, and vowed to be there the next weekend. What if I showed up and she wouldn't go out with me? That would be fun, wandering around Ocean City by myself, on foot. It just wasn't worth the chance. I was surprised by how little I felt about her. Wasn't she the prettiest girl I had ever seen? The moonlit night in the lifeguard stand had seemed like a dream even as it was happening, then, as the weeks passed, it also faded like one.

I didn't go back to Ocean City for the rest of the summer. Something changed in me when my father died, I didn't know what. All through the wakes and the funerals and the trip to Milwaukee, I didn't tell anybody that less than a week before he died he told me he was going to die soon. What good would it do now that he was dead? Should I have told my mother while he was still alive, before I left for Ocean City? What could she have done? I thought it would just upset her. And I had always kept his secrets—I never told her or anyone else the craziest, weirdest stuff he said to me in the Playroom. I knew that his telling me he was going to die soon was one of these secrets. That's how he meant it. A secret. Between the two of us, me and him. I didn't believe it when he said it, only the part of me that believed in the Greenies and his voodoo stories about curses and snakes and lightning. I thought I had outgrown all that. But I kept it secret anyway. And it had been true. Secrets were always true. And the truth was secret.

My grandfather died a couple of weeks after my father. Another body blow for my poor mother. I didn't feel a thing. She and my sister were flying back to Milwaukee for another funeral. My brother had returned to Laramie and he wasn't going to go (he had never been close to my grandfather). My mother said I didn't have to go either. So I didn't, not because I was still too upset about my father (as she seemed to think), but because I wanted to stay in Steeltown by myself, with the house and Skylark to myself. My mind immediately started clicking with the possibilities, my mental Rolodex. This was my chance to take a girl to bed. Bed! Not rumpling around in the Skylark, worrying about cops or bushwhackers. I set up a date for the night they left, with the sole exception to my two- or three-date rule.

Her name was Sally. She was sixteen, two years younger than me, a strawberry blonde with naughty green eyes. She was a majorette at Tumberg High School, which served rural areas and was famous for girls who Put Out, the explanation being that farm girls who grow up watching farm animals have sex become horny. But Sally didn't grow up on a farm. She lived on a street very much like my street, the pre-fabricated houses maybe a little smaller and cheaper. Her father was a milkman. But she certainly did Put Out. When she was fourteen and I was sixteen, I met her at the Hub Club and took her parking. She knew where we were going when we left the dance. One of the things I liked most about her was her inability to conceal her feelings, especially her sexual feelings, which were as profuse and robust as she was slim and demure. I was driving the White Sow that night. She sat as close to me as she could (like a farm girl in a pickup), Tumberg dating etiquette. I could feel her body heat. She kissed like Roto-Rooter. But, although she immediately and happily cleaned my tonsils as we rumpled about the capacious front seat of the Buick, she would not let me touch her breasts, or even her thighs, much less between them, clamping my hand every time it started to travel. I drove her home, thinking this was it for her. Kissy-face didn't cut it. I wouldn't be seeing her again. As we drove up her street, friends of her parents were leaving her house. She had gone to the Hub Club with her girlfriends and didn't want her parents to see her being dropped off by a strange boy. "Just keep driving," she said, ducking, smacking her ear onto my lap. I drove around the block and stopped in an alley. She sat up. It was late. I just wanted to get home. She wanted to wait at least ten minutes. I wasn't about to leave her on the street by herself even in her own neighborhood, but I may have acted a little impatient. I was tired of making out with her since I wasn't getting my rocks off, and if I couldn't get my rocks off, it was all a waste of time. As I sat there bored, gazing through the windshield at lawn ornaments, I noticed that she had let her left hand rest on my thigh. I looked at her and she smiled. I saw something in her eyes I hadn't seen before. I didn't kiss her. I put my hand over hers and, still looking into her eyes, pushed it up to my crotch. She went crazy. It was like a grenade had gone off inside her. Then I did kiss her, and we parked in the alley for another half hour. As she was masturbating me, she let me touch her wherever I wanted, and she wheezed and bucked in a way that made me wonder if she was having some sort of seizure. It took me a number of conversations with a number of friends to figure out what was happening to her. I never did figure out why she wouldn't let me touch her before she touched me, and I could never bring myself to ask her.

But, as a result, I did go out with her again — about once a month for my last two years of high school. She asked nothing of me. She never spoke about going steady. We both dated other people, but whenever I called her, with no exceptions I remember, she went out with me. I liked taking her to parties because she was pretty and cheerful and laughed at my jokes, and I liked taking her parking because she was hot. I knew something about her and she let me know it: that she was burning alive one-tenth of an inch under her skin and I could trigger it with the slightest touch or even a look. She made me feel I was the only one who could do this to her. I could dig a fingernail into her palm or press her hip while we were dancing or let our gaze lock for an extra second during a conversation with a group of friends and I'd know what she was feeling and that she was helpless to stop it. That's how I felt about sex, too: helpless to stop it. It seemed to take me, voodoo power, but I could use it on Sally and thereby stand outside it. We shared it but I also controlled it: getting her hot got me hot. Once we got going, she was gone. She was always ahead of me, as if I were pushing her and she were pulling me. She never stopped. I was always the one who stopped (because I ejaculated), and she would blink, and blink, as if she had just returned to her body from the planet Mars.

It was odd to be with her alone in my house. We had been together only in cars, drive-ins, movies, parties, the Charcoal for a cheese steak after parking. Giving her a tour of my house was like showing her an abandoned shell. I couldn't begin to show her the living things: the things I had done in each room, the things I felt. The hamper I hid inside to make my parents think I had run away was only a hamper, the warped pool table my father bought for me when I couldn't play football anymore was only a warped pool table, my father's nightstand and detective novels were only a nightstand and detective novels. And Topsy. Topsy was an old dog now, her eyes rheumy and her gums exposed. She greeted Sally at the door, barking and wagging her tail arthritically. Sally scratched her ears and was licked in return, made a face, and washed her hand in the kitchen sink. Topsy followed us from room to room and down the basement stairs into the Playroom. My father's drinking paraphernalia was still on the shelves behind the bar: stirrers, shakers, mixers, corkscrews, risqué cartoon-painted cocktail glasses, the empty bottles of liqueur with the novelty corks. It was like a museum exhibit behind glass. What could it mean to Sally? I locked Topsy in the basement when we went back upstairs. I undressed Sally in the hallway and stood behind her before the circular mirror where I had made gargoyle faces and practiced my bowling approach, five steps and slide on the throw rug, kaboom. I picked her up and laid her down on my sister's bed where Sharon had bent over in her slip and folded her clothes and asked me what I thought of this blouse or that halter top before wiggling into her skirt and kissing me on the cheek and leaving me sitting there dazed.

I thought we went All The Way that night, but we didn't. I didn't know what it felt like to be inside, so I didn't know what it felt like not to be inside. As Sally confirmed later, I was rubbing between her and the sheet. Could have fooled me. *Did* fool me. I announced to my friends that we had Done It.

I probably would have never known we didn't if it weren't for what happened when we did. We actually did it a few weeks later, at a party at Timmy Flaherty's house: the first time for both of us. Virtually every party we had that summer was when somebody's parents were away. Timmy's grandmother was home, but she agreed to stay upstairs after 8 P.M., when the party was to start. That afternoon Chuck and I bought a full keg of beer and chilled it in a washtub at one of my secret parking spots not far from Timmy's house. Chuck was dating Sally's best friend, a sprightly brunette named Sheri (who once racked him off in the backseat while her parents drove them to dinner—using her father's sport coat to cover Chuck's lap and returning it to its hanger before her father put it on in the parking lot on the way into the restaurant: those Tumberg girls!). We picked up Sally and Sheri in Chuck's Packard. Sally looked great as always. She had on a white blouse that showed off her tan. We dropped the girls off at Timmy's and fetched the beer. It had already started to rain, and soon it was raining harder, really hard, in sheets. At least fifty kids were invited to the party, and another fifty came who weren't. Among the guests was Corky Kellogg—who had rubbed me underwater the summer after eighth grade—and we exchanged droll collegiate witticisms. Since nobody could go upstairs (because of Timmy's grandmother) or outside (because of the rain) every room was packed wall-to-wall with kids spilling their paper cups of beer and smoking cigarettes. The beer keg was in the kitchen, the dancing was in the living room, and the dining room with its furniture stacked against the wall was the make-out room. There was only one bathroom, a half-bathroom next to the kitchen, with a toilet and sink and Timmy's mother's flowered guest towels and scalloped scented soap. I was drinking one beer after another and so was Sally. She got more ravenous the drunker she got, and I was entertained by it, knowing quite well that before the evening was out we would find someplace to do it, although I didn't know where. The promise of sex made me feel secure, confident, powerful. I was going to get it tonight. On the dance floor Sally was biting me and sticking her tongue in my ear and pulling my shirttail out so she could rub my bare back. She was drunk and so was I and so was almost everybody else. The air inside the house was thick with humidity. The music was loud and the dancing was steamy. We went into the makeout room and lay down on the floor among the humps of bodies like seals on a beach. We runched around for a while, kissing and rubbing and groping. "Give it to me," Sally whispered into my ear. "Give it to me give it to me give it to me." Okay, I thought, I'll do just that. But there was no place to go. Couldn't go outside: rain. Couldn't go upstairs: grandmother. There wasn't anyplace else. Then a soggy lightbulb lit above my besotted head, inside of which appeared two words: the bathroom. I took Sally into the bathroom and locked the door behind us. She giggled. There was hardly enough room for us to stand up, much less to lie down. We got out of our clothes. I sat on the toilet and she straddled me and then I was inside her. Actually. For real.

Unfortunately, I hadn't considered the fact that we would be occupying the only bathroom at a beer bash. The same reasons we couldn't go upstairs or outside to have sex applied to everyone else when they had to go to the bathroom. Nor are drunk teenagers with bladders full of beer a cultural subgroup particularly known for patience and courtesy. The first knocking began during the first thirty seconds and did not let up for the duration of our virginal act of love. Indeed, it became an increasingly tumultuous banging and yelling, "What's going on in there? Let us in! We need to piss!" Bang crash bang crash bang, the door nearly being pulled off its hinges. After a while, it got to me and I stopped. I wasn't enjoying myself, although Sally characteristically was. I switched on the light so we could find our clothes, and there was blood everywhere. A lot of blood. On my thighs, on the floor, on the walls, on Sally's white blouse. It looked like someone had slaughtered an animal in there. It shocked me to my toenails, but Sally was completely calm. "Are you all right?" I asked her. She said she was just fine, dreamy-eyed, still in her reentry mode. "You aren't having your period?" I asked. "No, silly," she said. "I would have told you." She wanted to kiss some more. People were still banging on the door. I didn't know what else to ask. I couldn't guess what happened since I was sure we had done it before.

When we finally got our clothes on, they looked like we had been rolling around in a meat locker. I wiped up the blood on the walls, floor, toilet, and sink with Timmy's mother's flowered guest towels. I washed my bloody hands with the scalloped scented soap. Then I opened the door. There was a line of about twenty people scowling at us. "Mike and Sally were in there together!" somebody yelled. "Jesus Christ, Pork," Timmy said to me.

It was already after one, and Sally was supposed to have been home at midnight. The sex seemed to make her drunker, or quieter. She sunk into an armchair and didn't want to leave. She said, "I just want to sit here and think." I found Chuck and asked him to drive us home. He had already driven Sheri all the way back to Tumberg and returned to the party. "I didn't know where the hell you went," he said. "The bathroom," I answered. He kindly agreed to drive yet again to Tumberg and back. I practically had to carry Sally over my shoulder to the car. Her white blouse had big smears of blood down the front. On the way home I tried to sober her up a little. She nodded at everything I said, and kept insisting she was fine. When we got to her house, I walked her to the front door. Everything was dark inside. Her parents were asleep. Lucky thing. I put my hands on her shoulders and spoke to her nose, since her eyes were going in and out of focus.

"Okay," I whispered. "Remember what I told you. Just go up to your room as quietly as you can, take off all your clothes and stuff them into the back of your closet. Tomorrow you can sneak them out to the laundry. Then just get into bed and go to sleep. Okay?"

"Okay," she said.

"Okay," I said. "Good night." I gave her a kiss.

"Good night," she said quietly.

I held the screen door for her and closed it behind her as noiselessly as I could. I turned to walk back to the car where Chuck was waiting, and, as I turned, I heard Sally shout at the top of her lungs, "Mother, I'm home!"

I ran. I jumped into the car, which was already moving. We drove back to Timmy's party, which was still going. There was still plenty of beer, and I began drinking it in earnest, one jumbo cup after another, like Gatorade. All that blood had upset me. I still didn't know if I had hurt her or something, though she said fifty times she was fine. Her parents were probably talking at this moment to the police ("We thought he was such a nice boy, Officer"). As I got drunker—really drunk—I began raving quite loudly about it: "Blood on the floor, blood on the walls, blood all over the fucking bathroom." I guess I was raving so loudly Timmy was afraid his grandmother would hear me. After a number of efforts to get me to shut up, he invited me to leave. This hurt my feelings, and I decided that I would show him once and for all by sleeping under a tree in the rain. I was staggering across a field toward the luxury accommodations of my choice when Chuck intercepted me. He insisted I get into his car. I was soaking wet. I told him I was too drunk to go home and therefore I was going to sleep under a tree, that very nice one right over there, not to worry I'd be fine. He pushed me into his car and took me to his house.

By this time it was about 4 A.M. He put me to bed on his living-room couch. I remember waking up to go to the bathroom, and walking to the far corner of the living room and peeing on his brother's graduation picture on top of the television set. It seemed like the right place to go at the time. I wasn't aware of doing anything untoward, and went right back to sleep. I didn't even think of it when Chuck woke me up to go home. That afternoon his mother was dusting the living room. She asked, "Chuck, what's this on Biff's picture?" I became a famous personage in their family.

Sally's parents didn't get out of bed when she shouted, so they never saw her bloody blouse. I dropped my soaked, soiled clothes into somebody's trash can on the way home from Chuck's. He woke me up at 7 A.M. by placing a clean T-shirt and a pair of his jeans on my face. I was still drunk, but at least I could walk and utter a more or less grammatical sentence. If my father died at 6 A.M.—on a Sunday morning, the morning after his biggest drinking night of the week, when he usually slept until at least midafternoon—he must have died drunk, and not just drunk, blind drunk. God knows what he thought or felt. Probably nothing. Hit by a train.

I got home before my mother and sister were awake. My mother knew I hadn't slept in my bed, but when I finally got up (at midafternoon) I told her it had gotten late so I had slept at Chuck's, not wanting to wake her in the middle of the night. It was sort of the truth. My mother always woke up when I came in. She was alert to me constantly. She waited on me hand and foot. I always felt her watching me, worrying about me, wanting me to be happy but also wanting me to be better, nudging, nagging me to be a good boy, telling me in every circumstance, as she had with my brother, what "a nice guy" would do. It took enormous energy to keep her out of my face, to hide who I really was, but over the years I had acquired great skill at doing so, and by this time it had become a collaboration, a masterful duet. *Don't tell me who you are*, she told me in a million ways, *I could not stand it*. Nor could I stand it. I was just too awful, and always had been.

But I had true kabongs. I had made myself what I imagined girls wanted, a pinch of JFK, a pinch of James Dean. I formed my personality around it: this drive to be wanted. I became it. With my father dead, I was the man of the house. He had stayed home almost all the time during the last year of his life, underneath us, in the Playroom, living in the basement like a troll. For months after his death, it seemed he was still down there, that one night he would simply walk up the stairs and pull another tallboy out of the refrigerator. I dreamed the same dream over and over again: he had been away on a trip; he had come back to see me but had to go away again and didn't know when he'd return. I'd cry when he said this to me in the dream and wake up crying. *Don't go away Daddy please don't go away*. Then I'd realize it had been the dream, I was in my room, I was eighteen years old, my father was dead. My mother stuffed his clothes into Goodwill boxes, and a truck came and picked them up. She asked me if I wanted any of his ties. There must have been three hundred of them blooming from his tie rack in his closet like some noxious multilayered vine that thrives in darkness. I took a couple of them, reluctantly. She threw his detective novels and *Alfred Hitchcock's Mystery Magazines* into the trash. She wanted me to look at everything else of his she sifted through, to see if I could use it, before she gave it away or threw it away. She gave me his watch. I wouldn't wear it, so she kept it for me for the day I would. (When I finally accepted it a couple of years ago, I who almost never lose anything lost it within a month.) I don't know what she did with his ring, the one with the diamond he had been given by the Greenies. She piled on their bed his violins and guitar and cuff links and tie clips and gold-plated pillbox. "I don't know what to do with these things," she said, breaking down and crying. They seemed too painful to keep and too valuable to throw away. She didn't touch the Playroom. Except for the open whiskey bottles, which were poured down the sink, for years afterward the bar stayed as it was the moment he died. It was not that she was preserving a memorial. This wouldn't have been the memorial she chose. She just didn't know what to do with it. The bar would have looked even worse stripped of all the paraphernalia on the shelves. Eventually, she moved the TV upstairs and hardly went down to the Playroom at all. She had never spent much time in the Playroom anyway. But with the bar intact it seemed for a long time that he was just out for the evening, gone out for a pack of cigarettes, drinking at the Keystone.

Topsy also died that summer, just before I left for Notre Dame. The city was digging a ditch for an alley behind our house, and Topsy climbed down into it to die. It reminded me of her going underneath the house in Groveland to have her puppies, away from human beings: her animal dignity. The week before graduation we had had a retreat at school, a week of classes replaced by our final moral instruction before we were sent out into the world, culminating in going to confession as a class. I decided I was going to make a sincere confession, maybe for the first time in my life, to give the Catholic religion one last shot. It had been a good year for me. Things were going my way. Maybe God wasn't so bad to me after all.

I was standing in the confessional line in front of Sam Pulaski, a Vocational major from Bunny's neighborhood who for all four years of high school dressed in black (sportcoat, chinos, skinny tie, and pointy shoes) and wore his dirty blond hair in a Detroit (a spiky flattop greased back on the sides). Although we had always been in the same homeroom because of the alphabetical proximity of our names, I had not exchanged a word with him in the four years. Neither of us saw a reason to. We lived in different worlds. On this occasion, we had acknowledged each other with our usual barely perceptible masculine nod.

"You know, Ryan, I've been watching you all this time," he said out of the blue to the back of my head.

I was startled that he had spoken to me at all, not to mention by what he said. I had actually been examining my conscience, to find words for my sins. I looked over my shoulder at him.

"Is that right, Sam," I said, flatly.

"That's right. I've seen you dating all those different girls, one after another. You've been all over the place."

"Hnnh," I said.

"Fact is, you go steady you get more."

I told him thanks for the tip. He nodded. This was all he had to say to me, just a little friendly advice.

In confession, I told the priest that I had committed the sins of fellatio, voyeurism, and bestiality. He didn't ask for details. He didn't respond at all, except to give me a penance of three Our Fathers and three Hail Marys, the sort of penance I used to get in fourth grade for disobeying my parents. What a joke, I thought. I didn't say the penance. It was the last time I went to confession. I told Chuck and Timmy that as a lark I had confessed every sexual perversion I could think of, and that the priest was so stupid he didn't know what the words meant. We had a big laugh about it. Fellatio, voyeurism, bestiality. They thought bestiality was a particularly good one.

THE FIGHTING IRISH

In 1964, Notre Dame was an all-male school. ND: No Dates. There were six thousand undergraduate men for the six hundred women at St. Mary's College across the road and the handful of townies from the nursing school and the beautician college in South Bend. Therefore, freshmen did not get dates. It was an axiom so incontrovertible it made Euclid's seem like whimsy. There may have been a freshman who actually got a date that year, but I didn't know him.

Without girls and dates, I came unglued almost immediately. After dinner every night I hung around the Clubhouse. The Clubhouse was one of two triples on my wing. The rest of the rooms were doubles (I lived in a double). Except for the difference in size, all the rooms were identical: the same brown linoleum floor and institutional green walls, the same chair, desk, and dark green metal locker for each occupant, the same porcelain sink and medicine chest in the corner, the same dark green metal bunk beds with the same brown Army blankets. There were about a half-dozen of us who hung around the Clubhouse, and we referred to ourselves, only half ironically, as the Clubhouse Gang. After dinner the Clubhouse accommodated a constant traffic until lights out. Coffee cups pilfered from the cafeteria overflowed with cigarette butts, the blankets were dotted with burn holes, the pillowcases doubled as napkins for the endless parade of junk food and late-night burgers 'n' fries from the Huddle. Anybody who wanted a study break or an evening of distraction would wander in, plop down on a bed, join the blackjack game in progress, or rifle a desk for juicy letters from somebody's girlfriend, which then would be given an expressive reading in a falsetto voice.

The freshman quad, five dorms each housing 300 eighteen-year-olds bursting with testosterone, was like a minimum-security prison, only with stricter rules. Freshmen were required to live on campus and could not own a car. We had to be in bed by midnight with lights out (1 A.M. on weekends). No drinking. No female visitors, except for two hours after home football games with a hardbound textbook (not a paperback), placed lengthwise, propping the door open. Overnight passes had to be requested three days in advance, and an address and phone number provided. Otherwise, you had to sign in every night, and once you signed in, you could not leave the dorm until morning.

The rector of my dorm was named Father Ziti, and it was the joy of his life to enforce these rules. The other priests at Notre Dame usually wore pants, but Father Ziti always wore his black cassock, which fit snugly from the slope of his narrow shoulders to his little paunch, then hung like a skirt to the tops of his shiny black shoes. He was dove-colored and podgy, shorter than the shortest of us, and wore old-fashioned black wire-framed glasses like a Fellini padrone. He had a high, musical voice, and when he was excited he said everything twice. Catching us at some infraction, he would start by shouting: "Boys. Boys. What's this? What's this?"

And he was perpetually catching somebody in some infraction. He began his patrol exactly at midnight (lights out), walking the corridors with a stick long enough to push into the cracks under the doors on either side to make sure we were not blocking a light from inside our rooms with a towel. We could hear his footsteps from inside our locked rooms. Sometimes he wore one shoe and one sneaker so he could run and it would sound like he was walking. If you knelt down by the door and watched carefully, you could see the tip of his stick flick into the crack underneath. To enforce the rule against drinking, on random nights Father Ziti stood at the sign-in desk and smelled everyone's breath. In response, some boys would eat raw garlic after an evening of guzzling beer, with predictable effects on their stomachs and the communal johns, especially on St. Patrick's Day, when green beer was the drink of choice. For every minute of the two visiting hours after home football games, Father Ziti patrolled the halls, checking for a suspiciously shut door.

We all hated Father Ziti, and he hated many of us, but I had the distinction, by general agreement, of being hated by him the most. Father Ziti did not think I belonged at Notre Dame and told me so. Besides the misfortune of living down the hall from his suite, I had the additional misfortune of being enrolled in his theology course. I preregistered by mail before I got to Notre Dame and met him. The course was called "The Bible as Literature." We were required to take a theology course freshman year, and this one sounded the least religious.

I stayed after the first class meeting. I wanted to impress Father Ziti with my deep thinking but it ended up with me arguing about whether or not the historical Christ was God and him accusing me of blasphemy and heresy. Had I waited a few more classes, I would have induced that his theological positions were somewhere to the right of the Grand Inquisitor. I did my best to avoid Father Ziti over the next few weeks, but it was hopeless. Every time he saw me in the dorm, he looked at me as if I had just been scraped off his shoe. I knew he was thinking, Blasphemy and Heresy. It was indeed the way his mind worked, attaching a little phrase to each of us, probably because he was in charge of three hundred boys whom he could distinguish only by some mnemonic device. (There were three Michael Ryans in the dorm and four in the freshman class.) Besides giving me a grade, which God knows was disastrous enough, he could make my life miserable.

He got his chance about six weeks later. I had already gotten away with getting drunk every weekend with the Clubhouse Gang—usually in the cemetery or on the golf course, in the freezing cold, passing around pints of Seagram's and chasing them with quarts of Budweiser (wiping the mouths of the bottles with our gloved hands before upending them down our throats), then stumbling around the St. Mary's campus in our humorous canvas hats and blue-and-gold Notre Dame jackets screaming hilarious insults at girls when they couldn't see our faces. We would come back to the dorm early, before the rush at curfew when Ziti was likely to be smelling breath or snooping around, and we'd screw around in the Clubhouse with the door locked until the coast was clear ("Ziti's taking a leak") to sneak to our own rooms and sleep it off.

But the first Engineering Club smoker of the year was on a weeknight—three bucks for all the beer you could drink during a four-hour discussion of thermonuclear furnaces and hydraulic nozzles in a rented banquet room in South Bend. Whoopee. Ergs and foot-pounds! I found I was able to drink a statistically exceptional amount of beer during such a discussion. I got back to the dorm just before midnight. I have no idea how. I was so drunk I could barely talk, much less walk, as drunk as I had ever seen my father.

Father Ziti was standing at the sign-in desk, and, without so much as sniffing my breath, invited me to his suite for an interview. I remember following him down the corridor, the blur of sympathetic faces peeking out their doors like death-row inmates as I marched to the gas chamber. The worst thing about it was not Father Ziti telling me I stunk and was disgusting and did not belong at Notre Dame, but the panic at not being able to talk when I knew I was in big trouble if I couldn't. I had to conceal the fact that I was drunk and I couldn't. Words came out as primordial mush, and I finally gave up and nodded my agreement with each of Ziti's insults and muttered a pathetic "Yerssh, Faaartherr" when he told me to go to bed and try not to vomit all over myself.

I was put on disciplinary probation for the year and campused for the rest of the semester. For my next offense, however minor, I would be expelled. My curfew was changed from midnight to 10 P.M., every night including weekends. I was also required to sign in at the dorm four times a day (at ten, two, six, and ten) and to obtain permission from Father Ziti to leave campus, which, for the next three months, excluding Thanksgiving and Christmas, he chose not to grant.

I don't remember much of what I did for the rest of the semester, except stay on campus and not get drunk. I didn't study any more than I did before. With a ten o'clock curfew, a date was impossible, but it had already been impossible. Although I knew the guys were still joylessly passing around pints of Seagram's in the cemetery and stumbling around St. Mary's, and they would tell me what a shitty time they had had in order to console me, I still felt very sorry for myself and unbearably lonely. After seven o'clock on Friday and Saturday nights, the corridors were empty, the bathroom was empty, all the rooms were empty. Father Ziti was right: I didn't belong at Notre Dame. I had ruined my life—in two months I had gone from being a hot shot with a cuntcar and two different dates a weekend to being utter scum in a deserted dorm who was flunking pop quizzes and couldn't get a date with dopey girls with bad haircuts and midriff bulge. Where in God's name was I? What had I done to myself?

I was at least smart enough not to complain aloud. Everybody felt sorry for me—even Lockheed. Lockheed lived across the hall. He was from the Upper East Side of Manhattan and had gone to prep school in Connecticut, and was dark and smooth and lean as a lizard. He had a long face and a large, sensual mouth, and puffed on his boxed filter-tipped Benson & Hedges with an audible ungluing of his lips. He dressed beautifully, in the softest fabrics, cashmere sweaters, calfskin loafers. The rest of us threw on anything to go to class or the cafeteria (who was there to dress for?), but Lockheed color-coordinated his outfits, and wore the thickest, whitest Turkish robe down the hall to the shower, his imported soap-on-a-rope slung over one shoulder.

Even Lockheed never procured a date locally, although he would disappear to Chicago virtually every weekend. On his way out one Friday, he dropped by my room. "I've got a little present for you," he said. It was a twenty-page typescript pornographic story. He had brought it back from Chicago, and it had been circulating through the dorm for a week. I was dying to read it. So was everyone else. Lockheed had made a list on adding-machine paper and kept it folded in his wallet, crossing off the name when the story was returned and personally handing it to the next guy. "Don't get the pages sticky," he'd say every time. He wasn't showing the list to anyone, but as far as I could tell from the traffic at his room, it was constructed according to the order in which those listed could do him a favor in return. Since I was in no position to do him a favor in return, I didn't expect to see the story until sometime in the next decade.

He made me promise not to tell anybody I had it. He didn't want a reputation for being soft. Instead of dreading when the dorm emptied out that evening, I began to look forward to it. At dinner in the cafeteria everybody noticed my changed mood. I lofted a few gobs of mashed potatoes from my lap across the cafeteria, using my spoon as a catapult. I was making jokes as if I had plans to jet to the Bahamas with Jane Fonda for the weekend. "Ryan's cracking up," somebody said. "It's finally got to him." When the Clubhouse Gang in their humorous canvas hats and blue-and-gold Notre Dame jackets trooped out for their usual Friday night entertainment, I waved them off cheerily, imitating my mom. "Definitely cracking up," they said, and made the screwy sign twirling their fingers at their temples.

I locked my room and slipped the story from where I had sequestered it between the mattress and the net of springs of the bottom bunk. I placed it reverently on the pillow and switched off the overhead light and switched on my tensor light and stripped off my clothes and climbed into the bottom bunk with a fresh roll of toilet paper I had filched from the john. I preferred the bottom bunk to the top; it was like sleeping in a hutch, a coffin, a womb. At this moment the bottom bunk, in the silence and tiny beam of the tensor light, was the only world I wanted: my own comfy private horizontal projection booth for the story.

I had never read anything like it. It was ostensibly a letter from a precocious fourteen-year-old girl to her best friend. The typescript made it seem real and, although I knew it wasn't real, I believed these things happened, that there were people who felt this way and were this way and did these things, because this is the way I felt and was, and these were the things I wanted to do. The "letter" was about the girl's cute new stepfather, spying on him and her mother through their cracked bedroom door, then having sex with him herself in the hallway, all sorts of sex, explicitly described, the sexual organs enormous and proficient, the characters nothing but appetite. Kaboom, I was gone. The rush must be what it's like to freebase coke: my first taste of real hardcore porno. I wasn't lying alone on the bottom bunk in an empty room in an empty dorm at Notre Dame anymore: I was inside this hot young girl. I felt what she felt, I was doing what she did to her stepfather and her stepfather did to her, I was watching them and I was them, both of them at the same time. It was pure sex. I wanted it. Dear God, I wanted it. I didn't want to talk to anybody, I didn't want to be anybody. I just wanted it.

The story gave it to me. It was more than enough. Time evaporated, which had been hanging around my neck in a choke hold (ten, two, six, and ten). Time didn't exist. I somehow managed to delay my first orgasm until I had finished the story (which ended with the girl exhorting her friend to visit her and have sex with her stepfather, too), then reading it again and dwelling on the parts I liked best—the spying, the girl's desire, her descriptions, the initial seduction, the dramatic turns and extensions—bringing myself to climax at each of my favorite moments, so that in four hours or so I read the twenty pages only twice. I knew from my dad's soft-core detective novels the more I read it the less effective it would be. I wanted to savor it and save it for the next night.

At about eleven the grinds began returning from the library, and at about midnight the clunk and clatter of the revelers: footsteps, doors slamming, voices: the real world. The stupid shitty real world. When I heard the Clubhouse Gang come in, I switched the tensor light off. They stopped at my door. "He's asleep," a voice said. "No, he's dead," another voice said, and they all laughed. "Knock on the door," a third voice said. "No, let him sleep," the first voice said. "Let him sleep."

The next day, Saturday, I was in a fog all day. After masturbating with the story again that night, I did get up and get dressed and went to the Clubhouse when people began coming in at about midnight. The same old stuff. The usual tipsy horseplay and tales and complaints. It didn't seem possible anymore, or all too possible: this was my life. I was very quiet and sad. "You look funny," someone said. "What have you been doing, whacking it all night?"

I didn't understand what the story did to me. Everybody in the dorm knew what it was about, but nobody but Lockheed knew I had read it. Nobody, including Lockheed, knew how much I relished it. It was the first time I felt desire for a young girl, a porno girl, etched thereafter into my brain (I can still see her in the hallway with her stepfather). It was a molestation story, of course, transfigured and disguised. I would have been repulsed by the story of a man seducing a little boy. But this was a girl's story, it was heterosexual, she loved the sex, she wanted it. All I knew was that I wanted it, too, and I resented I didn't know who or what for not giving it to me, and blamed myself for not being strong enough to get it. I couldn't even get a date, and that wouldn't have been it anyway. I scrolled through all the stories I had made from the chances I had blown—Bunny, Sharon, Luscious Laura—and masturbated, usually in silence, whenever I had ten minutes alone in my room, wanting to scream out loud in frustration.

At home over Christmas vacation, I pooh-poohed my mother's fretting over my disciplinary probation and joked to my friends about the "social life" at Notre Dame. There were parties and dates over Christmas, but I didn't see Sally. She had a steady boyfriend now. I had not written to her nor called her, much less invited her to visit me at college. I hadn't indicated to her that I wanted to continue dating. I had simply said nothing about it, half-expecting that she would be available during vacations, half-expecting to meet someone I liked more at school, at home, at a truck stop, anyplace: Keeping My Options Open. Against all reason, I was disappointed when I called her and invited her to a Christmas party and she told me she couldn't go. But I also felt relief. I was glad she had a boyfriend. I didn't want to string her along, which is what I knew I had always done. It was better to be alone.

At the parties I didn't mention being campused and on disciplinary probation. I didn't mention desperately wanting to transfer to another school and being afraid I couldn't because I was on disciplinary probation. I didn't want anyone to think I wasn't doing well. I said I was considering switching out of engineering. The freshman curriculum was identical for premed and engineering, so I wouldn't lose any credits if I switched. I thought maybe I'd become a psychiatrist. (Nobody blinked when I said that.) Yeah, it was tough to get into med school. I was doing okay, not great. I'd do better next term. For this first semester I'd probably pull down about a 3.4.

Until the moment I saw my grade report in print, I really believed I would get a 3.4 or a 3.2 or a 3.0 at the lowest. I had written my English compositions during class the day they were due; I had flunked pop quizzes and skipped half the labs in chemistry, physics, and math; I had done rotten on midterms; but during finals week I was going to pull all-nighters and ace all the final exams. I didn't even know enough to know I had bombed them; or I couldn't admit it to myself. Using the percentages the teachers had allotted for pop quizzes, midterms, and finals, I had spent more time calculating what grades I'd have to get on the finals to squeeze out the next highest grades for the courses than actually studying for them.

Our grade reports were delivered to the dorm mailbox, rows of slots covered with little golden metal doors with combination locks built in. Everybody was running around and comparing and yelling and whooping, although a few boys like me went ashen-faced and silently walked back to their rooms and lay down on their bunks. I couldn't believe my eyes, but there it was, in black and white: two B's, C, D, and F. 1.6. I felt dizzy and nauseated. It couldn't be true, but it was. A nightmare. I'd never be able to transfer to another (coed) university. Forget about being a psychiatrist or anything else. When I was finally able to arise from my bunk and compose myself enough to go to the Clubhouse, I told everybody I had gotten a 2.6, raising all my grades one letter, except the B from Ziti (an A would not have been credible) and math (which I raised two letters to a C). I said how disappointed I was, which was obvious from my pallor. Somebody didn't believe the 2.6 and asked to see my grade report. I said I had already ripped it up and flushed it down the toilet, which was true. Nobody said anything else, but they all suspected I was lying.

The next day the Clubhouse Gang was headed for Chicago for semester break. We were going to hitchhike in pairs and bivouac at a cheap hotel in the Loop. As we were signing out, Ziti stopped me and asked me where I thought I was going. I said the semester was over and I wasn't campused anymore. He said number one the first semester was not over until the first day of the second semester and number two it was his decision whether or not I was campused anymore. I saw myself leaping across the desk and ripping his face apart like a puffy loaf of bread. Luckily, this image kept me from picturing the breathtaking desolation of five days alone in the dorm, and I did not try to argue with him. My visible reaction was probably only crestfallen astonishment.

"All right," he said, "I'm going to let you go on your trip. But you're still campused when you get back until you improve your grades. One point six. That's disgraceful. That's disgraceful. You missed academic probation by one-tenth of a point. In addition to your disciplinary conduct, you are almost flunking out of school, my good fellow. A fine beginning to a distinguished college career."

He said this in front of the whole group at the sign-out desk. I was too mortified even to joke about it. As we stood next to the on ramp to the tollway with our cardboard sign ("ND→Chicago"), my hitching partner confided to me that everybody already knew I had pumped my GPA. "No way you pulled a B from Ziti," he laughed.

In Chicago two guys rented a room and eight of us slept there, and we did what we did in South Bend—got drunk and complained about not meeting girls. It was a Saturday night. There was an all-college mixer the next afternoon but nowhere to go that night. I hadn't been really drunk since the Engineering Club smoker, but I made up for it. The room was on the eighteenth floor, and it had one unusually tall window that hung on a vertical axis like a revolving door and doubled as the thermostat. Despite the room costing about twelve dollars a night, it was heated through the subzero Chicago winter like a sauna. Everybody else, in shifts, went out to walk around the Loop and look for bars that wouldn't card us, but I stayed in the room drinking, getting more and more pugnacious, feeling meaner and crazier. I was desolate. Nobody knew how desolate. I needed dates. I needed sex. I was stuck at Notre Dame. I was stuck in this life. The Clubhouse Gang. What a joke. More like the Shithouse Gang. The Dumbshit Gang. I said it out loud. The Dumbshit Gang. A group of guys returned after cruising the Loop, kicked out of bar after bar, their cheeks crimson from the thirty-below windchill. Their blue-and-gold Notre Dame jackets were like a signboard that announced "Don't serve me, I'm underage." They loved their jackets so much they didn't even bring a heavier coat (nor did I).

"Hi, you flaming assholes," I said when they came in. "Hi, you flaming asshole," they responded. "No, you're *really* flaming assholes," I said seriously, belligerently. Mostly they just gave me one of the what's-with-you looks they had already been giving me more and more frequently, but one guy, the second-drunkest after me, told me I was really a flaming asshole each time I told him he was really a flaming asshole. He was the originator of the term "flaming asshole," and it was a great hit, spreading from the special vocabulary of the Clubhouse Gang to popular usage in the dorm. His name was Scan O'Grady. He weighed about 110 and had a puff of red hair. He looked like a kitchen match. He was a peripheral member of the Clubhouse Gang, the only English major, articulate and bright, with a startlingly deep voice, a folk music DJ on the campus radio station. He had read what I had read in high school, only more. When he was drunk, he'd recite Dylan Thomas from memory, his role model for his idea that the truly sensitive were raging and wild. It was the first I had heard of that idea (or of Dylan Thomas), but it made great sense to me. We mocked the rest of the Clubhouse Gang for their Top 40 musical taste and conservative politics and conventional ideas, and we had intellectual discussions, just the two of us, about Bob Dylan's lyrics and the CIA "advisors" in Vietnam. I liked him very much.

Ludicrously, he had brought a bowie knife to protect himself in the big city, and walked around with it stuck inside the waistband of his pants under his blue-and-gold Notre Dame jacket. It was about two feet long in its leather sheath, and nearly poked through his khakis above the knee every time he took a step. Coming into the room, bright red and very drunk, O'Grady had tossed it into his suitcase, which, like the other seven suitcases, was lying open on the floor. I fished it out of his unwashed underwear and held it up like a lawyer displaying the crucial piece of evidence. Here it is, ladies and gentlemen, objective tangible proof that Sean O'Grady is really a flaming asshole, because who but a flaming asshole would bring such a weapon to the big city? Who did he think he was, Davy Crockett? Where was his coonskin cap? O'Grady had been a champion debater in prep school, his father was a partner in one of the oldest law firms in New England, and he was planning to go to law school himself. He responded that on the contrary I was the flaming asshole, as demonstrated by my 1.6, which I had surely unintentionally misread and misrepresented as a 2.6, and, furthermore, I was stupid enough to get caught drunk by Ziti and campused, which I used as an excuse to make everybody put up with my bullshit, and here I was with the temerity to be calling everybody collectively the Dumbshit Gang and individually flaming assholes whereas everybody knew I was the one absolute certifiable official dumbshit flaming asshole in this room and probably the city of Chicago if not the entire universe and to put the knife back in the suitcase where I had found it and go fuck myself and the horse I rode in on.

Before I knew what was happening, I had unsheathed the knife and said maybe it was a good thing the little shit weasel had brought it along to the big city since I was going to make good use of it right fucking now, and I took a staggering step in his direction. Then I was on the floor under three or four guys and somebody wrenched the knife out of my hand and everybody was screaming at me telling me I was really a flaming asshole. They let me up, and, as automatically as I had unsheathed the knife, I stepped up onto the windowsill and pushed open the window. I remember my surprise at being on the windowsill, at how easy it was going to be to step out of this world. Then I was tackled again, and being screamed at again. I had finally shocked everyone. I started crying for them to let me alone and let me do what I want, it was my life, it was none of their business. "We're going to have to watch him all night," somebody said, and everybody was quiet and tiptoed around the room and treated me kindly, as if I were sick. I even got one of the two beds, in the corner farthest from the window.

The next day they all said I had scared the piss out of them and was I okay? I said I was just drunk. I apologized to O'Grady. He apologized, too. He asked if I was really going to stab him. No, I said. Sorry about that, I said. Did I really want to kill myself? he asked. Many of the existentialists had committed suicide, he added. It was a philosophical decision. I said no way, I was just smashed, I didn't know what the hell I was doing. But after we talked for a while in the hotel coffee shop, I confided in him that I was at the end of my rope at Notre Dame. I said something had to change.

Something did, that afternoon. At the all-college mixer I met a neat girl. She even danced with me the first time I asked (unlike the St. Mary's girls). She had been leaning against a wall with her ankles crossed, her hand under her elbow, chain-smoking, observing the proceedings of what she called the meat market from within a tent of long straight soft brown hair that framed her face and hung almost to her waist. Only folksingers had hair like this. Her name was Candice Norris, and she most emphatically did not wish to be called Candy. She was all hair and cheekbones and lips, and big brown eyes. Even with her thick sweater and long wool skirt, it was apparent there was barely a wisp of a body underneath; she was five five and might have weighed a hundred pounds in a football suit and holding a large wet dog. Otherwise, it was ninety if she had eaten a big breakfast. But she had panache. She had a quick wit and sweet irony and could talk with a cigarette in her mouth, which was a good thing since there was one there almost constantly. After we danced, we went back to her spot against the wall and talked. She had read a lot of books. She worked part-time in a bookstore. She was a philosophy major at De Paul. I was dazzled. A philosophy major! She had grown up in the suburbs and knew Chicago up and down: coffeehouses where you could listen to folk music, jazz bars where they'd let you drink Cokes, used-book stores, places to sit alone by the lake. When she felt depressed about the state of the world, she went to the petting zoo. Her dorm faced the lake; there was a window seat in her room where she read for hours on stormy days, and drank hot mugs of tea, and talked to her brilliant two-hundred-pound roommate, who was demonstrating her belief in the holiness of passion by having an affair with a three-hundred-pound married man who owned a shoe store and called their sex Rolling Thunder. She had other unusual friends: a black history professor in his forties whom she met while registering voters on the South Side, a blind Russian countess who had known Tolstoy and been a patient of Freud. This was what Candice liked: people who were just them-selves, whatever they were, a blind countess or a three-hundred-pound shoe salesman. No phoniness, no games. She agreed with me that things would be so much better if people could just be honest. There were more games going on out there (she gestured to the dance floor) than at a carnival. "What about you, Michael Ryan?" she asked, focus-ing her bright gaze on me. "Are you just another bullshit artist?"

We left the mixer together, and she drove me back to the hotel in her parents' car, an old Oldsmobile as long as the White Sow, wheel-ing it one-handed through the Loop, a cigarette dangling from her pouty lower lip. I didn't try to kiss her goodbye. I wanted this afternoon to be exactly what it had been. I was in love.

We wrote to each other, and soon we were writing every day, some-times twice—long handwritten letters, four or five sheets, both sides. In the same gold mailbox where I had gotten my grade report, there was invariably an envelope plump as a heart that I did not open until I was locked in my room and installed in the bottom bunk under the tensor lamp—as with the "letter" from the fourteen-year-old girl about her stepfather, only this was pure love and Candice's letters were real and written in her beautiful, clear hand to no one but me. They were an epistolary novel, our courtship. Since Father Ziti would not grant me permission to go to Chicago again, I had to write to her right away that I was campused and on disciplinary probation for being drunk. She wrote back that if she went to Notre Dame with its stupid rules she would also be campused and on disciplinary probation for being drunk. I admitted to her that I had gotten a 1.6 in engineering for the first semester. She said that if she had been in engineering first semester she would have gotten a 0.6. She wrote that nothing I had ever done in my life before mattered to her. She knew I was a creative guy. She knew I was a great soul. It was just a question of finding what I really liked.

I switched my major to philosophy. During lectures I wrote in the margins of my notebooks, "Candice is the reason for my existence." At the same time, O'Grady, remarkably, introduced me to his honors English teacher, who, after talking with me for ten minutes, even more remarkably invited me to transfer into his honors English class, despite my 1.6, which he dismissed with a mumble and a flick of his hand. His name was Frank O'Malley. He was a legendary teacher at Notre Dame, in his final years. He was a bachelor and celibate and for thirty years had lived in a single room in Lyons Hall (the intellectual dorm) surrounded by undergraduates. He dressed immaculately in three-piece blue suits, silk ties, and French-cuffed starched white shirts that matched the sweep of white hair that haloed his blazing face. His class was at four on Tuesday and Thursday afternoons, and he did not teach a class that year before he had a few drinks and sometimes many drinks. None of us cared. He loved the books he taught, and he treated us as if we were destined to make great contributions to humanity. He spoke of great books and great ideas with great passion and made us believe in them and in ourselves. The honors freshman English class, with fifteen select students, was the only small class he taught. He announced the first day that we would all get an A in the course (which drove the English Department crazy). We would read five books, starting with Joyce's *Portrait of the Artist as a Young Man*, and we could respond to these books in any way we wished, discursively or creatively, in any genre, and we would share these responses with our colleagues (suddenly, I had *colleagues*!). The class itself was always the same. Professor O'Malley would walk in five minutes late, cigarette in hand and ancient buckled leather case under his arm stuffed with the papers we had turned in. He'd dig into the case, his hands shaking, smearing ashes on his vest, and pull out one of our papers. He'd hold it up with both hands like a sacred thing, pausing a moment as if he were recalling its many pleasures and profound wisdom. Then he'd ask, with the utmost deference, if the author of (he'd read the title, looking over the top of his glasses) would consent to share it with his colleagues. What a thrill it was when he spoke the title of something you had written. When the reading was finished, Professor O'Malley would invariably ask the same question of the class, "What has the author accomplished in this work?" He always managed to steer us to talking about it as a response to the book we had been reading and then to the book itself, about its spirit, about the way it addressed "the human condition." We talked a lot about "the human condition." On the days I read something I had written (which were many: I discharged reams of poems, stories, plays, and unclassifiable effusions), I would invent an excuse to speak to Professor O'Malley after class. I never had to use the excuse because, before I said a word, he'd mumble, "A great work, Michael, a great work," and literally bless me, making a just-perceptible sign of the cross with the two fingers of his right hand, between which was lodged his filter-tipped Salem like the burning crossbeam of the Crucifix.

Between Candice and Professor O'Malley, I imagined someone I could become: someone they thought I already was *in potens* (I used Latin terms at every opportunity), someone they loved and respected. Exactly who this person was was not clear, except for his value. He was a worthy person, a very fine person, sensitive, deep, alienated, tormented, unappreciated by the corrupt world but destined for triumph: an intellectual creative neat guy. And not bad-looking either.

But what good was a new self-image if it were not made public? Therefore, I announced to everyone I knew that when I was a senior I was going to be the editor of *The Juggler*. *The Juggler* was the campus literary magazine. Professor O'Malley was the faculty advisor. Each spring the next year's editor was appointed by the current editor in consultation with *The Juggler* staff, the elite coterie of intellectual creative neat guys who lived in Lyons Hall and won fellowships to Harvard and Yale and scholarships to Oxford and Cambridge and had their own extracurricular intellectual discussion group (by invitation only) on philosophical and literary topics, which they called, after Samuel Johnson's, the Wranglers. The appointment of the editor of *The Juggler* was tantamount in my mind to being named the top intellectual creative neat guy on campus by a jury of his peers. And this, I announced, was going to be me. "Sure it will"; "Fat chance"; "And I think I'll be editor of the *New York Times*," were representative responses, especially from the Clubhouse Gang.

I sold my blue-and-gold Notre Dame jacket for five bucks and threw my humorous canvas hat into the dumpster outside the Huddle. Instead of hanging around the Clubhouse at night, I went to the library and spent an hour a page on Aristotle's *Metaphysics*, trying to really understand the difference between a first and formal cause. After a brisk shower and a balanced breakfast, I'd claim a carrel by placing a stack of books in it topped by a yellow highlighter, and study there between classes and after dinner until my 10 P.M. curfew. On Friday and Saturday nights, my idea of a good time was to go to the library and write a short story or read an extra book Professor O'Malley had mentioned in passing.

When the Clubhouse Gang started riding me for becoming a grind and sitting with the fems in the cafeteria ("Aren't we sensitive enough for you anymore?"), I explained to them that they were a bunch of superficial assholes who were never going to do anything with their lives, and that I had better things to do with mine. I said this, in these words, in the Clubhouse, to four guys playing blackjack on an upside-down wastebasket in the middle of the room, and three more guys lounging on the bunks. WLS, the Top 40 AM radio station from Chicago, was as always blaring in the background; except for the DJ's brain-pulping chatter, the response was silence, until someone finally replied, "Well, excuse us poor peons, Mr. Sensitive Intellectual. If you just get the fuck out of here, we'll just go on with our superficial, worthless lives. And don't ever come back, asshole. You're not welcome here anymore." "Fine with me," I said without remorse.

It made them very angry. Despite the time I was spending in the library, it was impossible to avoid them. For a couple of days they snubbed me and I snubbed them, but then, no doubt as a group decision, every time I passed two or more of them together, they'd say, "Hi, Asshole." They said it in a friendly tone, as if they were saying "Hi, Michael." It happened at least ten times a day, sometimes when I was talking with people I didn't know very well, whose good opinion I wanted to cultivate, and once when I was walking Professor O'Malley part way to Lyons Hall before the turnoff to the freshman quad. He gave me a puzzled look. "Old friends of mine," I said. Since I would be expelled for fighting, I didn't have any other choice but to wait them out, and fighting would have led to more fighting anyway. I figured eventually they'd get tired of this tactic if they didn't get a response from me. And they did get tired of it, but their getting tired of it wasn't the end of it.

I had come back from the library as usual for the 10 P.M. sign-in, and, according to my new regimen, went directly to my room, wrote a letter to Candice, read over lecture notes for the next day's classes, and went to sleep. Sound asleep. The next thing I knew I had been hit hard in the face by something big. I jumped up and smacked my head on the top bunk, walked into a wall, slipped and fell, got to my feet, and bounced off my locker with a crash before I knew where I was or even if I was in three-dimensional space. I had no idea what happened. It took another minute before I realized I was shivering. I was dripping with ice-cold water. Or something. I turned on the light. Somebody had thrown in my face a wastebasket full of slush, turds, toilet cakes, and garbage, including approximately fifty slips of soggy scrap paper with "Fuck You, Asshole" typed on them. There was some kind of perfumed lavatory cleaner in the concoction that burnt my skin and smelled like a hospital. My bed was soaked, the floor was soaked, I was soaked. Everything stunk. I went to the Clubhouse door. It was locked, and dark inside. I said to it, as loudly as I could without waking Ziti, "I know you motherfuckers did this, and I'm going to get you for it." Luckily, they did not open the door. I was wild with fury. If they had opened the door, I would have jumped them and I would have been expelled, and they knew it. I'm sure they had decided in advance not to open the door.

The next day they greeted me with nods and smiles. I fumed, and expressed again my estimate of their worth and prospects, and they nodded and smiled some more. I don't know if they thought I'd do anything or not. They were simply waiting, as if saying, It's your move. The tension was palpable for about a week, and then it slowly deflated. I didn't do anything. I didn't want to cut my own throat. I never went into the Clubhouse again. My revenge would have to be slow and sweet. I would make something of myself. I would make the whole world admit it, including them.

It made O'Grady mad, because I couldn't retaliate. It offended his sense of fair play. He found an opportunity to tell Professor O'Malley that I was still being campused for a little innocent drinking bout first semester and that I was in love with a girl in Chicago I consequently couldn't go see. Professor O'Malley immediately scrawled a note for O'Grady to deliver to Father Ziti: "Dear Antonio," the note read, "For God's sake, please remove the disciplinary sanctions on Michael Ryan. He is a splendid student and a fine young gentleman. Sincerely, Frank O'Malley." O'Grady told me that Ziti turned his characteristic arresting shade of pink when he read the note. But the next week Ziti informed me I was no longer campused, although my disciplinary probation would remain in effect until the end of the semester.

Thereafter, I went to Chicago as often as I could, as often as Candice could find a place for me to sleep. We didn't sleep together. She was afraid of intercourse because, she said, she was so small, which had the compensation of making me feel big. Each time she promised we would do it, but not this time, and we'd roll around and grope. She was as light as a child, and, except for her makeup and hair and full, fleshy lips, when she was naked she looked like a child. I did not find this erotic, but sex was only erotic when it was bad, and this was love, and love was good. I had no other sexual prospects anyway, except myself and my fantasy partners, and I'd do it with them for five minutes a day, as quickly as possible, sometimes in a locked stall in the men's room in the library between chapters of Aristotle. It was like spitting. It was a bad taste in my mouth, a distraction from finer things, a feeling to get rid of, if I could.

THE PINCH

I became the editor of *The Juggler*, of course. An orangutan could have become the editor of *The Juggler* if he needed to as much as I did. From the second semester of my freshman year until the last month of my senior year, I studied ten hours a day, including weekends. I subscribed to the *New York Review of Books* and read it cover to cover. When it mentioned a composer, I went to the library and listened to his music; when it mentioned a painter, I looked him up in Janson's *History of Art*. Ditto the writers and philosophers, finding a way to casually drop their names into conversation with my professors. Through the championship of Professor O'Malley, I was accepted into the Committee for Academic Progress—the honors program—which meant I was exempted from all requirements, including the odious yearly theology requirement, and was allowed to register early for any course I wanted. I loved reading books, sitting in a comfy chair, the way the hours disappeared into that intimate voice from the page inside my head, but this happened increasingly only with novels, plays, and poems. I had never enjoyed reading Aristotle or Plato or whoever as much as the idea that I was reading Aristotle or Plato or whoever. I peppered my classroom comments with Kant and Hegel without cracking their dreary thick tomes, having picked up their general drift from Will Durant's *Story of Philosophy* or some other survey or encyclopedia. I pretended I read what I hadn't read when I thought I could get away with it and, as in high school, spoke as much and as often as the teachers, and twice as much and as often as any other student. I wanted to be educated and intelligent, but infinitely more than that, I wanted everyone to think I was educated and intelligent, and not only educated and intelligent but the most educated and intelligent (and creative) student on campus: the editor of *The Juggler*.

I broke up with Candice when I returned to Notre Dame at the beginning of my sophomore year. I didn't love her anymore. I didn't know why. Her letters started to seem cloying and clinging. To my surprise, I didn't miss her. Nights would go by and I'd climb into bed and realize I hadn't thought about her all day. Although the "social life" at Notre Dame wasn't appreciably different than it had been freshman year, I didn't want to go to Chicago and I didn't want her to visit me. "Why? Why?" she asked when I told her on the phone. But I didn't know why. "Is there somebody else?" she asked. There wasn't, but there was everybody else. Just seeing some girls gave me a buzz she didn't. Her fear of Doing It made me not want to Do It with her. She was so self-conscious, she seemed ashamed to take off her clothes. Sex with her wasn't sexy for me. I wanted it hot and dark, I wanted to be taken by it, and with her it was more like a negotiation. I sometimes got the feeling she'd just as soon not.

She insisted on seeing me one last time, and took a bus to South Bend. I met her at the bus station. She looked awful—skinny, red-eyed, pathetic, smoking constantly, her fingers shaking, her fingernails bitten. When she got off the bus, she said, "Don't look at me." She said she was taking the next bus back to Chicago. She didn't want to go anywhere to talk. We sat in the bus station cafeteria with the poor people, drinking coffee under the fluorescent lights, which made her look even worse. Since I couldn't explain why I didn't love her anymore, I said that we should keep in touch, that maybe I just needed to find myself. She kept making ironic references to my being lost and the big day when I'd find myself, laughing hollowly. She said ever since I dumped her, people seemed like cardboard cutouts. She said she had to see me to see if I also seemed like a cardboard cutout. "Do I?" I asked. "Yes," she answered. She gave me a Simon and Garfunkel album ("Hello darkness my old friend") and two books of poems— *Selected Poems* by George Seferis and *A Coney Island of the Mind* by Lawrence Ferlinghetti (an odd pair). They were goodbye gifts. Then she stepped onto the bus. I wondered if I should stand there and wave. That's what I did before whenever we parted, waving not only until we could no longer see each other but until the bus itself was out of sight. This time I walked away. I imagined her looking out the window and seeing the concrete post where I had stood, seeing my absence.

It made me sad, but it cleared the decks. I was alone now. Everyone, everything out of my way. I was going to be Great. I studied with a fury. I shared a room in Lyons with Sean O'Grady. We drew the last available room, an eight-by-ten double, in which we couldn't pass each other without walking sideways. There wasn't even enough space in it for a reading chair: just the bunk beds, the sink, and the lockers, and a narrow reinforced shelf nailed to the wall that could be used as a desk. But it was worth it to be in the same dorm as Professor O'Malley and rub elbows with the campus intellectuals. We both published poems in *The Juggler*, and were invited to join the Wranglers, which, for that year, was devoted to a study of Wittgenstein. The Wranglers met in the basement of a pizza restaurant off campus. We drank beer out of pitchers, but I'd drink no more than a glass or two, not like at the Engineering Club smoker. I was engrossed in the subject and exhilarated to be included in this company. These were the smartest people I had ever met. I memorized key sentences in German from Wittgenstein's books and popped them into the discussion at opportune moments, generously offering to elucidate the subtle-but-crucial distinctions between the English translation and the original. We spent one whole evening on the meaning of the last sentence of the

Philosophical Investigations: "About which one cannot speak, one must be silent" (or, as I eagerly pointed out, *"Was man kann nicht sprechen, worüber er müss schweigen."*)

The Wranglers were a close-knit group. Our teachers made us feel we represented the real Notre Dame, Notre Dame at its best. We were the ones in touch with the times, the cultural vanguard, as the sixties belatedly began to bleed into even the provincial, secure Notre Dame campus. We let our hair grow, we gave up our Christmas dinner in the cafeteria for black sharecroppers in Mississippi, we protested ROTC and Dow Chemical and CIA recruitment, and we experimented with drugs to expand our consciousnesses ("Better living through chemistry"). We questioned authority and we did not trust anyone over thirty. We defined ourselves against the public image of the school— the football team, the conservative Catholicism, the roaring boys in humorous canvas hats and blue-and-gold Notre Dame jackets—but the aggressive all-male competition that manifested itself in football and rugby and the annual campus boxing tournament in which boys pummeled one another bloody to the accompaniment of bloodthirsty cheering, such macho idiocies as we mocked and mimicked, we translated unconsciously into the sharp ironies and rhetorical gambits of the Wranglers. Underneath the bonhomie and camaraderie of the group, I saw that the idea was nonetheless the same: to win. To be Number One. We were all smart, but somebody got the prestigious awards and big fellowships, and somebody didn't, and I was going to be the one who did.

I enrolled in a Plato course with senior Wranglers and graduate students in philosophy. The only previous philosophy course I had taken was a freshman introduction. I was way out of my league and I knew it, but I studied each of the dialogues relentlessly, outlined their themes and arguments, noticed which character said what, read extra commentaries, took meticulous notes in class, and kept my mouth shut for a change unless I was sure of what I was talking about. Because our room in Lyons was so small, I did most of my studying in the library, but late the night before the final exam I was reading through my notes on my bunk when someone knocked on our door and said the boy who lived in the room directly below us had hung himself. He was also a sophomore. I hardly knew him. He played lacrosse and usually wore his blue-and-gold lacrosse jersey around the dorm. He had short blond hair and was always grinning. The ambulance came, and the police, and, weirdly, the fire department in yellow rubber boots and red hats carrying axes over their shoulders. The halls were filled with people until 4 A.M. His roommate was taken to the infirmary and his friends were crying. Many people were crying. Then the details started to come out. He had been found naked with *Playboy* foldouts all over the room. He had hung himself from the bottom bunk. I didn't understand at first. The bottom bunk? There were two metal crosspieces that supported the net of springs of the top bunk, and he had attached a short noose to one and lodged his ankles underneath the other. His death, it seemed, was an accident. Apparently, he had been reaching orgasm by choking himself. It was in *Justine* by the Marquis de Sade. The idea was to catch yourself after orgasm and before losing consciousness. This time he couldn't work his ankles loose. He had passed out before he could get the noose off.

I didn't sleep that night, and when I went into the exam the next morning, I was still rattled. I bombed it miserably and got a C in the course. It didn't even occur to me to ask to postpone the exam. Such things weren't done. You did not make excuses or ask for special treatment. Everything was impersonal and rigorous, especially in upper-level philosophy courses. Later, when I told the professor what had happened (omitting the details), he said he was sorry but he didn't see what he could do. It would be unfair to my classmates to allow me to retake the exam. My C would have to stand.

This is what I felt about the boy who hung himself: he made me get a C in Plato. I didn't feel anything else about him. I didn't identify with him at all. I wasn't like him. I never considered choking myself to orgasm. I didn't know such a thing was possible, and this certainly didn't tempt me to try it. I didn't see myself in the split between his clean-cut grin and his secret life: his locking his door, his stripping off his clothes, his carefully spreading the foldouts on the floor and bed beneath him before he slipped his ankles under the crosspiece and his neck into the noose. Did he have a favorite arrangement, Miss March here, Miss April there? Where did he stash them? And what about the noose? Did he stash it with the foldouts? Did he stash it tied or remake it each time as part of the ritual, from the same hallowed piece of rope?

It was just a creepy thing he did—this was the general attitude. His friends mourned the boy they knew. At the memorial service the way he died was of course not mentioned. O'Grady just shook his head and wouldn't talk about it, and neither would anyone else. It seemed ungenerous to remember him this way, for what he had kept hidden, instead of for his outgoing friendliness, brightness, and good humor.

We just went on with our lives. When we looked at each other, we didn't ask ourselves, What bizarre sexual shit is that guy into? The public reality was so extremely the opposite. A date was still big news in the dorm, at least among the sophomores—it was so rare anyone got one. O'Grady had not kissed a girl since grade school, and his (lack of) experience was not uncommon. I did not have my first date with a St. Mary's girl until months after I broke up with Candice. Her name was Vanessa Sheffield. When she agreed to go out with me, she said (sincerely), "I think I'm free two weeks from Tuesday." I hopped on it. We went out two weeks from Tuesday: a study date, culminating in two scoops of ice cream in the Huddle and a brisk walk back to St. Mary's.

Vanessa had very black hair and very white skin and very blue eyes, and was from an old Virginia family that lived on a former plantation and still employed black people as house servants. I hooted when she told me that. She was embarrassed by it and didn't try to defend it, but she also did not like me insulting her parents. They were prominent Republicans and patrons of the John Birch Society. Vanessa and I did not get along at all, the first time or subsequent times, but I continued to ask her out because she was pretty and I had no other prospects. I also wanted to have sex with her. The more she irritated me, the more I wanted her. Over Christmas vacation she broke her back horseback riding and dropped out of school, and I lost touch with her until I got a call out of the blue a year later, my second semester junior year. Since we had spent the vast majority of the time on our three or four dates bickering, I asked her why she had called me. "Because you wanted to fuck me," she said. In the intervening year, despite her broken back, she had taken eight guys to bed, including the stableboy. And, she told me, she was on the Pill.

I took her to my room in Lyons Hall the next Sunday afternoon. The rector of Lyons was the opposite of Father Ziti. You would have had to burst into his suite with twelve naked women and a wheelbarrow full of narcotics to be put on disciplinary probation. As soon as I closed the door, Vanessa suggested we dispose of our clothes and get down to business. We did it seven times. During sex she growled like a dog. After the third time, as we were lying in my bunk with her snuggled into the crook of my arm, she said, "How come you don't do anything that feels good?"

"What do you mean?" I asked, thus confirming the implication of her question.

She pulled me onto the floor and straddled me like an English saddle. "Just lie there," she said. "I'll do it."

And she did, apparently to her satisfaction. She was my girlfriend for the rest of the term. She had changed during her year at home. Now she was furious at her parents, their falsity and snootiness, the numbers they pulled on her. They wanted her to be their proper little lady to show off to the world. "Well, they can cram that," Vanessa said. We still argued all the time, but I liked the wild bitterness that seemed to fuel her sexual appetite. Her favorite word was bullshit. The "social life" at Notre Dame, especially, was bullshit. She had no patience whatsoever for the brutality and misogyny of Notre Dame "men" (she put quotes around the word with her voice) who, she firmly believed, were afraid of sex. Their brutality and misogyny was to hide their fear of sex. In her opinion, they could do all the moralistic Victorian Catholic loop-the-loops they wanted. It was all bullshit.

In the spring was the annual ROTC review. Notre Dame had the largest ROTC unit in the country outside of the military academies and Texas A & M. Each year Father Hesburgh reviewed the troops at an official ceremony complete with awards for the best cadets and a marching band and a review stand decorated with military bunting. Vanessa thought this was quintessential Notre Dame bullshit, and she agreed to accompany me to the anti-ROTC demonstration. "My father would have a cow," she giggled. I had participated in the anti-ROTC demonstration since my freshman year, when there were five demonstrators and fifty antidemonstrator demonstrators (including a couple of guys from the Clubhouse Gang). With the war in Vietnam growing and more American soldiers dying, this year (1967) we were up to about fifty demonstrators, but hundreds of students and parents attended the ceremony to honor the troops, and we were confined to a rope-enclosed space way off to the side where all we could do was walk in a circle with our handmade picket signs ("Hell No We Won't Go") surrounded by jeering boys in blue-and-gold Notre Dame jackets, some of them actually waving flags, screaming that we were traitors and cowards and faggots who would at a more opportune moment be getting the shit kicked out of us but good. We had decided after the obligatory tedious three-hour meeting on the subject to make our protest nonviolent according to the principles of Gandhi and Martin Luther King. (There had never been any other kind of Notre Dame demonstration.) We would ignore the heckling as much as possible; if we were attacked, we would drop into the fetal position with our arms covering our heads. (No one had ever been attacked at a Notre Dame demonstration.) The veterans of the civil rights marches in Mississippi and Alabama showed us how to do this, and how to go limp when the police arrested us. (No one had ever been arrested at a Notre Dame demonstration.) The last hour was spent debating whether or not St. Mary's students should be allowed to participate in a Notre Dame demonstration. Vanessa was one of the three St. Mary's demonstrators, and the only good-looking one, and every time she passed the worst knot of hecklers, their jeering became more anatomically specific. It was torture for me, but she seemed amused. I wanted her to ignore them. She started winking at them when we passed, which provoked them even more. They were screaming for her to strip, to see her pussy, that she was a whore, etc. It was ugly. As we were circling around again to where they were, I told her through clenched teeth to for God's sake stop winking, and she said, "Okay. Watch this." She pinched her miniskirt at the thigh and hiked it up an inch. When she got the deafening howl in response she had expected, she walked right up to the rope barrier and gave them the finger with both hands and laughed in their faces. I thought we wouldn't get out of there alive, but she knew them better than I did. They stayed behind the rope barrier. All they did was yell.

Vanessa had been a freshman when I met her, and wasn't able to finish the semester when she broke her back, so even completing this term when I was a second-semester junior, she would still be a freshman the following fall. She didn't know if she'd come back to St. Mary's or not. She had only come back this term at her parents' insistence and to get away from home. She decided she couldn't handle living at home for the summer, and said she'd let me know when she got to where she was going since she didn't know herself where that would be. I got a call from her in Steeltown a few weeks later. She had a job as a chambermaid in Provincetown, Massachusetts, and was living in a boardinghouse. She had a double bed and the nights were cool and she wanted me to come up and keep her warm—no, she corrected herself, not warm. Hot. Come up and keep her hot.

I had a summer job as usual (as Mister Softee, selling chocolate and vanilla SoftServe from the back of a truck in the poorest section of Steeltown). This was also the summer in which I was going to read all the Russian classics and write a novel. Vanessa argued that I could read all the Russian classics and write my novel just as easily in Provincetown, that on her chambermaid's salary she would support me in the style to which I was accustomed, and that if I didn't get my ass up there soon I would find my side of the bed occupied.

I put off going. I think I knew I wouldn't last in such a situation with Vanessa for very long. It was August by the time I got there and in fact

I stayed less than two weeks. I was twenty-one. It was my first experience living with a girlfriend and sleeping with her every night. The
room, on the third floor at the top of a creaky staircase, was not much
bigger than the bed. It was an old brass bed with very weak springs. You
couldn't move a millimeter without waking the other person, not to
mention the symphonic squeaking during sex. The boardinghouse was
run by a gay couple, and there were gay men in all the rooms who bellowed at the top of their lungs at orgasm and had terrible arguments in
which they called each other bitches and wore silk kimonos to the
bathroom down the hall. I didn't know anybody else in town besides
Vanessa, and the extravagant gay scene made me nervous. Nobody had
ever fluttered his tongue at me before. Vanessa got up at six A.M. and
came back about four P.M., and had to go to sleep at ten. I stayed up all
night writing and reading. When she woke up at six, she wanted to have
sex, and when she came back at four, she wanted to have sex, and before she went to sleep at ten she wanted to have sex. After a few days it
wasn't fun anymore. I was drained dry as a saltine. I thought she would
do as well with any reasonably firm inanimate cylindrical object—a
fireplug, for example. I suggested this to her, and we fought. We had
sex only once a day for a couple of days and she complained. We fought
some more, and I stuffed my novel and my Russian classics into my
gym bag and got onto the bus to Boston. She still didn't know if she
would be going back to St. Mary's, and I didn't know if I'd ever see her
again. It surely seemed like goodbye, but to make it easier we didn't say
so. We said we'd probably see each other at Notre Dame in a couple of
weeks. I thought my side of the bed would be occupied before the bus
passed through Wellfleet.

My friend Timmy Flaherty would be at Boston College in a week,
and I could crash in his room and hang out with him, but this still left
a week to kill. I called Sean O'Grady in Hartford, and he said sure,
come and stay with his family for the week. He said I would be bored
shitless, but I wouldn't starve. Sean's family lived in an enormous
white clapboard house on ten acres overlooking the city. It had four

porches, one with a porch swing that could seat six, although there were only three people in the family, not including Elizabeta, their ancient Hungarian maid. Sean was adopted. Whereas he was small, red-haired, and bird-boned, both his parents were dark, robust, and tall. His father (the lawyer) had played football for Notre Dame (class of '34) and had been a fighter pilot in the South Pacific. He had a Royal Air Force mustache and a nose like a stepladder—the nose as the souvenir of a legendary landing on an aircraft carrier under fire during a storm. He had no patience for nonsense. His time was valuable and he let you know it. He was always jetting to Washington to consult with the finance minister of some third-world country his firm represented. Troubleshooting, he called it. During that week he was home for one meal, the first one, during which I sat on my tongue while he lectured on the International Communist Conspiracy that had to be faced down in Vietnam and wherever else it reared its ugly head for however long it took, by God.

By contrast, Sean's mother was a nervous, elegant woman who doted on her son and loved his friends. She was in her fifties and always wore a single strand of pearls and gathered her long black hair up in a bun with a lacquered Chinese stick through it. I had met her already. She had come to Notre Dame for Parents Weekend, by herself, since Sean's father was in Saudi Arabia or someplace troubleshooting. She kissed me the first time we met, then apologized for it. "I just feel I know you so well from everything Sean has told me." I didn't think anything of it, since she kissed all of Sean's other friends, too. As we were standing uncomfortably around the dorm lounge with a couple of Wranglers and their parents, none of whom had previously met one another, she asked me suddenly and apropos of nothing what I thought of T. S. Eliot. I, who was almost never speechless when given the chance for self-display, was speechless. Sean quickly made a joke about his mother always trying to turn any gathering of three or more people into a literary salon.

Sean picked me up at the bus station, and when I walked into their house, his mother embraced me, then held my shoulders in both of her hands. "Look at you," she said.

I had no idea what she meant by that, and I tried to cover it with a smile.

"You're so tanned and healthy and young," she explained, her eyes teary. "You boys break my heart."

Her husband was already seated at the head of the dinner table, acutely inconvenienced because the meal had been delayed by my arrival, and chronically uninterested in his wife's enthusiasms, especially for the health, youth, and skin pigment of Sean's friends. He stood up with his napkin in one hand and firmly shook my hand with the other and told me to wash up for dinner. I washed up and we sat down to dinner, served by the Hungarian maid who referred to Sean as "Butchska," which was when we got the lecture on the International Communist Conspiracy. It may have been triggered by my hair. Sean's father kept eyeing it when he thought I wasn't looking, and before the dinner was finished, he told Sean he was due for a haircut, although Sean's hair wasn't half the length of mine. It looked like it was going to be an interminable week, but Sean told me after dinner that his father was going away on business the next morning and to ignore his mother, who was wigged out because the summer was almost over and Sean was going back to Notre Dame and leaving the two of them alone together. He said that, despite appearances, it was easier for him to handle his father than his mother. He said he probably should have warned me, but frankly he was overjoyed when he got my call. He was so bored, his brain was about to start dripping out of his nostrils.

There was in fact not much to do. We were going into our senior year at Notre Dame and, unlike me, Sean didn't have friends at home from high school. He had gone away to prep school, so he had never associated with local kids; his attitude toward them was a little snobbish and superior. He wasn't athletic and he never had a summer job, so he never met anybody in those ways either. He swore this was the last summer he'd ever spend at home. He had been reading the Russian classics, too, and also trying to write a novel (because I was, I thought), which he characterized as "an egregious piece of shit." His father believed Sean was wasting his time. He wanted Sean to intern at the law firm, but Sean insisted that (like me) he was going to get a Ph.D. in English, and his father had been needling him about it at every opportunity. His mother, on the other hand, thought it was just wonderful. Sean could not wait for the fall semester to begin so he could get out of there.

We sat on the big porch swing with his mother and drank dark rum and grapefruit juice, while his father locked himself in his study with a stack of documents about the Saudis he had obtained from the State Department. He was gone by the time we got up the next morning. In the afternoon we went swimming (in their private pool). We went to Hartford for an ice cream. We went to a movie. We sat around and read. We watched something dumb on TV. In whatever room we were (and there were many in the house), his mother wanted to be there also. She tried very hard to leave us alone, and kept saying things like "Pardon me for bothering you two" and "I know you two have things to talk about a mother shouldn't hear"—a lot of "you two" this and "you two" that. Finally, sighing, Sean said, "Mother, we're really very happy to have your company." Thereafter, she left us alone during the day but spent the evenings with us.

She told me about twelve times each day how happy she was I was visiting Sean. She kissed me in the morning when I came down for breakfast and kissed me good night when she went upstairs to bed. She touched me frequently—when I passed her, when she spoke to me— usually on the arm, but a few times on the thigh when we were sitting on the porch swing. I started touching her in response, which surprised her. One night, out of boredom, Sean and I went through the family albums. There were baby pictures of him in a plastic swimming pool with his mother leaning over in a bathing suit revealing large firm breasts and plenty of cleavage. These pictures were twenty years old, but I started fantasizing about her. I liked the weird way it made me feel. It had been a few days since I had been having sex constantly with Vanessa, and I started to want sex again, to really want it.

In response to Sean's complaints about there being nothing to do, the next evening after dinner Sean's mother suggested a game of three-handed bridge. I was to leave the day after next. Sean's mother had reserved theater tickets in Boston for the three of us, and afterward they'd drop me at Boston College, spend the night at the Ritz-Carlton (in their usual suite), and visit the museum the next day. She said she was already starting to miss me. We'd deal a dummy and bid our hands, and one of us would play the contract while the other two defended. "What should we play for, Michael?" she asked me. My knee touched hers under the table. She did not move hers away. I slipped off my sandal and soon I was rubbing up and down her calf with the instep of my bare foot. It put me in my trance. She started misdealing, trumping when she still had cards in the suit, overtaking her partner's kings with aces, wasting trick after trick, and giggling nervously. "Are you drunk, Mother?" Sean asked.

When she went to bed, she kissed me good night as usual. Sean was in the room. But the next morning I woke up with her standing next to my bed in a light green negligee.

"Elizabeta's at the market and I've sent Sean downtown to get his hair cut," she said. She had let her hair down. It was the only time I saw her without her lacquered Chinese stick.

That's all I remember. I fell back asleep immediately. She must have awakened me about 9 A.M., and every day Sean and I had been sleeping to noon. We had drunk a lot of dark rum and grapefruit juice while we played cards, and more of it after she went to bed. He had confided in me that unless she were going through some advanced stage of menopause he really thought she was losing her mind. How she managed to get him up before 9 A.M. for a haircut is a mystery, but, except to hear her say this one sentence whose implication didn't register on me, I couldn't wake up. By the time I did wake up and come downstairs, Elizabeta was back from the market and Sean's hair was neatly trimmed above the ears. "Fucker scalped me," he said.

I took my breakfast dishes into the kitchen where Sean's mother was standing by herself facing the sink.

"I'm sorry I didn't wake up this morning," I said.

"Don't think twice about it," she snapped. She wouldn't look at me. Insane as it was, I *was* sorry. I would have had sex with her. I wanted to have sex with her. She was almost three times my age, she had liver spots on her hands and purses of flesh under her upper arms—not to mention the facts that she was somebody else's wife and my friend's mother. None of that mattered to me when I went into my erotic trance, and it was in fact what made it erotic. Sex with a girl my own age might be fun, but it wasn't erotic. It was expected and accepted and appropriate. This was forbidden and secret and dirty. I wanted it and she wanted it. And as I had done so many times before in these situations, I had blown it.

She was furious. She couldn't wait to get me out of her house. She didn't address me or look at me again, much less kiss me or touch me. I don't think Sean noticed the difference. "I'm going to leave you two alone today for your last day together," she said to him. The next morning she canceled their trip to Boston because of a migraine and didn't come down from her room for breakfast and sent her fond farewell to me through Sean, who drove me to the bus station and apologized for his mother being such a neurotic flake.

I didn't tell anybody what had happened. I didn't know what to think about it. Part of me felt relief that I had not had sex with an old woman. It seemed almost funny that I had wanted to. I laughed on the bus at how crazy it was. But it also excited me, and with the necessary revision became a regular masturbatory fantasy, everything happening just as it happened but at the moment of my orgasm doing it to her seventeen ways from Sunday in a condensed blinding flash, then wiping myself off and throwing the Kleenex away and not thinking about it until the next time I felt like masturbating.

I saw Sean much less during our senior year. I couldn't see him without being reminded of what he didn't know and what he would feel if he did. We weren't roommates anymore. I had a prized single in Lyons, where I could bring girls whenever I wanted to. As one of *The Juggler* staff members said, "You can't knock on Ryan's door after 8

P.M. without interrupting his intellectual foreplay." Everybody laughed. Affectionately, I thought. Admiringly. Enviously. I liked having the reputation as a stud.

I got a letter from Vanessa a month into the semester. She had married a carpenter who had been doing repairs at the motel where she was a chambermaid. She said her parents were trying to have her declared legally insane so they could get it annulled. All I could think was that I had been right. She was probably in bed with him before my bus passed through Wellfleet. Maybe she had been screwing him at the motel during the day while she was sleeping with me at night. Why had she even written to me? In case her parents contacted me for some sort of testimony? They never did and I never answered her letter.

I was glad she didn't come back. I didn't want a girlfriend. I was very busy, a very important person on campus. Besides editing *The Juggler* and being a senior member of the Wranglers, I wrote and directed experimental films with the Experimental Cinema Group and experimental plays with the Experimental Theatre Group (the Impersonal Pronouns), read my poetry sitting on a high stool under a spotlight in the local coffeehouse, and led protests against the war, the draft, and campus recruitment by the CIA, GE, and Dow Chemical. There was always something cooking, people to see, arrangements to be made, issues to be decided, but I scheduled my classes in the afternoon and stayed up all night in my room reading and writing and drinking instant coffee and smoking cigarettes. The more I did, the more I could do, and the more I got, the more I wanted. I felt entitled to everything there was. I didn't care about money or material things—they were beneath me—but I wanted all the honors, all the glory, and all the girls. My fame was entirely of the local variety, but it was no less convincing to me. Everybody I met, including professors and St. Mary's girls, had heard of me. I had done what I had set out to do. I had made myself into what I was: the editor of *The Juggler*. A testimony to my will, my true kabongs.

At the beginning of second term, the nominees were announced for the big national fellowships. There were eight nominees for the

Woodrow Wilson and four for the Danforth, but I was one of three seniors nominated for both of them. I had been right about this, too.
Somebody got the big fellowships and somebody didn't. Whatever
pious bullshit was thrown at you, it came down to this: winners and
losers. And I was going to be a winner.

After the nominations came the interviews, and the winners were
announced in late spring. The Danforth was more money, but it had a
religious overtone (Notre Dame usually got at least one) and it was
therefore in my mind less prestigious than the Woodrow Wilson. The
first of the two interviews was the Danforth, at the Drake Hotel in
Chicago. To my surprise, there was only one interviewer. He was probably in his thirties, but didn't look much older than I was. He was
dressed in khakis, a tweed sport coat, and a tie—an A-level handball
player or mile-a-day swimmer, an ex-athlete who kept his hair short
and his body trim. I liked him immediately. He had that skill psychia-
trists have of looking at you steadily without blinking, along with other
verbal and bodily gestures that draw you out. Whatever I said he
seemed to turn over carefully in his mind, considering it from every
angle, furrowing his brow. We were sitting in a grand suite with tall
windows and lavish drapes in high-backed chairs that might have
come from the palace at Versailles, yet here was a modest man in
khakis, with a disarming manner, apparently completely fascinated by
my ideas. I forgot why I was there, and just spoke from my heart—
about the war, the artist's role in society, my poetry, the plays and films
I had done and the ones I was planning to do, the function and purpose of *The Juggler* for the Notre Dame community. I thought he liked
me as much as I liked him. I thought we had a great talk. At the end of
it he checked his watch and said how much he regretted that our hour
was up, it went so fast. I thought, I got a Danforth! Then, after a long
pause in which he was no doubt considering how to imply this to me
unofficially and discreetly, he said, "You know, Michael, I really don't
think you should go to graduate school."

I was sitting facing him, the windows were to my left, and I watched
my Danforth Fellowship rise from inside my folder on his lap and fly

right out the window on a pair of feathery white wings. How could I be so stupid as to forget why I was there talking to this man?

"But I want to study literature," I said weakly.

"I think you want to be a writer," he answered. "Just think about it." He stood up and shook my hand. "I enjoyed meeting you," he said. I knew he meant it. I felt like smacking myself in the head.

The Woodrow Wilson interview was a week later at the University of Indiana in Bloomington, a 150-mile drive south from South Bend on a two-lane highway. I borrowed a rickety old Dodge from a Wrangler who lived off campus. It was a cold Saturday in late March. As soon as I got on the highway, it started sleeting. In no time it was like driving on glass. The Dodge probably had last had its wheels aligned during the Pleistocene era, and the tires were as bald as Jell-O. If I took my hands off the wheel for a moment, the car took a sharp right turn. The wiper blades had chunks bitten out of them like ears of corn. I couldn't slow down too much or I'd miss my interview, but I wasn't doing any passing either. It was enough to keep the car on the road.

About an hour from Bloomington, not more than twenty yards ahead, a car coming from the opposite direction pulled out to pass. It would have been a head-on collision at fifty miles an hour, but instinctively I pulled the wheel to the right, where the car wanted to go anyway. What followed could not have taken more than ten seconds, but I experienced it in excruciatingly slow motion, as if in a dream. There was a generous gravel shoulder on each side of the highway, a couple of yards wide, and the shoulders were even more icy than the road. After I pulled the wheel to the right, I started sliding at high speed into a ditch. I knew I had to pull the wheel back to the left, but I also sensed that there was a car behind me that I first had to let pass. If I pulled the wheel back too soon, I'd crash into it. I glanced out my side window out of the corner of my eye and saw an old black pickup truck with a square cab. Out of its passenger window, shattered like a spider's web, a man was staring at me. His head was turned to stare full-faced at me as the pickup truck went by. Then I pulled the steering wheel back to the left and the car did a 135-degree spin, so it was now perpendicular to the highway and going into the ditch on the other side. I pulled the steering wheel to the right once again and the car turned 90 degrees and stayed on the highway but in the wrong lane, with cars heading toward me. The first car swerved to the right into the ditch to avoid me, and the next car swerved to the left into the other ditch to avoid me, then I swerved into the ditch to avoid the rest of the cars coming toward me, and hit the brakes and slid gently into a white wooden fence around a pasture, my front bumper just tapping it. It didn't even crack the paint. Four cars ended up in the ditches on both sides of the road. None of them were damaged and nobody was hurt. A miracle. Traffic stopped on the highway. A tow truck with a winch and cable pulled all the cars out of the ditches, including the Dodge, which was apparently no worse for the experience. I was. I was shaky, but I couldn't think of anything but to continue driving to Bloomington for the interview. I didn't know what they'd do if I missed it, and it was even further back to Notre Dame.

I arrived for the interview five minutes late. Unlike the Danforth, there were five interviewers sitting in a half-circle in a classroom, with the interviewee's chair in the middle as for an interrogation by the secret police. All that was missing was the naked lightbulb hanging from the ceiling by a cord and the bloody instruments of torture casually lying about. The interviewers were introduced to me with the names of their universities, departments, and professorial titles, including the full titles of their endowed chairs. Five cannons pointed at a squirrel. I apologized for being late, saying I had a car accident on the way down in which I was almost killed.

"Yes, we get one of these every year," one professor said impatiently with a German accent. He was bald and portly, with white tufts of hair above his ears, and was wearing a red sweater-vest under his suit jacket and smoking a swan-neck Bavarian pipe with an oversize ivory bowl. Noting (with disapproval) the predominance of English and philosophy courses on my transcript, he then began with an aggressive question about the (lack of) difference between logical and aesthetic meaning. A positivist, eh? Right up my alley. I hauled out my

Wittgenstein, quoting the last sentence of the *Philosophical Investigations* in German. This apparently touched a nerve. He corrected my German pronunciation, then disputed my application of Wittgenstein, in the traditional Teutonic academic style. It seemed funny to me, and I laughed openly at him, which neither he nor the other four interviewers appreciated. He huffed indignantly and they were visibly embarrassed. It seemed funny to me because I was sitting up on the ceiling, completely dissociated, watching myself in this classroom in Bloomington, Indiana, being viciously attacked by this self-parody of a German professor. How could he hate me? He didn't know anything about me. I had just nearly been killed in a car accident. And the old black pickup truck with the square cab I had hallucinated I hadn't seen since I was five years old. It was Bob Stoller's.

So the interview did not seem real to me, nor the classroom, nor the five professors, nor even myself. What did any of this matter? The interview was eventually over, and when it was over, I didn't care if I got the fellowship or not, because it was abundantly clear that I didn't.

When I told my friends at Notre Dame about hallucinating the old black pickup truck and the man staring at me through its shattered passenger window, they said, "Far out." Nobody asked if I recognized the pickup. They did ask if I recognized the man, and I said "No," which was true. It wasn't Bob Stoller. It was a face out of Bosch: small and squinched and demonic. His head was shaved or bald, an inmate in a locked ward pressing his face against the window. "Really far out," everyone said. "Yeah," I said. But it was seeing the truck that shook me. I had never forgotten Bob Stoller, but I never thought about him either. I thought he was just something that happened a long time ago, when I was five years old. What was the sense of thinking about him, much less talking about him? But hallucinating his pickup truck like that, at a moment like that, *was* far out. Was he still with me?

A couple of weeks later, for the first time I told someone that I had been molested. Unfortunately, it was not in the most therapeutic of circumstances.

The person I told was my teacher. His name was Richard Mueller, and we were drinking bourbon in his apartment together, and he had just propositioned me. "I propose sex," he said. He was in his late twenties, fresh from Berkeley, in his first tenure-track job. He was slender and tawny, one of those people who move with such fluidity it seems they don't have bones in their body. He carried his books in a green drawstring canvas bag slung over one shoulder and marched with us in the campus demonstrations and taught his classes sitting cross-legged on the floor and made references to the latest Mothers of Invention album. Much of the time he spent hunched over, smoking, listening intently, but when he was excited by an idea, he would quickly sit up straight as if he had been shot. He had a wicked wit and loved to laugh at folly, especially of the midwestern conservative variety, and his classes were fun. I had been his student all year in his Great Books Seminar. Our syllabus consisted of the European classics of philosophy and the history of ideas with a few big novels sprinkled in. When the subject was literary, he deferred to me, as if I were the real authority on this subject. Needless to say, I loved this. We all called him "Mr. Mueller," and he used "Mister" when addressing us or referring to us in the third person. Late in the year, when he asked me to call him "Richard," he confided to me that he used Mister with all of his students to remind them of the formal distance he wished to maintain between him and them — which was a way of telling me he no longer wished to maintain the formal distance between us.

I didn't know he was gay, or, more accurately, I knew he was gay but could not acknowledge it to myself. I admired him enormously, I was flattered by his admiration, and I wanted to be his friend. To acknowledge he was gay would have forced me to understand everything differently, in a way I simply didn't want to understand it. And so I didn't. Homosexuality was a taboo subject at Notre Dame. Nobody declared his homosexuality openly. An openly gay student probably would have been beaten up and certainly harassed mercilessly. A gay professor would have been boycotted or worse. We all knew this, and I never heard any speculation about anyone's homosexuality, especially about a professor everyone liked. Just the gossip alone would have been too damaging.

When I told my friends that "Richard" had invited me to his apartment for a drink, they didn't blink. I was proud he had invited me. It wasn't something I had to hide. I had been to his apartment before; he had even loaned it to me to shoot my latest experimental film. And he didn't exactly say that there wouldn't be anyone else there but us. He just said, "You want to come over Saturday night for a drink?" It was in the context of talking about grad schools. I had started hearing from the grad schools I had applied to. Harvard: no. Yale: no. Stanford: no. Curt form letters wishing me success in my graduate studies elsewhere. I was crushed and baffled. I was being rejected by every place I applied to, except for my two sure shots, one of which was Claremont Graduate School, in California, which Richard had suggested. I had never heard of Claremont Graduate School. Now it looked like I would be going there. He said that when I came over for a drink he would tell me things that would make me happy at that prospect.

His apartment was a studio in downtown South Bend: a living room with books stacked to the ceiling against all the walls except the one that hid a Murphy bed and was hung with a Beardsley print. He poured us each a tumbler of bourbon on the rocks and I sat in his reading chair and he sat across the room cross-legged on the floor. It took him about one minute to tell me why I was going to be happy at Claremont (it was small, flexible, and less stuffy than all the big-name schools I had applied to; the professors cared as much about teaching as about publishing; I could actually get an education there). Then we just drank and talked, talked and drank. And drank. Many hefty tumblers of bourbon. I don't remember much of what either of us said before he said "I propose sex." My memory is of sitting in his chair in his dimmed apartment, the tumbler of bourbon in my left hand, a cigarette in my right. It is a memory very much like my memory of Bob Stoller, of a man's attention focused on me, a man I liked. The sex was part of the attention, the attention was part of the sex. I understood this. I did it to girls. But they never did it to me, at least in this way, and I liked it being done to me. Once, when Richard filled my glass, he touched my fingers and I didn't move them. I liked doing what we were doing, in this dark place, alone.

So when he said "I propose sex," I wasn't shocked or surprised. I did think it was a dorky, academic way of putting it. I told him I had never had sex with a man, and he said that was okay, he liked going to bed with straight men. It was kind of his specialty. He said he had seduced most of his married friends. He said this with relish, like my relish when I repeated the *Juggler* staff member's line about my intellectual foreplay, about being a stud. I was listening with one ear. As soon as I said I had never had sex with a man, I remembered Bob Stoller.

"Actually, that's not true," I said.

"Whatever could you mean?" Richard asked. He thought I was disputing his claim that he seduced his married friends.

"I have had sex with a man."

"Really," Richard said.

"I was five years old," I said.

Richard didn't respond for a moment. There was one moment of silence in which I was waiting for his response. Then he said, "That's kind of young."

"Kind of *young*?" I said. "I should think so." His response infuriated me. I don't know what I expected. Sympathy, I guess. Something. Now I see that he was in his own erotic trance: he was inside his own aggrandizement, telling me about how he liked seducing straight men, feeling he was going to seduce me. Having to deal with this information was a turnoff, an obstacle to his erotic momentum. But I told him, as opposed to everyone else I had ever known, because I was still ashamed of what I had done with Bob Stoller, that I had had his cock in my mouth and mine in his, and I knew I didn't have to be ashamed of that with Richard because he was proposing that we do the same thing, which he did all the time, and apparently was not ashamed of.

I wanted him to say something that would take my shame away. When he said what he did, I thought, Fuck it. Then I said it out loud: "Fuck it."

"What's *that* supposed to mean?" Richard asked.

"Just fuck it," I said. I put down my drink and deliberately crushed my cigarette in the ashtray. I got up and walked over to Richard and stood over him, my crotch at his eye level. He looked up at my face coolly, but smiled nervously. He had no idea what I was about to do.

"Well?" he asked.

"Well fucking what?" I answered, and knelt down and kissed him on the mouth. His hair was light, but his beard was heavy. It must have been after midnight and he hadn't shaved since that morning. His skin was scratchy around his lips. I had never kissed a man before and I didn't like it. It reminded me of my father chafing his whiskers against my face.

"Out of our clothes," Richard said after the kiss was finished. He hopped up and unhooked the Beardsley print and pushed the chair I had been sitting in across the room and all the rest of the furniture out of the way and pulled the Murphy bed out of the wall. I helped him. It took a few minutes. "Out of your clothes," he said again, and disappeared into the bathroom.

I undressed alone, sitting on the edge of the bed to unlace my shoes and pull down my pants. When I was naked, I lay back and waited for him to come out of the bathroom. I heard him peeing. What was I doing here? This grim apartment, all these paperback books stacked up to the ceiling, the way he lived alone. I wanted to be like this? I felt an overwhelming bitterness, against Richard, certainly, but more against life. What an ugly fucking thing it was.

Richard came out of the bathroom naked. His body was smooth and almost muscleless, like the boy Picasso painted leading the horse. He was round-shouldered and, I noticed for the first time, pot-bellied. You couldn't tell when he was dressed. We started kissing again, but apparently he didn't go for kissing that much, and almost immediately he shot down my body and started sucking me. I was soft, and embarrassed that I was soft. It just felt like weird slurping and tickling and put my nerves on edge and made me fidgety.

"Wait a minute wait a minute wait a minute," I said, pulling him up by the shoulders.

"What?" he said.

"This isn't doing anything," I said. "Isn't there something else to do?"

"What would you suggest?" He seemed both amused and irked by my question.

"Nothing's happening for me," I said.

"For me either," he said, a little bitchily.

"Let me go down on you," I said. He was soft, too, and pathetically small. I didn't want to put it in my mouth. I didn't know how to do it and he had just been pissing. I put my hand on it and rubbed for a couple of minutes. Nothing. It felt like a small dead bird.

"Let's have a cigarette," he said. He put two cigarettes in his mouth, lit them both, and handed one to me. We lay next to each other not touching, both with one hand under our heads.

"It might help if I hadn't been fucking all last night," he said.

"I was, too," I said. It was true. I had slept with the star of my film. Her name was Christy Hedges. She was a St. Mary's freshman, cute and blonde. I had noticed her around campus for a couple of months, but had never met her before I went up to her in the Huddle and said, "How would you like to be in a movie?" All along I planned to get her into bed, and the night before, I had succeeded. Richard had met her when we arrived at his apartment for the filming. As a compliment to me, he now observed that "she has a body that won't quit."

He said he had come four times last night with three different guys. The four of them went through a half lid of Tijuana Gold and a bunch of poppers. It was pretty wild, pretty hard to follow that tonight. Believe it or not, he said, he hadn't been planning to do anything with me tonight, although he admitted the thought had crossed his mind before. We commiserated for a while about how drained we were and had a couple of cigarettes and a couple of jokes and started to feel better. Just talking at all about how we were feeling reminded me of my regard for him, that he was Richard Mueller, not some anonymous gay guy with a little potbelly who had somehow managed to seduce me. But it was still too weird to be lying in bed with him. He crushed his cigarette and said he was ready to try it again. He said if I got hard he'd get hard. There didn't seem to be any polite way of stopping him. He went down on me and began sucking, but it felt the same way it did before, and I was still soft.

I said, "It's not happening, Richard."

"Give it a minute," he answered, and kept it up.

"It's really not happening," I repeated, but he didn't stop. I started laughing, softly at first, nervously, hollowly, the way Candice had in the bus station. This did make him stop, but I kept laughing, more and more loudly—a little hysterically, I realized, even as I was doing it. He sat on the edge of the bed with his back to me. I kept laughing. I knew I was pissing him off. I wanted to piss him off.

"Let's get dressed," he said over his shoulder.

"What a fucking joke," I said. "You have no idea."

"Let's get dressed," he repeated. "And please stop that obscene laughter."

He drove me back to campus. We spoke about how we'd try it again on a night when we weren't both so played out, etc. He asked for my "discretion," which of course went without saying. We parted amicably, shaking hands as I got out of the car. It was strange to shake hands with him now.

I felt awful when I got into my own bed, lying in my room in the dark. I stared at the ceiling. I wasn't drunk anymore, although I must have had at least a half-quart of bourbon. How could I do such a thing? What was wrong with me? I felt sick at the thought of it. I went to the bathroom and threw up until there was nothing left but bile.

When I woke up the next day, I felt even worse. I had gone to bed with a man. With Richard Mueller. Bob Stoller. I had rubbed his pathetic cock (thank God I hadn't sucked it). He had sucked me. Was I queer? It was hell seeing my friends. They asked how my drink with Richard went. I told them what he said about Claremont, but unlike the many times before when I had hidden the truth, this time I almost broke down and started crying. I had to tell somebody.

It was a Sunday, but I called up Christy Hedges at St. Mary's. As everybody said, she looked like a doll: perfect features, blonde hair, vacant expression. She was an eighteen-year-old freshman from St. Cloud, Minnesota, and had had about as much contact with male homosexuality as with the more esoteric sects of Islam. But there was no way I could tell any of my male friends, and I had just had sex with her so she knew I wasn't really gay.

I took her to my room in Lyons. We sat down on the bed and I took both her hands in mine. God knows what she thought I was going to tell her—something directly affecting her, no doubt: that I had an exotic venereal disease or that somebody had reported her sleeping with me to the president of St. Mary's and she was going to be expelled. When I told her about Richard, she was visibly relieved. "Oh, you poor guy," she said. She put her arms around me, and I pushed my face against her breasts and cried my heart out, soaking her angora sweater, which shed onto my cheeks. It was like crying to my mother about Betty Short taking me under the abandoned house, except Christy didn't send me to confession. It was just sexual experimentation, she said. A lot of people were doing it these days. I realized she didn't quite understand (but I didn't tell her about Bob Stoller). Talking to her, I also realized that I couldn't go to Richard's class anymore. I couldn't handle sitting there with my classmates pretending nothing had happened. All his admiration of me seemed fake, just a way to seduce me. Plus he wasn't the same person: he pretended to be so solicitous and humble. What bullshit. We could never be just teacher and student again, and I had really liked being just teacher and student.

So I didn't go to his class anymore. There was less than a month to graduation, but after I missed two classes, my friends asked me what the story was. I had never missed a single class before, I enjoyed it so much. I said I was simply too busy. I had the final issue of *The Juggler* to get out, there was the big anti-ROTC demonstration coming up at the annual ROTC review, my experimental play was in rehearsal with the Impersonal Pronouns, I had term papers to write, and, if there was any time left over, I still had a film to edit. "Just tell Richard," I said. "He'll understand."

They did tell Richard, and he did understand, but he sent a message to please call him. I didn't call him. But he came to the opening of my play, and I couldn't avoid him there. The play was called *And/Or* (ironic allusion to Kierkegaard). The main characters were named Vivaldi and Telemann because the form of the play, I allowed, was patterned after the fugue. It began:

Telemann: I can't talk to you anymore.
Vivaldi: Why not?
Telemann: I have to take a shit.

(Sound of toilet flushing offstage, and a little boy yelling, "Mommy, I'm fin-ished.")

Vivaldi: That's you all right.
Telemann: What do you mean?
Vivaldi: Always wanting someone to wipe your ass for you.
Telemann: I do not.
Vivaldi: You do so.
Telemann: I do not.
Vivaldi: You do so.
Telemann: Do not.
Vivaldi: Do so.
Telemann: Do not.
Vivaldi: Do so.
Etc.

Richard came to the cast party afterward and cornered me in the kitchen.

"Marvelous play," he said. "Trenchant. Witty."

"Thanks, Richard," I said.

He hesitated a moment. He looked at me sheepishly and smiled his charming smile. "It's fine you're not coming to class."

I looked him hard in the eyes.

"I know it's fine," I said.

He blinked, and his expression became somber and sincere. "You've been really great about this, and I just wanted to thank you."

"No problem," I said, and pushed past him into the living room. What a smarmball, I thought. He's scared shitless. The thought of reporting him hadn't crossed my mind. I was much too ashamed of my part in it. He hadn't raped me at gunpoint. Despite myself, I felt sorry for him. But it was all very confusing. I couldn't stand seeing him much less talking to him.

My mother and sister came to graduation, and they met him at one of the receptions. I walked away while he was chatting with them. "Professor Mueller said you were his best student," my mother said, after I pulled her away to meet another teacher.

"That's what they all say, Mother," I said, steering her by the elbow. "So I guess it must be true."

My sister laughed. "Oh, you," my mother said, giving my forearm a pinch.

THE SEX KING

And strange it is
That nature must compel us to lament
Our most persisted deeds.
        —ANTONY AND CLEOPATRA, V, i

In spring 1981, my last semester at Princeton, I taught a small seminar in contemporary poetry that met in a mahogany-paneled office with leaded cathedral windows that looked as if it had been transported intact from Oxford University. My eight students and I crowded around a short table. Although most of them were from wealthy families, they all dressed down for class in jeans and sweatshirts—except for one young woman who wore cashmere sweaters with her (designer) jeans and always looked as if she had just had her hair done. It was luxuriously long and chocolate-brown, and through the New Jersey winter she was improbably tanned and wore pale shades of lipstick and a thin gold-chain necklace. She almost never spoke in class, but while she was listening, she would sometimes pull the gold chain across her lower lip, slowly, toying it with her tongue. I don't think she was trying to be provocative. It was an unconscious gesture, like twirling the ends of her hair around her index finger, which she also sometimes did. I never had sex with this student, nor did I ever get to know her—she was from an old Princeton family and was not particularly interested in poetry or in me. But when she pulled her gold chain across her lip, my mind would go blank in the middle of the sentence I was speaking. I'd try to cover by calling on someone to read a poem, which most likely had no connection whatsoever to the subject we had been discussing that I couldn't remember anyway, and I'd sit there with my heart slamming my breastbone like a hammer. When the reading was over, I was going to have to say something, and if what I said made no sense, the eight faces of my students would stare at me as if I were insane. These full-blown panic attacks — like the ones my father had when he had to drive across a bridge — were in my case caused by a collision of worlds: what I was supposedly doing in this classroom (teaching) and what this young woman's mouth could be doing to me instead of to her gold chain. The membrane between these two worlds had by this time been worn to nothing. I could barely maintain the distinction between fantasy and reality or impulse and action: if I could imagine it, I would do it if I could, no matter how unlikely, difficult, dangerous, or destructive it was.

I had begun teaching at Princeton in the fall of 1979. I was thirty-three. I had spent three semesters at Claremont and four years at Iowa, then taught at Southern Methodist University and Goddard College. Most people either hadn't heard of these schools or weren't impressed by them, but now when I met people and told them where I taught, they did seem impressed. I'd wait for them to ask what I did, so I could say, "I teach at Princeton" — exactly as I had waited for them to ask what the "D" stood for on my baseball cap when I was nine years old so I could recite my scintillating pitching record. My mom was thrilled. She didn't really understand what my poetry awards meant, but if I was teaching at Princeton, I must be doing very well. My father visited the campus once on a business trip, and wrote her a long letter describing it. She read the letter to me. He said Princeton represented the highest level of human civilization and the finest education this country had to offer. How proud of me he would have been now.

I found a studio apartment not far from campus, on a wide street with big lawns. It was in the upstairs wing of a large expensive house that belonged to a divorcee whose five children were grown and gone. The apartment had a separate entrance, but to use the laundry room I had to walk through the downstairs, which I did when the landlady wasn't home. The walls and bookcases and tabletops were jammed with silver-framed photographs of her children at every stage of their lives, engaged in every conceivable healthy American activity from softball and scouts to piano recitals and proms. It was eerie—these perfect frozen smiles, this roomy family house once alive with noise and energy now so silent and empty. Four of the children were girls, all of them cute. I'd pick up the photos and study their pubescent bodies in tennis whites and swimsuits. Their mother was in her sixties, skinny and mannish, her peppery hair tightly curled and cut squarely upward like a hedge. She started every evening with hefty cocktails at five o'clock, by herself, on the patio beneath my window (while the weather was still warm). She acted like she had seen everything and was very tired of it, and spoke gruff no-nonsense with a patrician New England accent. Shortly after I moved in, she put her hand on my thigh as she was giving me a ride to the grocery store, but after I pretended not to notice, she didn't do it again. Even I realized it would be insane to have sex with her—not because I wasn't attracted to her (that never stopped me before if the person were sufficiently inappropriate) but because I was planning to have sex with lots of women at my apartment and I didn't want to think about getting any interference from her.

I taught two courses that first semester: a poetry-writing workshop and a precept for Walt Litz's Modern Poetry. Precepts were small discussion groups of a large lecture class. Princeton is one of the few schools that could afford to have faculty instead of graduate students teach precepts, and this was regarded as a singular feature of the Princeton undergraduate education. It was an honor to be teaching a precept for Walt Litz. He was the chairman of the department and universally admired. A big man with sandy hair, light eyes, and almost translucently pale skin, he had the quickest mind of anyone I had ever met, and he spoke as quickly as he thought, with rapier wit. Writers entertained him. He liked twitting me about being the brooding, suffering, sensitive Poet. I knew he had chosen me as one of his preceptors because he also wanted to look me over. There had been discreet hints that I might be considered for director of the Creative Writing Program the following year. I couldn't wait to be able to say *that* to people: "I direct the Creative Writing Program at Princeton."

Initially, everything went swimmingly. My students were as good as I'd thought they'd be—no better than the best students at Iowa, SMU, or Goddard, but more of them, and more competitive, even combative. They'd know what I didn't know, so I tried to know everything. We covered a poet a week, and I read extra books about each one. I also had to give a lecture late in the term on the poet of my choice, and I chose Wallace Stevens because I knew the most about him. But Litz himself had written a superb book about Stevens, so I started working on my lecture immediately, determined to wow him and all the students with my brilliance.

I also got a girlfriend right away—a twenty-year-old senior, stunningly beautiful and bright, with a dark sense of humor and an even darker sexuality. Just my type. Her name was Marcia. She is the one who said, "You are like another person when we go into sex." That was where I wanted always to be. I appeared functional because I worked so hard, but working so hard made me want sex even more. It was a strain to pretend I was thinking about anything else. I'd think about the women I had had sex with and the ones I was going to have sex with—rarely the ones I was actually having sex with—or pop in one of my mental videos about hot teens or hungry housewives: paperboy fantasies honed over the years for maximum effect but still the same paperboy fantasies. Talking to a friendly telephone operator on the phone could propel me into fantasy, or seeing a pair of eyes in a rearview mirror, or breasts or legs on the street. "Holy shit," I'd say under my breath, as I did when I first saw Marcia walk into Walt Litz's class. I liked seductions, especially with students. When one of them showed regard for me, it switched on the magnet in my solar plexus. I watched her eyes, I watched her body language. I noticed how she dressed for class and especially for conferences, and how often she stopped by my office. I sexualized words and gestures and concocted strategies and scenarios, relishing the anticipation. But after we actually went to bed together, it was over for me. Then she was a real person I might or might not like or be attracted to—most often not. Even when I did like her and was attracted to her (not just to the seduction), I'd have to find some way to stay inside sex with her, and even if I could, it didn't satisfy my need to be cultivating and fantasizing and seducing. I couldn't go shop for a quart of milk without hungering for a hi or a smile that would lead to something wild. Every time I went to a movie, I'd try to sit next to the sexiest stranger, preferably a teenage girl with The Look.

This made long-term relationships difficult, to say the least, and monogamy impossible. I dealt with the latter by admitting it up front (if the subject arose), and dealt with the former through power. I liked students because I had power over them. Although I was teaching only two courses, Marcia was getting three grades from me, the third being her senior thesis on John Donne, which I was directing. I slept with other women that semester, but she was the only student. One of her jokes was that she was the little Dutch girl with her finger in the dike, protecting all other Princeton coeds from the flood—a joke I enjoyed because it implied I was an inexorable sexual force. Dark. Dangerous. Devastating. The only way I could stay inside sex with her was for her to participate in this myth by surrendering completely to the Sex King. Such self-ironic honorifics were designed to defuse this dynamic between us, but they were serious jokes. I was certainly a magnet for some women, as some women were for me—suicidal women for whom sex was both validation and self-annihilation, an intense temporary escape from the pain of being themselves (as it was for me). Many of them had also been sexually molested, some of them by their fathers. I could pick them out the minute I walked into a room. Their hunger is what made them sexy to me and, no doubt, vice versa. We always at least half-hated each other, the half that was a mirror.

Marcia was such a knockout I wanted to squire her about to show her off, but she would have none of that. She insisted our relationship be secret. She made me pick her up in alleys downtown. When her friends asked her how she had spent the weekend, she made up a story. Some of the undergraduate boys complained to me that they couldn't get to first base with her and speculated that she must be dating some honcho lawyer or actor in New York. How I loved smiling to myself then. It was as if her beauty were my inner strength. Maybe some similar part of her enjoyed having the secret, too, but as the semester went on, it got harder for her. She was my student during the week and my lover on weekends. She said she felt invaded. She said she didn't know where I ended and she began.

I just wanted more and more of her, to take her further sexually than she had ever gone and then some—further than she ever would go again. This fantasy was the way I could stay inside sex with her, and why she thought I was like another person when we went into sex. I *was* another person: I was her molester. To be invaded, to be confused about where the other person ends and you begin: this is what it feels like to be molested. It is an assault on the nervous system. I couldn't figure out why she was so angry. She'd say cruelly perceptive things about me, like "There must be something wrong with you, wanting to be with a twenty-year-old." I'd usually just deflect them. "Men are pigs," I'd answer. Or "Men bad. Women good."

But once I didn't. She said, "I get the feeling we're both just sleeping with each other until something better comes along." I responded, "I think that's right." We had this exchange a few days before I was to deliver my lecture, and it was probably then she decided to break up with me, but she waited another month until the semester was over and I had turned in her grades (two A's and an A+). When I accused her of this, she said she hadn't wanted to interfere with my work on my lecture. I screamed, "Bullshit!" but knew she was telling at least a partial truth. She knew how important the lecture was to me. And were it not for her insistence that I keep our relationship secret, Walt Litz would have eliminated me much sooner for the director's job. After my lecture he invited me to coffee in the faculty common room. He said it was one of the best lectures on Stevens he had ever heard. I was ecstatic. His saying this meant so much to me I almost wept. We sat in studded leather armchairs and had the kind of conversation that only two people steeped in a subject they both love can have. As we were leaving, he asked almost offhandedly if I would be interested in directing the Creative Writing Program, should the job in fact come open as anticipated. With as much aplomb as I could muster, I said I would be.

Checking afterward with people who knew Litz well, they said it meant I had the job. He wouldn't have even mentioned it otherwise, they said. This was his style, the Princeton style, to downplay the real business at hand. I was impressed. I thought, this is how the powerful conduct themselves: a friendly chat, then one casual sentence by which all is understood. I felt like I had been at Potsdam or something. I had made it. I was in.

But when the job was advertised in the spring, it called for a poet with at least one published critical book. This wasn't me. I hadn't published a critical book. I was shocked. All anyone would tell me was that the decision was to hire someone who would be acceptable to the English Department, who could teach courses in both creative writing and literature. But I *was* teaching courses in both creative writing and literature. I had a Ph.D., I could publish a book of essays about poetry in a couple of years, and it was Litz's call anyway. What about our conversation after my lecture? I couldn't figure out what had happened.

What had happened, of course, was that he heard I was sleeping with students, which I was, conspicuously, by the spring. Marcia broke up with me after Christmas, a week before I was to go to a reception honoring poets at the White House. I had wanted to take her with me, but there would be other Princeton people there, besides which, how could she tell her parents about me? Was she supposed to lie about going to a reception at the White House? I didn't argue with her. Instead, I invited an ex-girlfriend from Dallas. Marcia said it didn't bother her, but she probably had already made up her mind to break up with me when she said it. Nothing much bothered her during our final month, nor did she have much time for me because she was studying for finals and furiously writing papers (including one I graded: A+).

The day I got back to Princeton after Christmas, she called (collect, from a pay phone). She was supposed to come back early, to spend a few days with me before my rendezvous in Washington. She said she would not be coming back early, nor when she did come back would she be sleeping with me anymore, etc. She said it had been too much for her, too much Michael Ryan. I was surprised at how little it surprised me. I actually understood her point of view. The only thing that irked me was her waiting to tell me, because now my week was ruined. I wouldn't have come back to Princeton early except to be with her. Everybody was gone for Christmas break. I immediately called my ex-girlfriend from Dallas to see if I could meet her sooner. She said how funny, just that moment she was about to pick up the phone. Something had come up, she said. She was very sorry, but she had to cancel.

It would have been easier to learn that my best friend had been killed in a plane crash. The apartment was furnished with a cheerful plaid overstuffed armchair I sat in whenever I talked on the phone. I sat in it trying to calm myself. I was in a situation here. For days I had been feeling flush. I had my ducks lined up: the week with one knockout and the weekend with another. Now I had zip. I no longer had a girlfriend. Again the trapdoor had opened underneath me. You couldn't trust anybody or anything, especially women. When the hell was I going to learn that? I picked up my little black book and checked A to Z for somebody to ask to the White House or somebody to sleep with that night or somebody to at least make a date with. There were a couple of hundred names, some going back a decade, many of which could instantly propel me into nostalgic memory-fantasies, but none I could call now and wanted to call. The week ahead yawned like a shark. A week of solitude with no obligations would be heaven to some people, but to me it was hell. It scared me. I had been through it before and done frightening things, especially when a girlfriend had just broken up with me.

I managed to get through the week with a couple of dates in New York, and the thought that I might meet somebody new at the White House. President and Mrs. Carter had invited three hundred poets and a hundred poetry patrons for a celebration of contemporary poetry. It was the brainchild of John Frederick Nims, the editor of *Poetry*. His idea was to try to build a foundation of private financial support by creating a prestigious national event that could attract big money the way opera and ballet did, and which would also raise the public stature of American poets by an official presidential recognition. Fat chance on both counts was my opinion, but of course I went anyway, for my own reasons.

The lines at the White House were very long by the time I got there. All invitees had to send in their acceptances two weeks in advance so security checks could be done. Now guards were verifying names and identifications, and walking everybody through a metal detector. I didn't see anyone I knew. It was late afternoon, always a rough time for me if I didn't have an assignation set up for the evening. I checked out the women in line. The likeliest prospect was standing right behind me, accompanied by a couple but no escort. We exchanged a few pleasantries. They were patrons, not poets, which I had inferred already from the way they were dressed. The woman had on an ankle-length sable coat and diamonds the size of kumquats. Her name actually was something like Mrs. H. Huntington Huffington. She was in her late thirties, a few years older than me but meticulously maintained. I asked her where she lived. She said, "I winter in Palm Springs and summer in Newport." I waited for her to ask where I lived so I could say, "Princeton. I teach at Princeton."

She was very chummy. She asked if I had come alone and I said I had. She said she had, too. Her husband canceled at the last moment. Business. I didn't ask what business. Her friends were amused by meeting a real live poet—apparently I was their first. "He certainly seems alive," Mrs. H. Huntington Huffington said. "And I certainly need an escort." Whereupon she hooked her arm into mine. Her friends laughed uproariously at that. She kept holding my arm as the line inched slowly forward. I really didn't know how to handle this. On the one hand, I was Dying For It and here was a rich woman ready for a lark. On the other hand, I didn't want to be her lark, and I definitely didn't want her hanging on me at the reception, because maybe I could pick up somebody I liked more.

My dilemma was solved when we reached the metal detector. Mrs. H. Huntington Huffington's name was not on the prescreened invitation list. Her friends' were, and mine was, but hers wasn't, nor was her husband's. She unhooked my arm and dug into her Louis Vuitton bag for her engraved invitation. Sorry. Not good enough. Everyone had to be prescreened. She could not be admitted under any circumstances. Embarrassment. Insult. Indignation. "Do you know how much my husband contributed to the Carter campaign?" Etc. I left her arguing there and walked through the metal detector. The black security guard winked at me. "You're clean, poet," she said. "Go right on in and meet the president."

Everyone flooded toward the reception in the Great Hall upstairs. I didn't expect the White House to be shabby, but I also didn't expect it to look like an imperial palace: marble walls and staircases and dew-drop crystal chandeliers, every one of which would feed twenty families for a year. I thought it was obscene, a proper symbol of the real business of government—making the rich richer—some of whom I was rubbing elbows with, one of whom I had allowed to hold my arm. All the repugnance I couldn't consciously feel about my sexual exploitations I projected onto these symbols of economic ones. I was inside the belly of the beast. And I was dishonoring myself.

An announcement was made that President Carter would stop in later. In the meantime, Mrs. Carter and Amy and other dignitaries formed a receiving line. I went through an ethical crisis about whether or not to shake Mrs. Carter's hand. When I did, I glared at her so furiously she literally recoiled. She must have thought a crazed assassin had snuck through security. Then I hooked up with some friends and started drinking, mocking everything and everybody, which none of my friends wanted to hear. None of them felt like I did. They just wanted to have fun. Marcia would have enjoyed my bitter jokes and chimed in with her own, a sardonic duet for which the reception was merely raw material. That would have been the real event for me. Plus she would have knocked everybody's eyes out and I could have basked in that glory—of all possible glories, the most important to me—to show off my sexual prowess, to prove my sexual magnetism by being with the most beautiful woman there (wherever "there" was). It was commensurately unbearable being alone, but something wouldn't let me leave, a little devil's voice goading me to push it, to make myself feel worse. Or better. Or something. To just not feel like this. The only way out, as always, was into sex. The place was jammed and noisy, everybody schmoozing and making connections, which I also disdained. Careerists and operators were beneath my contempt. The only person I wanted to connect with was some hot babe.

But every woman there was with someone. Every single one. I checked. I left my friends and started prowling, exactly the way I sometimes prowled through a disco by myself at midnight, circling the periphery, drinking in the bodies, the gyrations, looking looking looking. This was the first phase of a secret ritual that usually ended with me drunk and aiming my car at the strut of an overpass to see how close I could get before I turned the wheel, with a stopover in between at a gay bar or porno house where I could pick up a man and have anonymous sex. I had been doing this a few times a year for about two years, and continued doing it during my two years at Princeton—after a girlfriend broke up with me, or when I just couldn't stand being in my own skin. The more beautiful women I had, the better I felt; to have none, and, worse, to have sex with men, was my deepest degradation. It enacted my calcified childhood shame. Of all my shame-based sexual behaviors, this was the most shameful to me—not the worst thing I did to others but the worst thing I could do to myself. Which is why I did it. I also did it because I had to have sex, any kind of sex, and it put me inside sex so deeply I no longer recognized myself. I began to get that familiar dream feeling of starting down the sliding board into oblivion, made singularly more intense by the fact that I wasn't in some blue-collar disco in Trenton but at a presidential reception at the White House. I had always cruised places where I wouldn't be recognized. Never before had I gone into this particular trance when I was among people I knew. John Frederick Nims grabbed me and introduced me to Harvey Shapiro, the editor of the *New York Times Book Review*. I chatted with them as if I were rising young poet Michael Ryan, not knowing where the words from my mouth were coming from, and really not caring. When I left them, I resumed being no one, for a while still hoping to pick up a hot babe, finally out of frustration hunting specifically for Mrs. H. Huntington Huffington, preferring the self-degradation she represented to the one I was heading for. But she wasn't there. I lamented not picking her up when I could have and blowing off this whole miserable fiasco. There was always a specific moment in the ritual when I realized how the evening was going to end, a moment when I stopped resisting and began to welcome it, and this is the moment when I began to welcome it at the White House. There was no going back after that. Fuck it, I said to myself (as I had said to Richard Mueller). Just fuck it.

After the reception there was a private dinner with eminent poets at a fine restaurant, which I attended (in body), and after the dinner there was a big party in one of the budget hotels, which I didn't attend. I had made a reservation at a hotel near the White House, but I didn't even check in. I shook loose from the group I had dinner with, implying I had "other plans," and took a cab to the gay area of Georgetown. I walked into a fern bar carrying my overnight bag. Nobody laughed. Nobody seeing my bag said, "That's what I call optimism." Nobody particularly noted my entrance. I had walked into gay bars before— but only sleazy ones, with names like The Ramrod—and never wearing a suit. At bars like that, especially near closing time (the only time I ever went into them), all heads turned at the sight of fresh meat. Not here. This was civilized. Lots of men were in suits: stockbrokers and government functionaries. There was an enormous mirror behind the bar. I watched myself drinking cut-glass ditches of Jack Daniels on ice until it seemed that the man in the mirror might indeed be fictional, maybe an assistant deputy undersecretary coming out of the closet. The suit helped me not to be me. I never wore a suit. Nobody in the world knew where I was. They didn't know who I was either. I had felt this my whole life, but I had never felt it more intensely, a bitter self-pity impacted to the core, a hatred of human beings—especially myself—and of being human, of being alive. To rip it out of me would have killed me because it *was* me. This was the closest I could come to it, digging into the wound.

The man I was going to go home with came in with another man, a man who laughed inhaling instead of exhaling so it sounded like a wheeze. He kept thumping the man I was going to go home with on the back—hard, then very hard, then *extremely* hard, nearly sending him headfirst over the bar. It was very odd. After each thump the man I was going to go home with told the man he came in with to stop it, but he didn't. It seemed that he couldn't—which was also very odd—and after about an hour and the climactic resounding hollow thump as loud as a slit gong, the man I was going to go home with shouted at the man he came in with to go away and leave him alone. So the man did, immediately. Without so much as a word. Just put on his coat and walked out. This, too, was odd.

By this time I was staring.

"He's crazy," the man I was going to go home with said to me.

"I'd say so," I said.

"He thinks it's funny. Hitting people is funny."

We were now the only two men at the wide U-shaped bar, but he stayed where he was, around the bend to my left. He looked like any guy on the street outside: neatly trimmed black hair, collegiately dressed in a dark crew-neck sweater and pin-striped shirt. He was about my age, or a couple years younger. I don't remember his name, or any of their names, or occupations, except of the hairdresser in Dallas who told me as I left his apartment abruptly afterward that I was rude but that he understood. I know he was a hairdresser because he gave me his card, which I tried to flip straight up into the air doing ninety down the freeway in my jaunty red Fiat Spyder, but it flew back and stuck to my cheek for a few seconds before I swatted it off like a hornet. "A hairdresser, what else!" I yelled at the top of my lungs. I got gonorrhea from that experience, which so easily could have been the strain of HIV before anybody had heard of HIV that supposedly spread throughout the country from Dallas. This was the first time I performed my disco-prowl–gay-pickup–suicide-drive ritual (a girlfriend had just broken up with me), and I enjoyed the sex, but I didn't enjoy how I felt afterward coming out of the trance (like blowing my brains out). I didn't want to want to do it. I was terrified that I might really be gay, that what I really wanted was to have sex with a hundred strangers a night, and I fantasized about going to the warehouses and detached semitrailers parked on Eighth Avenue I heard of where men did that in the dark in a frenzy of anonymous body parts. I was afraid I'd commit suicide if I did that. I got pretty close, to both doing it and committing suicide.

The man in Georgetown may have been the only person I met that year whom I did not tell that I taught at Princeton. I told him I was a high school English teacher from Trenton named Michael Riley. I did say I had just been to a reception at the White House—maybe to impress him, but more because the truth was so strange I knew he wouldn't believe it. But when he finally moved to the stool next to mine, he spotted the overnight bag at my feet.

"You really don't have a place to sleep tonight?" he asked.

I said I didn't, and he asked what I was planning to do.

I looked at him. "I'm planning to go home with somebody." I could see it got his attention, until his better self took over again.

He said, "You could get murdered doing this."

I shrugged, as if to say, who cares?

He lived three doors away from the bar in a second-floor walk-up. I left my overnight bag at the door with my coat. Then we sat down in the living room across from each other. I was drunk, as I always was by this time in the ritual. He poured me more Jack Daniels from a dry bar, and watched me over the rim of his glass as he sipped his own drink. He was still wary, still trying to figure out if I was dangerous. I don't think he believed anything I had told him about myself. He got up and picked an encyclopedia off a shelf and sat back down.

"Give me the name of a poet," he said.

"What is this, a pop quiz?" I asked.

"Just give me the name of a poet," he repeated.

"Wallace Stevens," I said.

"Here he is," he said, looking him up. He began reading, "Wallace Stevens was born in—"

"Reading, PA," I said. "In 1879."

"That's *right*," he said, surprised. He continued reading, "He published his first book—"

"*Harmonium*. At the age of forty-four."

"Right *again*," he said. "Word for word. That's amazing."

"Enough?" I asked. It wasn't. I had to complete a few more sentences.

"Wow," he said. "Can you do that with any poet?"

That's when I realized I still had my engraved invitation to the White House in the inside jacket of my suit pocket. I pulled it out of the envelope so he couldn't see my real name and address, then handed it to him.

"You really *were* at the White House today," he said. But it just baffled him more. "Who *are* you? What are you doing here?"

"You don't have to be afraid of me," I said. "I'm not going to hurt you."

Then we went to bed, but nothing went right. It was like being with Richard Mueller, only he was the one who quit first. He said, "I have to get up for work tomorrow."

It was 3 A.M. I went back to the living room and poured myself another Jack Daniels and sat in the chair where I had aced the Wallace Stevens quiz. A row of bonehead best-sellers were alphabetized under the encyclopedia in the one bookcase, and the rest of the shelves were filled in with curios. There was a huge oil painting of a red setter on the wall (his boyhood dog?), and some family photos in frames. Pretty strange life, I thought, but less strange than mine. At least there was some coherence here: this person was more or less the same person all the time. Picking up guys three doors away, dating some lunatic who compulsively thumps him on the back, working nine to five every day in an office—as little sense as it made to me, it made more sense than my life.

The first train back to Princeton didn't leave until 7 A.M. I sat in the living-room-in-outer-space until six. As I left, I wrote the man a note thanking him for the place to stay—in childish block letters to disguise my usual printing because I thought he might try to trace me from my handwriting. Why he might try to do that, since he had no reason whatsoever to try to do it, did not enter my thinking. I just thought he might try, maybe through the White House, since he knew I had been there. I regretted showing him the invitation.

I was drunk at that moment, but that doesn't alter the fact that I was also insane. It was a functioning insanity, since I didn't rave in public or take instructions from a voice inside my head, and I rarely experienced such paranoia as I did writing the note. But in fact I had the severe delusions, both cognitive and emotional, of an advanced stage of sexual addiction—a disease nobody recognized then and still seems to some people like a joke. It determined what I thought and what I felt. My personality was formed around it. All of my talents, all my good qualities as a human being, were devoted to serving it, and I was willing to sacrifice anything to it. Although I could perform practical tasks perfectly well, it was running my life, and had been for a long time.

But now it was costing me more and more: it wanted more and more of me. I got to the train station and back to Princeton just fine (except for wanting very much to be dead). It was one of the few times on a train I had no desire to sit next to a hot teen and rub up against her. I didn't walk the length of the train before I chose my seat as I usually did. I just sat down with the commuters on their way to work, men in suits who might have stepped out of the fern bar in Georgetown or been guests at the White House. I had thought I could do anything and it wouldn't affect me because I was so strong-willed, but this experience proved me wrong. The boundaries of my personality got fuzzed. I became disoriented more frequently by my awareness that I was not who people thought I was. And I became more reckless, especially with female students.

I found one quickly to replace Marcia. I had noticed her around campus for a couple of months, because she had The Look. In spades. She was almost a dead ringer for Bunny, the girl who sat behind me in high school history class—much more elegant and sophisticated, but with that same haunted aspect, the same bruised look about the eyes, the same pinholes-into-your-brain-stem burning stare. She also did the same little pout thing with her mouth, as if she were about to growl. Her name was Ronni Slater. Like Marcia, she was my student, but in only one of my classes. I touched her at a party after a poetry reading— secretly, the way I liked it, the way I did with Bunny. This seemed to be her thing, too. I was talking to her, the first time we had ever spoken, our butts propped on a low bookcase, half-leaning, half-sitting, both facing the clot of dancers in a dimly lit room, when I noticed that her calf was suddenly flush against mine. I inched my butt toward her until we were joined from hip to ankle like Siamese twins, and that's how we stayed, rubbing a little as if to the music, until we got up to dance, after which I handed her a cocktail napkin and asked her to wipe the sweat from my face, which she did, slow and sexy. It was a reckless public display, and I didn't care. Marcia was at the party, too, and grabbed me when I went to get a drink.

"What's the deal with you and Ronni Slater?" she asked.

"What's it to you?" I replied.

"Don't you think people can see what you're doing? It's all anybody's talking about."

"What do they expect me to do in Princeton, stick my dick in a blender?"

"But *Ronni Slater*?" she said, as if the name itself appalled her. "*Ronni Slater*?"

Ronni Slater. I dated her openly the whole semester. Like Marcia, she refused to go out with me anymore when the semester was over, after I had graded her paper (A-) and turned in her grade for the course (A). And I'm sure she felt invaded, too—or violated. Maybe more so if she was acting out her own compulsion. After the party, she didn't know what to do because I was coming on so strong. Should she date me or not? She discussed it with everyone, at large crowded tables at her eating club, asking for advice. For a few weeks, it was apparently a general topic for debate on campus: Should Faculty Date Students? Fuck what anybody thinks, I thought. I picked her up at her dorm and chatted with her suitemates while she was getting ready. I took her home from class, the class I had just taught in which she was my student, leaving the room with her while the other students stared. I scoffed at Princeton propriety, which is all I believed I was violating.

"You can't get away with this at Princeton," Marcia warned me. She was the one who reported what Ronni was saying about me in public.

"So you want to start sleeping with me again?" I asked her. She just laughed

"You must think I'm as crazy as you are," she said.

So I slept with Ronni Slater instead. I quickly discovered that I didn't like her very much, although that hardly seemed to matter anymore. Not liking her was part of the sexiness. I didn't really get to know her at all. For me she was nine-tenths Bunny, whom I still fantasized about. I knew it wouldn't last, with Ronni Slater or anyone else, so what difference did it make if I liked her or not? It was one of the better ways I had to spend a night, which, alone in my apartment without a date, had become like sitting in a roomful of pepper gas.

I slept with other students, too, that semester—and a painter from Philadelphia, and a horror-movie actress in New York, and a Princeton stockbroker, and a dental hygienist who did the casinos in Atlantic City on weekends and whose last boyfriend was a hit man in Trenton, currently and fortunately (for me) incarcerated. Et alia. The same old story. For each woman I seduced, there were two more I tried to seduce, and ten more I wanted to seduce but couldn't. So what I experienced most of the time was failure and frustration.

There was a goodbye party for graduates of the Creative Writing Program during graduation week, a couple of weeks after most of the rest of the students had left town. No faculty were going, but I went, late, alone. It was supposed to be a blowout. Orange-and-black Princeton Tiger towels were draped over the lampshades for that *demimonde* effect. I knew I was intruding, that all the students were looking at me wondering what I was doing at a student party. I could hear them thinking, Get a life, you sicko. I stood in the shadows near the dance floor, sucking beer from a bottle. The music was blasting, nobody was talking to me and I didn't talk to anybody. I felt like I did in a disco: anonymous, only worse, because I wasn't. Then I saw Ronni Slater ten feet away. She was arm in arm with a boy I didn't know, each of them with a beer bottle in their free hands. I thought she looked right at me, then I saw her hand drop from the boy's waist to his butt, then down the back of his thigh and up again. The boy turned to her and they kissed, long and lingering, still holding their beer bottles, a mutual tonsillectomy. I stared at them, mesmerized. I realized I had to get out of there immediately. I walked upstairs. There were a dozen students, male and female, in one of the bedrooms. A TV and VCR was set up at the foot of the bed. They were about to watch a porno video. On a dare. Lots of forced, self-conscious jokes were being made. The young women who had never seen a porno movie were trying to act blasé, and the boys were saying they wouldn't last ten minutes. I was standing there when one of the boys pushed the play button. I said, "This isn't a good idea." Nobody responded. Maybe I hadn't actually spoken aloud as I thought I had. Maybe I was invisible. On the TV screen, a nurse walked into a room where a curly-haired man was lying on a hospital bed. "It's time for your sponge-bath, Mr. Smith," she said. I said, "This is a mistake," and walked out. A couple of my students were in the other bedroom sitting on the bed. They had decided the porno video was going to be embarrassing and had passed it up. In two minutes the porno video room began emptying, and in five minutes the porno video had been turned off. Sure enough, everybody was embarrassed, including the boys who had proven their point. I was glad that I had said what I said and left, but I had watched hundreds of porno movies, some of them in hellish-smelling booths in adult book-stores pumping in quarters every ninety seconds. Had I been alone I would have watched this one. So what kind of victory was it? Even my walking out of the room was a kind of lie. My best actions and noblest impulses were hypocritical jokes. I went downstairs intending to go straight out the front door, but I couldn't help one little peek at Ronni Slater before I left. She wasn't in the room where she had been and neither was the boy she had been touching and kissing. "Where's Ronni?" I asked a student whose name I didn't know. I had to yell over the music to be heard. He looked at me as if I were demented. "I think she went for a walk," he said.

I walked outside and got into my Fiat. It was a two-seat convertible, the same one I had in Dallas when I tried to flip the hairdresser's card into the air. The top was down now, too. I drove the residential Princeton streets looking for Ronni and the boy, up one and down the next. The enormous trees made heavy shadows over the side-walks like black pits I couldn't see into. There was no one on those streets. All the houses were dark. Every normal human being was asleep. Then I saw them up ahead. They had walked about ten blocks toward campus, away from the party, much farther than I thought they could get on foot. They must have left as soon as I went upstairs. I knew very well what they were going to go do. I pulled up next to them.

"You guys want a ride?" I asked cheerily. God knows what I was thinking. The car couldn't fit three people anyway.

They both shook their heads slowly no. I believe the boy said, "No, thanks." Ronni Slater looked shocked to her shoes. I'm sure she was.

I drove away. When I got home, I felt like I did on the train back from Washington, the first time I had ever felt like this when I wasn't drunk and hadn't picked up a man. This was, if anything, worse.

Yet it didn't stop me from calling Ronni Slater again. She moved out of the dorm into a house with about ten people. I don't remember how I got her new number. I didn't call her for a while, then I tried again. I told myself I only wanted to straighten things out with her. I even left that message with her roommates when she didn't return my calls, but she still didn't return my calls. "Sorry, she's not home," I was told every time. "When will she be home?" "[X] o'clock." I'd call at [x] o'clock. "Sorry, she's not home."

But finally she was. It was about dinnertime. A boy answered. When I asked for Ronni, he said, "Just a minute."

Then I heard the boy saying, "I already told him you were here." Laughter in the background. I pictured her ten roommates at the dinner table. "What do you want me to say?" the boy said. More laughter. He was laughing himself. Then he said into the phone, "I guess she's not home after all." Much more laughter. Big chorus of guffaws.

"Thanks," I said, and hung up.

Within a year I was fired for having sex with one student and propositioning another: surprise. What *was* surprising is that I knew all along what was happening to me, or, more accurately, *that* it was happening to me. The evidence was abundant that my compulsion to glorify myself sexually was being taken over by a compulsion to humiliate myself sexually. Months before I was fired, I wrote a poem called "The Gladiator" which begins by describing a clay figurine I saw in a book called *The Erotic Art of Pompeii*:

> *His cock is bigger than he is*
> *and thickens out from his thighs*
> *until it touches earth and curls*
> *back to attack him with a mad dog's head:*
> *jaws stretched, bared teeth, going for his throat.*

The figure struck me because it was an image for my own sexual self-destructiveness. I knew that perfectly well. I wasn't in a blackout. I was fully conscious the whole time. But I was on automatic pilot, as if my brain were being beamed in from Mars. I knew I was headed for trouble, but there was nothing I could do about it.

And that's exactly what I said when I first saw the student who later reported me to the dean: "There's trouble." I said it aloud under my breath. I will call her Melanie. She was standing outside my classroom with her hips cocked—wearing jeans, boots, and a brown leather vest. My seduction of Melanie was no more remarkable than my seduction of any of my other students over the previous decade: conferences, coffee after class, call me if you'd like to come over. However, she was the first one who could no longer bear to sit in my classroom afterward (which was also my response to Richard Mueller, although that didn't occur to me at the time; nor did it ever occur to me that I might be making my students feel the way Richard Mueller made me feel). She told me on the phone that she had made a mistake sleeping with me. When I asked why, she said, "Because I don't love you." Say what? I never uttered the l-word. I firmly believed sex had nothing to do with love, and was, if anything, its opposite: a demonic force. My problem, I thought, was reconciling my superior demonic sexuality with bourgeois and fundamentally pedestrian social mores (blah professorial blah). Still, I knew this didn't quite account for the undermining I was experiencing, the almost physical sensation that the ground underneath my feet was giving way. And there were those panic attacks in my other class when that young woman dragged her gold chain across her lower lip. They were becoming so severe I dreaded the days I had to teach.

I encouraged Melanie to come to the last class before spring break, and to reconsider her decision to drop the course during the vacation. She came to the class, we talked in my office afterward, and I thought everything would be fine. I left town for a week of poetry readings in Ohio (where I seduced every woman I could). When I returned to Princeton, waiting in my mailbox was a letter from Melanie's father which concluded by assuring me that he was very concerned for my future. There was also a letter from the dean of faculty asking me to make an appointment at my earliest convenience.

Needless to say, what followed was a nightmare: a month of hearings, a month of appeals, with a story and my picture on the front page of the *Daily Princetonian*, the gossip spreading throughout the poetry world, being held up as an example of male poets exploiting female students. The saddest thing to me now is that I believed I had done nothing wrong. There was no rule in the Princeton Faculty Handbook explicitly forbidding sex with students. (There is now.) I admitted to having sex with Melanie, and denied unsuccessfully propositioning the other student. I did proposition the other student, of course; it was easier to admit "success" than failure. Although it was overwhelming to go through a public humiliation for my sexual behavior, what I was prosecuted for was "normal" in the eyes of some people. But I knew I wasn't normal. I was not being prosecuted for the secret things I did. Nobody knew about those things, but I knew about them.

The dean heard about Ronni Slater, but she didn't file a formal complaint against me. Nor did Marcia. Technically, I was not fired. Melanie, by her own account, had "responded or participated in the sexual act" and I had "cooperated fully with the inquiries," so I was suspended with pay from my teaching activities for that academic year. I was not allowed to finish my last weeks of classes. I became notorious. Who would ever hire me again? Who could read my poems without thinking, "This is the guy who was fired by Princeton"? I was sure I'd never get another teaching job the rest of my life.

After the newspaper stories were published, Melanie's father wrote a letter to the dean, which became part of the file I was allowed to read. He said that Melanie felt guilty for having reported me, and (with remarkable kindness) he expressed the hope that this experience might cause me to reevaluate my behavior (which it finally did, although it took another decade of pain and loss as a result of my sexual behavior for me to realize I had not been treated unjustly). When I first read his letter sitting in the dean's office, I was glad Melanie felt guilty. She *should* feel guilty, I thought. But I was wrong. Her guilt was part of my abuse of her, every bit as much as my guilt was part of Bob Stoller's abuse of me. It's true that she was nineteen years old and I had been five, but I had power over her and I used it—it was only more insidious if I could make it seem to both of us that I wasn't using it. She was only one in a long line of students with whom I reenacted my own sexual abuse, from the other side, as the molester, as if I could escape its unhappy imprinting by being Bob Stoller and not myself.

A BEGINNING

I dreamed only once in my life about Bob Stoller—in August 1991, the week Jeffrey Dahmer was arrested in Milwaukee, eight months after I wrote out my bottom-line behavior on the plane to California and almost a year after I found myself driving to upstate New York for the purpose of seducing my friend's fifteen-year-old daughter. I was working on this book, and trying to break the pattern of compulsive seductions one day at a time, to see exactly what was behind it and if I could begin to become a person who could be happy. For the first time in my life I was not having sex with anyone by my own choice. I also thought I might be in love with a woman in Chicago (it turned out I was), and I wanted to be faithful, also for the first time in my life.

I dreamed I had somehow gotten in touch with Bob Stoller, and he had written back to me enclosing maps to his apartment, a group of maps. The one that got me there had a drawing of a baseball diamond, behind which was a number of tall buildings, including his apartment building, in an urban setting, maybe Chicago. The map was three-dimensional, more like a view of the place than a map of it. Also included in the papers were some brochures about Officer Training School, which somehow he was going to help me get into, or something—he was going to do something good for me. My mother went with me to his apartment. I told her I was going to confront him about molesting me. (At the age of forty-five, I had still never told her I had been molested.) She went with me, but tentatively, fearfully, so I was psychologically pulling her along. She was trying to be supportive, but couldn't be.

Then we were with Bob Stoller inside his apartment. It was like the newspaper descriptions of Jeffrey Dahmer's: dreary, dark, dirty, a life isolated by his perversity. Bob Stoller looked pathetic—my age but juvenile. He didn't look his age (as I didn't). He had brown hair the length of mine. But his body was not like mine: he was slim and potbellied like Richard Mueller. The three of us sat down, my mother in an easy chair in the background. For a while we talked about the ostensible reason why I had come: Officer Training School. And Bob Stoller really did have a way to get me through it quickly that appealed to me. He could do that for me, and was very willing to, apparently out of genuine generosity. Then I got tired of the charade. He left the room for a moment and I told my mother I was going to confront him when he came back. She was fearful, tentative, as before. But I was determined. He came back, and I immediately said to him, "Do you know you molested me?" It was hard to say it—not so hard that I couldn't say it, but I had to entirely switch the subject, a feeling of shifting momentum, of absorbing the force of a strong current coming toward me and turning it in the opposite direction. But I did it, without my mother's help. He denied molesting me. He said it wasn't true. He was lying on the floor, wriggling. For the briefest moment it seemed maybe it wasn't true, that I had made it up (a feeling I've never had in my life—I've never doubted that it happened). My mother was willing to entertain this, that I had made it up. But I knew this was a lie. I stood up from my chair and stood over Bob Stoller; he was wriggling on his back on the floor, and I pointed down at him and said, "You *know* it happened." He said I don't know, I'm not sure—a less certain denial, which, I realized, came from his awareness that he had in fact molested many children and was still doing it. It was denial in its psychological sense, but with the awareness of living deceptively (that I always had), of having a secret life. He said coyly, "I saw you walking with your girlfriend." When he said that, I could see in my mind two little children five years old walking in heavy coats. They were identical and tiny, like salt and pepper shakers. I saw them at a distance on a dark day walking through a mist. But I didn't have a girlfriend when I was five years old, so I was trying to figure out what he was talking about, when he suddenly shouted, "I wanted to fuck HER more than anything." It was what I felt when I first saw Marcia and Melanie and Ronni and my friend's fifteen-year-old daughter—what I felt when I saw teenage girls with The Look. And this was Bob Stoller's admission of the truth, that he had molested me. I said there it is, that proves it, and he was saying, no, I don't know, wriggling on the floor on his back, trying to make me feel sorry for him. It gave me a momentary sexual feeling, of resolving our conflict by having sex with him, but I didn't indulge the feeling and it passed through me. My mother stayed back, sitting in the easy chair, watching, not helping me. But I didn't need her. I saw how pathetic and sick he was, that he was irrelevant to me now, to my well-being. He just didn't matter anymore.

My mother and I left. I felt sorry for her for being so fearful. We talked a little about what had happened, but it also didn't matter what she said. It was to me a simple fact, no longer painful: This was the way it was for Bob Stoller, not for me. This is who *he* was. It was too bad for him but not for me. I had done something important for myself and was ready to go on.

I awoke with this feeling of having had a momentous experience that I could not have in life and was given in a dream. I hadn't seen Bob Stoller since my sister and I waved goodbye as he drove off in his old black pickup truck with the square cab. I didn't know if he was dead or alive, or how to begin to find him, and I didn't want to know. But I had been given the experience of confronting him in my dream.

I got up and wrote this in my journal:

I am no longer Bob Stoller. Being him holds no appeal for me anymore: he is a wriggling worm. Nor am I in his power anymore. The gift of the dream was to have this *experience*. No amount of talk could have done it: I experienced Bob Stoller as I am now and I separated myself from him. For all these years, he has been my false self. He isn't inside me anymore. A benevolent, loving God has replaced Bob Stoller. This is the gift, a surprising gift, better than anything I could have asked for or imagined: myself. I can begin to be my (God-given) self.

—

A COUPLE OF weeks later I told my mother about being molested. My father has been dead for more than thirty years. My mother has lived alone all this time, half a mile from my sister's home. My sister's family is the new family, a very different one than the one I grew up in, and my mother has been a part of it, helping to raise my sister's children, who are now in their early twenties and about to start their own new families. They are big fans of my mother's, and I can see why: I look at her through their eyes and see the caring, spirited, good-humored old woman they see, whereas for my whole adult life I have seen her through a plastic shield of resentment for her inability to protect me from Bob Stoller and my father and for giving me her guilt and shame. My sister's family is an unusually happy family; the kids are great, her husband's a mensch, my sister is a powerhouse with a big heart for the engine. I don't know how she turned her suffering into the ability to love, but she did: they are loving to one another, and loving toward me, and have always invited me in. But I have never been able to let them know me. How could I? I couldn't visit my mother without stopping at the adult bookstore on the way and kissing her hello with a porno paperback tucked under my shirt. I would stay a day or two every year or two; I couldn't stand any more than that, not because of them but because of me. It was too much like being the guilty child hiding himself. They knew nothing about Princeton, nothing about my secret life, nothing about me except what I showed them: my cynical wit, my intellectual vanity, my literary trophies, and a parade of pretty wives and girlfriends. And still they invited me in.

I don't know if they needed to know the truth about me, but I needed them to know. I had told my sister on a previous visit that I had been molested by Bob Stoller (which is when she told me she remembered that he took her picture but that was all). I couldn't yet tell her or my mother about my sexual addiction and its consequences, but telling them I was molested was the first step in eradicating the secret that had had so much power over me. And I believed it was a family secret, too. I believed my mother knew it already somewhere in her heart.

I sat down across from her at her dining-room table as soon as I had carried my bags in. My mother is a small, sturdy woman in excellent health; at eighty she walks a couple of miles a day and does double acrostics. Her hair, I'm sure, is white, but I have never seen it white. One of her few indulgences is to go to the beauty shop once a week and have it lightly tinted. The first thing she always asks me after I arrive at her house is if I want something to eat, and I always do; she has always spent the day cooking the dishes I liked most as a child. But this day I arrived in midmorning and we were going out to lunch with my sister, so we just had coffee together. She usually drinks instant, or ground coffee from a can, but I like mine with freshly ground beans, so that's how she made it, with a grinder I had given her one Christmas that she stores at the back of a cabinet except when I am home. I told her I had something I had to tell her, then told her that I had been sexually molested by Bob Stoller for about a year when I was five years old. She cried and said, "I'm so sorry." She said she didn't really remember Bob Stoller. She asked if the Stollers were the family that moved into the Gerstlers' house up the block, and I said yes. She couldn't remember Bob Stoller taking my picture. That seemed odd to me. His eight-by-ten glossies of me are still in the drawer of the secretary in her living room, and he was so obviously my "friend" that when I went back to the neighborhood about ten years ago the first thing the mother of my best friend Kenny asked me was if

I had ever seen that strange guy Bob Stoller again. I told this to my mother.

"Did he do something with Kenny?" my mother asked me.

That wasn't the point. The point was that Bob Stoller was so obviously my "friend."

"I have no idea, Mother. I was five years old."

She said almost wistfully, "He seemed like such a nice guy."

I said that he had probably made himself seem like a nice guy so that he could molest children.

"It seemed okay," my mother said, referring to his taking my picture.

I noticed that we had gone from her not remembering who he was or his taking my picture to his being a nice guy and its seeming okay. I got a little vehement despite myself.

I said, "Mother, Mother, a twenty-three-year-old man and a five-year-old boy. Think about it. Let it sink in. Didn't that seem strange?"

She said she didn't know I was going to his house. I know she knew I went to his house, although she surely didn't know how often I went there. But this was turning into a cross-examination, with me as the prosecutor, and I didn't want it to. She cried some more, yet what I had told her didn't seem to register. Apropos of nothing, she started talking about her father, about being her daddy's little girl (where was this coming from?); then with no transition she switched to asking me where I thought she should be buried—she owned the plot next to my father in Milwaukee, but it seemed ridiculous to send her body all the way back there, didn't it? What did I think?

I thought, I'd better go upstairs by myself, and I did. I was pretty upset. I said a prayer. The important thing was to tell the secret and just let it go. I wasn't doing this for my mother, I was doing it for me.

We left for lunch. We drove to the restaurant in two cars. I went with my sister, and my mom went with the kids, who needed a car to go somewhere afterward. I told my sister what happened. She told me that my mother had come over to her house after watching an Oprah Winfrey show on child molestation a couple of weeks before and had said to my sister what my sister already knew—that the guy who had lived up the block from us in Milwaukee was funny that way, that he had tried to get Kenny to take down his pants and Kenny had run away.

It flattened me. My mother knew who Bob Stoller was and knew he was a child molester. She acted exactly as she had in my dream, only worse. She knew about Kenny, but she had never asked me if Bob Stoller tried to touch me. Why not I could not imagine. Nobody mentioned such things in those days, but Kenny's mother had told her. And I vaguely began to remember Kenny saying something bad about Bob Stoller to me and me defending him. My God, I thought. My whole life with this. And half of my mother's. We have both been carrying this shame for so long.

I didn't know what to do. I was leaving the next morning—a one-day visit as usual, although I hadn't stopped at the adult bookstore this time. I was angry. The way I have always expressed my anger toward my mother is through coldness, a steel-plate hardness a hundred inches thick, and a subtle diminishment of her, to make her feel stupid (which she isn't), because she values intelligence and education so much. I iced her for the rest of the day—genius work, a masterpiece. We had dinner at my sister's house. I didn't look at my mother, except when she was speaking—to show her by my ultrapatient expression how boring she was, one of those subtle, fleeting gestures no one else would notice but between a mother and her grown child have entangled roots a thousand feet deep. My mother and I are virtuosi of these. The way she sets her mouth to express her disappointment explodes inside me like a depth charge. My imperceptible lifting of an eyebrow tells her she is being unbelievably ignorant again. After dinner the two of us were alone together for the first time since the morning. We turned on the TV, an excuse for both of us not to talk. At a commercial, out of the blue she told me a story she had told me many times about Rocket Ismail being nice to my nephew when they were both students at Notre

Dame. My mother loves Notre Dame and Notre Dame football and thought it was great that Rocket Ismail, a famous football star, would go out of his way to be nice to people. This anecdote involved Rocket Ismail inviting my nephew to sit at his table when the dining hall was crowded. It was not overly stirring to me the first time I heard it, and was not one of those stories that gains in the retelling.

I glanced at her sideways once or twice as she spoke, and otherwise watched the commercial. When she finished speaking, I didn't respond. Nor was I going to.

"How about some comment?" she asked.

"You've told me that story before, Mother," I said. "About twenty times, at a rough estimate."

She didn't say anything. I hurt her good.

I sat there for five minutes or so, and said good night and walked upstairs. The beds in my mother's guest bedroom are the same twin beds my brother and I slept on. My old chest of drawers is still in the closet. I closed the door to the room and lay down on my bed without getting undressed—the same bed where I had masturbated 6 zillion times into the hydrangea-size wads of toilet paper and pressed the thermometer against the lightbulb so I could stay home from school, the same bed to which I carried Topsy and rubbed against her. I thought, I don't do that anymore. And I don't humiliate people, especially old ladies, especially my mother. I don't need to do that and I don't want to do that and I can't do that.

The next morning I went downstairs for breakfast. My mother had gone to early mass and stopped off at the bagel bakery because I like fresh bagels. She had eggs on the counter, and Oscar Mayer bacon if I wanted it, and fresh orange juice; the day before, she had made a fruit salad. The coffee grinder was full of coffee beans. She had made some chicken sandwiches and wrapped them in foil for me to take on the plane. She packed them in a brown bag with a napkin and a perfect red apple. I ate breakfast and she waited on me. We had not spoken another word about my being molested since our conversation before lunch the previous day.

My sister came in after her morning run and sat down at the table to my left. I finished eating. My mother sat across from my sister, to my right. They were making small talk, just talking, but it was pretty obvious what we were not talking about.

I took one of their hands in each of mine, and held them. I said to my mother, "Mom, no matter what you knew or didn't know, I want you to know I don't blame you for it. I know you wouldn't hurt me on purpose." I told this truth. She would never have hurt me on purpose. That was as much as I could say to her then. She cried bitterly—I couldn't have let that happen, she said, I couldn't have let that happen. My sister cried and so did I. I told my mother it was okay. I told her I didn't want to be angry with her anymore, that I didn't have to blame her anymore for who I am.

And I don't. I don't have to blame her or my father or even Bob Stoller—the triumvirate that ruled my soul. I don't have to blame anyone for who I am anymore because I'm not ashamed of who I am anymore; one day at a time I don't have to do things I'm ashamed of in order to feel ashamed. There's a slogan in my 12-step program that has helped me a lot: if you want to feel self-esteem, do estimable acts. (Not prestigious: *estimable*.) Every day, I have to do a few (small, modest) estimable acts, loving acts, preferably ones nobody knows about. This is now my secret life.

But that's not enough. For almost thirty years, as the only available representative of my internalized triumvirate, I blamed my mother for everything I suffered as a child. I mean everything. Of course she was terrified of being blamed by me when I told her I had been molested: all I ever did was blame her—silently, obliquely, with masterful efficacy. I cannot fathom the pain I must have caused her. I nursed my wound and kept it open and held her responsible for it, because it justified my monstrous addictive behavior. I could do anything I wanted as long as it was her fault. It was a great way to avoid responsibility for myself. I do not think I should be awarded the Albert Schweitzer Medal for telling my mother I don't blame her anymore for my being who I am. I need to ask her forgiveness for punishing her for it for almost thirty years.

—

ONE FINAL STORY, which took place about four months after I wrote out my bottom-line behavior on the plane to California and four months before my dream about Bob Stoller: I see it now as the connection between those two events, between stopping my most shameful sexual behavior (through the grace of God) and expunging the imprint of the molester from my soul (ditto). I also want to end with it because after a lifetime of desperate attempts to feel worthwhile—driving myself mercilessly, clamoring for approval and impossible sexual validation—I actually *felt* worthwhile for the first time in my life: by doing a small kindness for a female student instead of seducing her. I don't think this one's going to win me the Albert Schweitzer Medal either. It's the sort of thing that teachers do all the time, and probably the reason some men become teachers instead of founders of *Playboy* or *Penthouse*— the reward, as dopey and improbable as it sounds, is richer because it comes from giving, not getting, because it's the by-product, not the goal, of the action, not the satisfaction of the will, which only demands to be satisfied again. How sweetly ironic and humbling that my mother tried to teach me this all along, and I thought it was pious bullshit straight out of Mom School.

This was my first *experience* of it. My student's name was Kathleen. The course was entitled "Autobiographical Writing." In the first meeting I told the class I was writing an autobiography about keeping the secret of being sexually molested when I was five years old (that was as frank as I thought I ought to be in describing this book), and I asked them what story they would write if they were going to write it right then. We went around the room. I heard one extraordinary story after another. Each one of them had a remarkable story, which I believe everyone does if he or she is willing to tell it. It doesn't have to be a shameful story, but it must be the one that formed you and you must be ready to tell it with compassionate dispassion that can be at least encouraged if not acquired by the act of writing itself. This is what I said to my students that day. When it was Kathleen's turn, she said one sentence: she was going to write about being sexually molested by her father and being given away by him to other men.

And she did. She made a couple of false starts with the beginning of her piece, and needed an unusual number of conferences. I liked her and obviously identified with what she was trying to write, but I did not come on to her sexually. I had not had sex with any of my students, nor had I been sexual with any of them, not even a lingering look. But my awareness of sexual signals was still highly attuned, and I could see where Kathleen wanted this to go. I could also see why. Her trauma, like mine, made her believe down to the microbes in her blood cells that her human value equaled her sexual value. She was trying to confront this subject bravely. I thought she was projecting her desperation to be healed onto me, and if she was she would experience that desperation as sexual desire. How many times I had experienced this myself. ("I wanted to fuck HER more than anything": Bob Stoller's sudden shout was like a battering ram breaking down the door.)

For a long time I had understood intellectually that my sexual compulsion was an attempt to feel my human value: as before my dream, I had just never experienced my understanding. Now I saw what I could do for myself by doing something for Kathleen, in a small way. I could show her that I valued what she was writing—that I valued her as my student, as a writer, and as a smart and courageous person—and confirm it by not having sex with her. I could show her that she didn't have to have sex with me for me to value her (as she did with her father). So when she propositioned me openly, I was ready with my answer. She did it over the phone, probably because she knew how I would respond, and did not want to face the embarrassment in person, but still couldn't stop herself from doing it (which, needless to say, I also understood). I told her I was touched by her feelings for me, but I was her teacher, and there was a boundary between us that could not be crossed; I could not jeopardize my integrity or my livelihood, so nothing sexual was ever going to happen between us. It didn't take long to say it. I didn't tell her anything about my history, and I don't think she knew anything about it. She was silent for a minute. I said I loved what she was writing and I hoped I could help her with it. You are helping me, she said. A lot. I said, Good, because I really want to. I said I'd see her in class. She said, "Thank you," and hung up. I said, "Thank *you*" after she hung up. She had no idea what she had done for me. I had felt the pull, and I'd surely feel it again, but the magnet in my solar plexus had lost some of its power.

I asked everyone in the class to xerox the first five pages of their pieces, and we'd discuss them together. Kathleen's opening pages were among the last we discussed. It had been a couple of weeks since she propositioned me, and I had not talked to her in conference since then or seen these pages. She walked in late and handed them out and began reading. Her name was Kitty, her father's name for her. She was eight years old and lying in her bedroom. He was sitting in the next room in the dark. Before he came to her room, he would always sit in the next room in the dark and sing three Irish songs. When she heard the first song, she knew he would be coming into her room. She still knew all the words to these songs. When she got to the part about listening to him sing, and knowing what would happen when the songs were over, she started singing herself, right there in the classroom. She had a gorgeous voice and sang a gorgeous, heart-rending ballad the way you'd hear it in an Irish pub. All of her feeling was in that song. It was breathtaking. When she finished, she broke down sobbing, bent over, her face in her hands. The class sat there stunned.

I usually drink a glass of water when I'm teaching. Without thinking about it, I got up from my desk and walked over to her and gave her a drink of my water. I squeezed her hand. The student next to her gave her about an armful of Kleenex and rubbed her back. Returning to my desk, I made a few jokes. I said I, too, knew some songs—show tunes from *Carousel* and *Oklahoma* and *South Pacific*. I threatened to sing "My boy Bill. . . ." It was not the most hilarious joke of all time, but Kathleen laughed. The class laughed, and the laughter broke the tension. Then we talked about the five pages, in a way that was encouraging and useful. That wasn't hard. Everybody was knocked out by what Kathleen had written.

If I had slept with her, I would not have known what to do when she began crying. I would have been afraid to go to her or to touch her in front of the class. I would have been worried that she was somehow going to expose our secret. I would have been thinking of myself. Instead, my response was automatic: I treated her as my student and a human being, a human being to whom I had an important connection that was not sexual.

After class I walked to the men's room and looked at myself in the mirror. There I was—not the man in a suit staring at himself in the mirror over the bar in Georgetown and trying to be no one. I was alive and I wanted to live. I said to myself, "You just did something really good." Maybe it was good for Kathleen—I don't know if it helped her. But it helped me, and I knew it did, although I didn't know yet how much.